the DEVIL DOES EXIST Volume 1

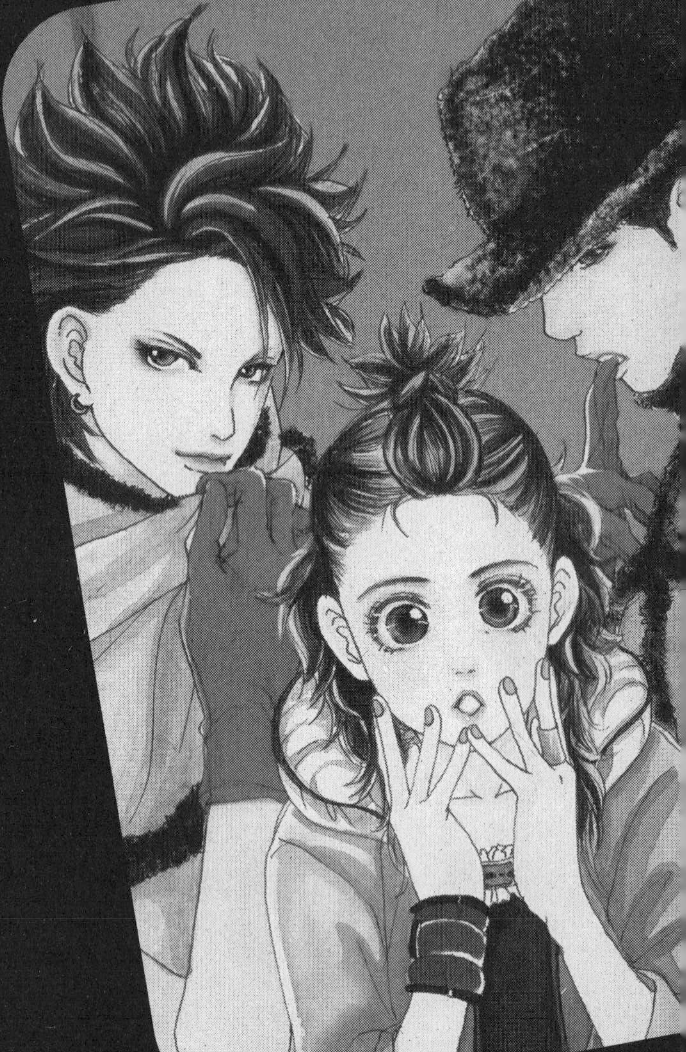

By Takanashi Mitsuba

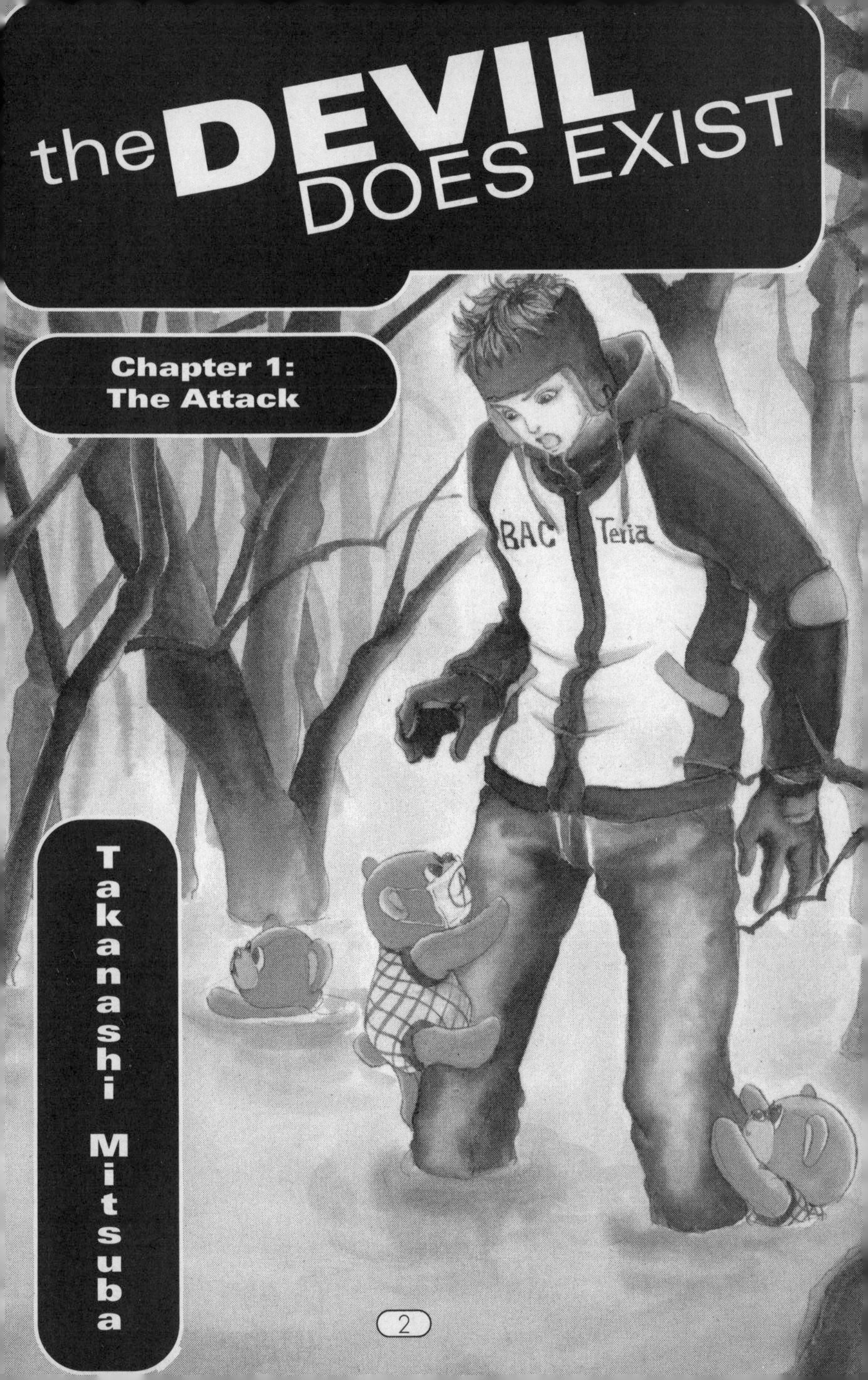
the DEVIL DOES EXIST
Chapter 1: The Attack
Takanashi Mitsuba
BAC Teria

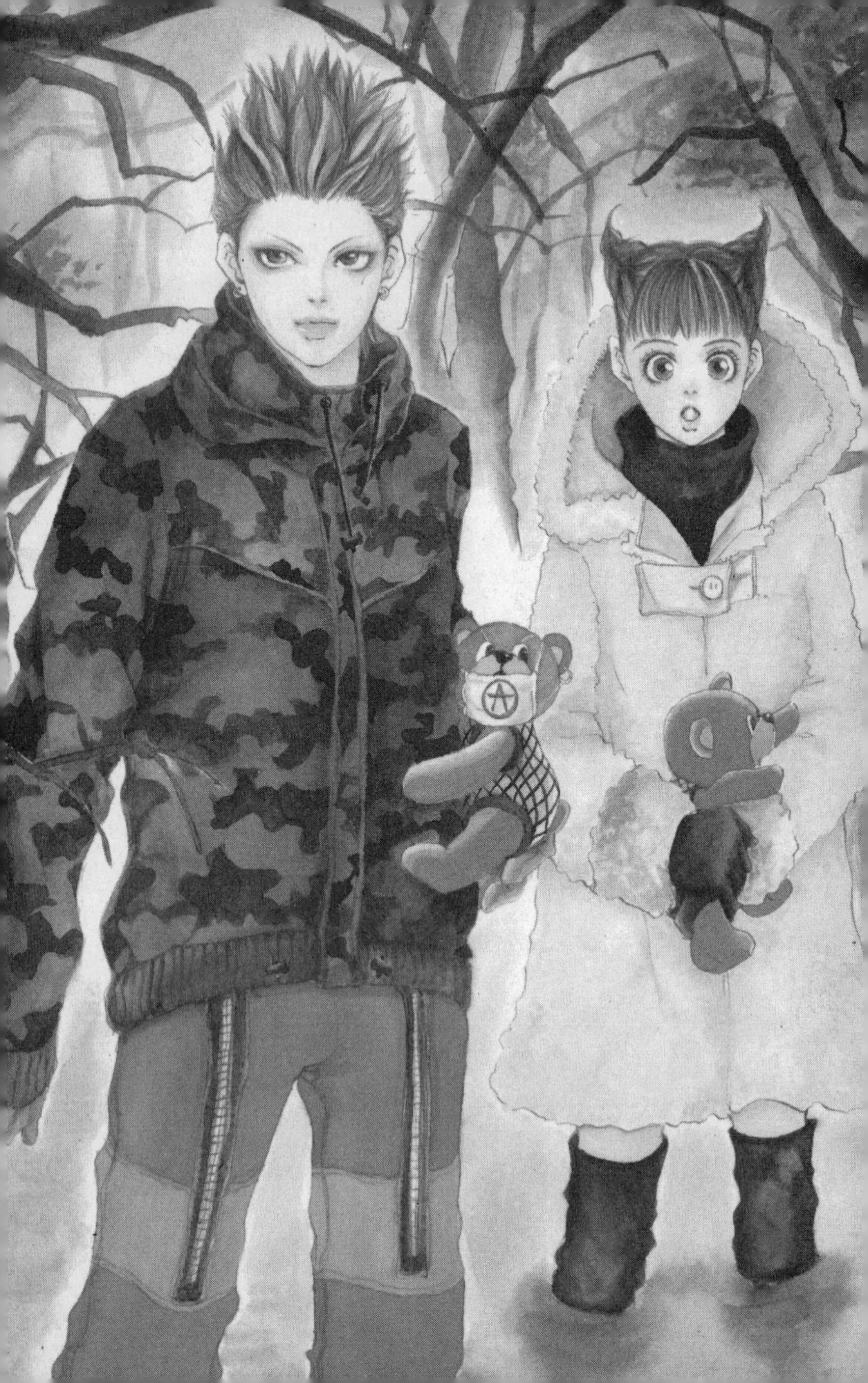

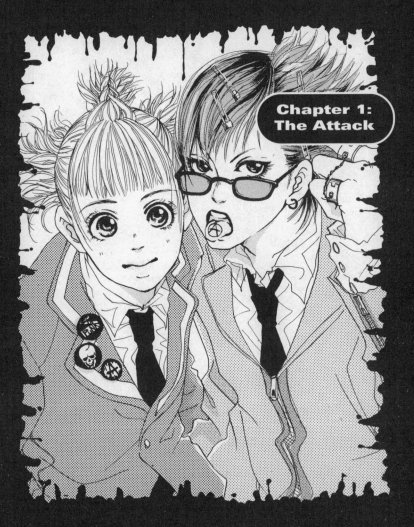

Chapter 1:
The Attack

the **DEVIL**
DOES EXIST

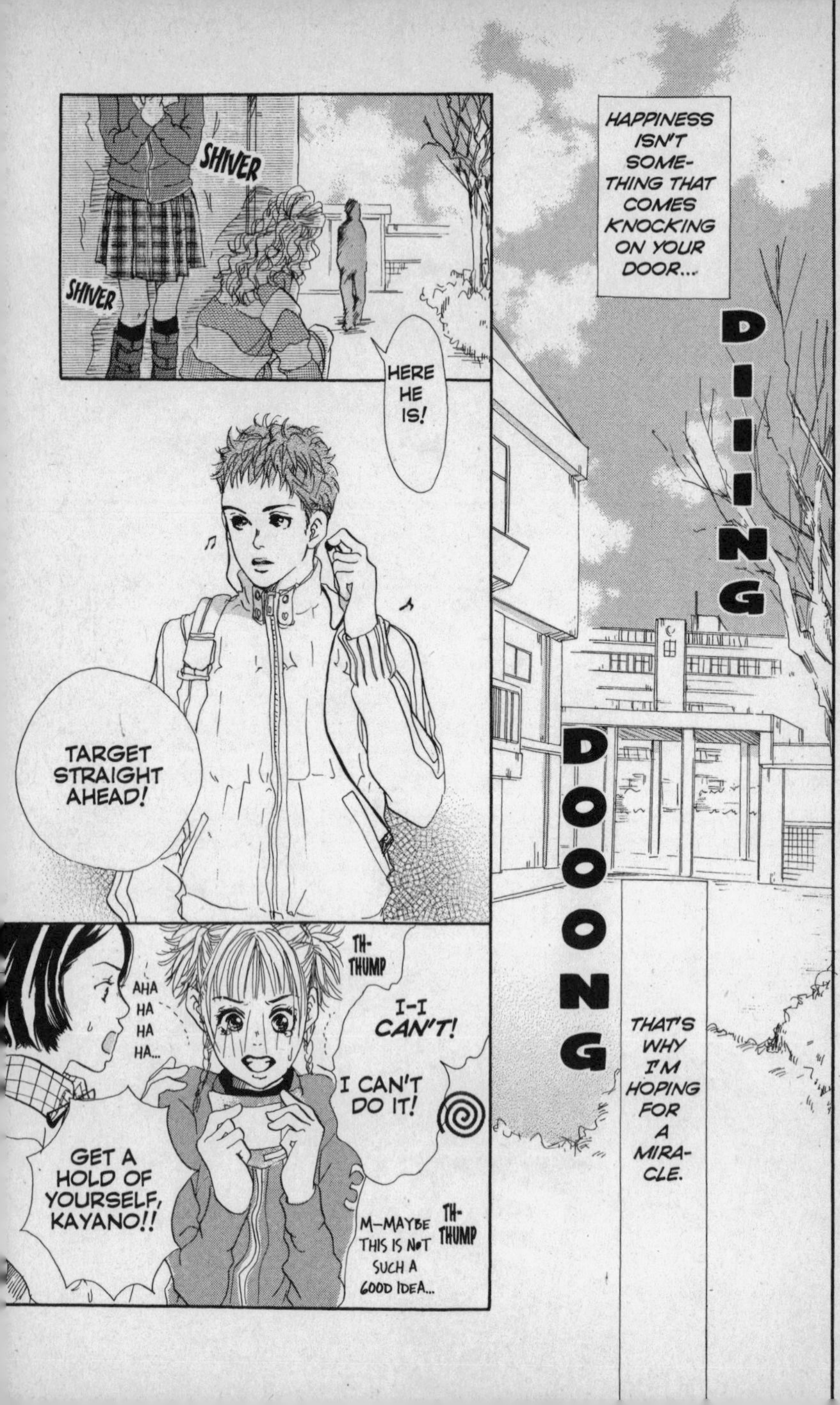
HAPPINESS ISN'T SOMETHING THAT COMES KNOCKING ON YOUR DOOR...
DIIING
DOOOONG
THAT'S WHY I'M HOPING FOR A MIRACLE.
SHIVER
SHIVER
HERE HE IS!
TARGET STRAIGHT AHEAD!
TH-THUMP
I-I CAN'T!
I CAN'T DO IT!
AHA HA HA HA...
GET A HOLD OF YOURSELF, KAYANO!!
M-MAYBE THIS IS NOT SUCH A GOOD IDEA...
TH-THUMP

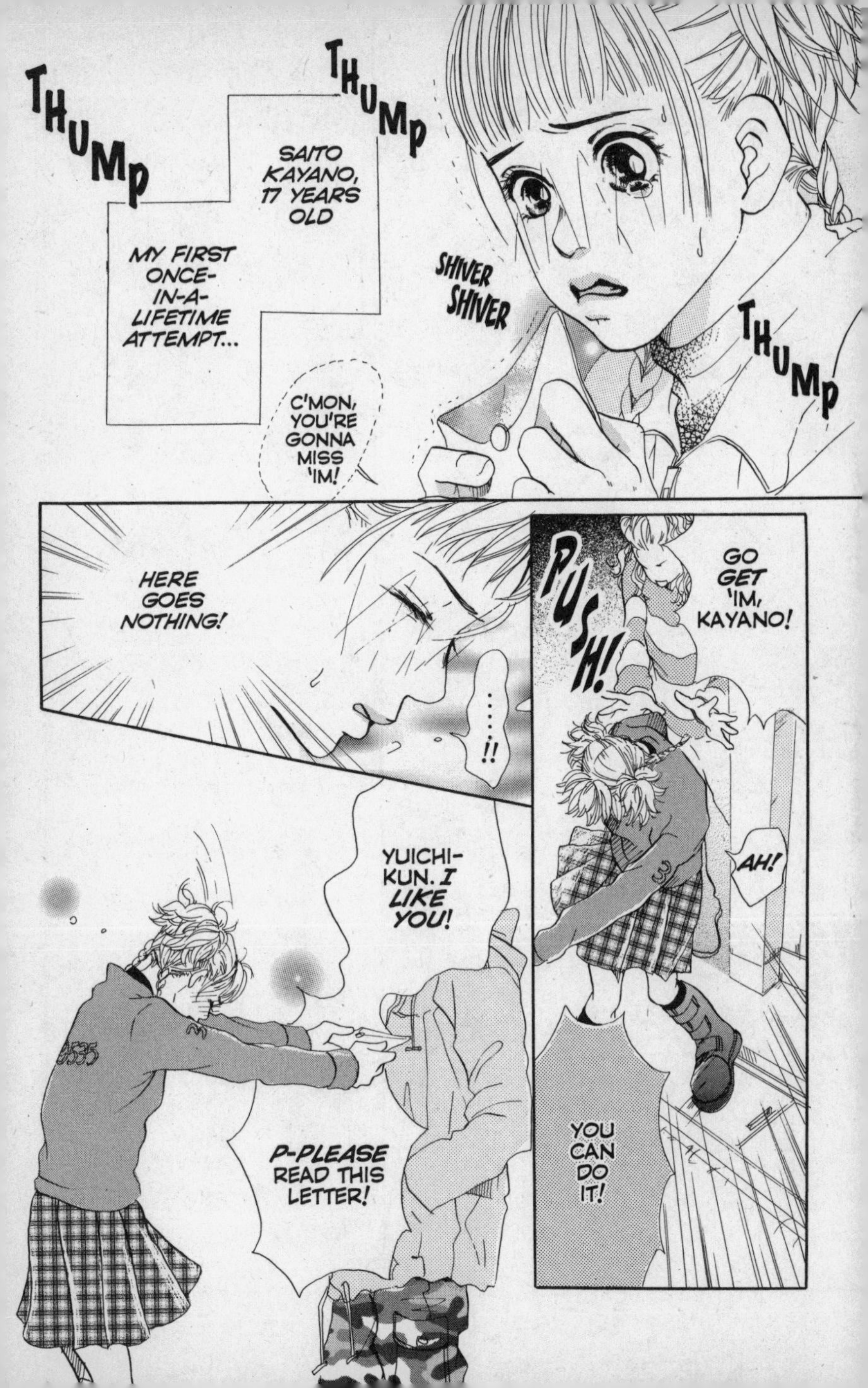
THUMP
THUMP
SAITO KAYANO, 17 YEARS OLD
MY FIRST ONCE-IN-A-LIFETIME ATTEMPT...
SHIVER SHIVER
THUMP
C'MON, YOU'RE GONNA MISS 'IM!
GO GET 'IM, KAYANO!
PUSH!
AH!
YOU CAN DO IT!
HERE GOES NOTHING!
......!!
YUICHI-KUN. I LIKE YOU!
P-PLEASE READ THIS LETTER!

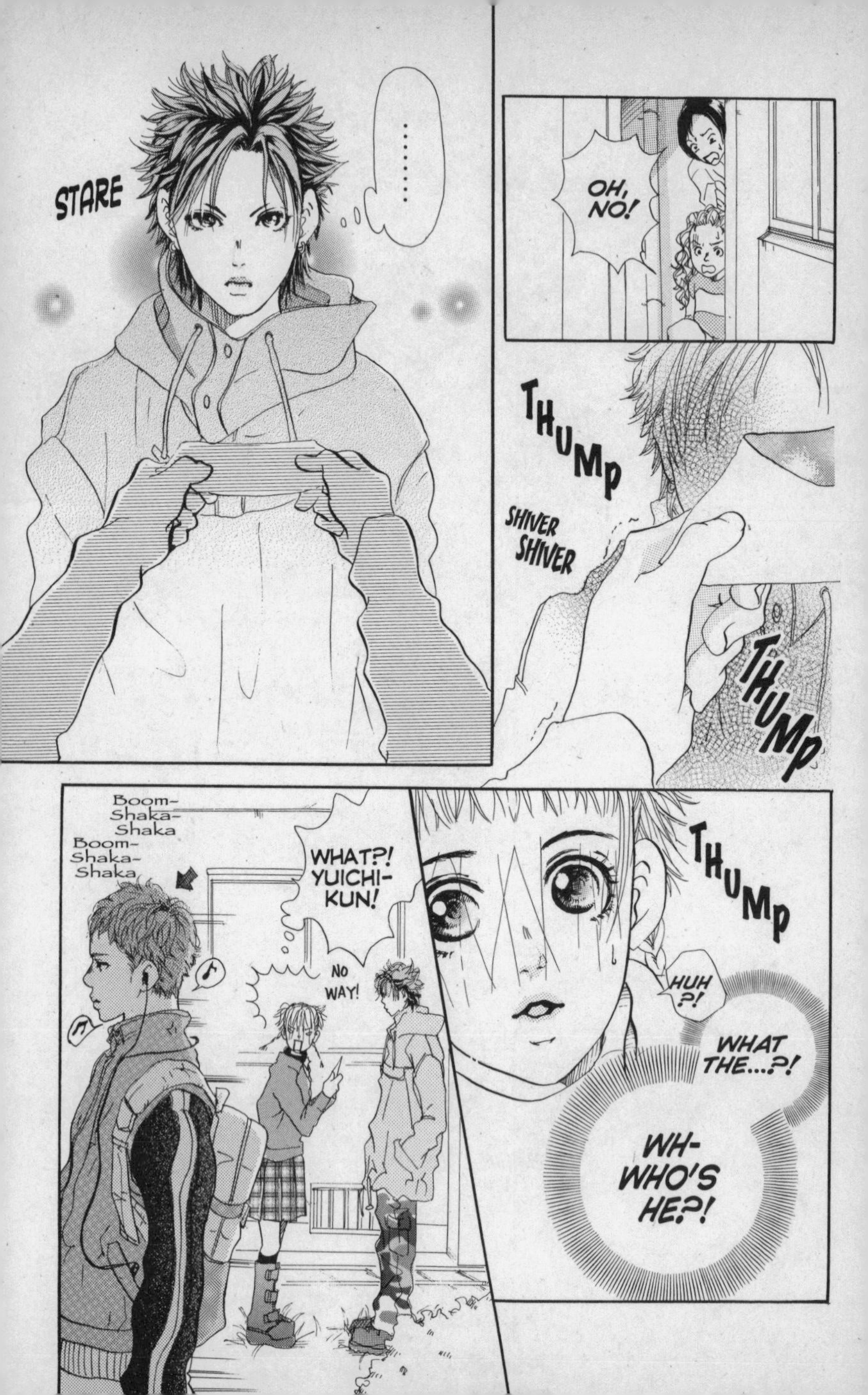
OH, NO!
THUMP
SHIVER SHIVER
THUMP
STARE
......
THUMP
HUH?!
WHAT THE...?!
WH-WHO'S HE?!
Boom-Shaka-Shaka Boom-Shaka-Shaka
WHAT?! YUICHI-KUN!
NO WAY!

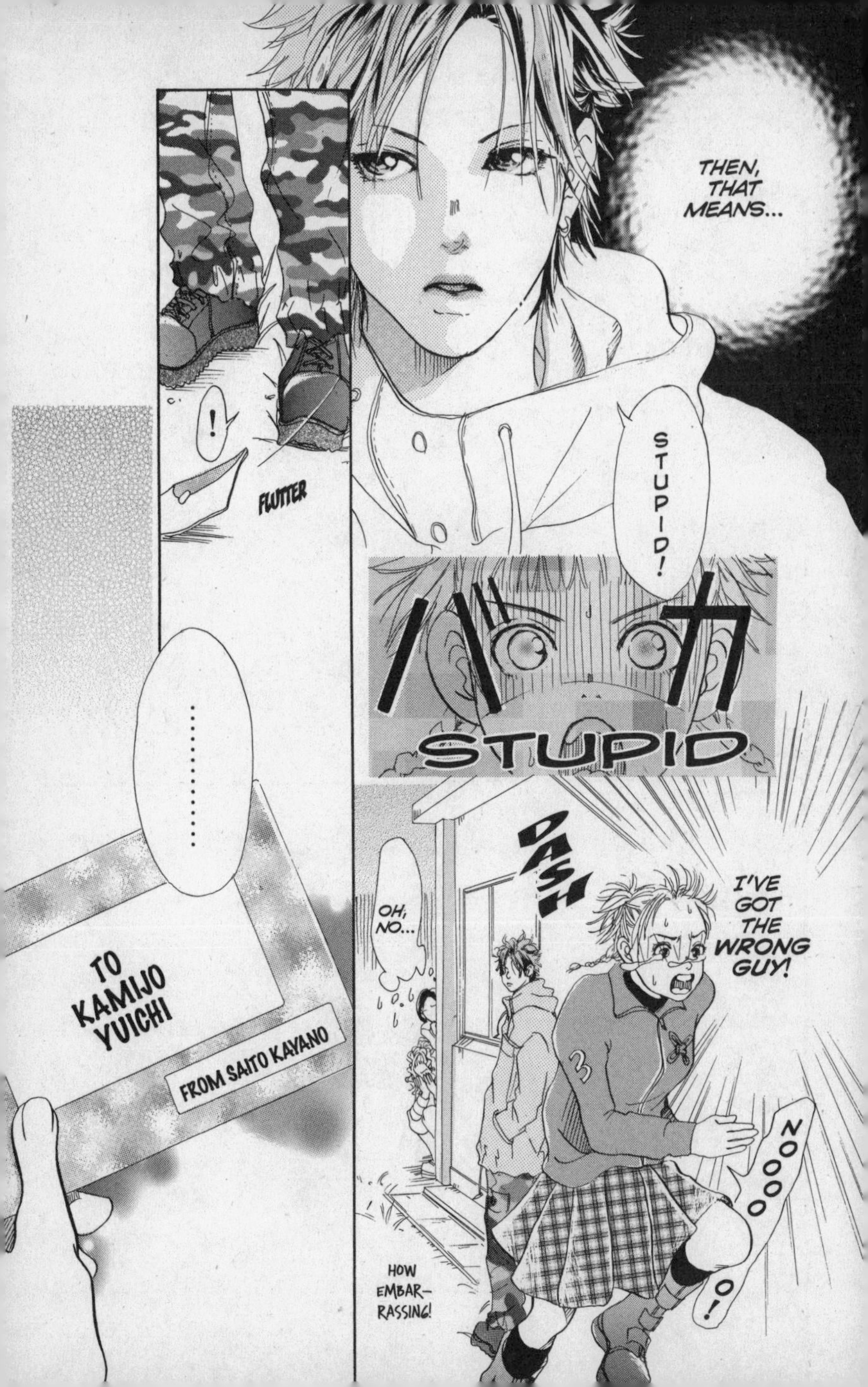
THEN, THAT MEANS...
STUPID!
バカ
STUPID
DASH
I'VE GOT THE WRONG GUY!
OH, NO...
NOOOOO!
HOW EMBAR-RASSING!
!
FLUTTER
......
TO KAMIJO YUICHI
FROM SAITO KAYANO

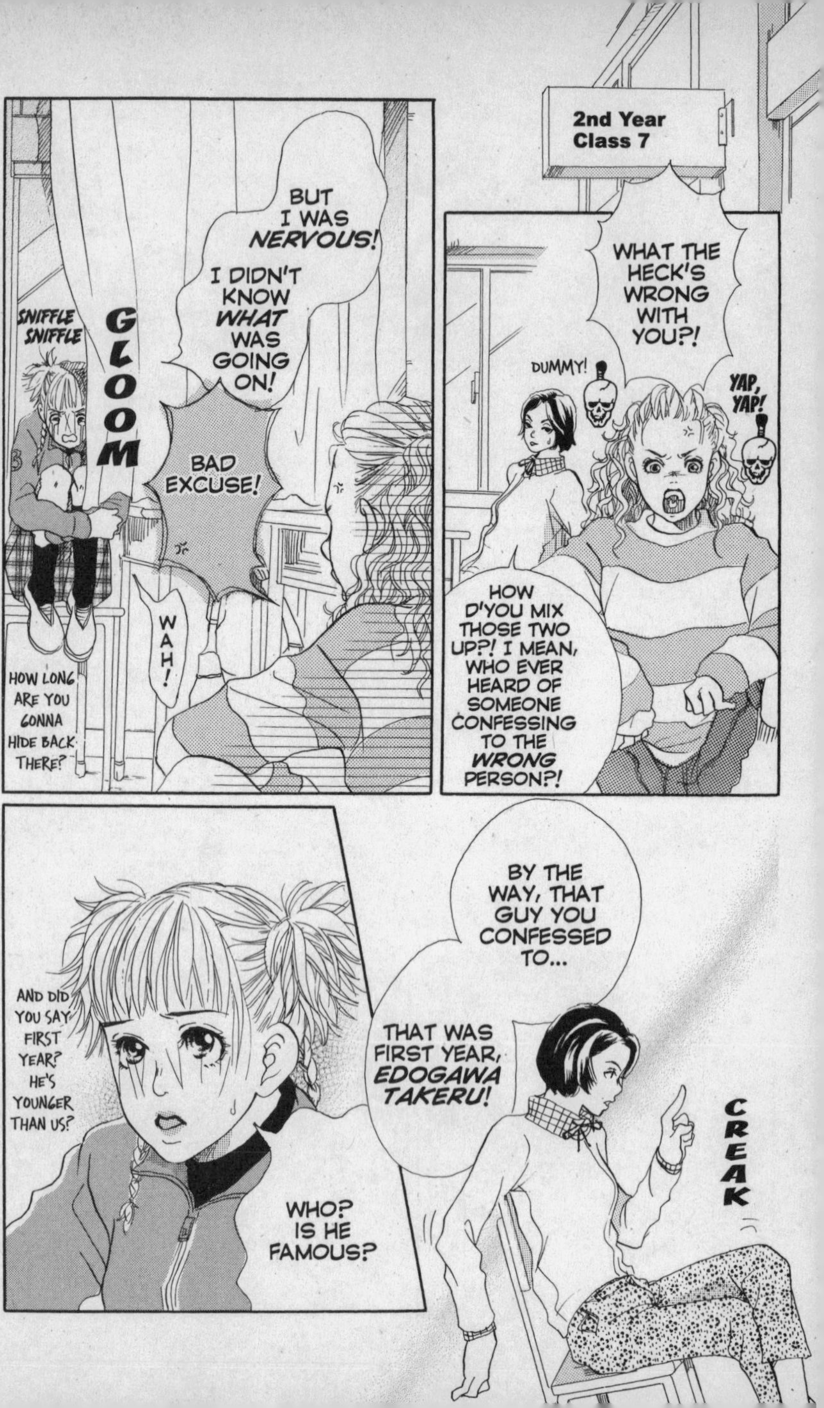
2nd Year Class 7
WHAT THE HECK'S WRONG WITH YOU?!
YAP, YAP!
DUMMY!
HOW D'YOU MIX THOSE TWO UP?! I MEAN, WHO EVER HEARD OF SOMEONE CONFESSING TO THE *WRONG* PERSON?!
BUT I WAS *NERVOUS!*
I DIDN'T KNOW *WHAT* WAS GOING ON!
BAD EXCUSE!
GLOOM
SNIFFLE SNIFFLE
WAH!
HOW LONG ARE YOU GONNA HIDE BACK THERE?
BY THE WAY, THAT GUY YOU CONFESSED TO...
THAT WAS FIRST YEAR, *EDOGAWA TAKERU!*
CREAK
WHO? IS HE FAMOUS?
AND DID YOU SAY FIRST YEAR? HE'S YOUNGER THAN US?

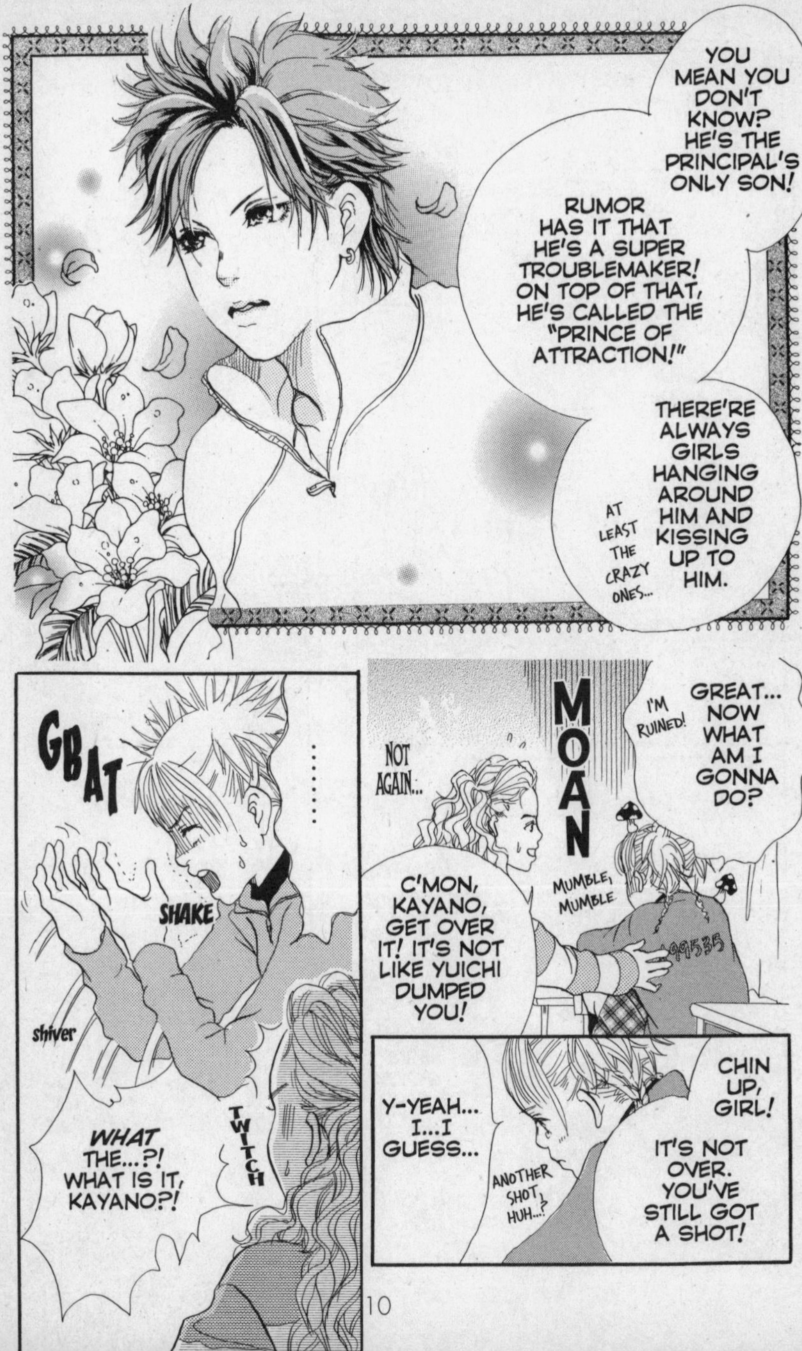
YOU MEAN YOU DON'T KNOW? HE'S THE PRINCIPAL'S ONLY SON!
RUMOR HAS IT THAT HE'S A SUPER TROUBLEMAKER! ON TOP OF THAT, HE'S CALLED THE "PRINCE OF ATTRACTION!"
THERE'RE ALWAYS GIRLS HANGING AROUND HIM AND KISSING UP TO HIM.
AT LEAST THE CRAZY ONES...
GREAT... NOW WHAT AM I GONNA DO?
I'M RUINED!
MOAN
NOT AGAIN...
MUMBLE, MUMBLE
C'MON, KAYANO, GET OVER IT! IT'S NOT LIKE YUICHI DUMPED YOU!
CHIN UP, GIRL!
IT'S NOT OVER. YOU'VE STILL GOT A SHOT!
Y-YEAH... I...I GUESS...
ANOTHER SHOT, HUH...?
GBAT
......
SHAKE
shiver
TWITCH
WHAT THE...?! WHAT IS IT, KAYANO?!

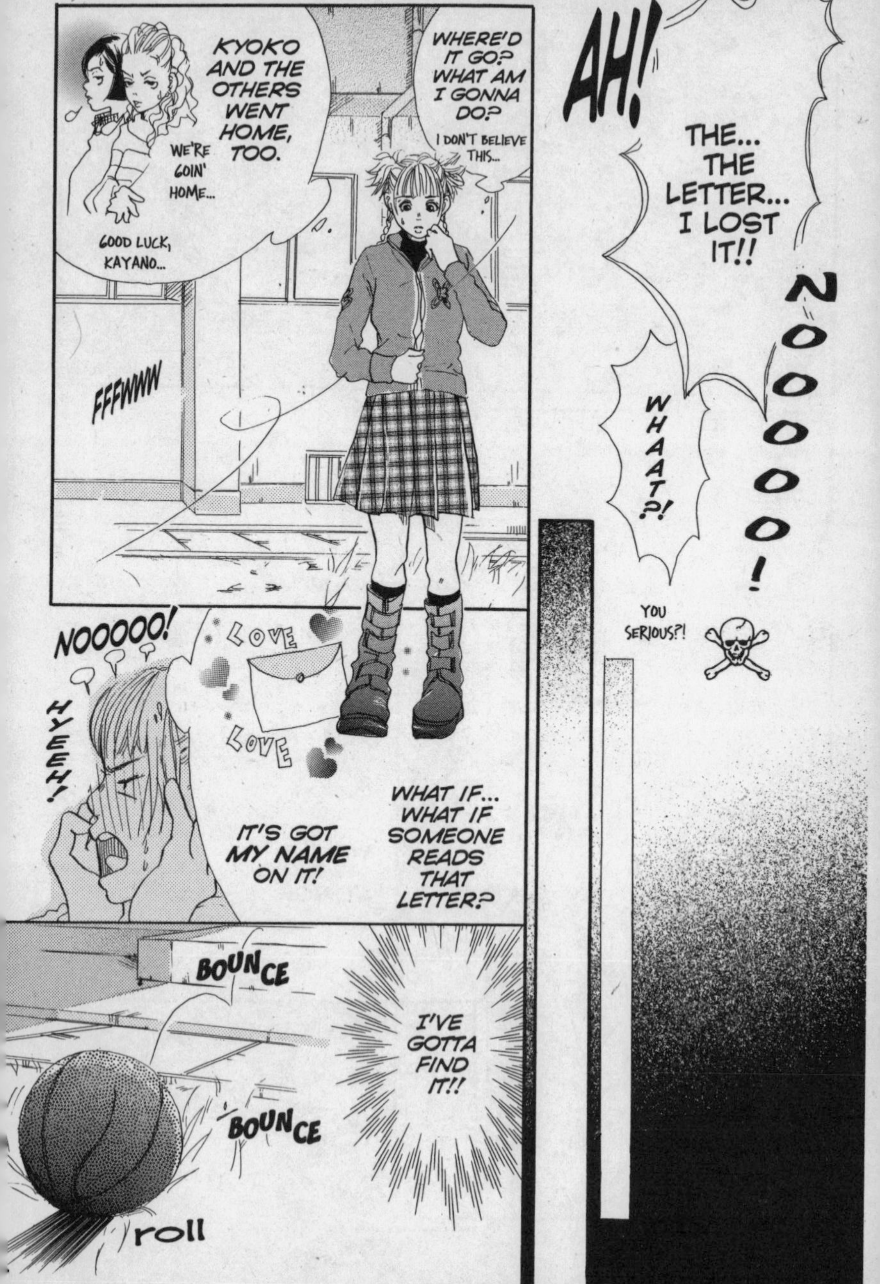
AH!
THE... THE LETTER... I LOST IT!!
NOOOOOO!
WHAAAT?!
YOU SERIOUS?!
WHERE'D IT GO? WHAT AM I GONNA DO?
I DON'T BELIEVE THIS...
KYOKO AND THE OTHERS WENT HOME, TOO.
WE'RE GOIN' HOME...
GOOD LUCK, KAYANO...
FFFWWW
WHAT IF... WHAT IF SOMEONE READS THAT LETTER?
IT'S GOT MY NAME ON IT!
LOVE
LOVE
NOOOOO!
HYEEEH!
I'VE GOTTA FIND IT!!
BOUNCE
BOUNCE
roll

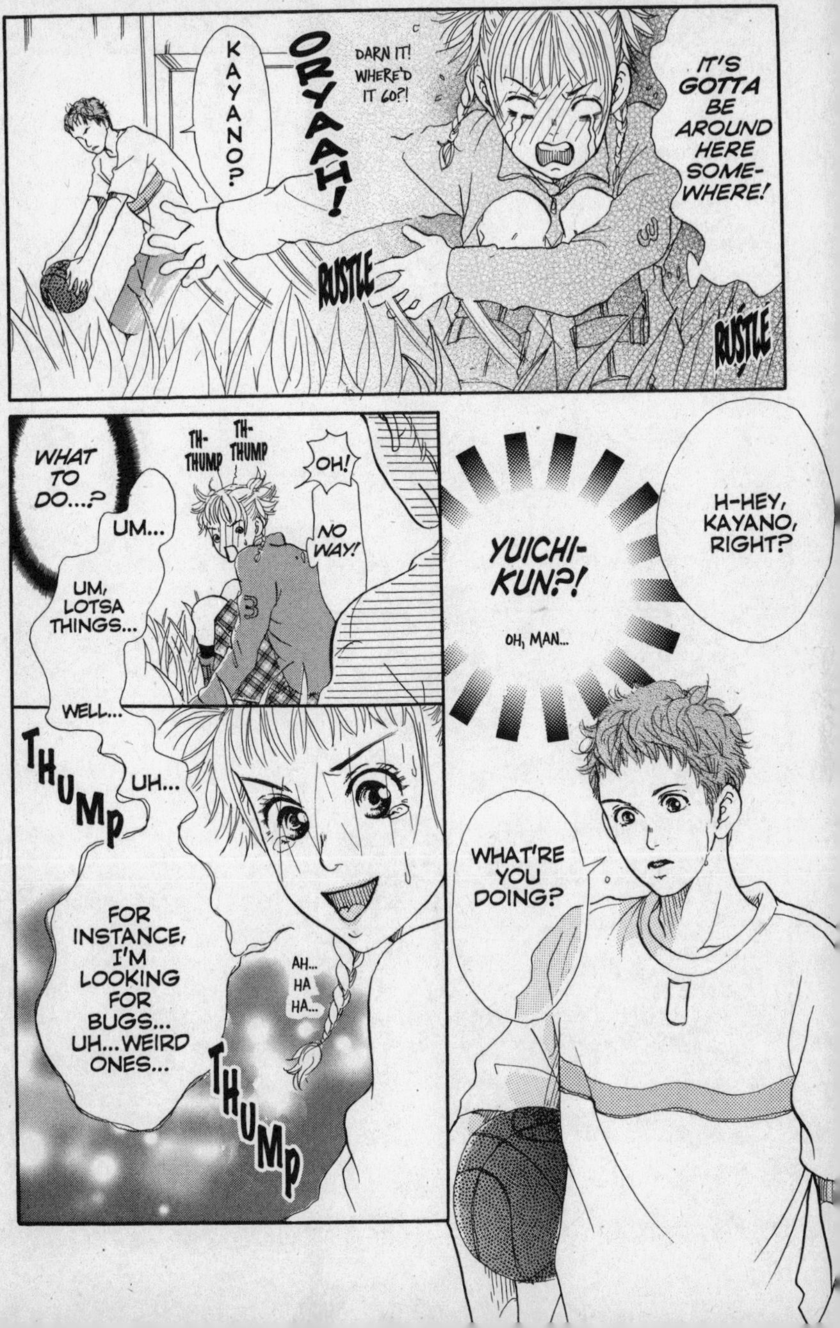

IT'S GOTTA BE AROUND HERE SOME-WHERE!
DARN IT! WHERE'D IT GO?!
ORYAAH!
KAYANO?
RUSTLE
RUSTLE
H-HEY, KAYANO, RIGHT?
YUICHI-KUN?!
OH, MAN...
WHAT'RE YOU DOING?
OH!
NO WAY!
TH-THUMP
TH-THUMP
WHAT TO DO...?
UM...
UM, LOTSA THINGS...
WELL...
UH...
THUMP
FOR INSTANCE, I'M LOOKING FOR BUGS... UH...WEIRD ONES...
AH... HA HA...
THUMP

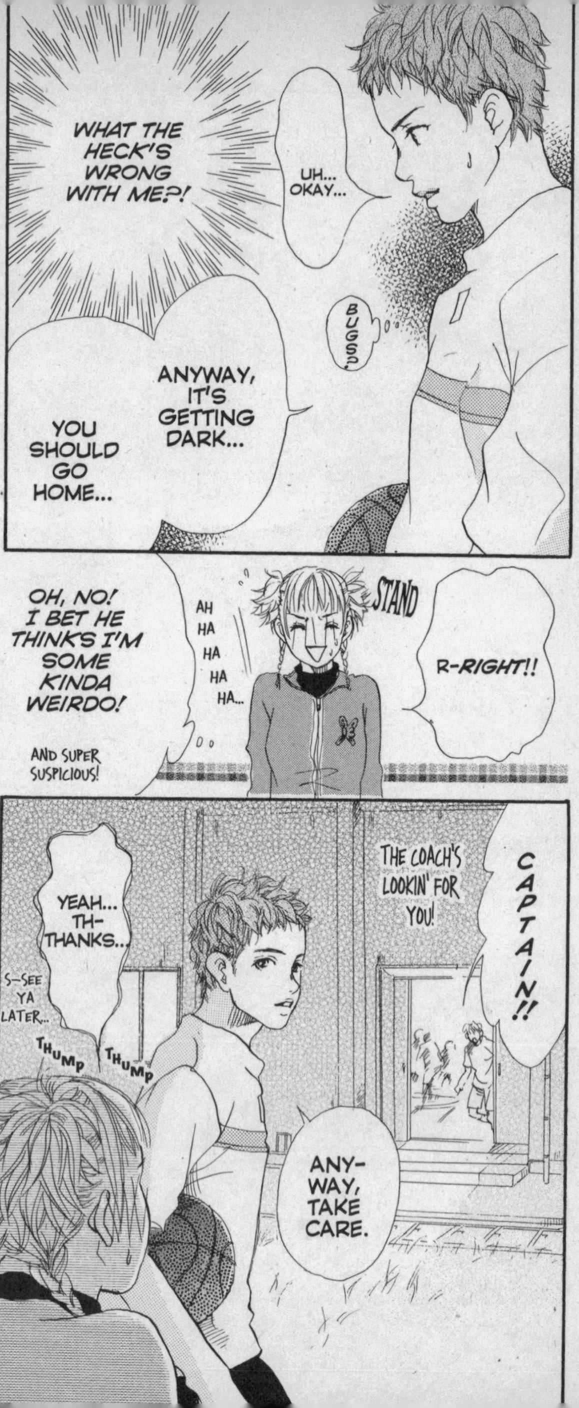
UH... OKAY...
WHAT THE HECK'S WRONG WITH ME?!
BUGS?
ANYWAY, IT'S GETTING DARK...
YOU SHOULD GO HOME...
R-RIGHT!!
STAND
AH HA HA HA HA...
OH, NO! I BET HE THINKS I'M SOME KINDA WEIRDO!
AND SUPER SUSPICIOUS!
CAPTAIN!!
THE COACH'S LOOKIN' FOR YOU!
ANY-WAY, TAKE CARE.
YEAH... TH-THANKS...
S-SEE YA LATER...
THUMP
THUMP

1

MitsuBa CLUB

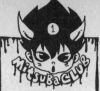

Good evening----!!

(The Outlaw of Bessatsu Maraget Magazine)

I'm Takanashi Mitsuba. How is everybody? The book is finally out: "The Devil Does Exist" vol. 1. It's certainly something to be grateful for. I want to thank everyone. Thank you all. I thought I would take the rare opportunity to talk about the serialization in this sidebar. As much as possible permits, I will answer everyone's questions. Yes. First of all, let's start with the title: "AKUMA DE SORO"--The Devil Does Exist. Well, I really only chose it because it had a nice ring to it, and I thought this piece would only be a one-shot story. Rather extravagant for a simple piece. But I liked it. So when talks of running the title as a series, I thought about the title for inspiration to expand the story. I suppose the feeling of the title allowed me to create this story.

Continued.

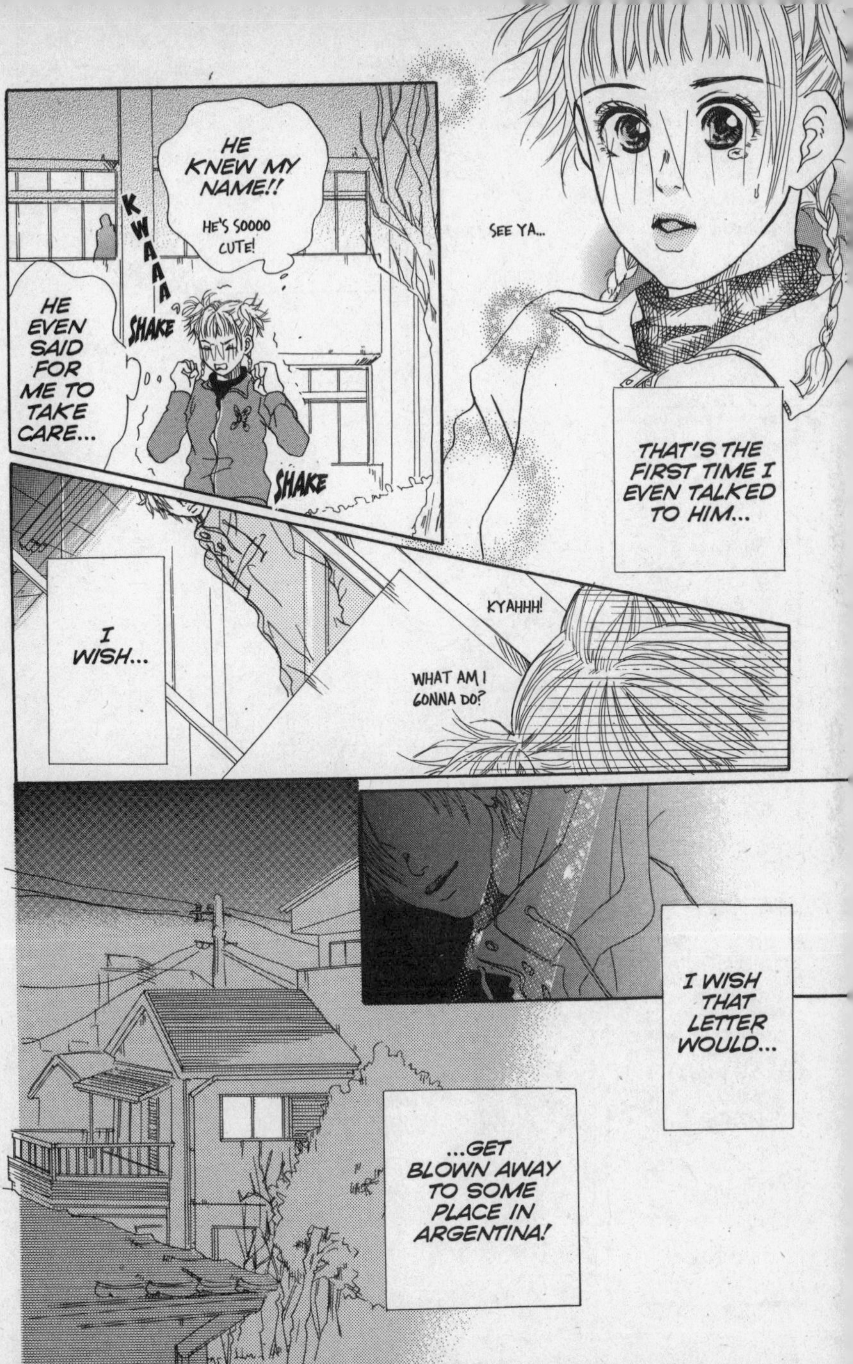
SEE YA...
THAT'S THE FIRST TIME I EVEN TALKED TO HIM...
HE KNEW MY NAME!!
HE'S SOOOO CUTE!
KWAAAA
SHAKE
HE EVEN SAID FOR ME TO TAKE CARE...
SHAKE
KYAHHH!
WHAT AM I GONNA DO?
I WISH...
I WISH THAT LETTER WOULD...
...GET BLOWN AWAY TO SOME PLACE IN ARGENTINA!

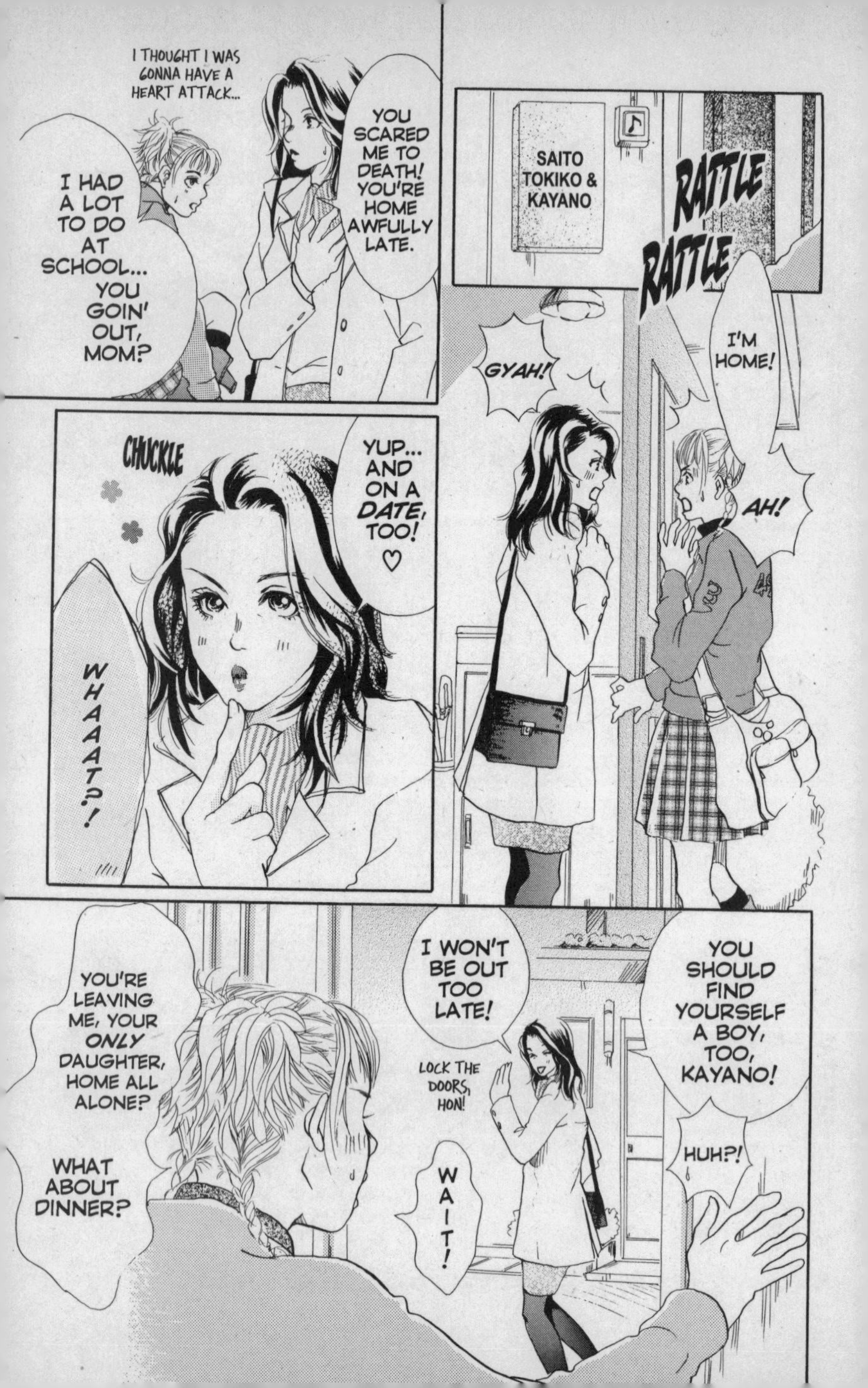

SAITO TOKIKO & KAYANO
RATTLE RATTLE
I'M HOME!
GYAH!
AH!
YOU SCARED ME TO DEATH! YOU'RE HOME AWFULLY LATE.
I THOUGHT I WAS GONNA HAVE A HEART ATTACK...
I HAD A LOT TO DO AT SCHOOL... YOU GOIN' OUT, MOM?
YUP... AND ON A *DATE*, TOO! ♡
CHUCKLE
WHAAAAT?!
YOU SHOULD FIND YOURSELF A BOY, TOO, KAYANO!
HUH?!
I WON'T BE OUT TOO LATE!
LOCK THE DOORS, HON!
WAIT!
YOU'RE LEAVING ME, YOUR *ONLY* DAUGHTER, HOME ALL ALONE?
WHAT ABOUT DINNER?

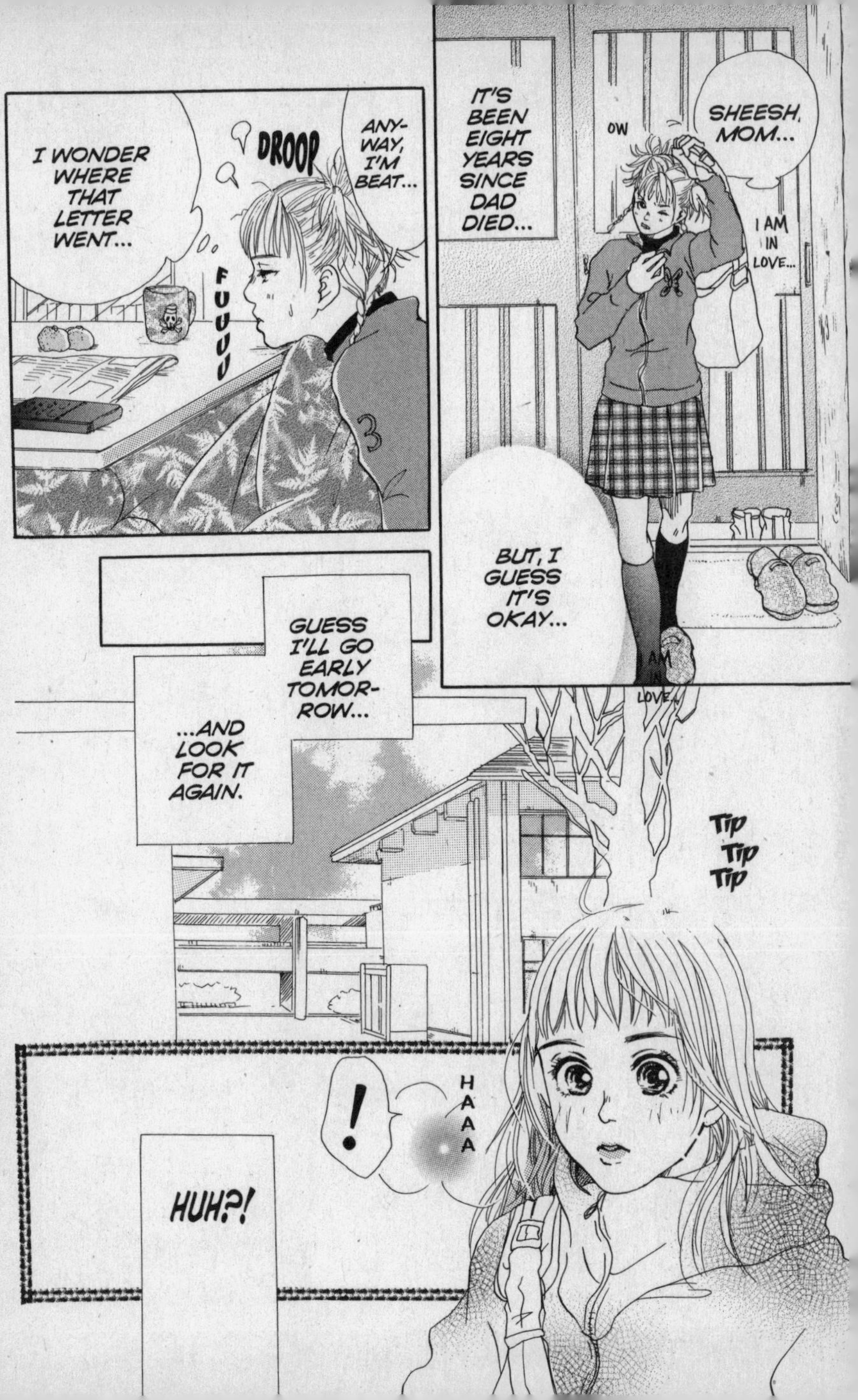
SHEESH, MOM...
OW
I AM IN LOVE...
IT'S BEEN EIGHT YEARS SINCE DAD DIED...
BUT, I GUESS IT'S OKAY...
I AM IN LOVE...
ANY-WAY, I'M BEAT...
DROOP
FUUUU
I WONDER WHERE THAT LETTER WENT...
GUESS I'LL GO EARLY TOMOR-ROW...
...AND LOOK FOR IT AGAIN.
Tip Tip Tip
HAAA
!
HUH?!

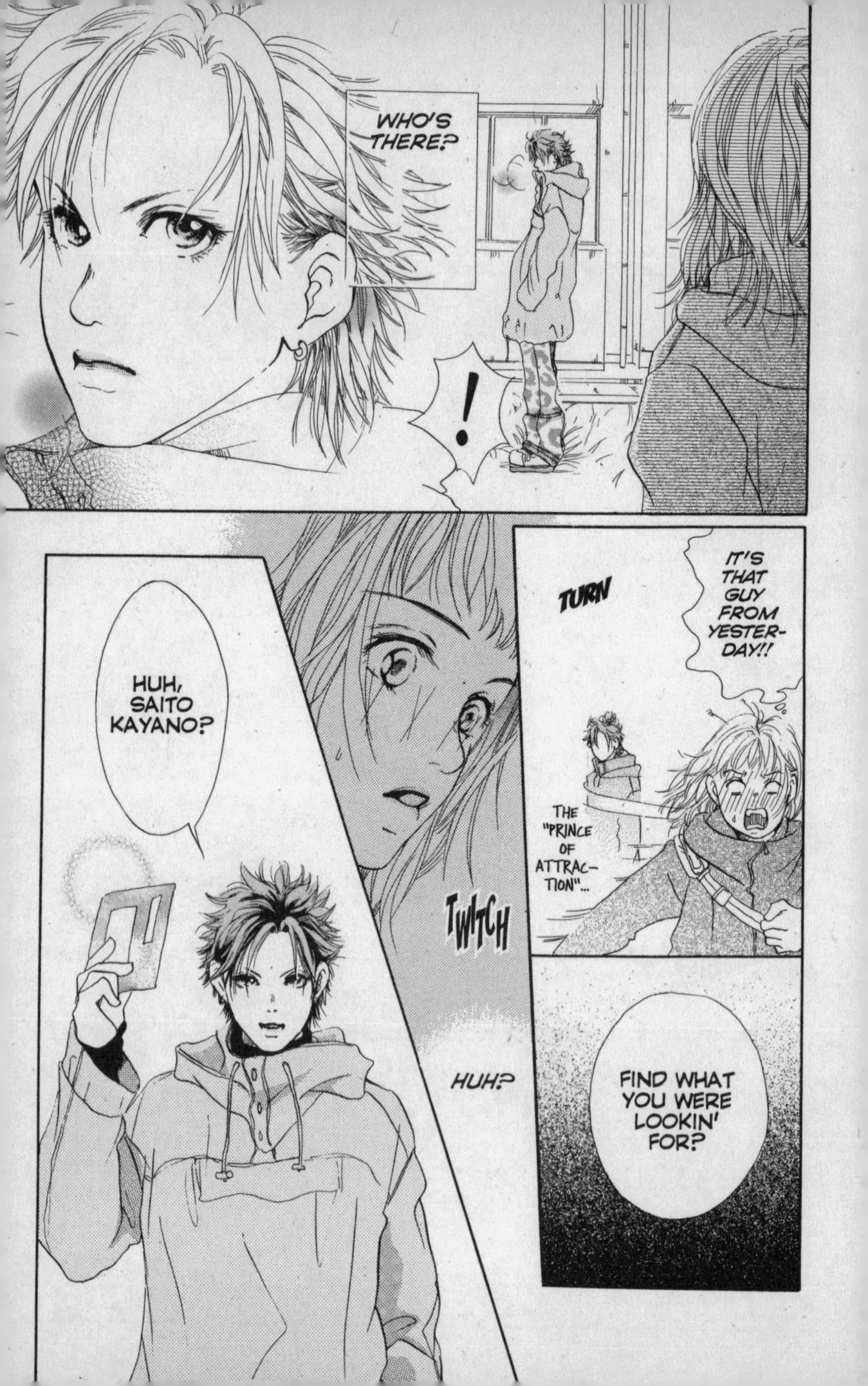
WHO'S THERE?
!
TURN
IT'S THAT GUY FROM YESTER-DAY!!
THE "PRINCE OF ATTRACTION"...
FIND WHAT YOU WERE LOOKIN' FOR?
TWITCH
HUH?
HUH, SAITO KAYANO?

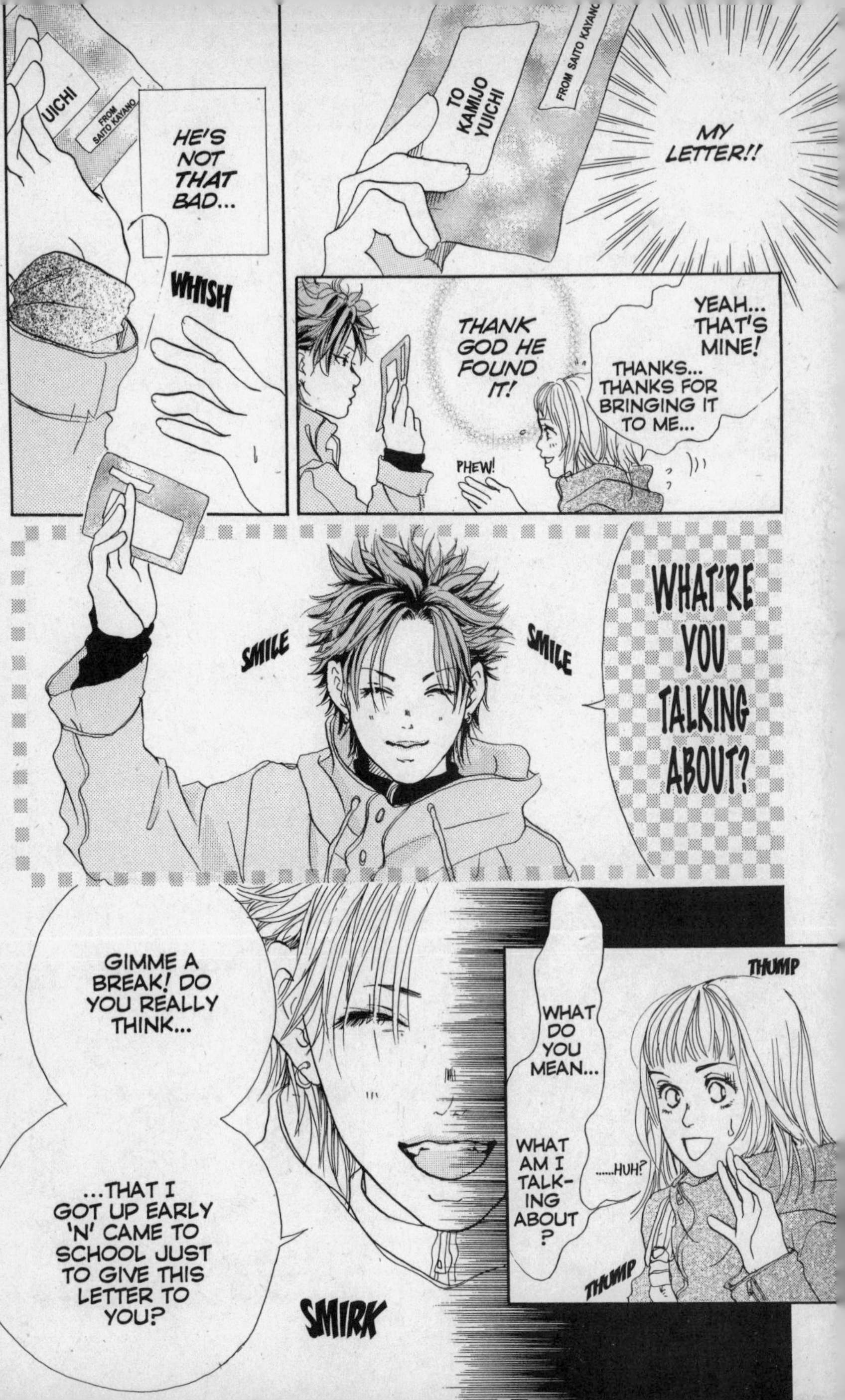
TO KAMIJO YUICHI
FROM SAITO KAYANO
MY LETTER!!
YEAH... THAT'S MINE!
THANKS... THANKS FOR BRINGING IT TO ME...
THANK GOD HE FOUND IT!
PHEW!
UICHI
FROM SAITO KAYANO
HE'S NOT THAT BAD...
WHISH
WHAT'RE YOU TALKING ABOUT?
SMILE
SMILE
THUMP
WHAT DO YOU MEAN...
WHAT AM I TALK-ING ABOUT?
......HUH?
THUMP
GIMME A BREAK! DO YOU REALLY THINK...
...THAT I GOT UP EARLY 'N' CAME TO SCHOOL JUST TO GIVE THIS LETTER TO YOU?
SMIRK

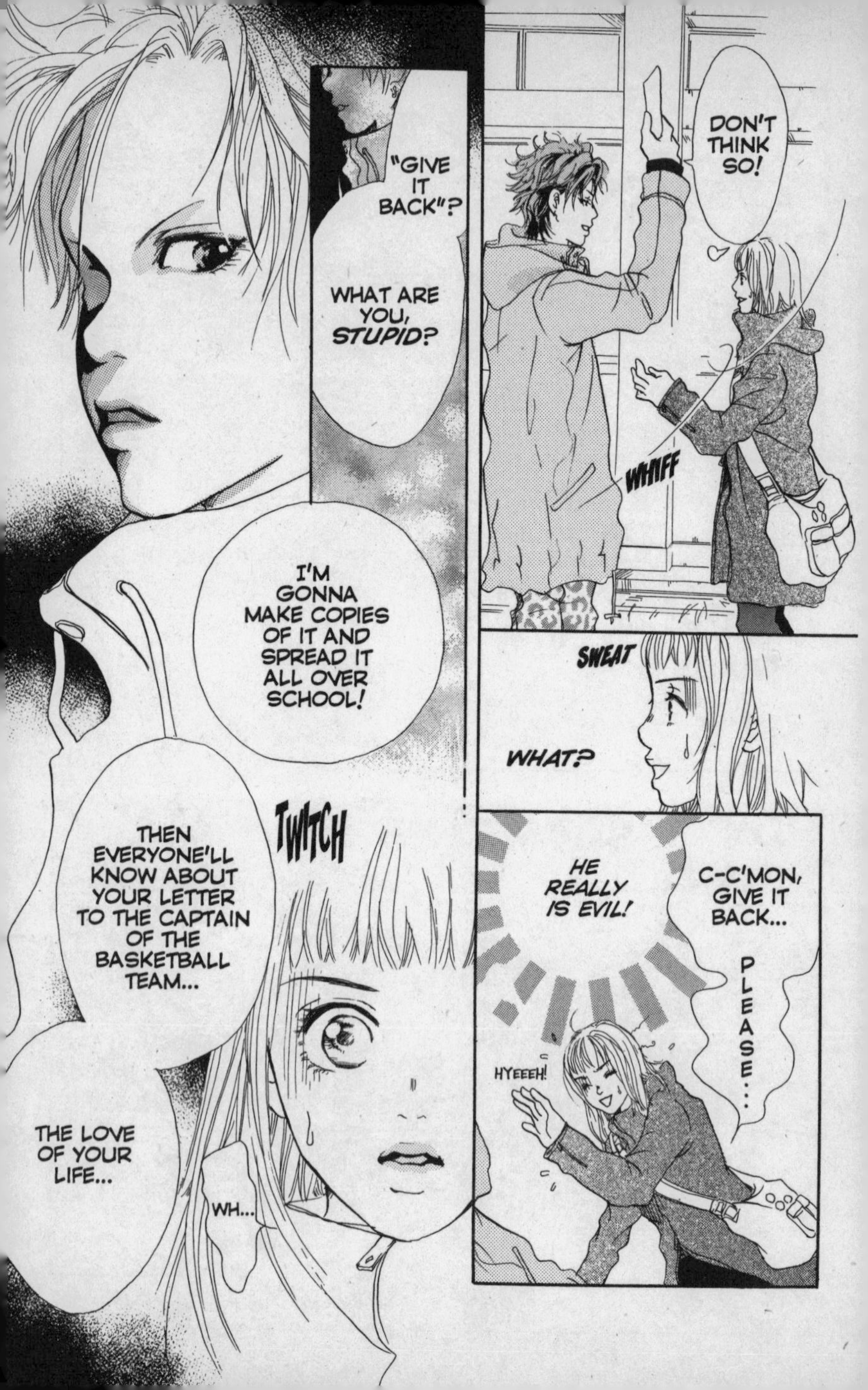
DON'T THINK SO!
WHIFF
SWEAT
WHAT?
C-C'MON, GIVE IT BACK...
HE REALLY IS EVIL!
PLEASE...
HYEEEH!
"GIVE IT BACK"?
WHAT ARE YOU, STUPID?
I'M GONNA MAKE COPIES OF IT AND SPREAD IT ALL OVER SCHOOL!
THEN EVERYONE'LL KNOW ABOUT YOUR LETTER TO THE CAPTAIN OF THE BASKETBALL TEAM...
TWITCH
THE LOVE OF YOUR LIFE...
WH...

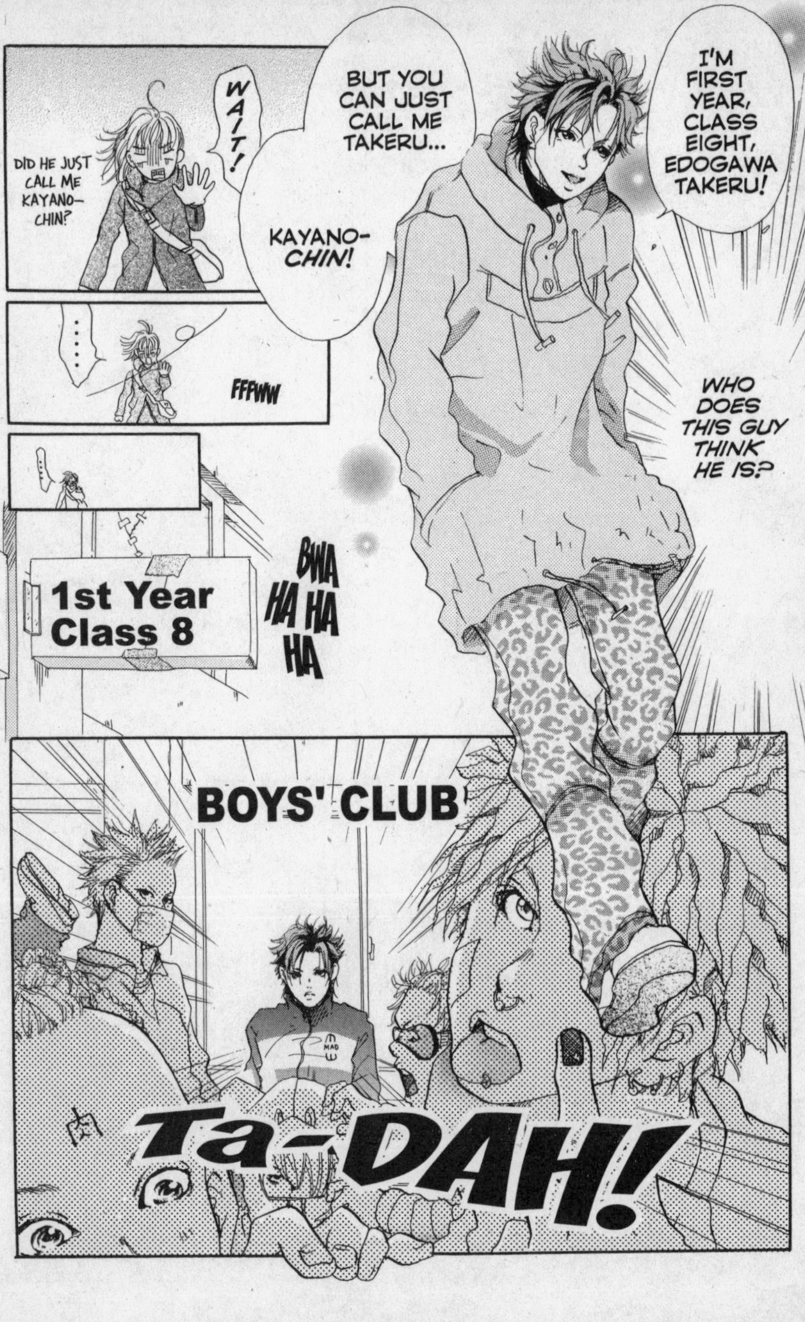
I'M FIRST YEAR, CLASS EIGHT, EDOGAWA TAKERU!
BUT YOU CAN JUST CALL ME TAKERU...
KAYANO-CHIN!
WHO DOES THIS GUY THINK HE IS?
WAIT!
DID HE JUST CALL ME KAYANO-CHIN?
......
FFFWW
...
1st Year Class 8
BWA HA HA HA HA
BOYS' CLUB
Ta-DAH!

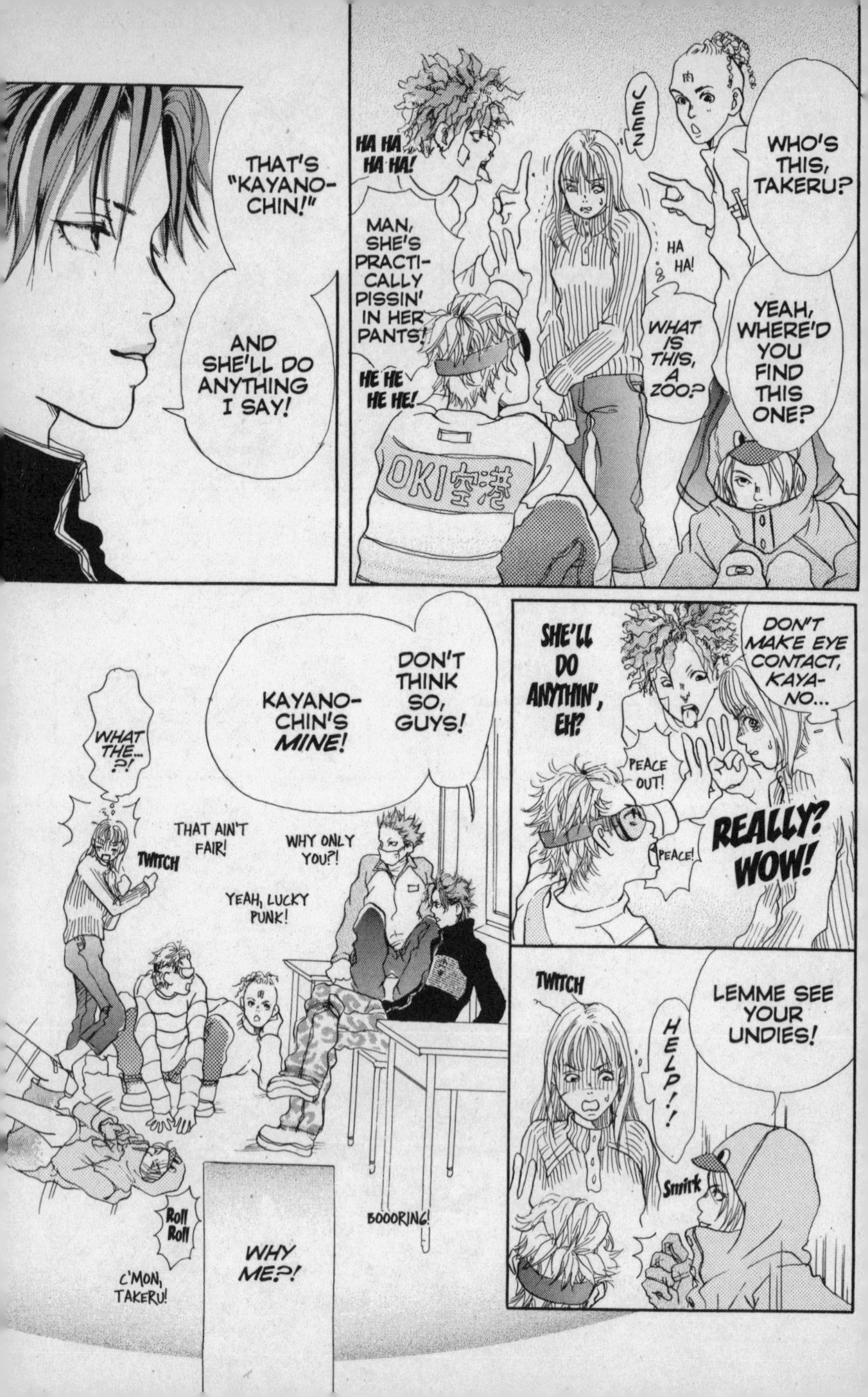
WHO'S THIS, TAKERU?
JEEZ
HA HA HA HA!
MAN, SHE'S PRACTI-CALLY PISSIN' IN HER PANTS!
HA HA!
YEAH, WHERE'D YOU FIND THIS ONE?
WHAT IS THIS, A ZOO?
HE HE HE HE!
OKI空港
THAT'S "KAYANO-CHIN!"
AND SHE'LL DO ANYTHING I SAY!
DON'T MAKE EYE CONTACT, KAYA-NO...
SHE'LL DO ANYTHIN', EH?
PEACE OUT!
REALLY? WOW!
PEACE!
LEMME SEE YOUR UNDIES!
HELP!!
TWITCH
Smirk
DON'T THINK SO, GUYS!
KAYANO-CHIN'S MINE!
WHAT THE...?!
WHY ONLY YOU?!
THAT AIN'T FAIR!
TWITCH
YEAH, LUCKY PUNK!
BOOORING!
Roll Roll
WHY ME?!
C'MON, TAKERU!

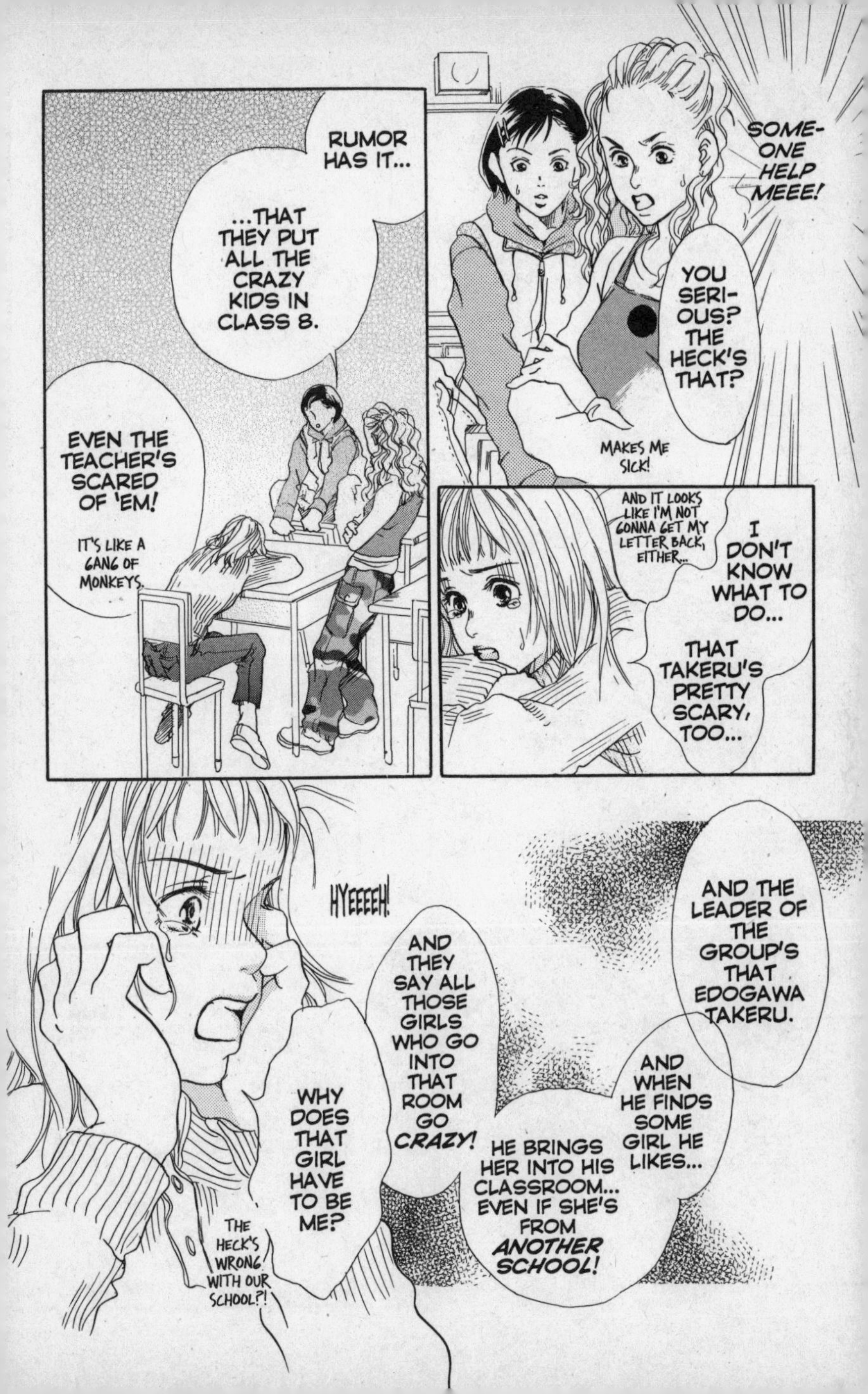
SOME-ONE HELP MEEE!
YOU SERI-OUS? THE HECK'S THAT?
MAKES ME SICK!
I DON'T KNOW WHAT TO DO...
AND IT LOOKS LIKE I'M NOT GONNA GET MY LETTER BACK, EITHER...
THAT TAKERU'S PRETTY SCARY, TOO...
RUMOR HAS IT...
...THAT THEY PUT ALL THE CRAZY KIDS IN CLASS 8.
EVEN THE TEACHER'S SCARED OF 'EM!
IT'S LIKE A GANG OF MONKEYS.
AND THE LEADER OF THE GROUP'S THAT EDOGAWA TAKERU.
AND WHEN HE FINDS SOME GIRL HE LIKES...
HE BRINGS HER INTO HIS CLASSROOM... EVEN IF SHE'S FROM *ANOTHER SCHOOL*!
AND THEY SAY ALL THOSE GIRLS WHO GO INTO THAT ROOM GO *CRAZY*!
WHY DOES THAT GIRL HAVE TO BE ME?
HYEEEEH!
THE HECK'S WRONG WITH OUR SCHOOL?!

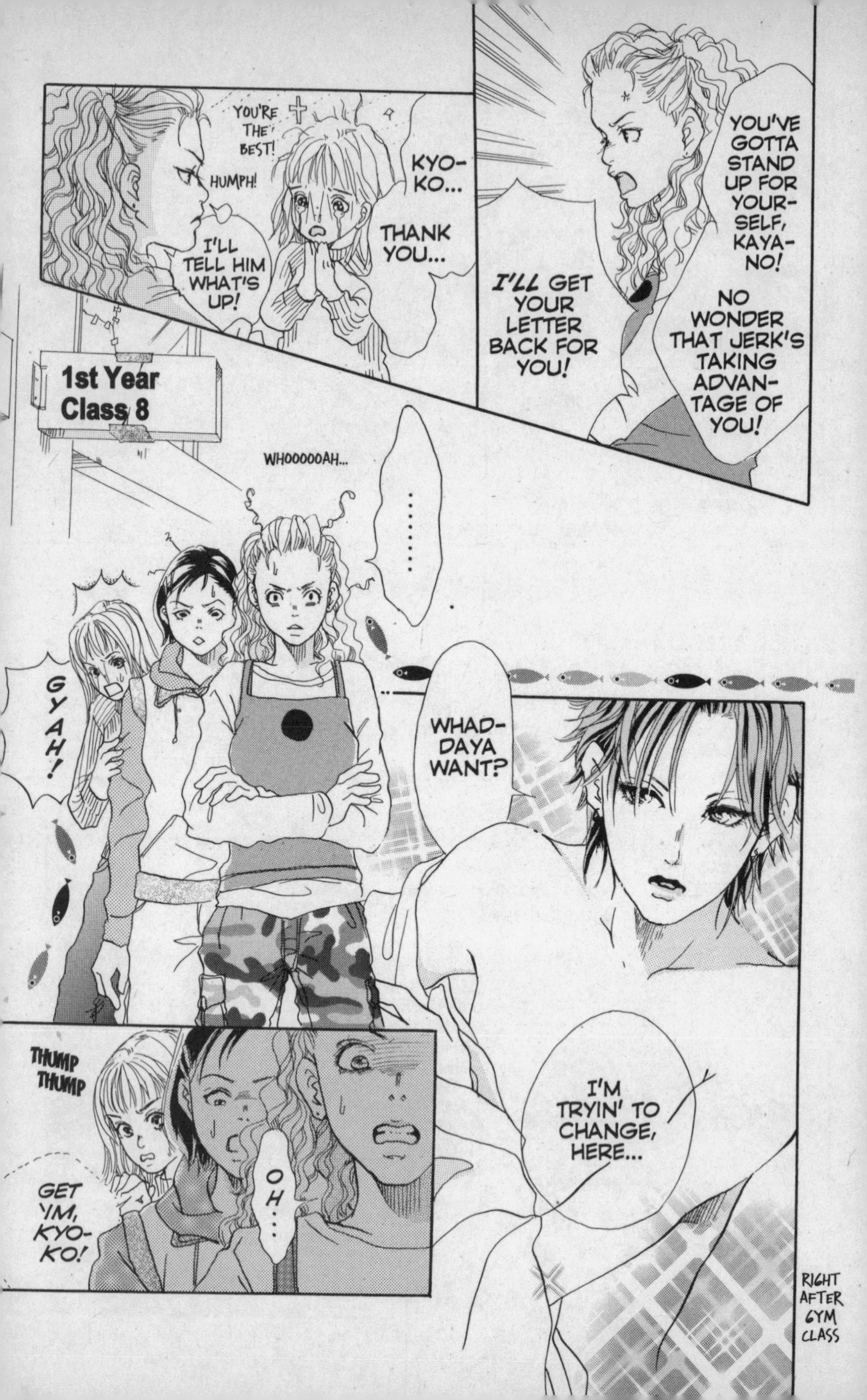
YOU'VE GOTTA STAND UP FOR YOURSELF, KAYANO!
NO WONDER THAT JERK'S TAKING ADVANTAGE OF YOU!
I'LL GET YOUR LETTER BACK FOR YOU!
KYO-KO...
THANK YOU...
YOU'RE THE BEST!
HUMPH!
I'LL TELL HIM WHAT'S UP!
1st Year Class 8
WHOOOOOAH...
......
GYAH!
RIGHT AFTER GYM CLASS
WHAD-DAYA WANT?
I'M TRYIN' TO CHANGE, HERE...
THUMP THUMP
OH...
GET 'IM, KYO-KO!

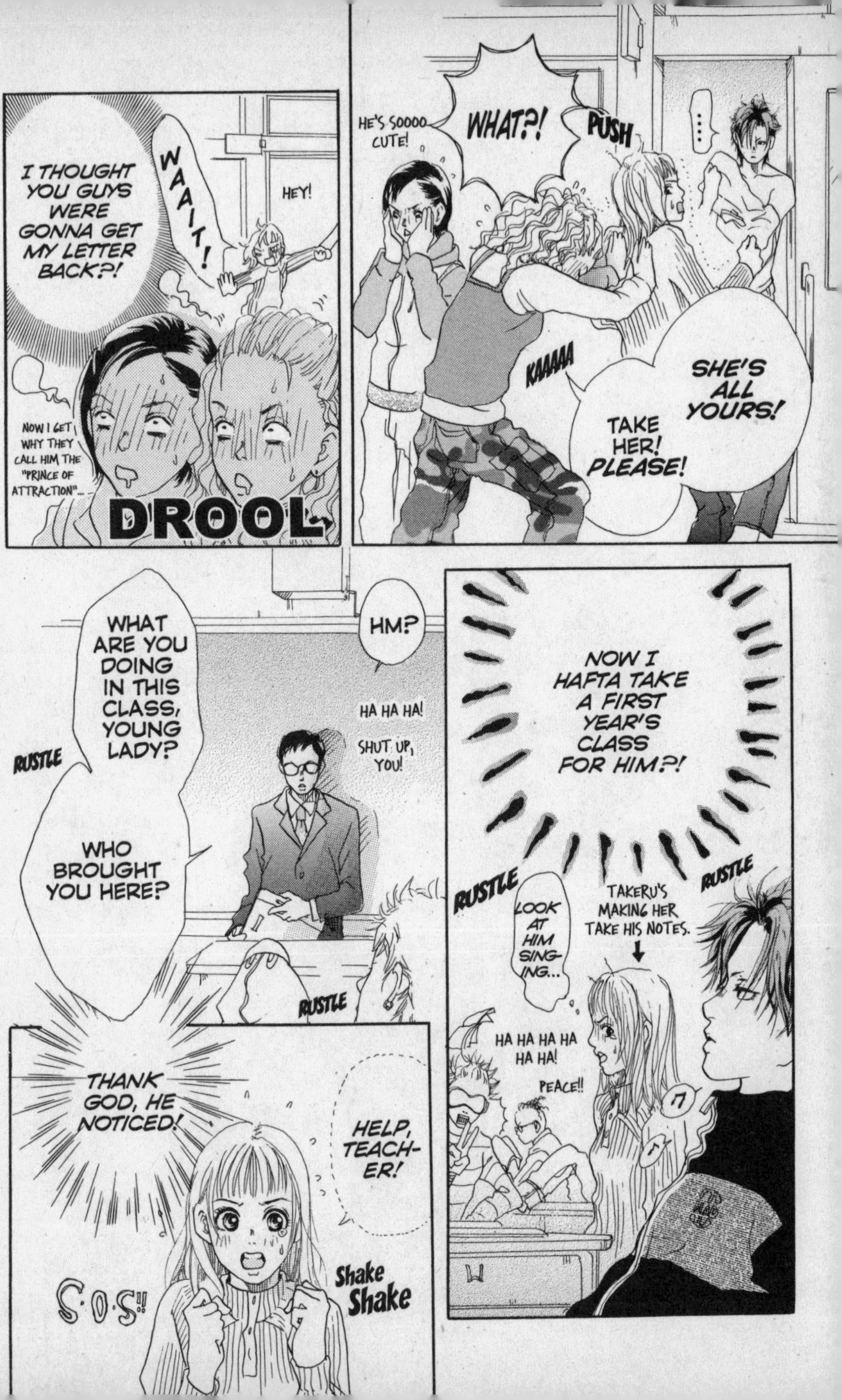
....
PUSH
WHAT?!
HE'S SOOOO CUTE!
SHE'S ALL YOURS!
TAKE HER! PLEASE!
KAAAAA
WAAAIT!
HEY!
I THOUGHT YOU GUYS WERE GONNA GET MY LETTER BACK?!
NOW I GET WHY THEY CALL HIM THE "PRINCE OF ATTRACTION"...
DROOL
NOW I HAFTA TAKE A FIRST YEAR'S CLASS FOR HIM?!
RUSTLE
TAKERU'S MAKING HER TAKE HIS NOTES.
LOOK AT HIM SINGING...
RUSTLE
HA HA HA HA HA HA!
PEACE!!
HM?
WHAT ARE YOU DOING IN THIS CLASS, YOUNG LADY?
HA HA HA!
SHUT UP, YOU!
WHO BROUGHT YOU HERE?
RUSTLE
RUSTLE
HELP, TEACHER!
THANK GOD, HE NOTICED!
Shake Shake
S.O.S!!

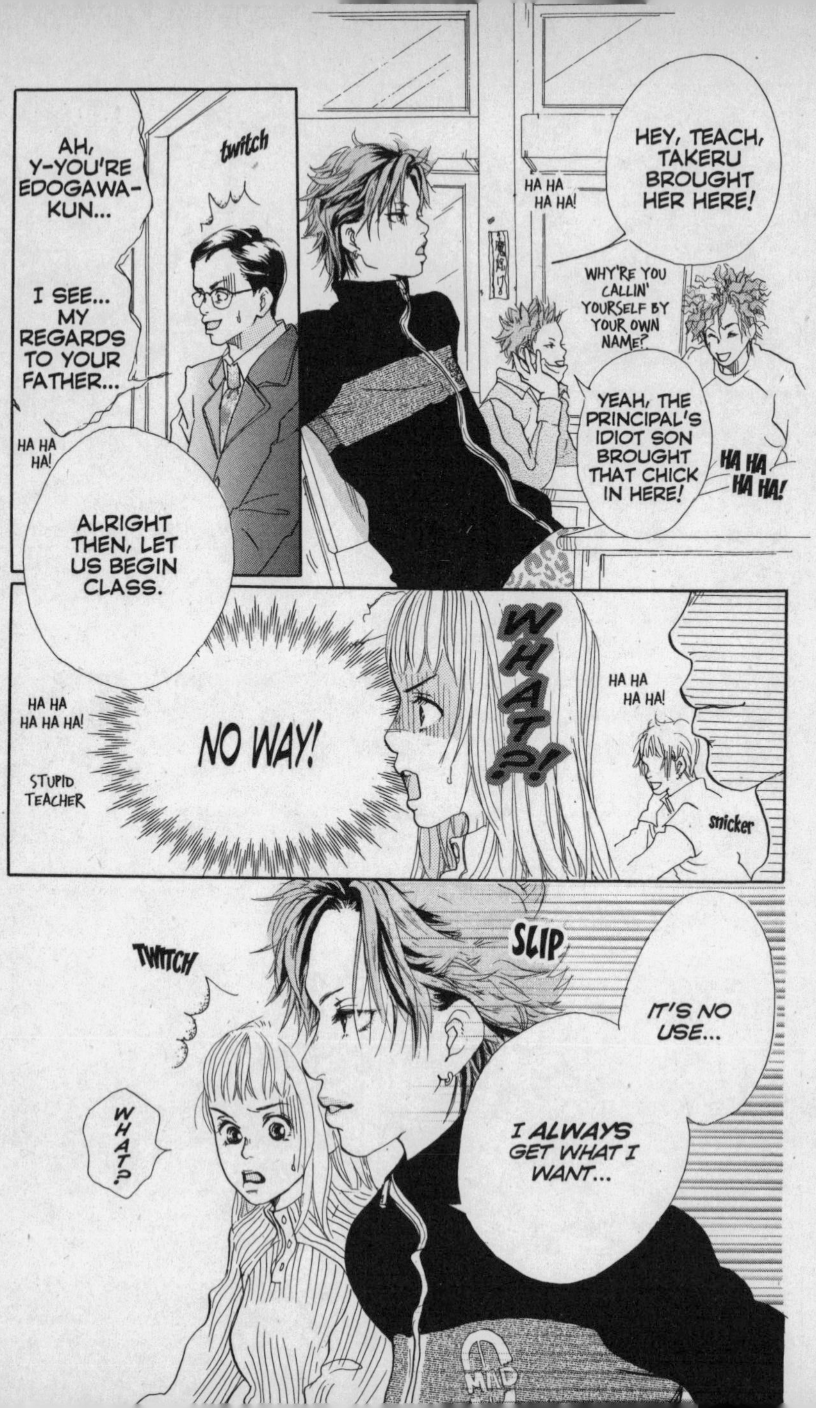
HEY, TEACH, TAKERU BROUGHT HER HERE!
HA HA HA HA!
WHY'RE YOU CALLIN' YOURSELF BY YOUR OWN NAME?
YEAH, THE PRINCIPAL'S IDIOT SON BROUGHT THAT CHICK IN HERE!
HA HA HA HA!
twitch
AH, Y-YOU'RE EDOGAWA-KUN...
I SEE... MY REGARDS TO YOUR FATHER...
HA HA HA!
ALRIGHT THEN, LET US BEGIN CLASS.
WHAT?!
HA HA HA HA!
snicker
NO WAY!
HA HA HA HA HA!
STUPID TEACHER
SLIP
IT'S NO USE...
I ALWAYS GET WHAT I WANT...
TWITCH
WHAT?
MAD

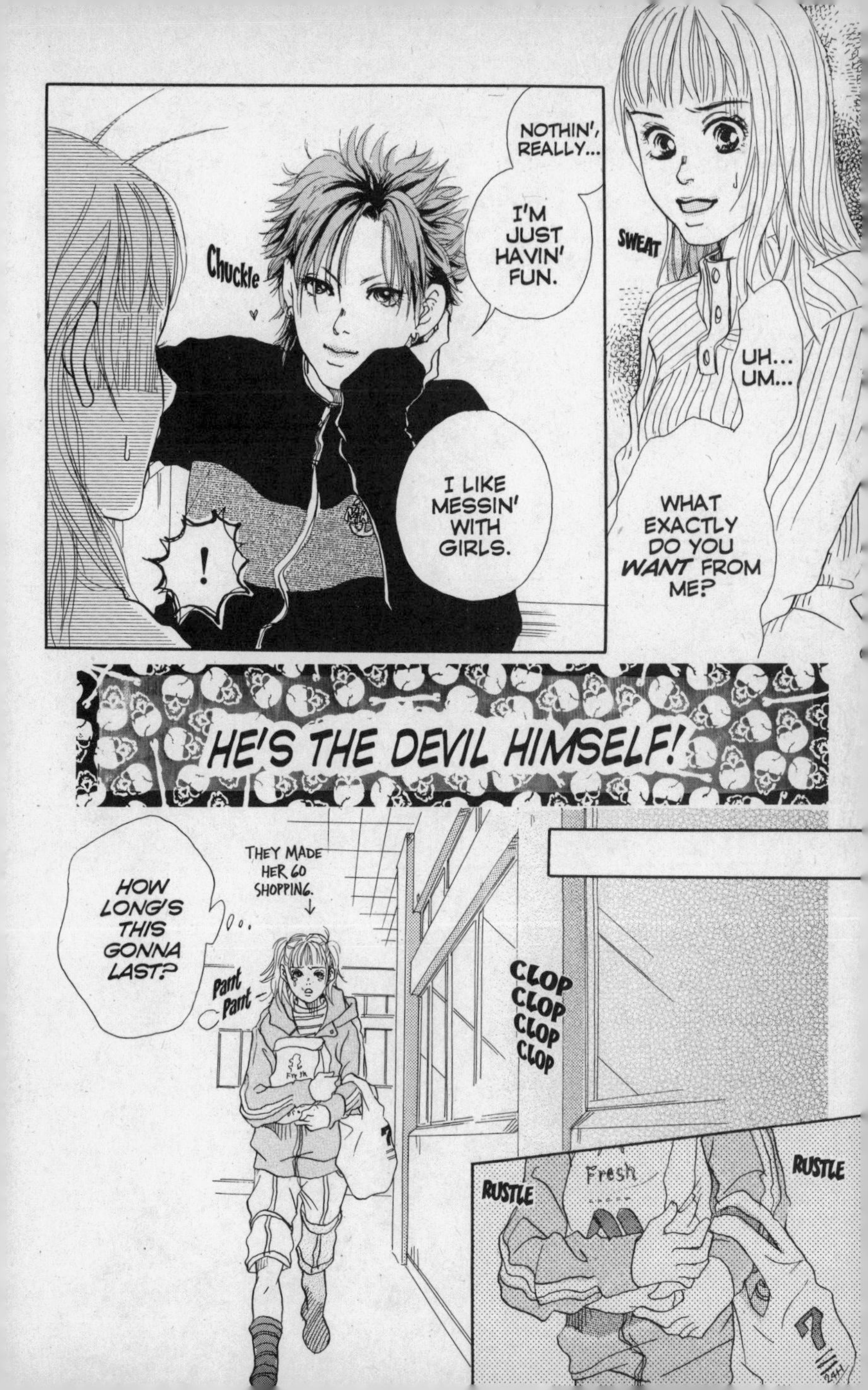
SWEAT
UH... UM...
WHAT EXACTLY DO YOU WANT FROM ME?
NOTHIN', REALLY...
I'M JUST HAVIN' FUN.
Chuckle
I LIKE MESSIN' WITH GIRLS.
!
HE'S THE DEVIL HIMSELF!
RUSTLE
Fresh
RUSTLE
CLOP CLOP CLOP CLOP
THEY MADE HER GO SHOPPING.
HOW LONG'S THIS GONNA LAST?
Pant Pant

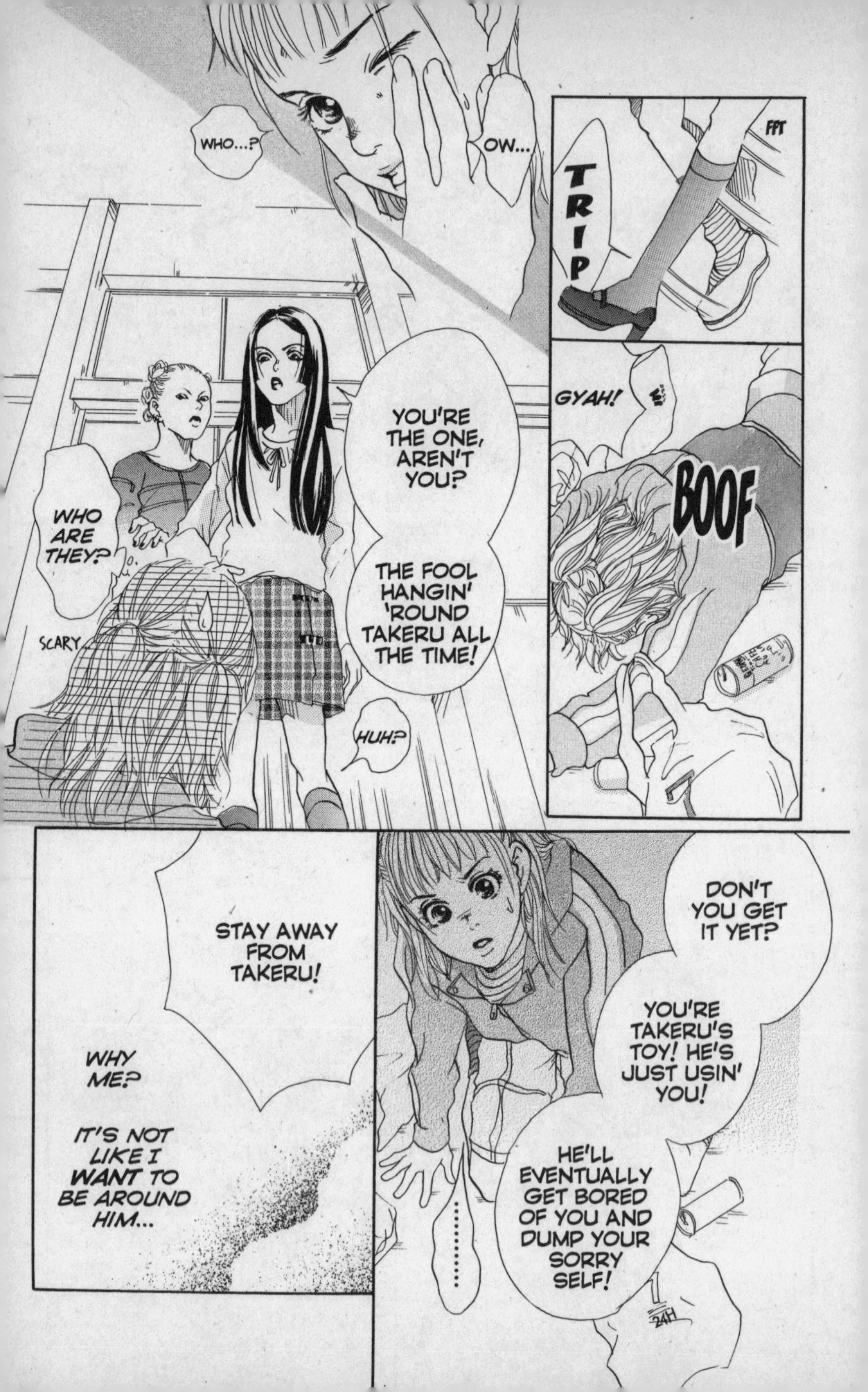
FPT
TRIP
GYAH!
BOOF
OW...
WHO...?
YOU'RE THE ONE, AREN'T YOU?
THE FOOL HANGIN' 'ROUND TAKERU ALL THE TIME!
WHO ARE THEY?
SCARY...
HUH?
DON'T YOU GET IT YET?
YOU'RE TAKERU'S TOY! HE'S JUST USIN' YOU!
HE'LL EVENTUALLY GET BORED OF YOU AND DUMP YOUR SORRY SELF!
......
STAY AWAY FROM TAKERU!
WHY ME?
IT'S NOT LIKE I *WANT* TO BE AROUND HIM...

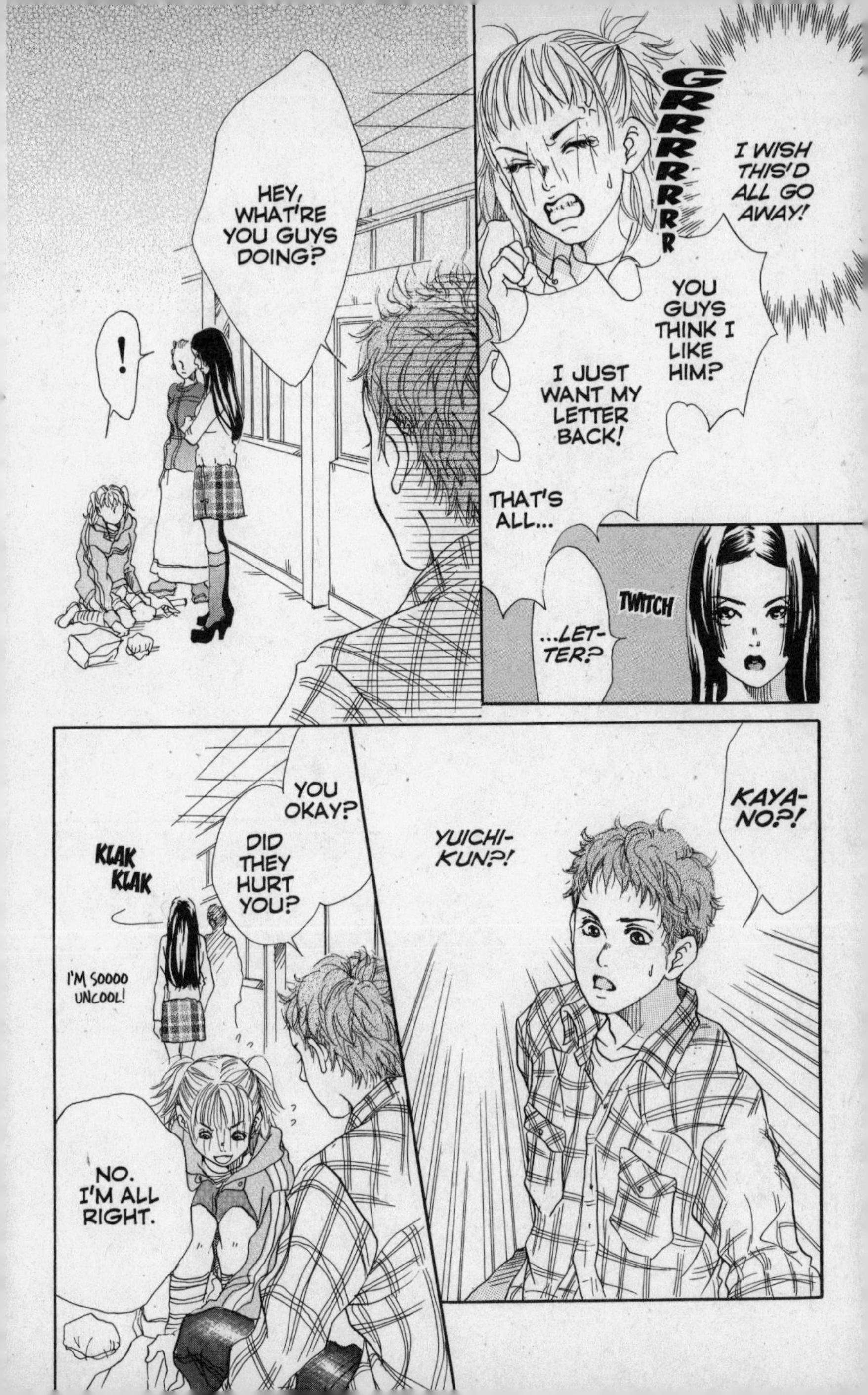
GRRRRRRR
I WISH THIS'D ALL GO AWAY!
YOU GUYS THINK I LIKE HIM?
I JUST WANT MY LETTER BACK!
THAT'S ALL...
TWITCH
...LET-TER?
HEY, WHAT'RE YOU GUYS DOING?
!
KAYA-NO?!
YUICHI-KUN?!
YOU OKAY?
DID THEY HURT YOU?
KLAK KLAK
I'M SOOOO UNCOOL!
NO. I'M ALL RIGHT.

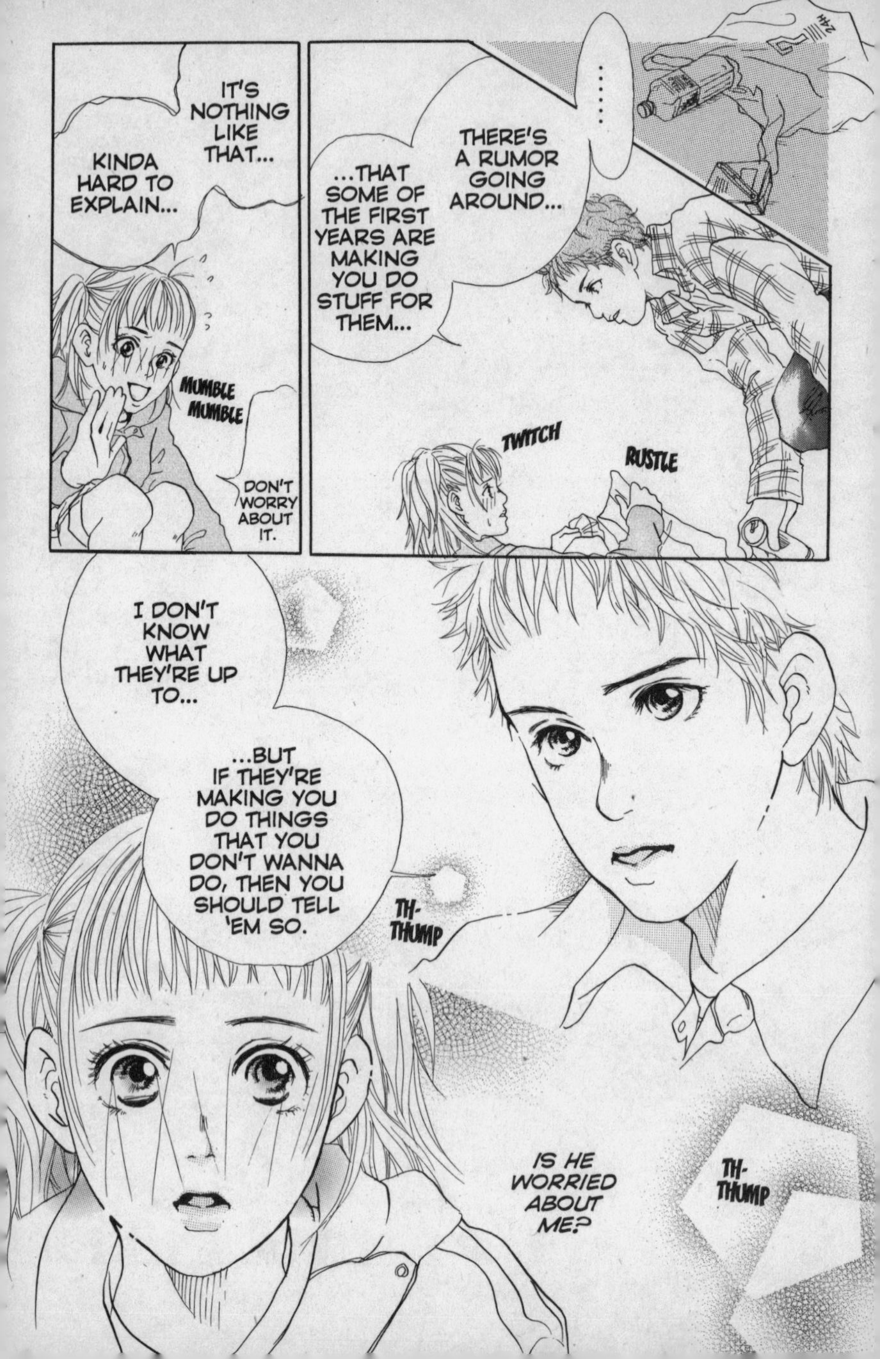
……
THERE'S A RUMOR GOING AROUND...
...THAT SOME OF THE FIRST YEARS ARE MAKING YOU DO STUFF FOR THEM...
TWITCH
RUSTLE
IT'S NOTHING LIKE THAT...
KINDA HARD TO EXPLAIN...
MUMBLE MUMBLE
DON'T WORRY ABOUT IT.
I DON'T KNOW WHAT THEY'RE UP TO...
...BUT IF THEY'RE MAKING YOU DO THINGS THAT YOU DON'T WANNA DO, THEN YOU SHOULD TELL 'EM SO.
TH-THUMP
IS HE WORRIED ABOUT ME?
TH-THUMP

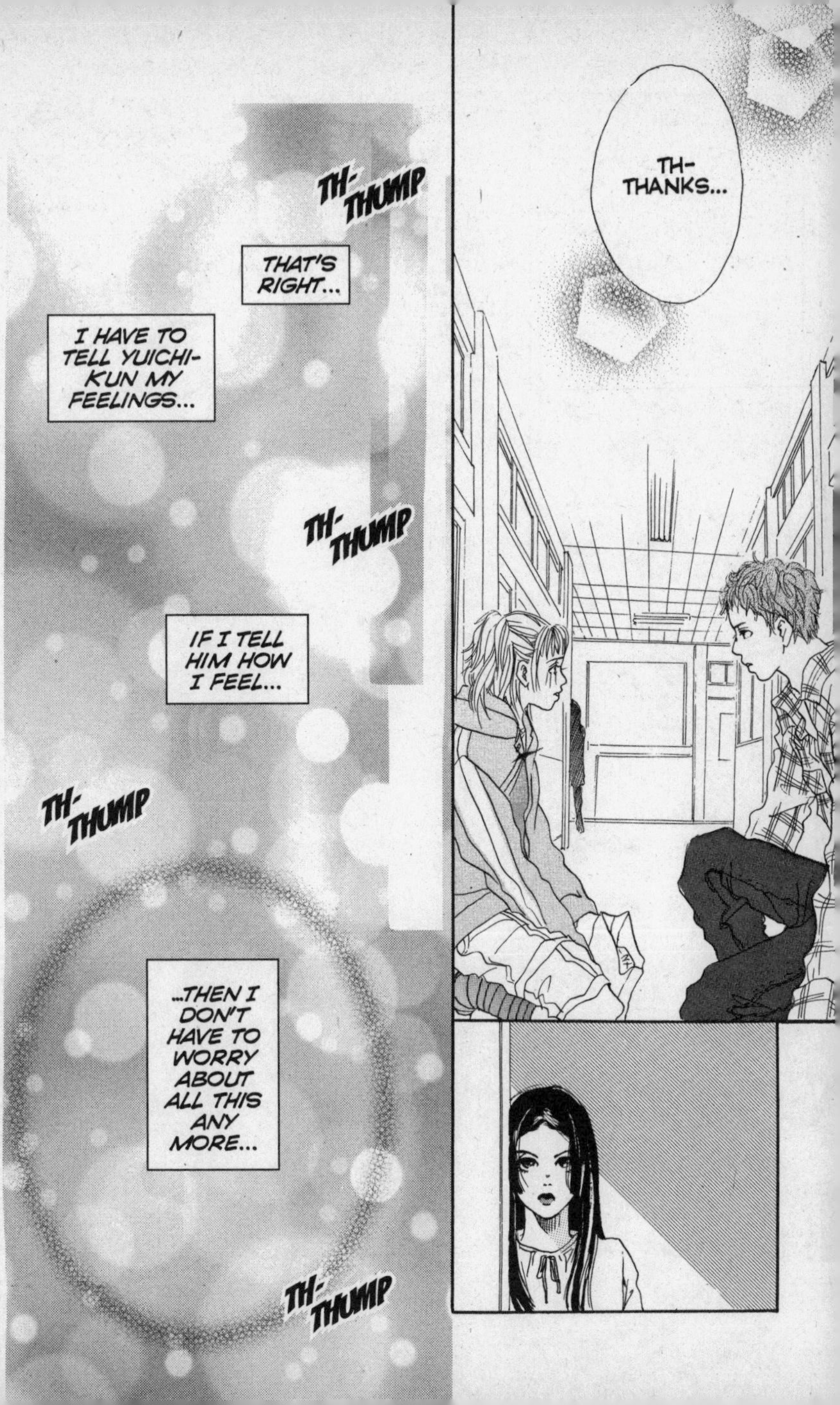
TH-THANKS...
TH-THUMP
THAT'S RIGHT...
I HAVE TO TELL YUICHI-KUN MY FEELINGS...
TH-THUMP
IF I TELL HIM HOW I FEEL...
TH-THUMP
...THEN I DON'T HAVE TO WORRY ABOUT ALL THIS ANY MORE...
TH-THUMP

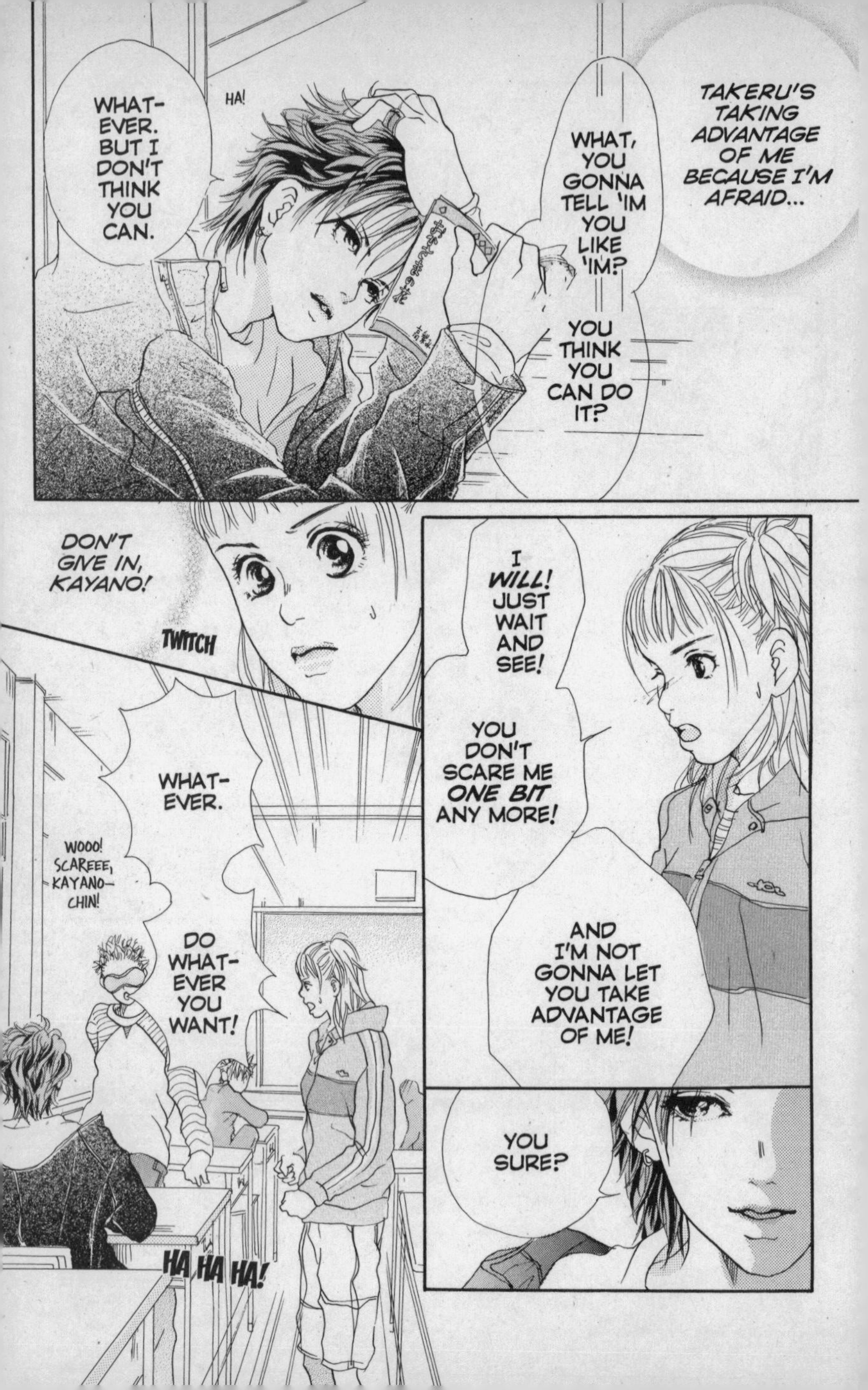
TAKERU'S TAKING ADVANTAGE OF ME BECAUSE I'M AFRAID...
WHAT, YOU GONNA TELL 'IM YOU LIKE 'IM?
YOU THINK YOU CAN DO IT?
HA!
WHAT-EVER. BUT I DON'T THINK YOU CAN.
I *WILL!* JUST WAIT AND SEE!
YOU DON'T SCARE ME *ONE BIT* ANY MORE!
AND I'M NOT GONNA LET YOU TAKE ADVANTAGE OF ME!
YOU SURE?
DON'T GIVE IN, KAYANO!
TWITCH
WHAT-EVER.
DO WHAT-EVER YOU WANT!
WOOO! SCAREEE, KAYANO-CHIN!
HA HA HA!

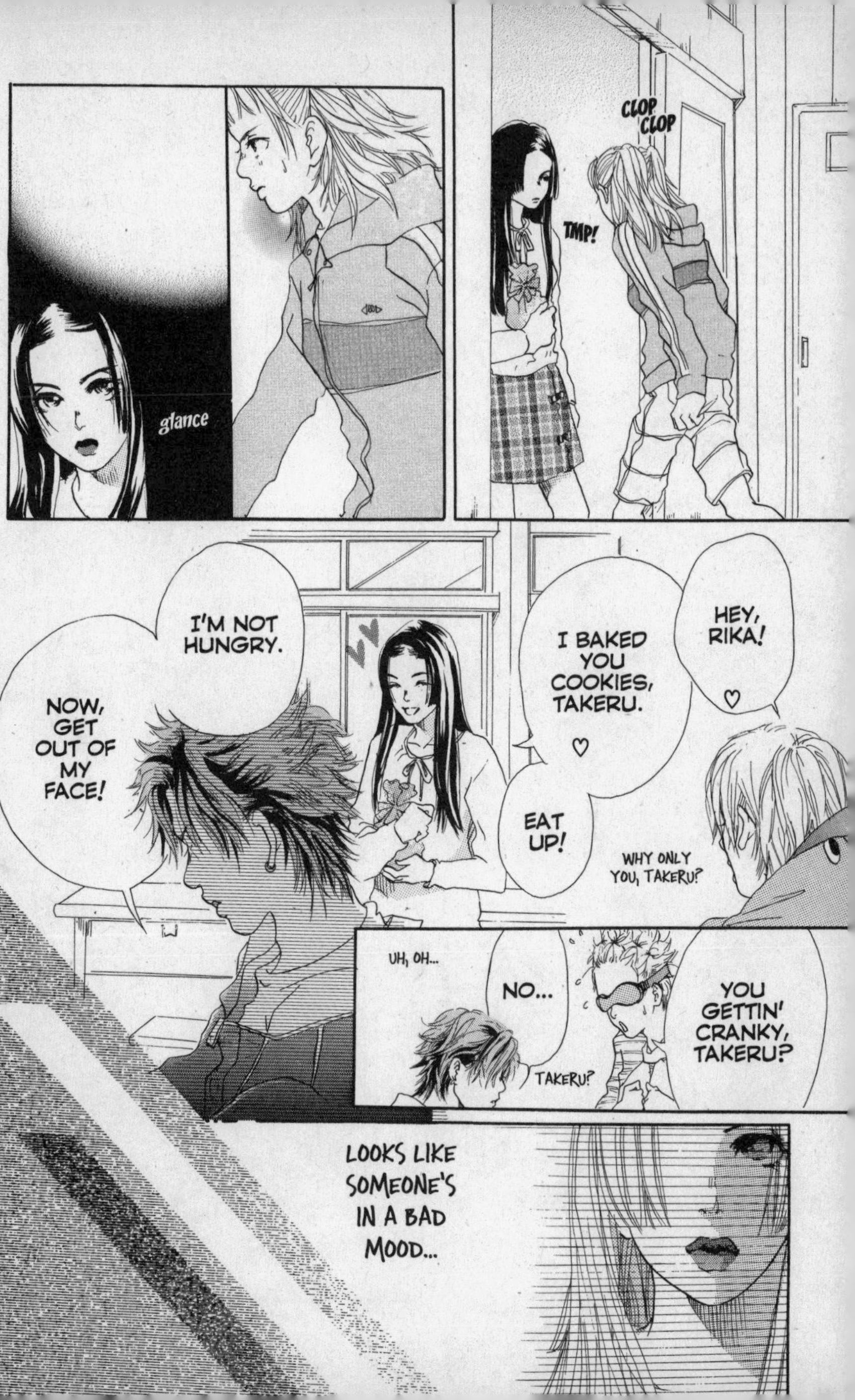
CLOP CLOP
TMP!
glance
HEY, RIKA! ♡
I BAKED YOU COOKIES, TAKERU. ♡
EAT UP!
WHY ONLY YOU, TAKERU?
I'M NOT HUNGRY.
NOW, GET OUT OF MY FACE!
YOU GETTIN' CRANKY, TAKERU?
NO...
TAKERU?
UH, OH...
LOOKS LIKE SOMEONE'S IN A BAD MOOD...

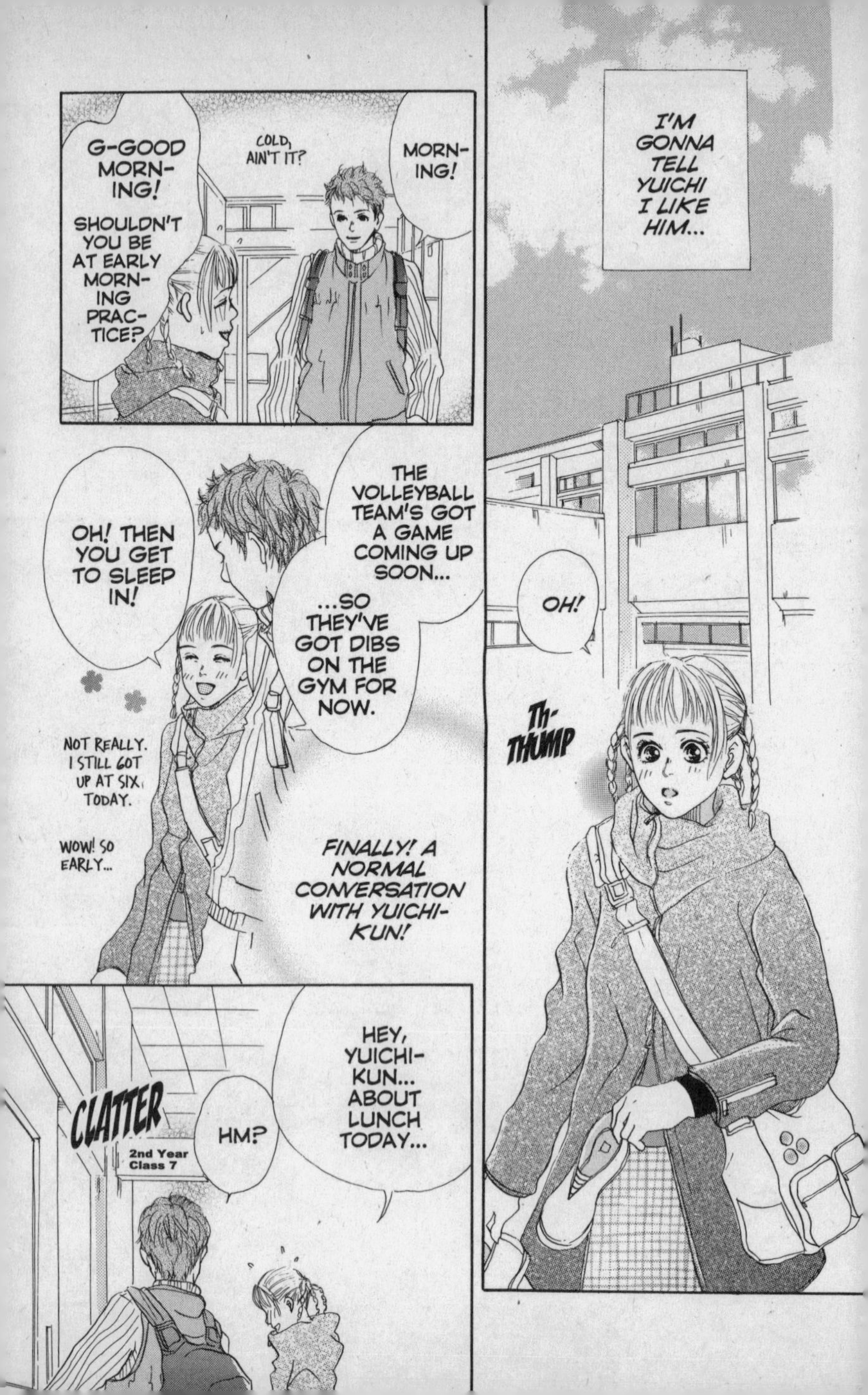
I'M GONNA TELL YUICHI I LIKE HIM...
OH!
Th-THUMP
MORN-ING!
COLD, AIN'T IT?
G-GOOD MORN-ING!
SHOULDN'T YOU BE AT EARLY MORN-ING PRAC-TICE?
THE VOLLEYBALL TEAM'S GOT A GAME COMING UP SOON...
...SO THEY'VE GOT DIBS ON THE GYM FOR NOW.
OH! THEN YOU GET TO SLEEP IN!
NOT REALLY. I STILL GOT UP AT SIX TODAY.
WOW! SO EARLY...
FINALLY! A NORMAL CONVERSATION WITH YUICHI-KUN!
HEY, YUICHI-KUN... ABOUT LUNCH TODAY...
HM?
CLATTER
2nd Year Class 7

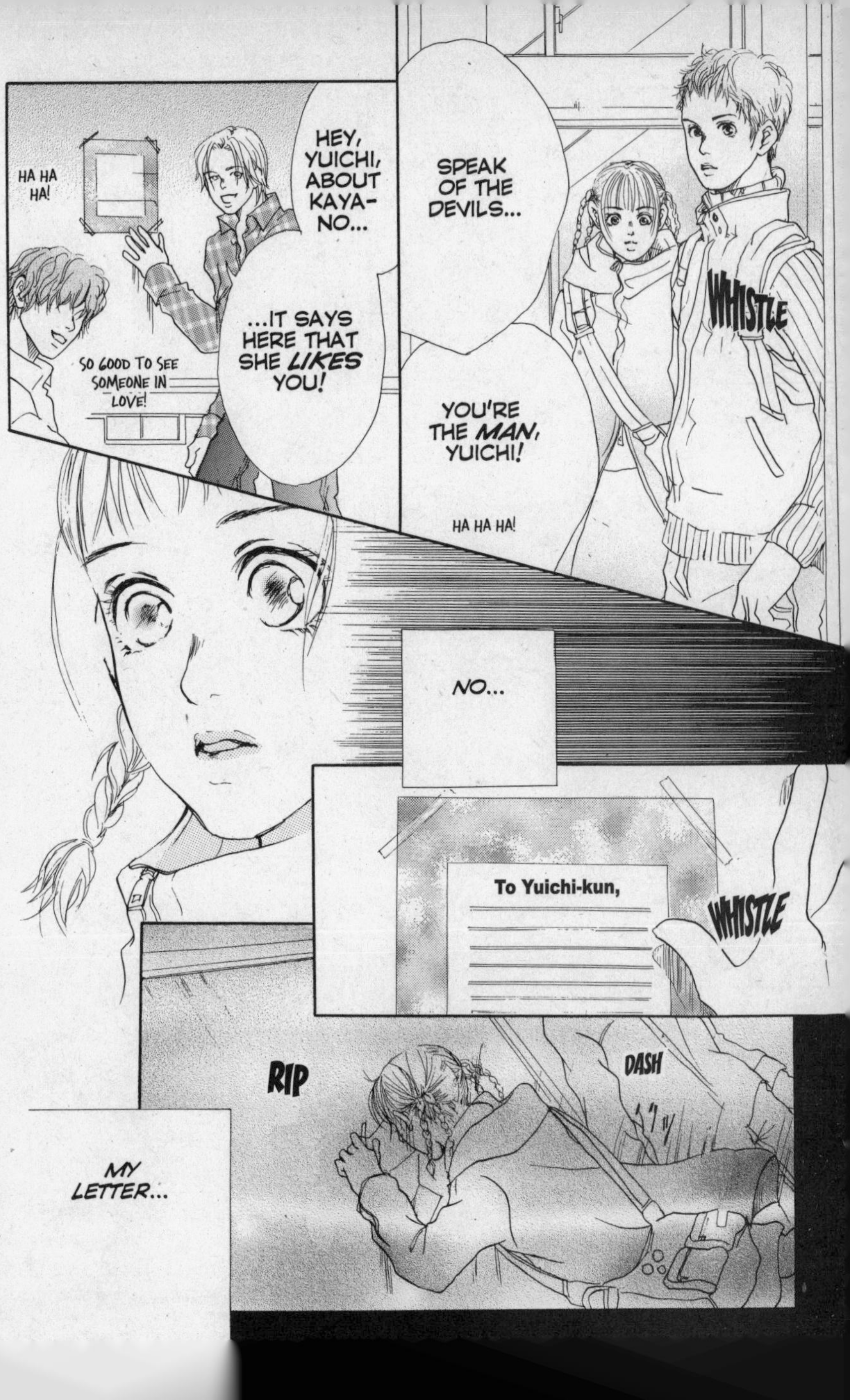
SPEAK OF THE DEVILS...
WHISTLE
YOU'RE THE *MAN*, YUICHI!
HA HA HA!
HEY, YUICHI, ABOUT KAYA-NO...
HA HA HA!
...IT SAYS HERE THAT SHE *LIKES* YOU!
SO GOOD TO SEE SOMEONE IN LOVE!
NO...
WHISTLE
To Yuichi-kun,
DASH
RIP
MY LETTER...

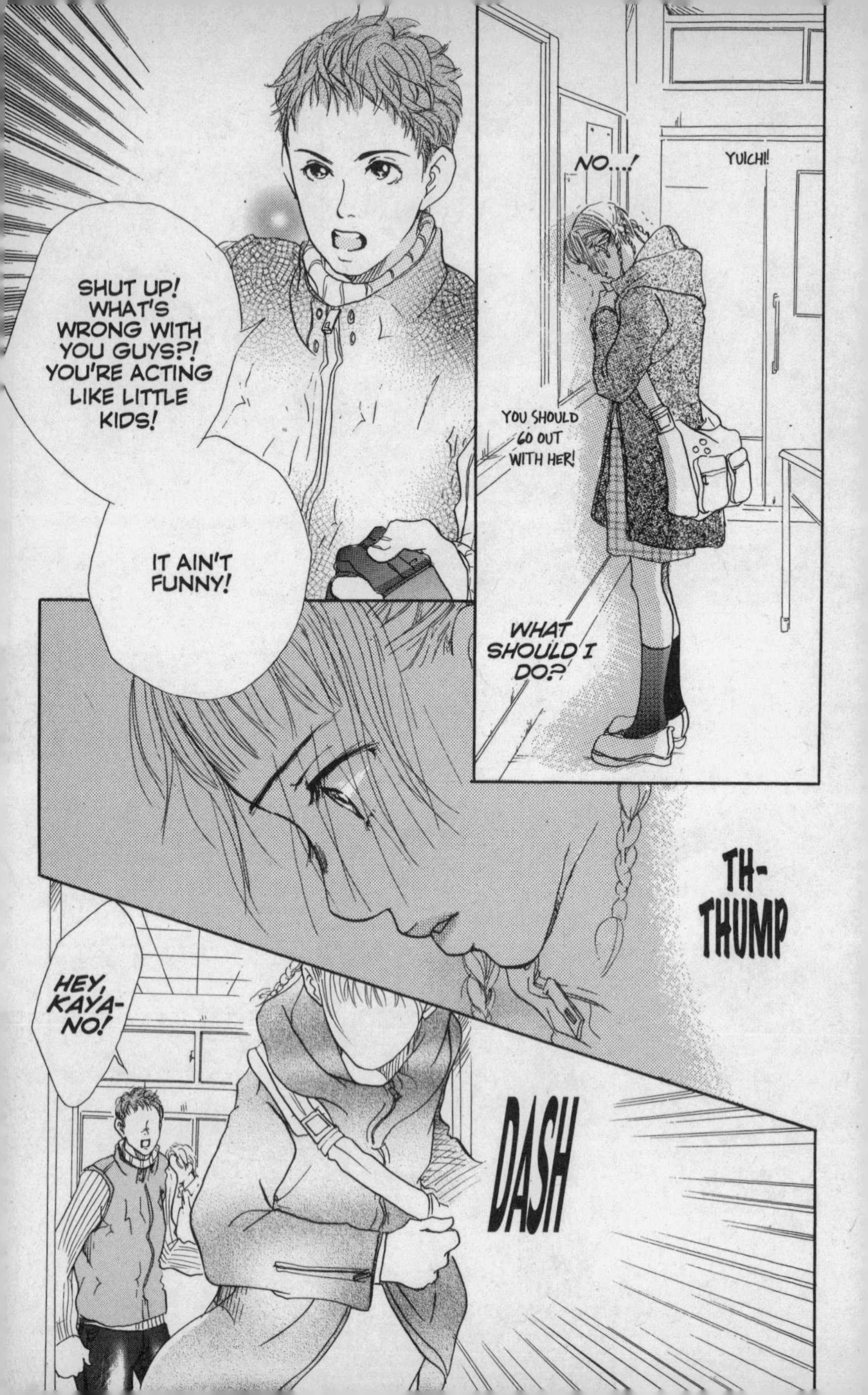
YUICHI!
NO...!
YOU SHOULD GO OUT WITH HER!
WHAT SHOULD I DO?
SHUT UP! WHAT'S WRONG WITH YOU GUYS?! YOU'RE ACTING LIKE LITTLE KIDS!
IT AIN'T FUNNY!
TH-THUMP
DASH
HEY, KAYA-NO!

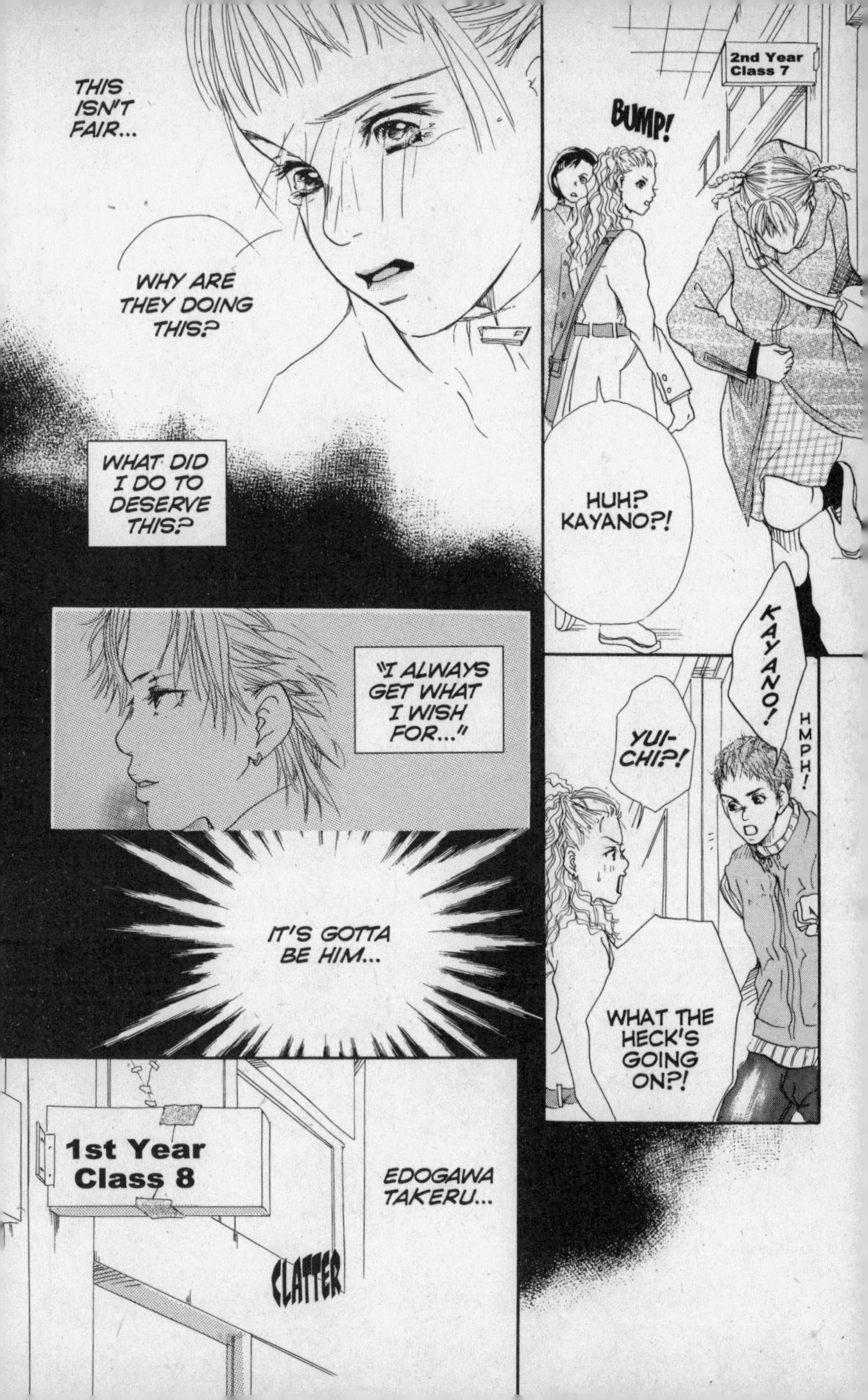
2nd Year Class 7
BUMP!
HUH? KAYANO?!
THIS ISN'T FAIR...
WHY ARE THEY DOING THIS?
WHAT DID I DO TO DESERVE THIS?
KAYANO!
HMPH!
YUI-CHI?!
WHAT THE HECK'S GOING ON?!
"I ALWAYS GET WHAT I WISH FOR..."
IT'S GOTTA BE HIM...
1st Year Class 8
EDOGAWA TAKERU...
CLATTER

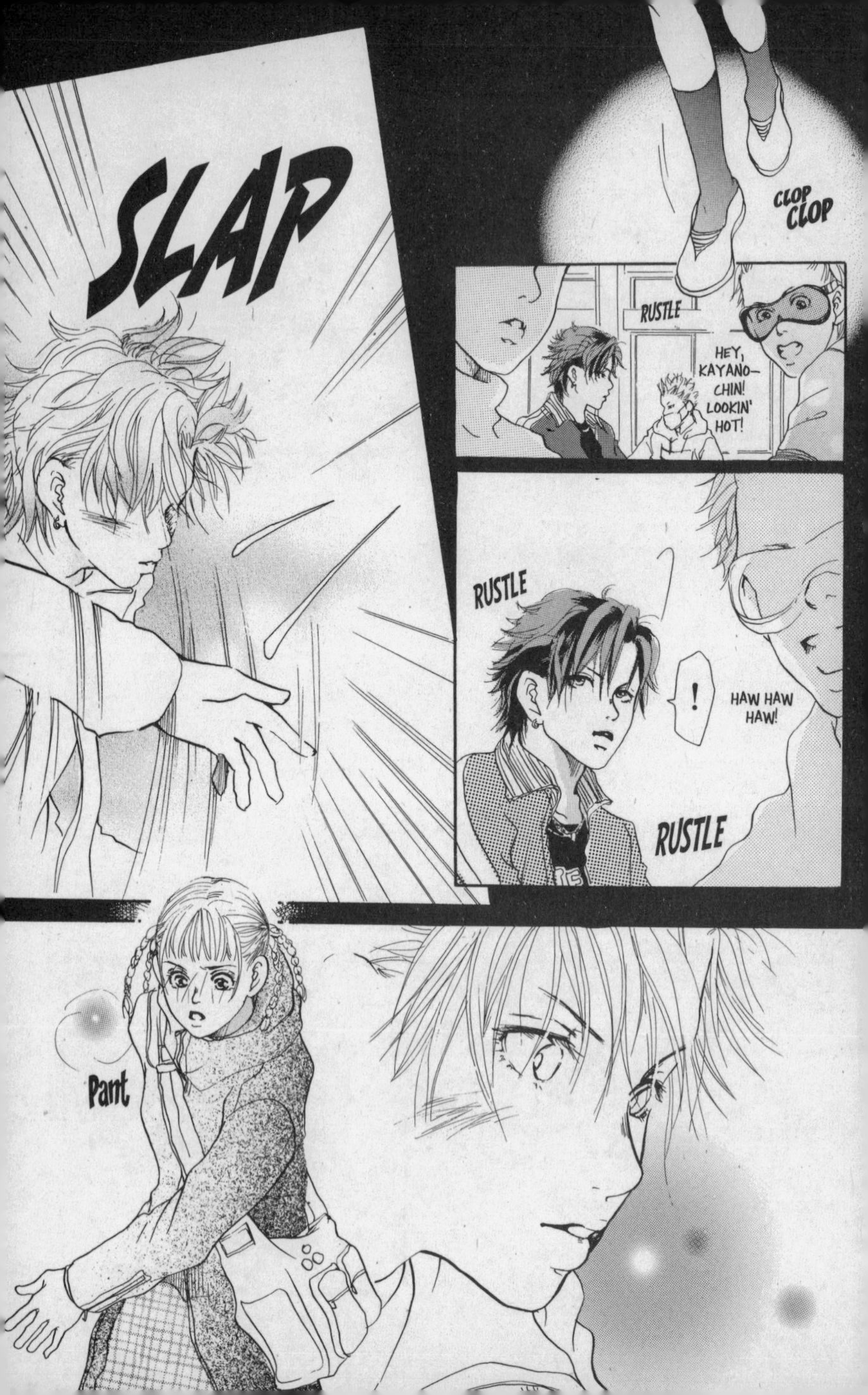
CLOP CLOP
RUSTLE
HEY, KAYANO-CHIN! LOOKIN' HOT!
RUSTLE
HAW HAW HAW!
!
RUSTLE
SLAP
Pant

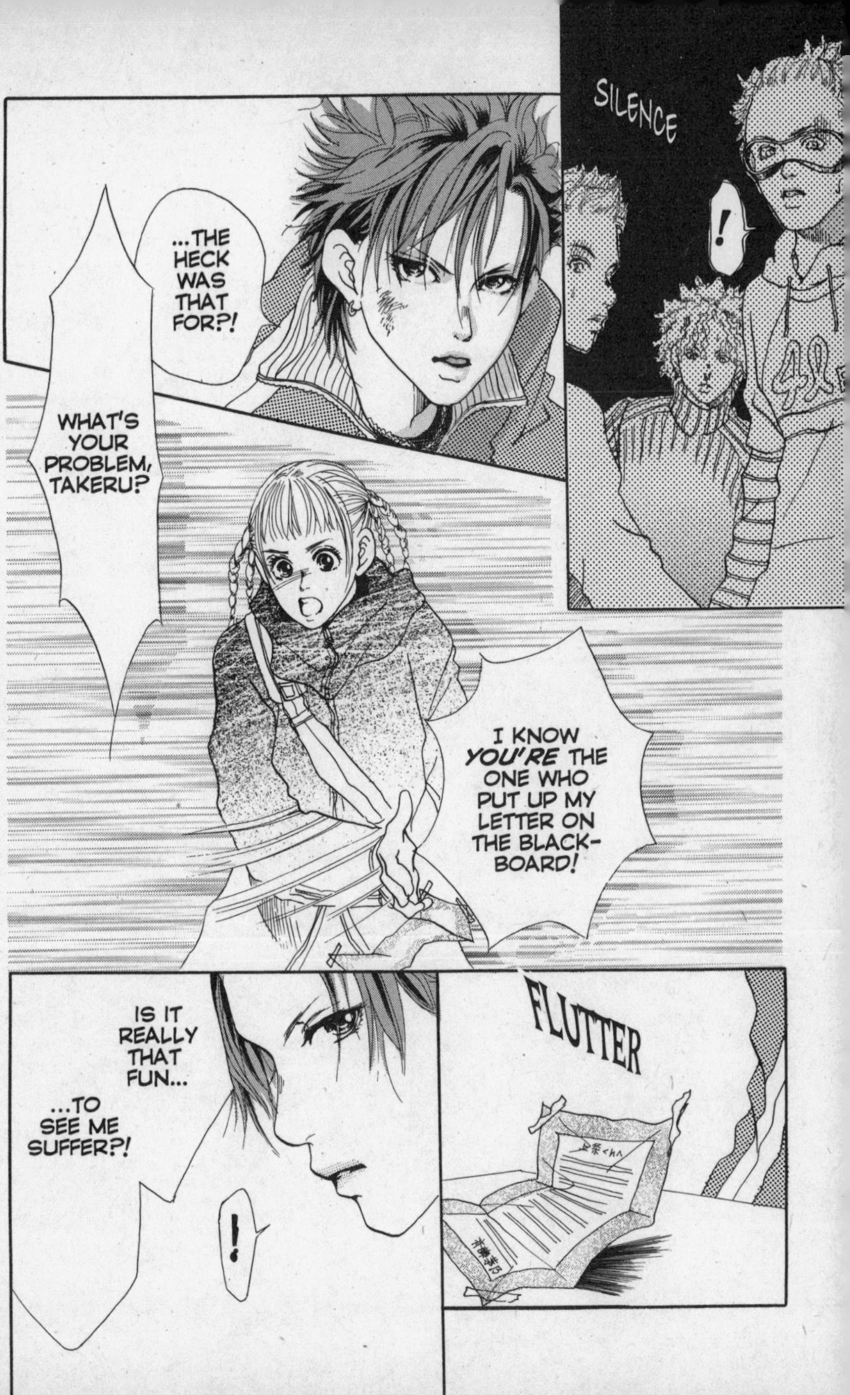
SILENCE
!
...THE HECK WAS THAT FOR?!
WHAT'S YOUR PROBLEM, TAKERU?
I KNOW *YOU'RE* THE ONE WHO PUT UP MY LETTER ON THE BLACK-BOARD!
FLUTTER
IS IT REALLY THAT FUN...
...TO SEE ME SUFFER?!
!

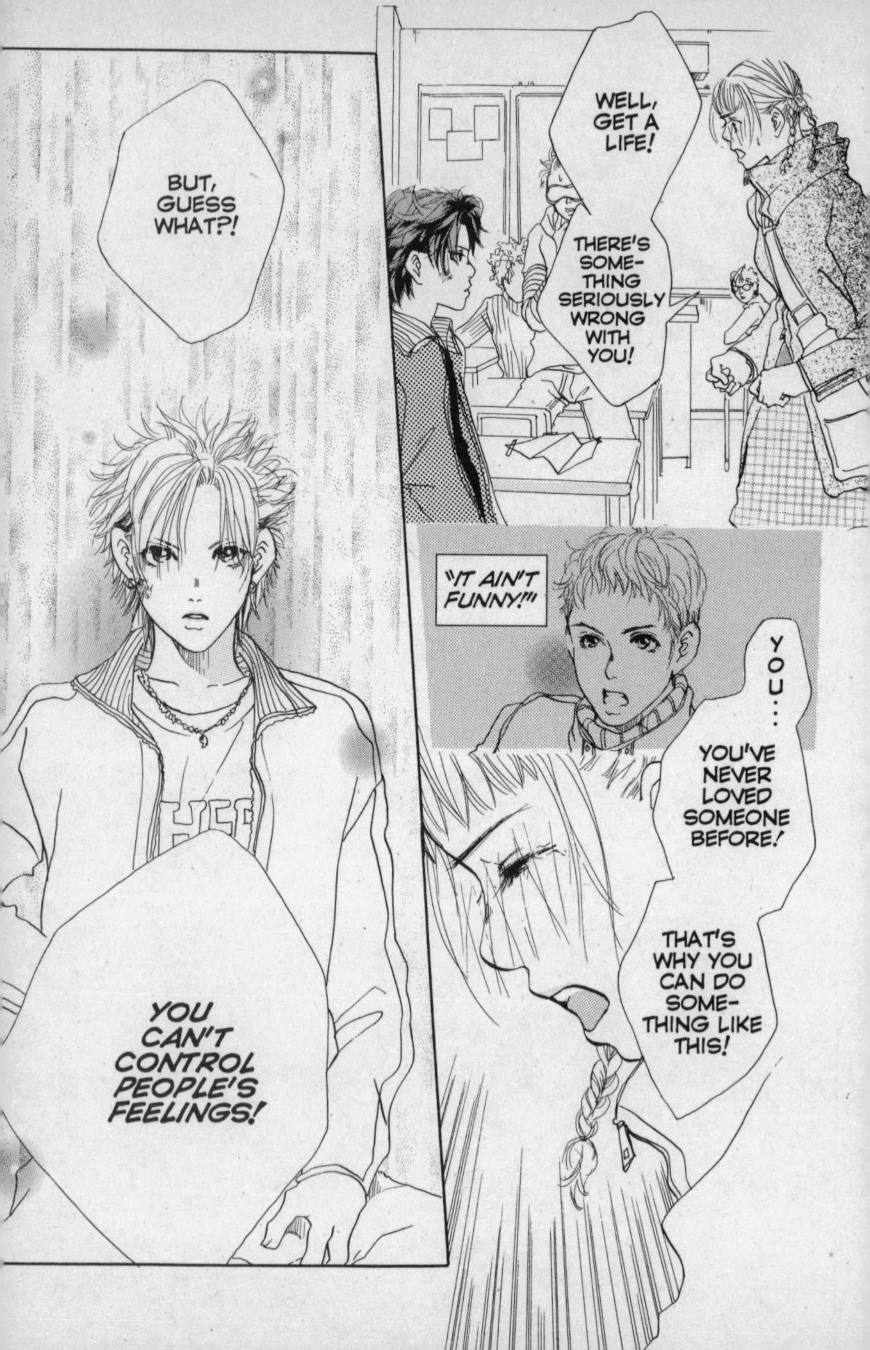
WELL, GET A LIFE!
THERE'S SOME-THING SERIOUSLY WRONG WITH YOU!
"IT AIN'T FUNNY!"
YOU...
YOU'VE NEVER LOVED SOMEONE BEFORE!
THAT'S WHY YOU CAN DO SOME-THING LIKE THIS!
BUT, GUESS WHAT?!
YOU CAN'T CONTROL PEOPLE'S FEELINGS!

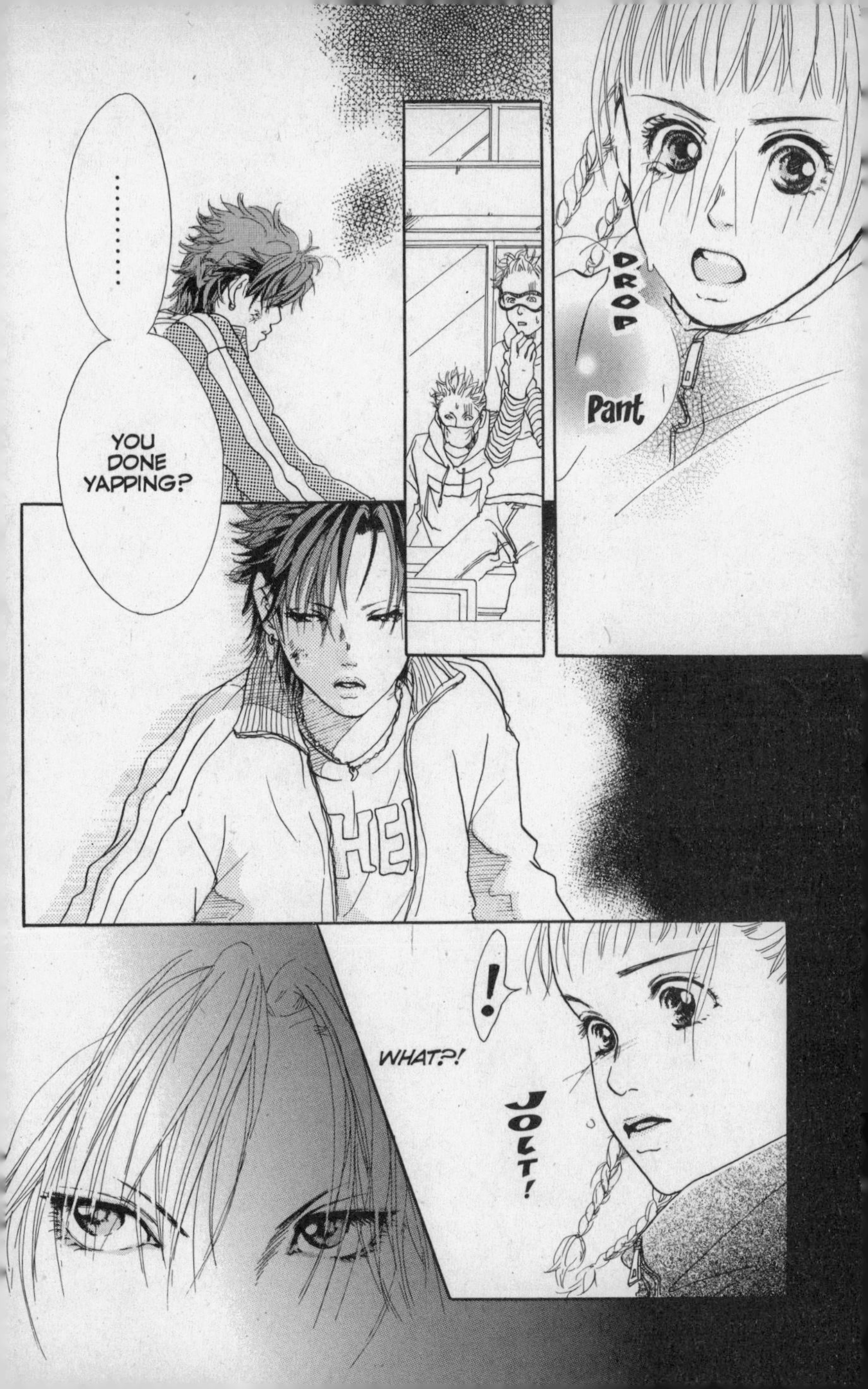
DROP
Pant
......
YOU DONE YAPPING?
!
WHAT?!
JOLT!

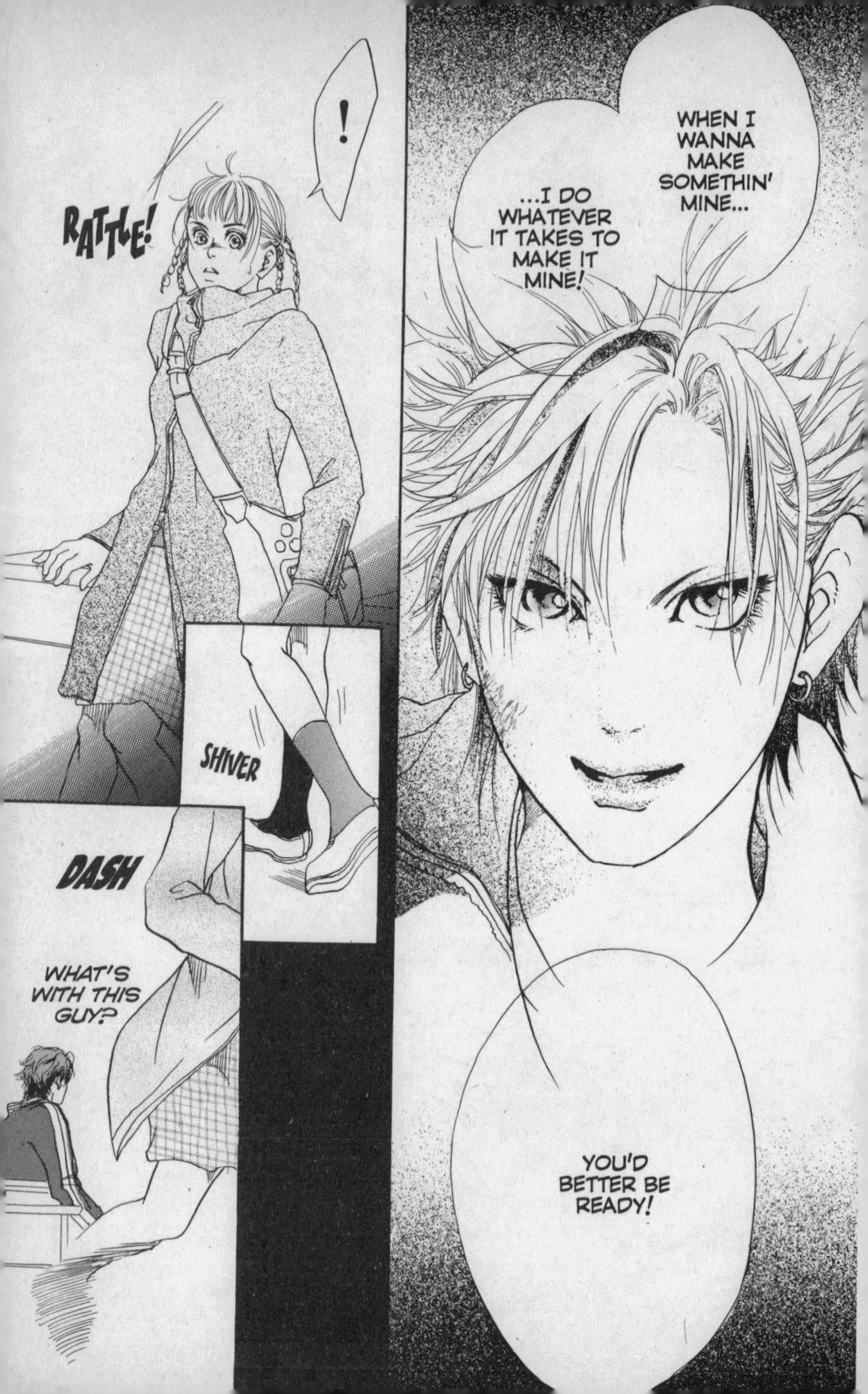
WHEN I WANNA MAKE SOMETHIN' MINE...
...I DO WHATEVER IT TAKES TO MAKE IT MINE!
YOU'D BETTER BE READY!
!
RATTLE!
SHIVER
DASH
WHAT'S WITH THIS GUY?

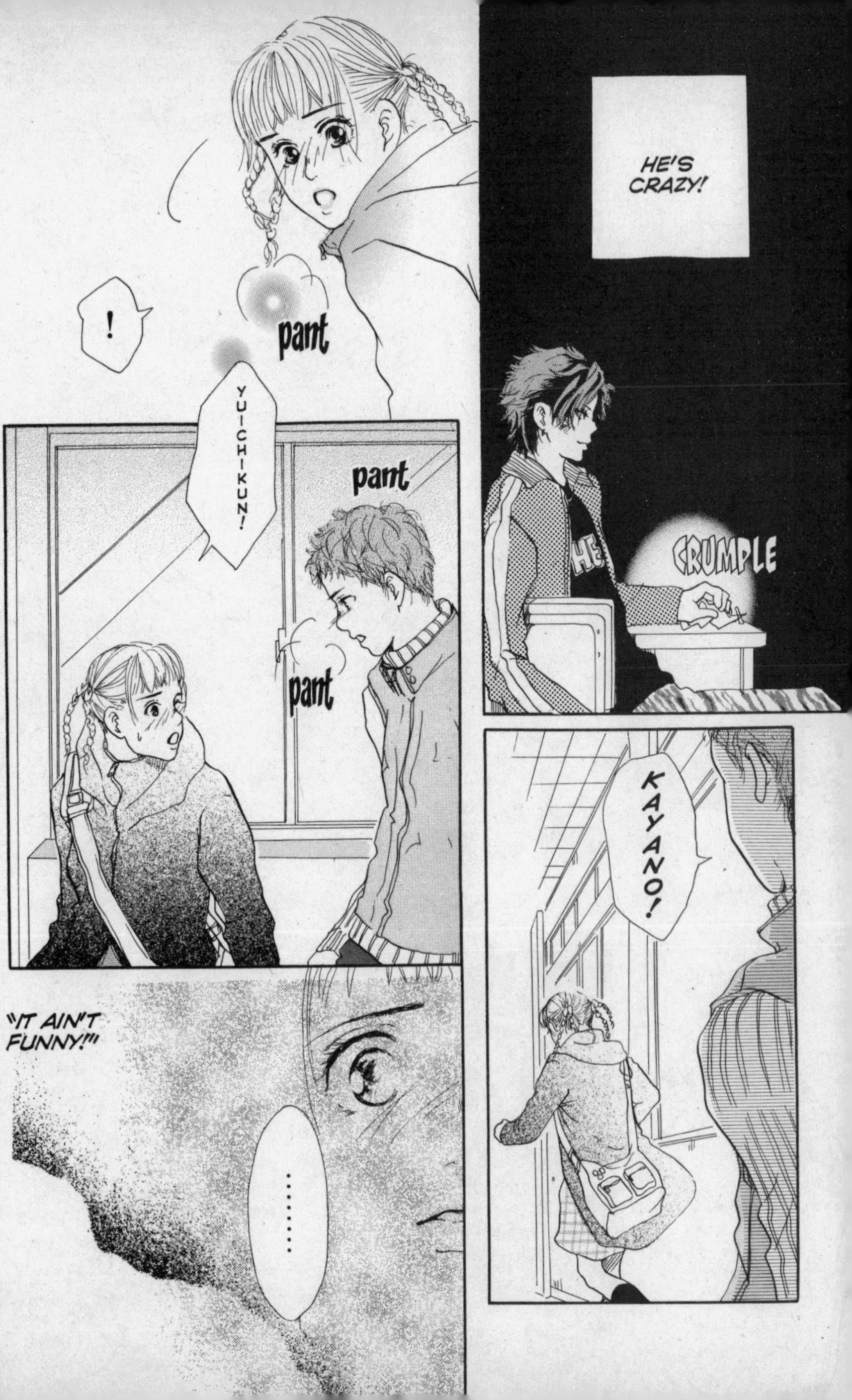
HE'S CRAZY!
CRUMPLE
KAYANO!
!
pant
YUICHI-KUN!
pant
pant
"IT AIN'T FUNNY!"
....

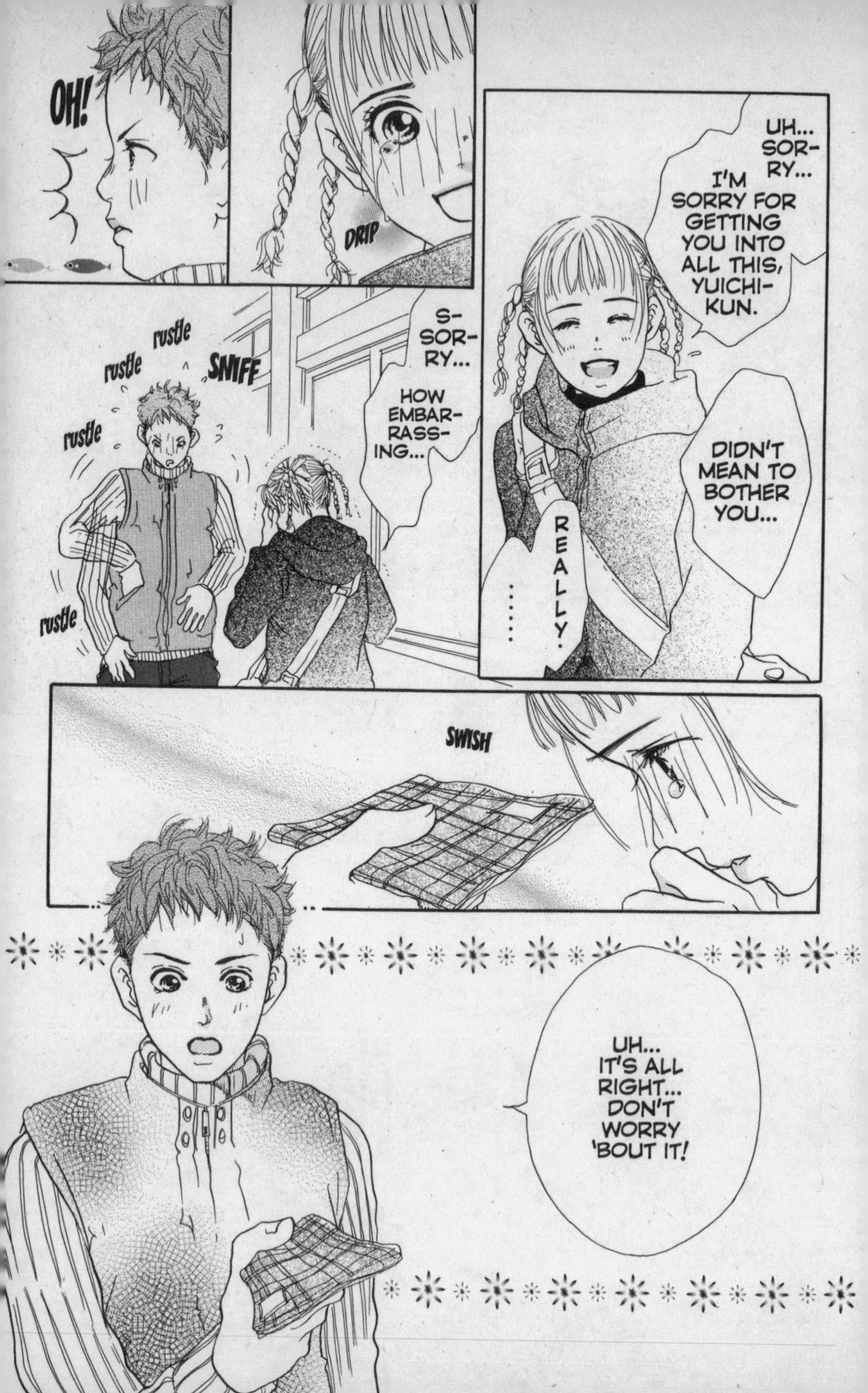
UH... SORRY...
I'M SORRY FOR GETTING YOU INTO ALL THIS, YUICHI-KUN.
DIDN'T MEAN TO BOTHER YOU...
REALLY.
......
DRIP
OH!
S-SORRY...
HOW EMBARRASSING...
SNIFF
rustle
rustle
rustle
rustle
SWISH
UH... IT'S ALL RIGHT... DON'T WORRY 'BOUT IT!

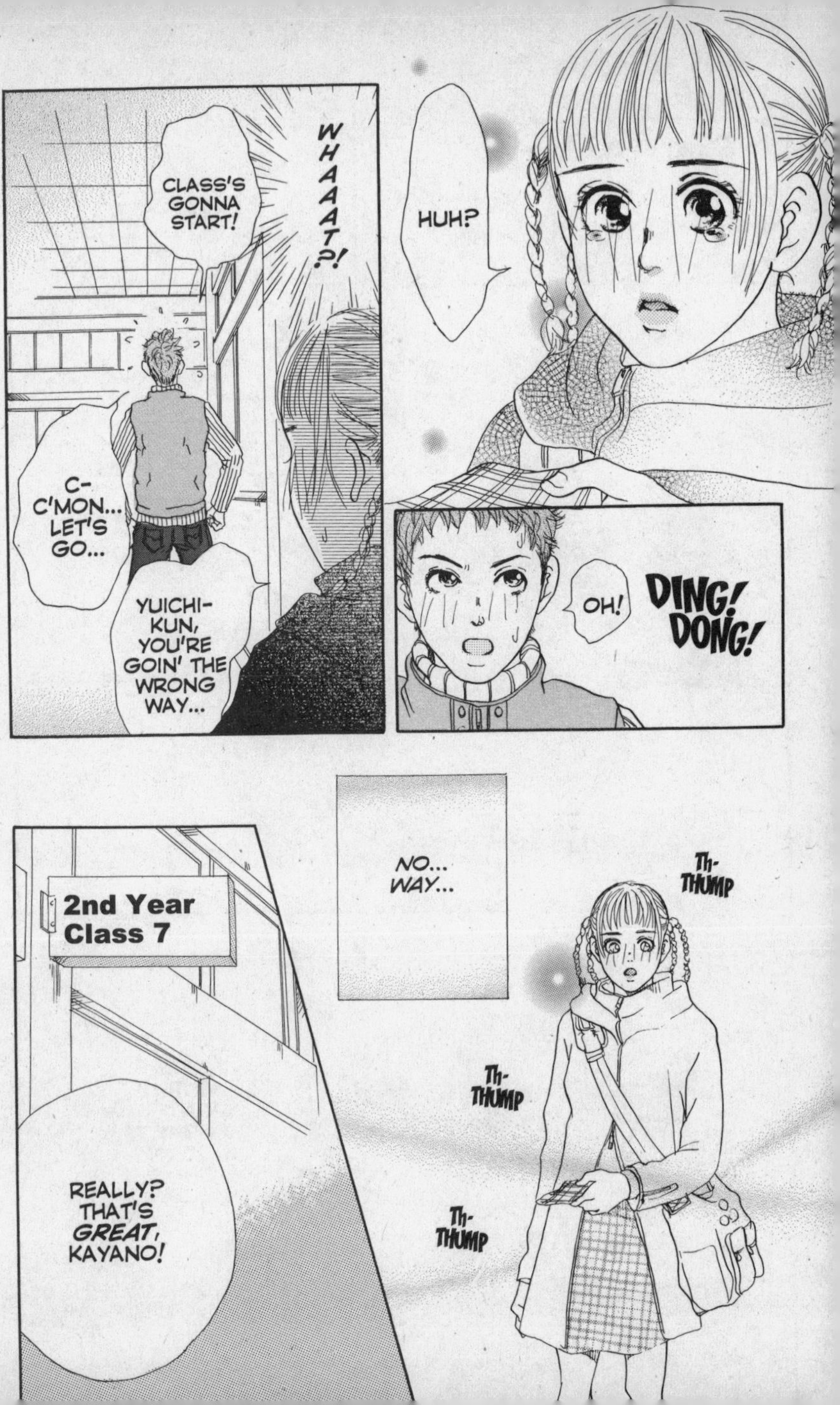
HUH?
OH!
DING! DONG!
WHAAAAT?!
CLASS'S GONNA START!
C-C'MON... LET'S GO...
YUICHI-KUN, YOU'RE GOIN' THE WRONG WAY...
NO... WAY...
Th-THUMP
Th-THUMP
Th-THUMP
2nd Year Class 7
REALLY? THAT'S *GREAT*, KAYANO!

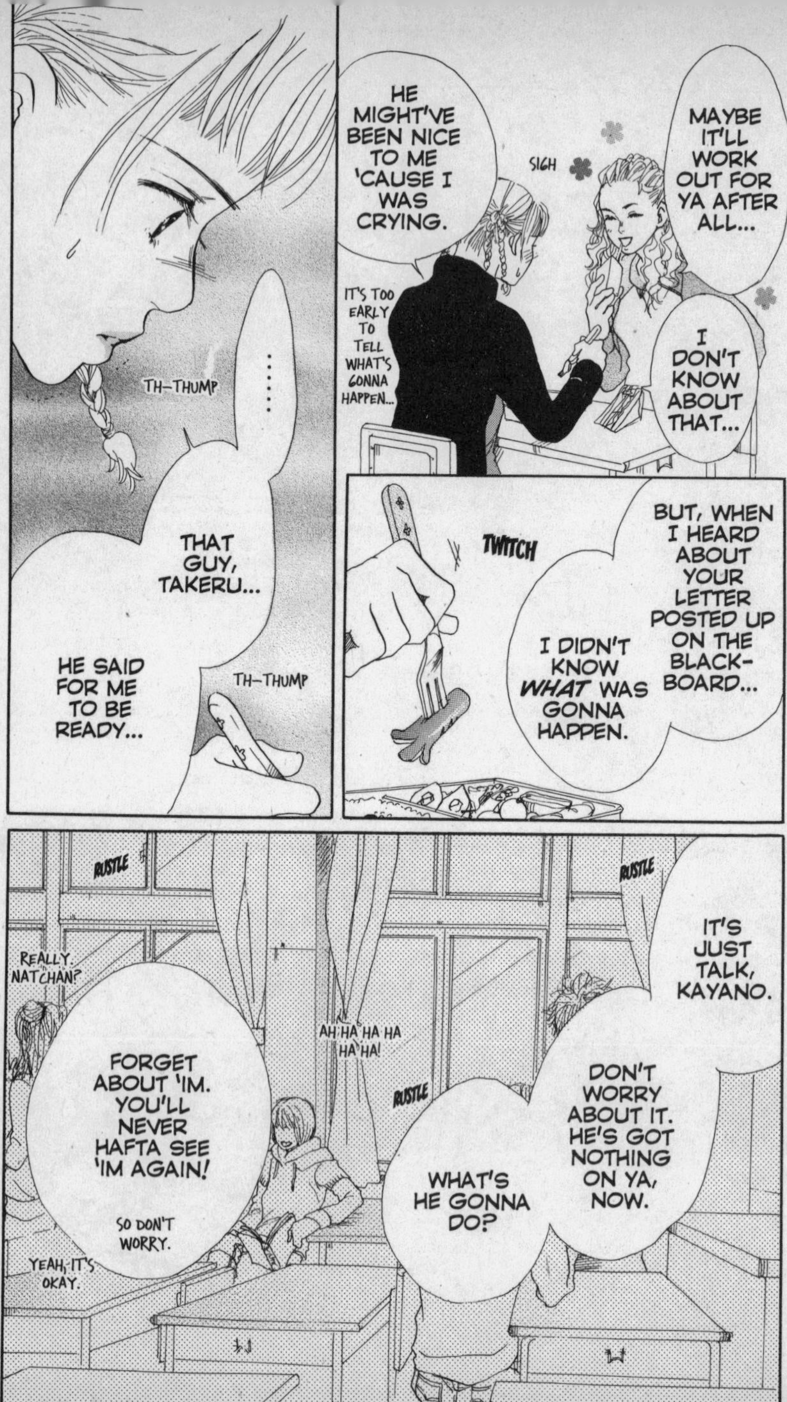
MAYBE IT'LL WORK OUT FOR YA AFTER ALL...
I DON'T KNOW ABOUT THAT...
SIGH
HE MIGHT'VE BEEN NICE TO ME 'CAUSE I WAS CRYING.
IT'S TOO EARLY TO TELL WHAT'S GONNA HAPPEN...
BUT, WHEN I HEARD ABOUT YOUR LETTER POSTED UP ON THE BLACK-BOARD...
TWITCH
I DIDN'T KNOW *WHAT* WAS GONNA HAPPEN.
......
THAT GUY, TAKERU...
TH-THUMP
HE SAID FOR ME TO BE READY...
TH-THUMP
RUSTLE
IT'S JUST TALK, KAYANO.
DON'T WORRY ABOUT IT. HE'S GOT NOTHING ON YA, NOW.
WHAT'S HE GONNA DO?
RUSTLE
AH HA HA HA HA HA!
RUSTLE
REALLY, NAT-CHAN?
FORGET ABOUT 'IM. YOU'LL NEVER HAFTA SEE 'IM AGAIN!
SO DON'T WORRY.
YEAH, IT'S OKAY.

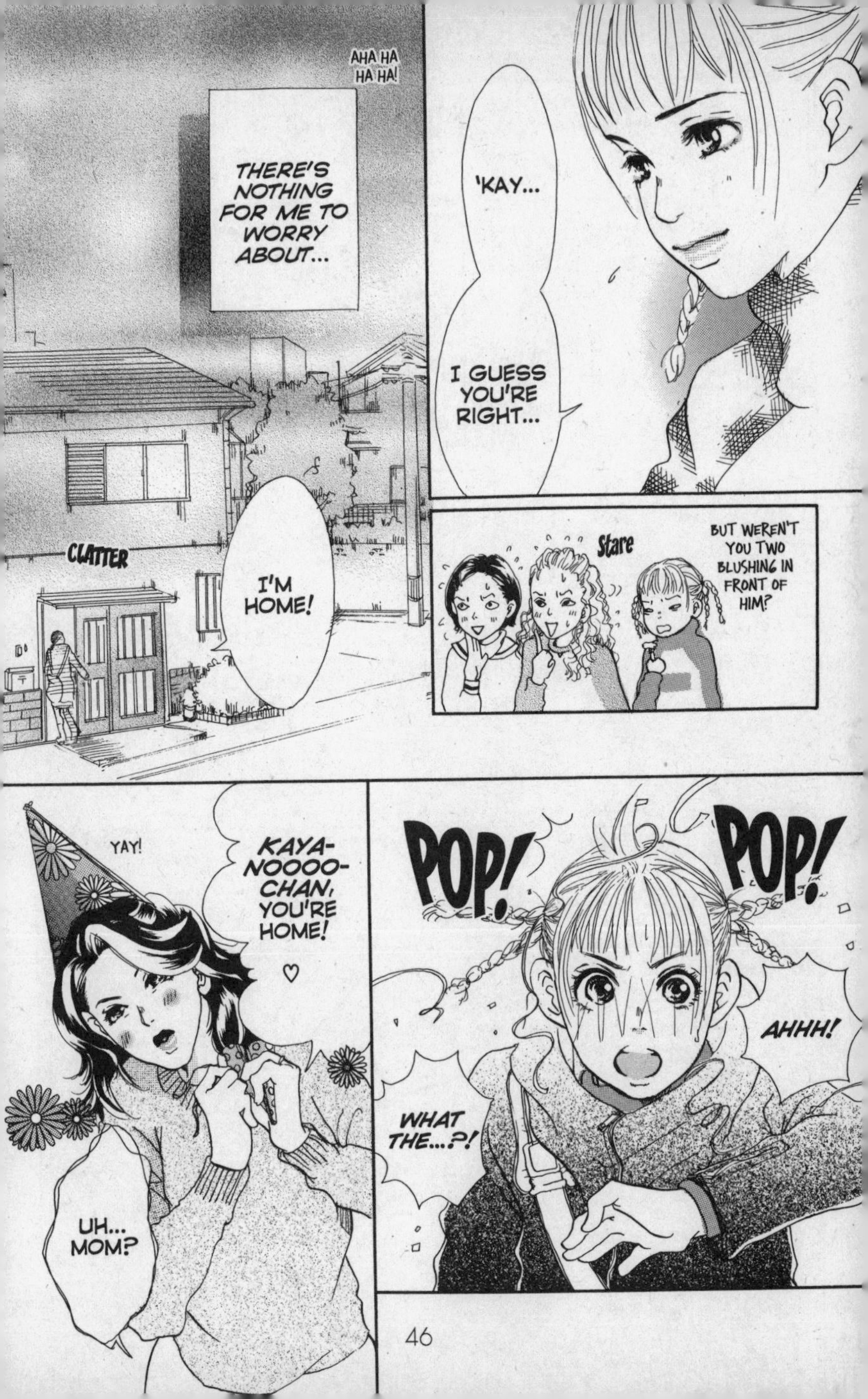
'KAY...
I GUESS YOU'RE RIGHT...
Stare
BUT WEREN'T YOU TWO BLUSHING IN FRONT OF HIM?
AHA HA HA HA!
THERE'S NOTHING FOR ME TO WORRY ABOUT...
I'M HOME!
CLATTER
POP!
POP!
AHHH!
WHAT THE...?!
KAYA-NOOOO-CHAN, YOU'RE HOME! ♡
YAY!
UH... MOM?

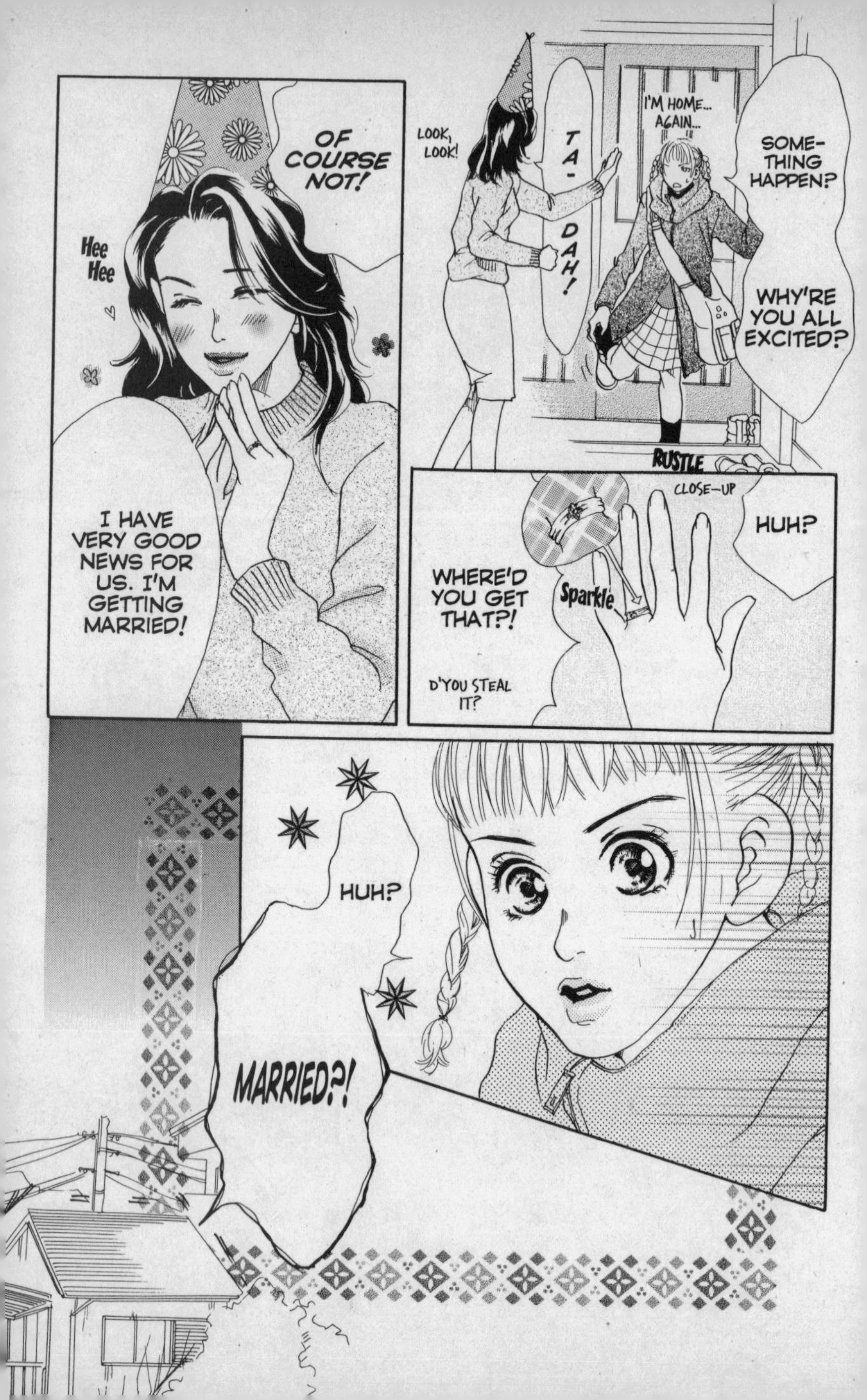
I'M HOME... AGAIN...
SOME-THING HAPPEN?
WHY'RE YOU ALL EXCITED?
TA-DAH!
LOOK, LOOK!
RUSTLE
HUH?
CLOSE-UP
Sparkle
WHERE'D YOU GET THAT?!
D'YOU STEAL IT?
OF COURSE NOT!
Hee Hee
I HAVE VERY GOOD NEWS FOR US. I'M GETTING MARRIED!
HUH?
MARRIED?!

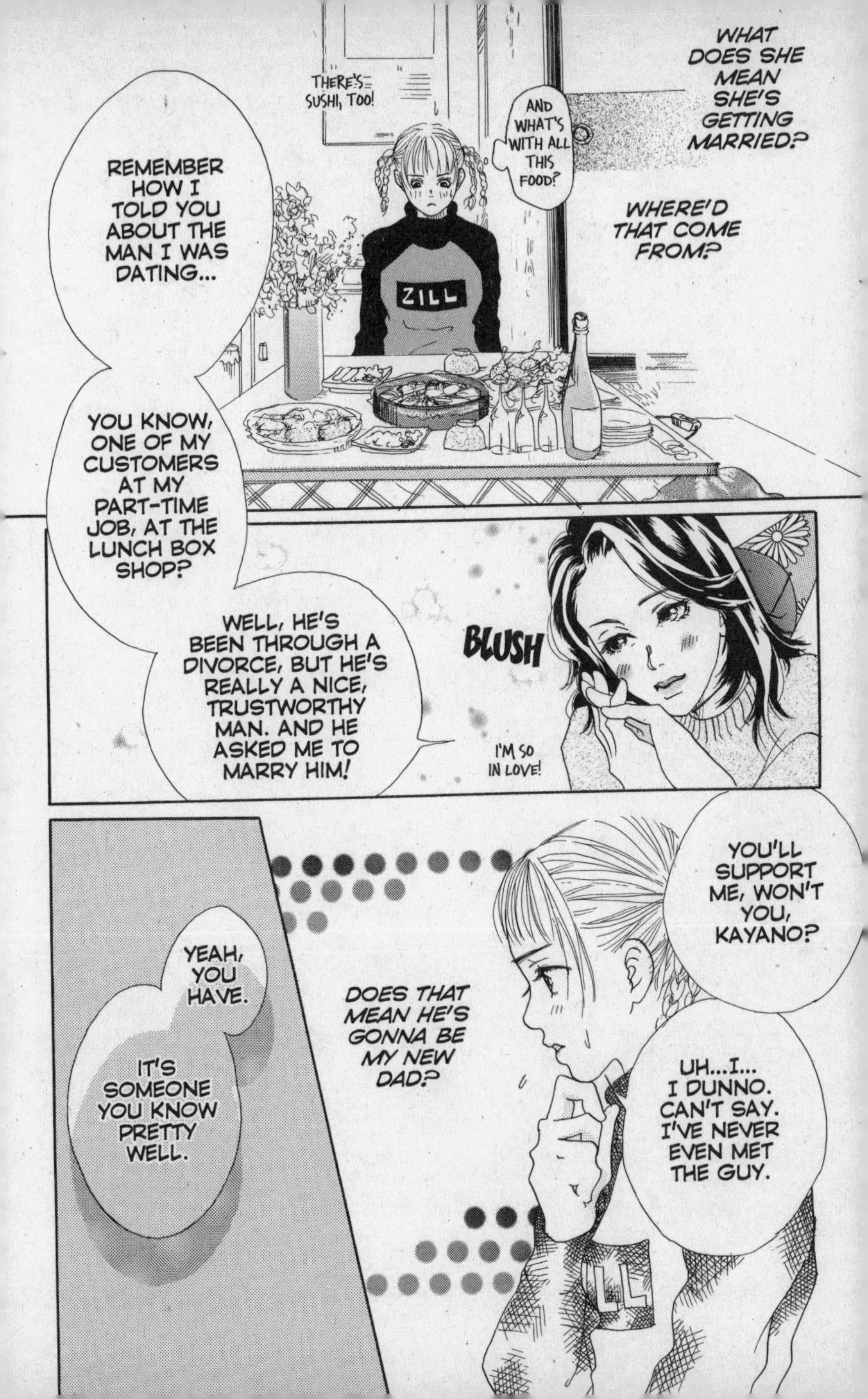
WHAT DOES SHE MEAN SHE'S GETTING MARRIED?
WHERE'D THAT COME FROM?
AND WHAT'S WITH ALL THIS FOOD?
THERE'S SUSHI, TOO!
ZILL
REMEMBER HOW I TOLD YOU ABOUT THE MAN I WAS DATING...
YOU KNOW, ONE OF MY CUSTOMERS AT MY PART-TIME JOB, AT THE LUNCH BOX SHOP?
I'M SO IN LOVE!
BLUSH
WELL, HE'S BEEN THROUGH A DIVORCE, BUT HE'S REALLY A NICE, TRUSTWORTHY MAN. AND HE ASKED ME TO MARRY HIM!
YOU'LL SUPPORT ME, WON'T YOU, KAYANO?
UH...I... I DUNNO. CAN'T SAY. I'VE NEVER EVEN MET THE GUY.
DOES THAT MEAN HE'S GONNA BE MY NEW DAD?
YEAH, YOU HAVE.
IT'S SOMEONE YOU KNOW PRETTY WELL.

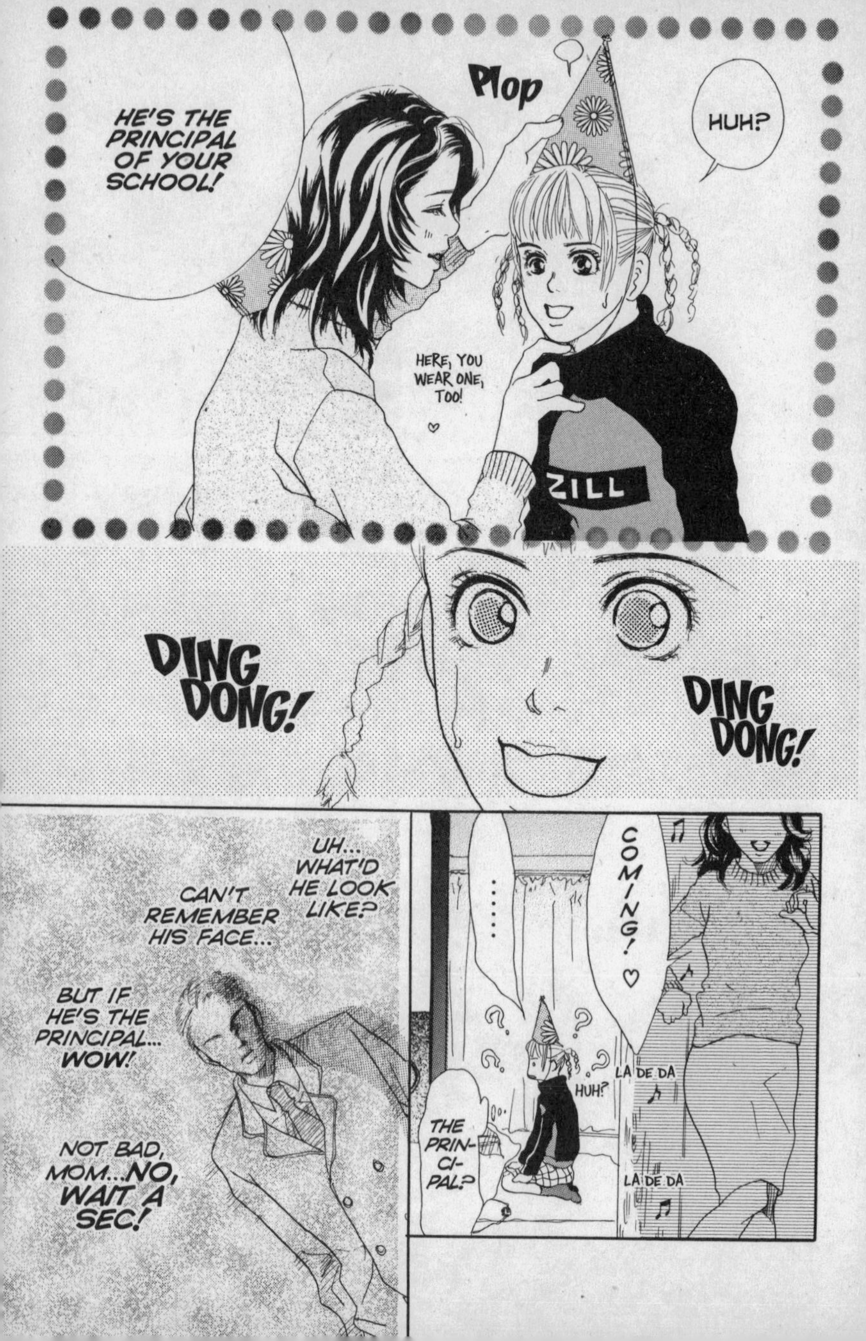
HUH?
Plop
HE'S THE PRINCIPAL OF YOUR SCHOOL!
HERE, YOU WEAR ONE, TOO! ♡
ZILL
DING DONG!
DING DONG!
COMING! ♡
......
LA DE DA
HUH?
LA DE DA
THE PRIN-CI-PAL?
UH... WHAT'D HE LOOK LIKE?
CAN'T REMEMBER HIS FACE...
BUT IF HE'S THE PRINCIPAL... WOW!
NOT BAD, MOM...NO, WAIT A SEC!

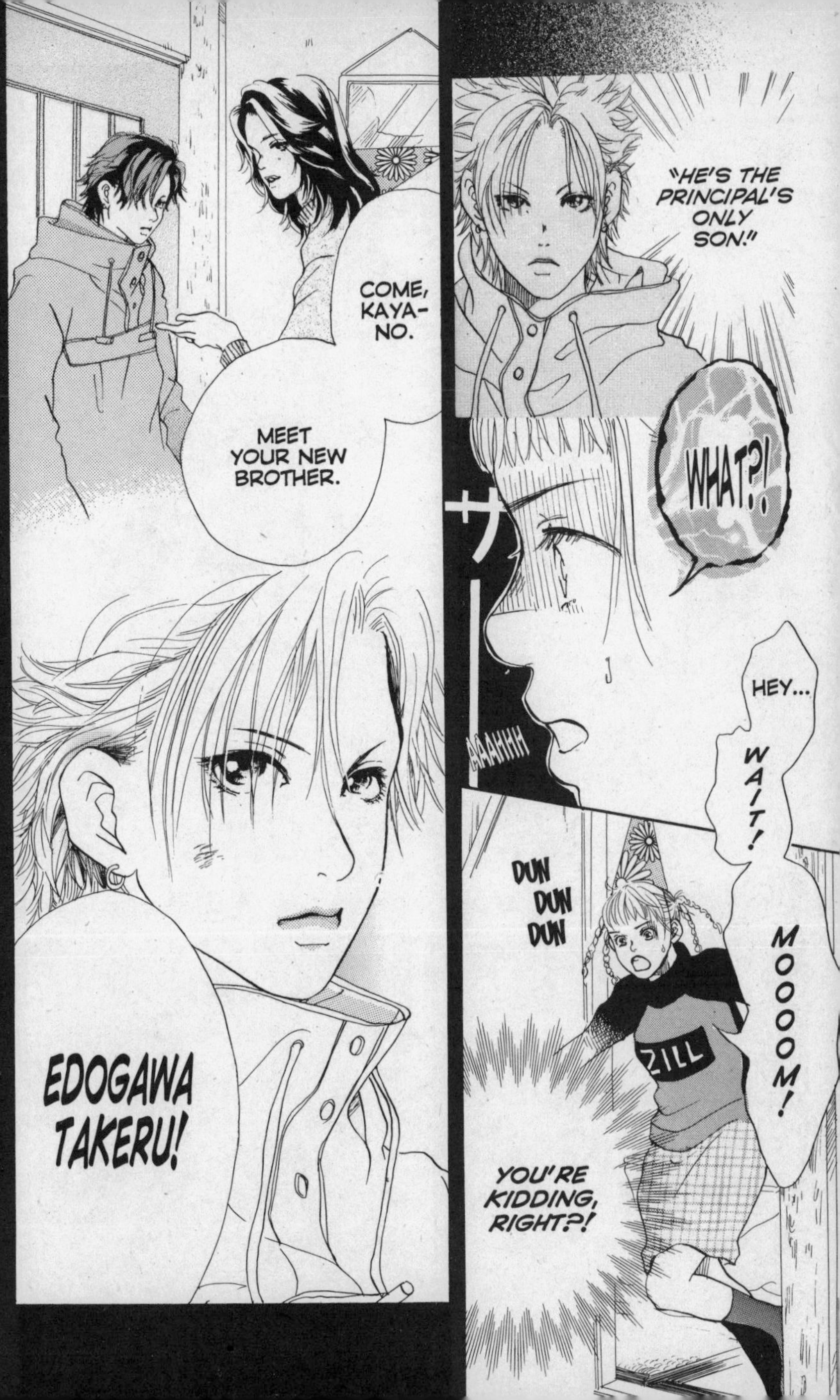
"HE'S THE PRINCIPAL'S ONLY SON."
WHAT?!
AAAHHH
HEY...
WAIT!
MOOOOM!
DUN DUN DUN
YOU'RE KIDDING, RIGHT?!
COME, KAYA-NO.
MEET YOUR NEW BROTHER.
EDOGAWA TAKERU!

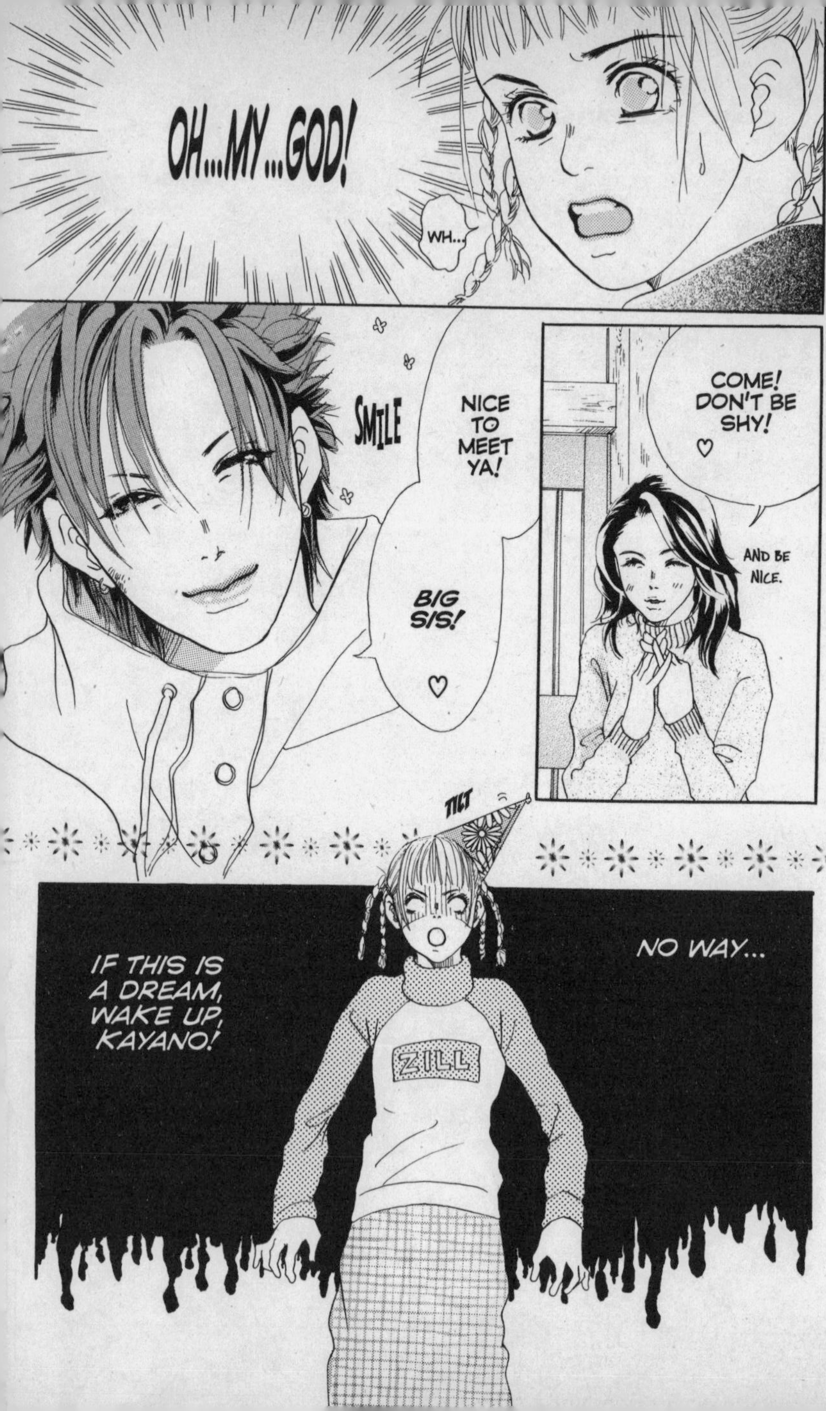
WH...
OH...MY...GOD!
COME! DON'T BE SHY! ♡
AND BE NICE.
NICE TO MEET YA!
SMILE
BIG SIS! ♡
TILT
NO WAY...
IF THIS IS A DREAM, WAKE UP, KAYANO!
ZILL

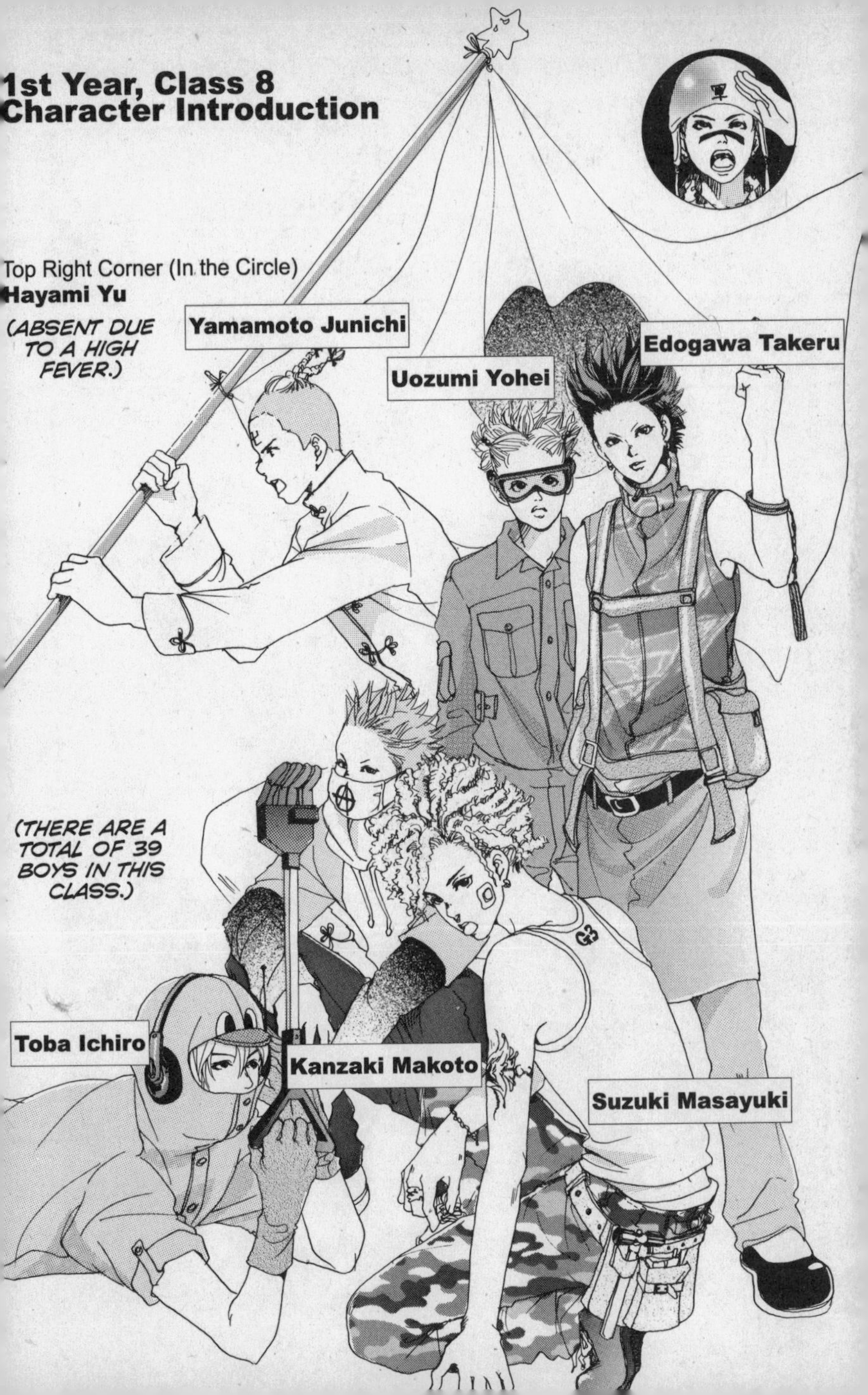
1st Year, Class 8
Character Introduction
Top Right Corner (In the Circle)
Hayami Yu
(ABSENT DUE TO A HIGH FEVER.)
Yamamoto Junichi
Uozumi Yohei
Edogawa Takeru
(THERE ARE A TOTAL OF 39 BOYS IN THIS CLASS.)
Toba Ichiro
Kanzaki Makoto
Suzuki Masayuki

Chapter 2: The Plunder

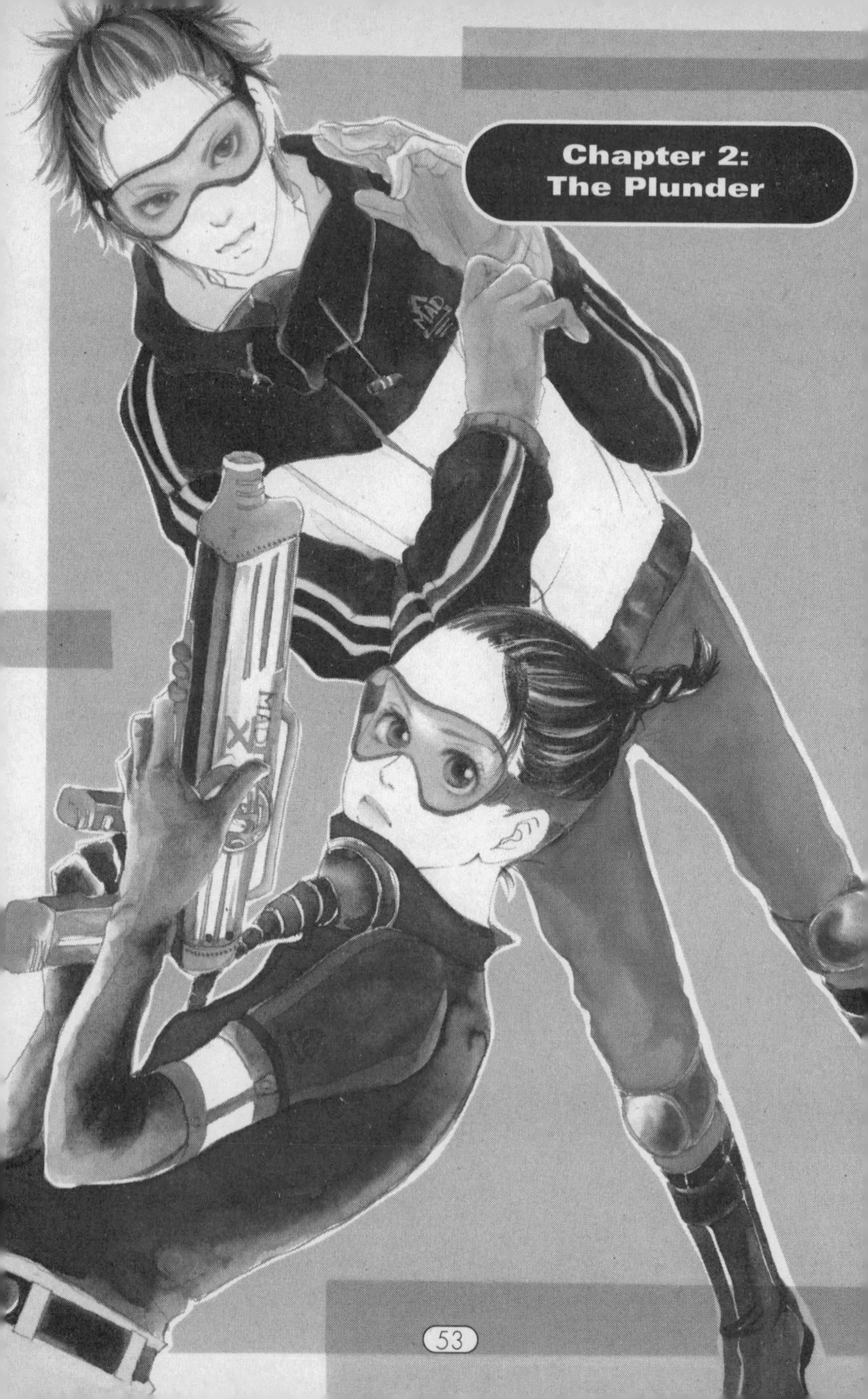

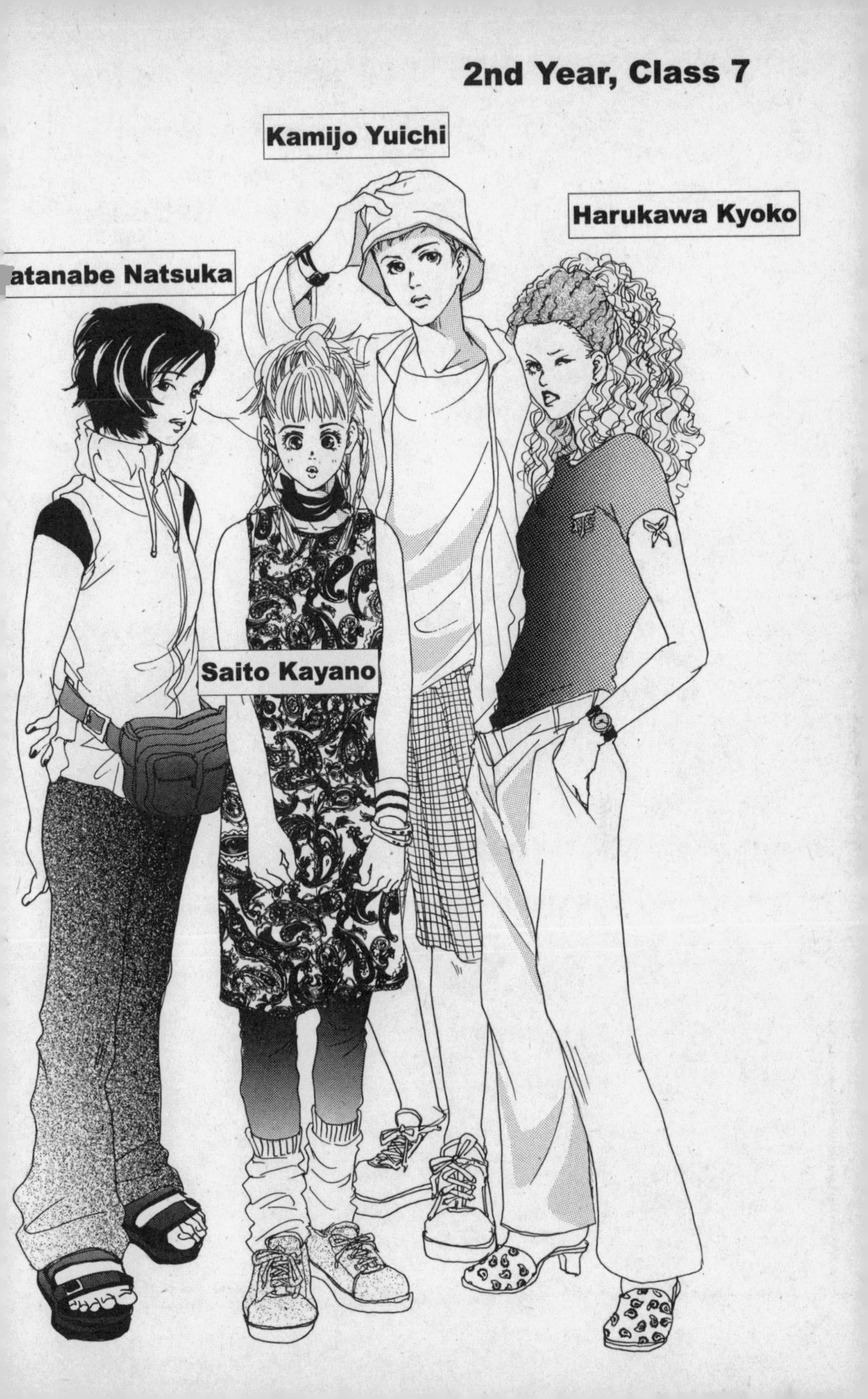
2nd Year, Class 7
Kamijo Yuichi
Harukawa Kyoko
atanabe Natsuka
Saito Kayano

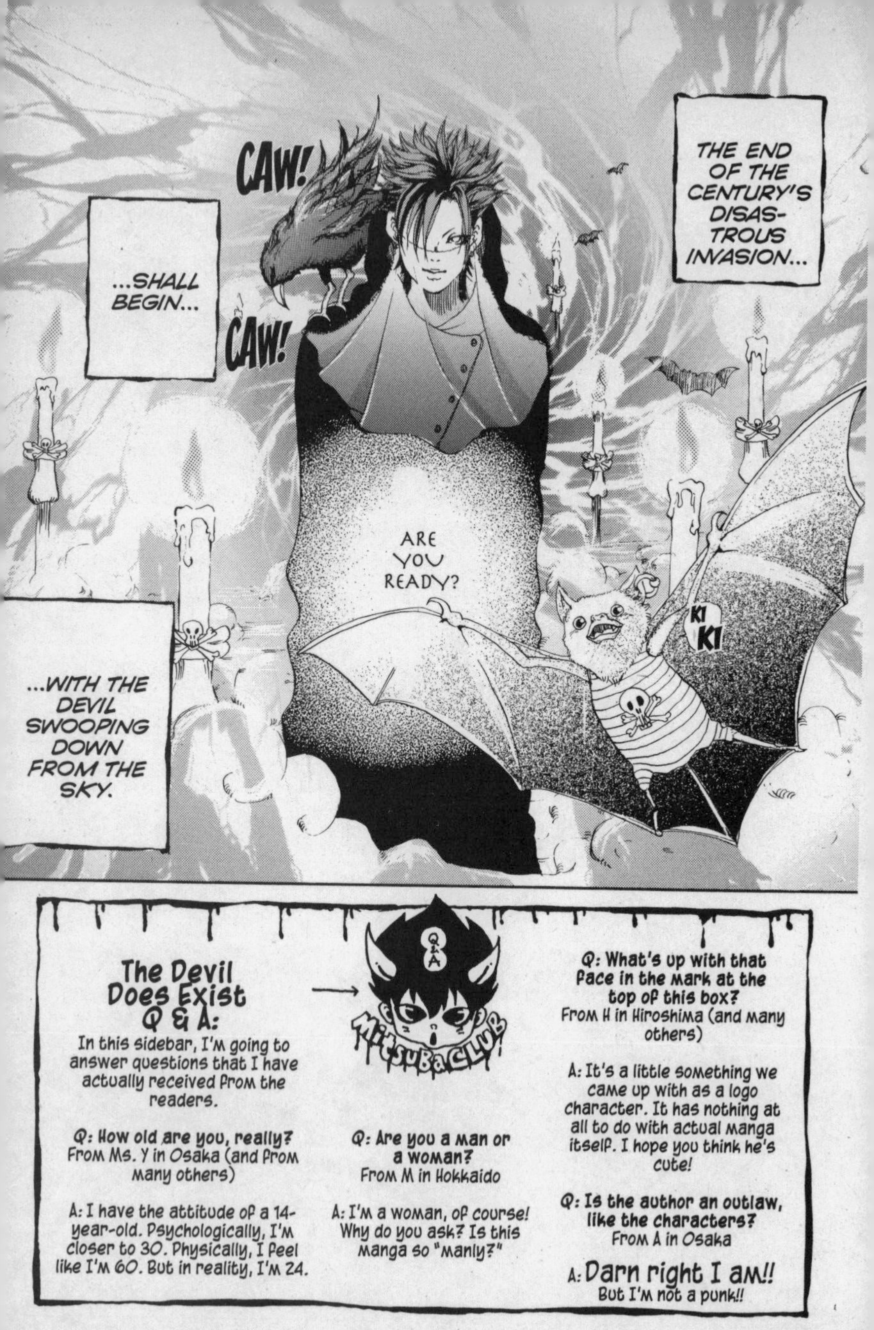
THE END OF THE CENTURY'S DISASTROUS INVASION...
CAW!
...SHALL BEGIN...
CAW!
ARE YOU READY?
KI KI
...WITH THE DEVIL SWOOPING DOWN FROM THE SKY.

The Devil Does Exist Q & A:

In this sidebar, I'm going to answer questions that I have actually received from the readers.

Q: How old are you, really?
From Ms. Y in Osaka (and from many others)

A: I have the attitude of a 14-year-old. Psychologically, I'm closer to 30. Physically, I feel like I'm 60. But in reality, I'm 24.

MITSUBA CLUB

Q: Are you a man or a woman?
From M in Hokkaido

A: I'm a woman, of course! Why do you ask? Is this manga so "manly?"

Q: What's up with that face in the mark at the top of this box?
From H in Hiroshima (and many others)

A: It's a little something we came up with as a logo character. It has nothing at all to do with actual manga itself. I hope you think he's cute!

Q: Is the author an outlaw, like the characters?
From A in Osaka

A: **Darn right I am!!**
But I'm not a punk!!

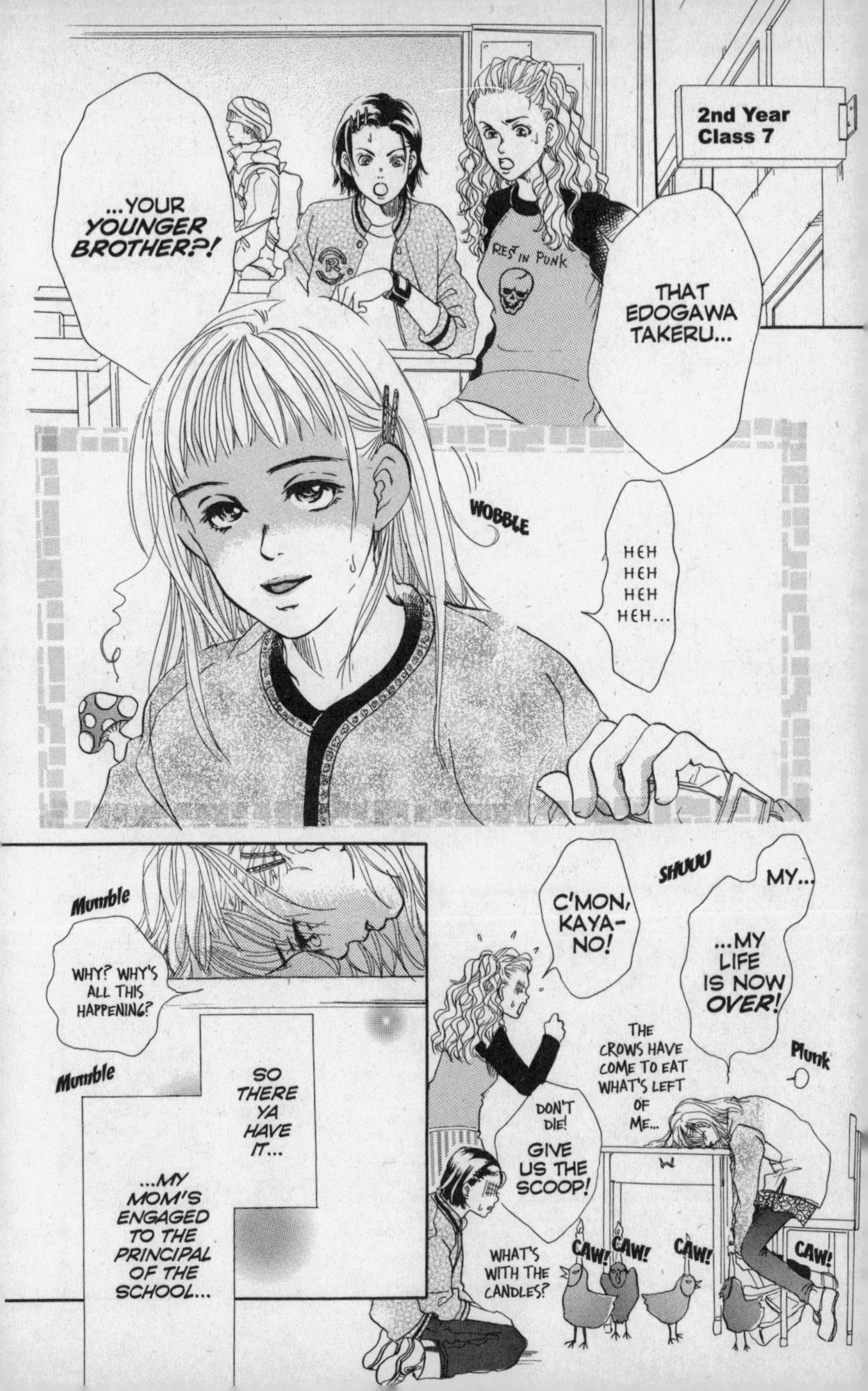
2nd Year Class 7
THAT EDOGAWA TAKERU...
...YOUR YOUNGER BROTHER?!
WOBBLE
HEH HEH HEH HEH...
SHUUU
MY...
...MY LIFE IS NOW OVER!
C'MON, KAYA-NO!
THE CROWS HAVE COME TO EAT WHAT'S LEFT OF ME...
Plunk
DON'T DIE! GIVE US THE SCOOP!
WHAT'S WITH THE CANDLES?
CAW!
CAW!
CAW!
CAW!
Mumble
WHY? WHY'S ALL THIS HAPPENING?
Mumble
SO THERE YA HAVE IT...
...MY MOM'S ENGAGED TO THE PRINCIPAL OF THE SCHOOL...

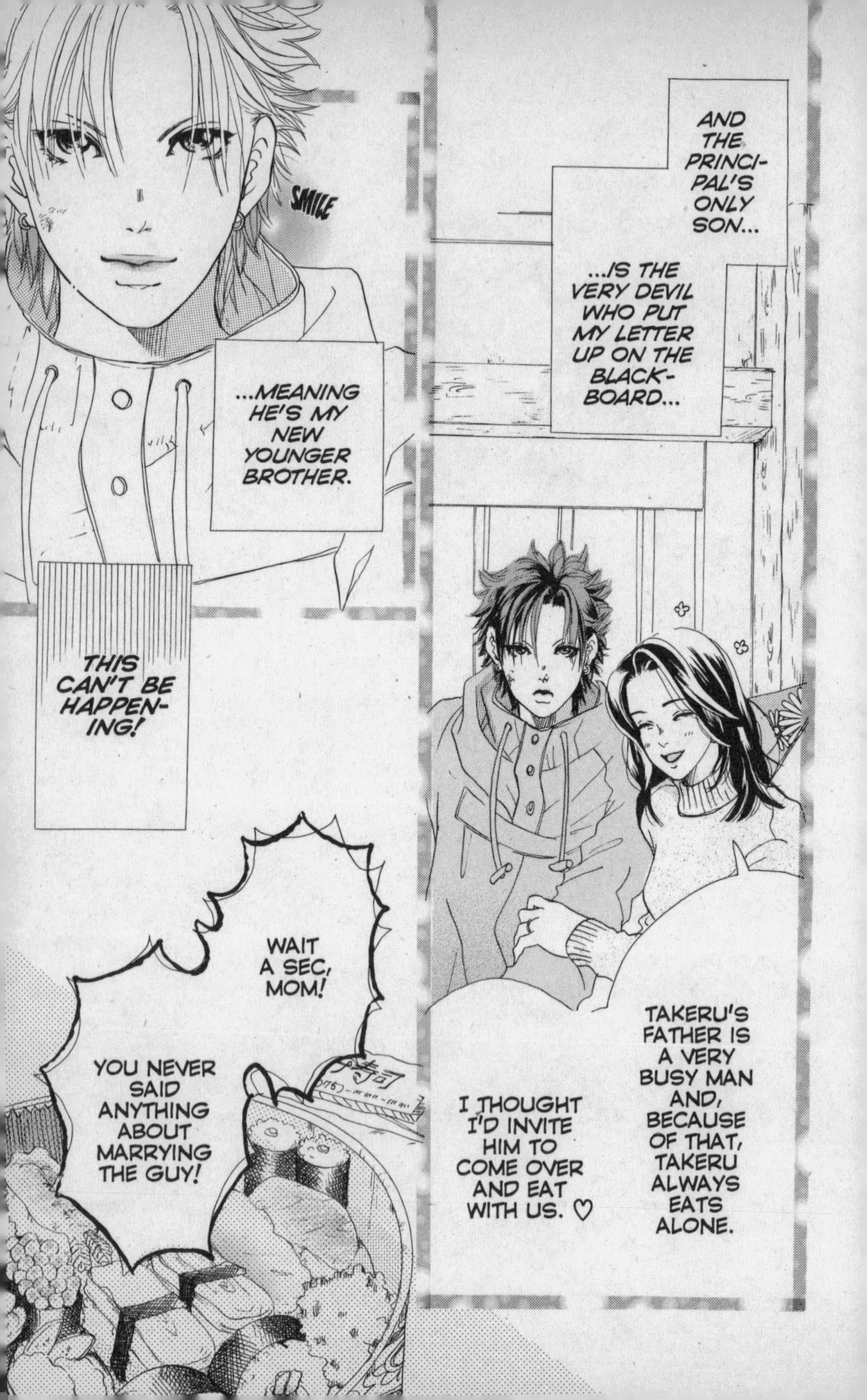
AND THE PRINCIPAL'S ONLY SON...
...IS THE VERY DEVIL WHO PUT MY LETTER UP ON THE BLACKBOARD...
TAKERU'S FATHER IS A VERY BUSY MAN AND, BECAUSE OF THAT, TAKERU ALWAYS EATS ALONE.
I THOUGHT I'D INVITE HIM TO COME OVER AND EAT WITH US. ♡
SMILE
...MEANING HE'S MY NEW YOUNGER BROTHER.
THIS CAN'T BE HAPPENING!
WAIT A SEC, MOM!
YOU NEVER SAID ANYTHING ABOUT MARRYING THE GUY!

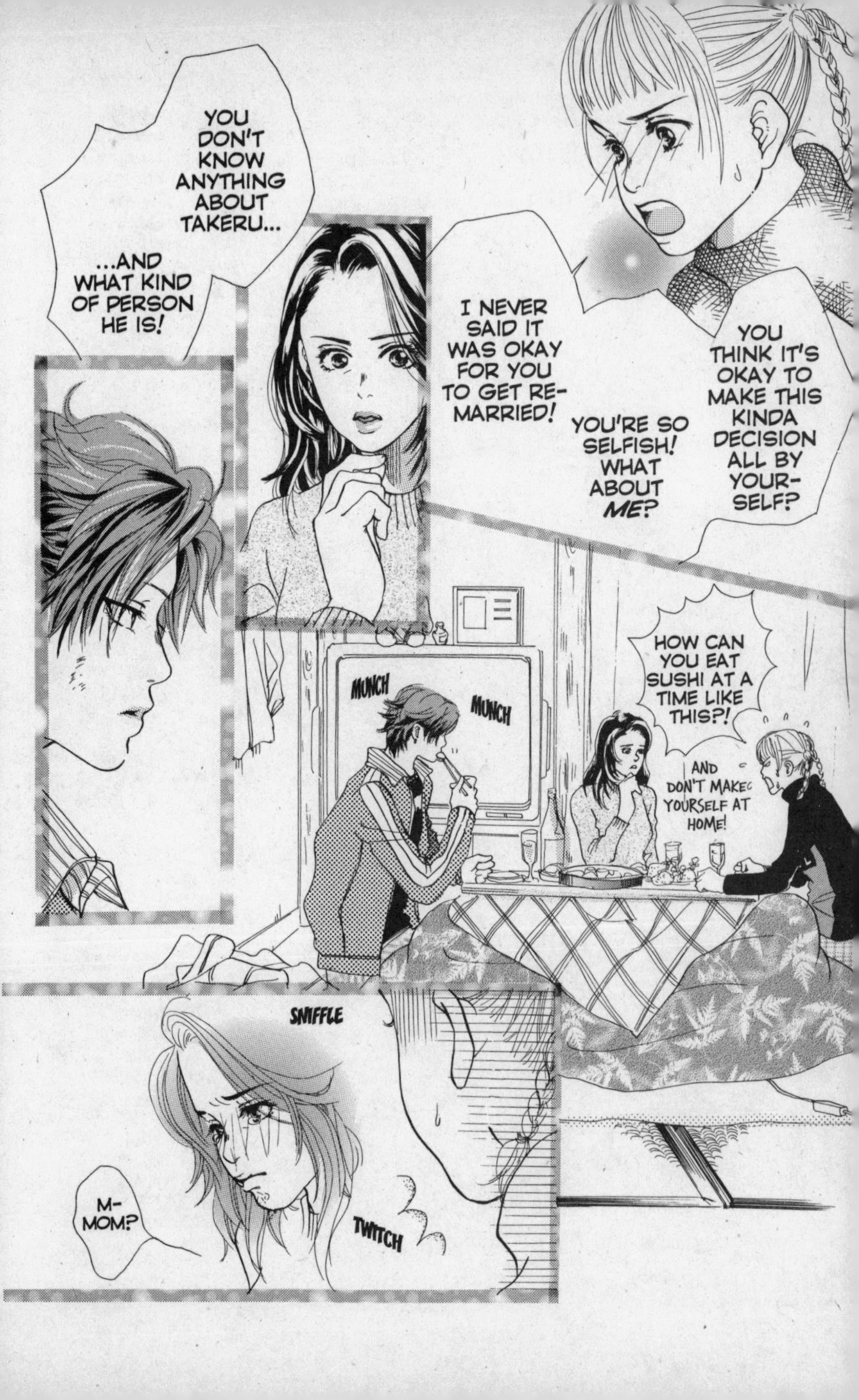
YOU THINK IT'S OKAY TO MAKE THIS KINDA DECISION ALL BY YOURSELF?
YOU'RE SO SELFISH! WHAT ABOUT *ME*?
I NEVER SAID IT WAS OKAY FOR YOU TO GET RE-MARRIED!
YOU DON'T KNOW ANYTHING ABOUT TAKERU...
...AND WHAT KIND OF PERSON HE IS!
HOW CAN YOU EAT SUSHI AT A TIME LIKE THIS?!
AND DON'T MAKE YOURSELF AT HOME!
MUNCH
MUNCH
SNIFFLE
TWITCH
M-MOM?

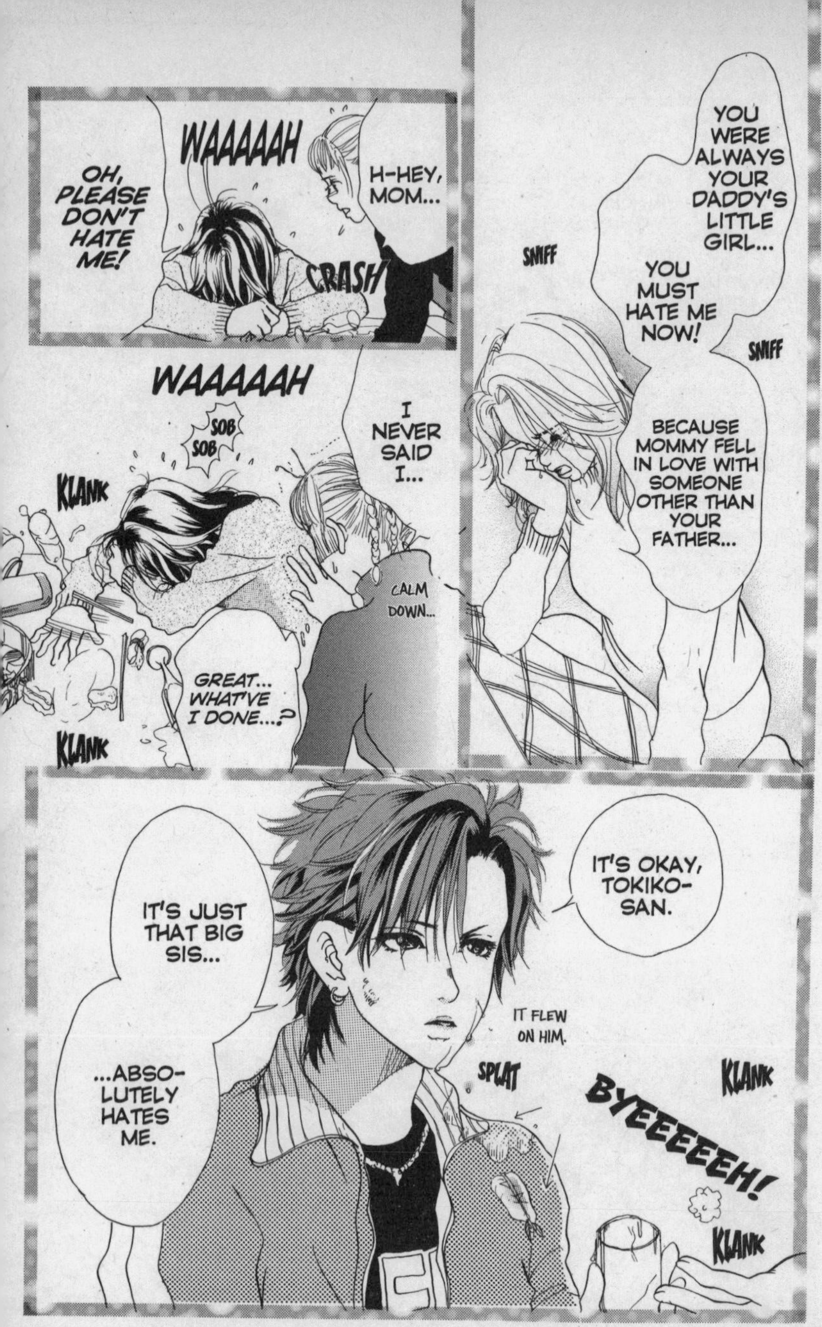
YOU WERE ALWAYS YOUR DADDY'S LITTLE GIRL...
SNIFF
YOU MUST HATE ME NOW!
SNIFF
BECAUSE MOMMY FELL IN LOVE WITH SOMEONE OTHER THAN YOUR FATHER...
WAAAAAH
H-HEY, MOM...
OH, PLEASE DON'T HATE ME!
CRASH
WAAAAAH
I NEVER SAID I...
SOB SOB
KLANK
CALM DOWN...
GREAT... WHAT'VE I DONE...?
KLANK
IT'S OKAY, TOKIKO-SAN.
IT'S JUST THAT BIG SIS...
IT FLEW ON HIM.
SPLAT
KLANK
BYEEEEEEH!
...ABSO-LUTELY HATES ME.
KLANK

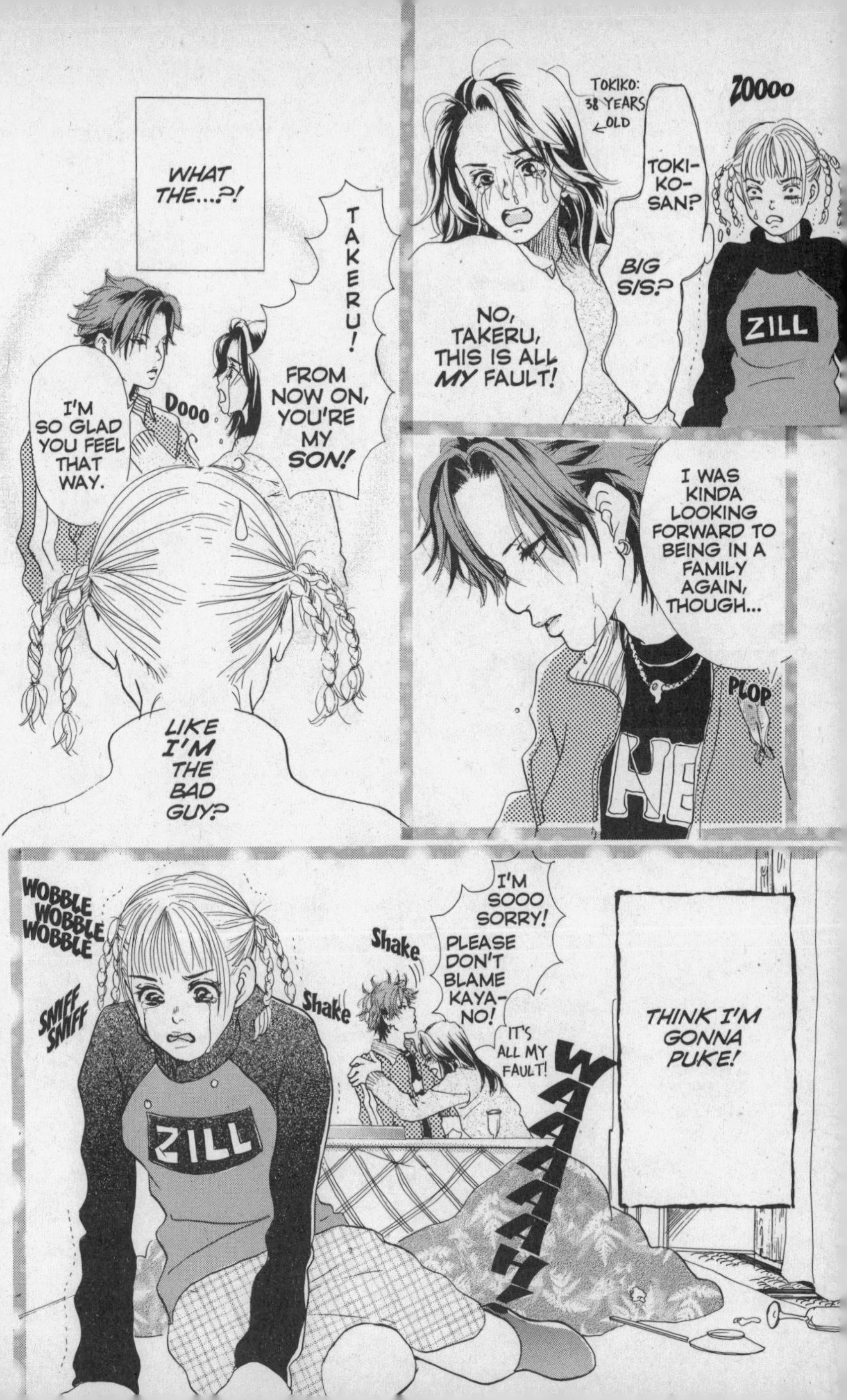
ZOOOo
TOKIKO: 38 YEARS OLD
TOKI-KO-SAN?
BIG S/S?
NO, TAKERU, THIS IS ALL MY FAULT!
I WAS KINDA LOOKING FORWARD TO BEING IN A FAMILY AGAIN, THOUGH...
PLOP
WHAT THE...?!
TAKERU! FROM NOW ON, YOU'RE MY SON!
Dooo
I'M SO GLAD YOU FEEL THAT WAY.
LIKE I'M THE BAD GUY?
THINK I'M GONNA PUKE!
WAAAAAH
IT'S ALL MY FAULT!
I'M SOOO SORRY! PLEASE DON'T BLAME KAYANO!
Shake
Shake
WOBBLE WOBBLE WOBBLE
SNIFF SNIFF

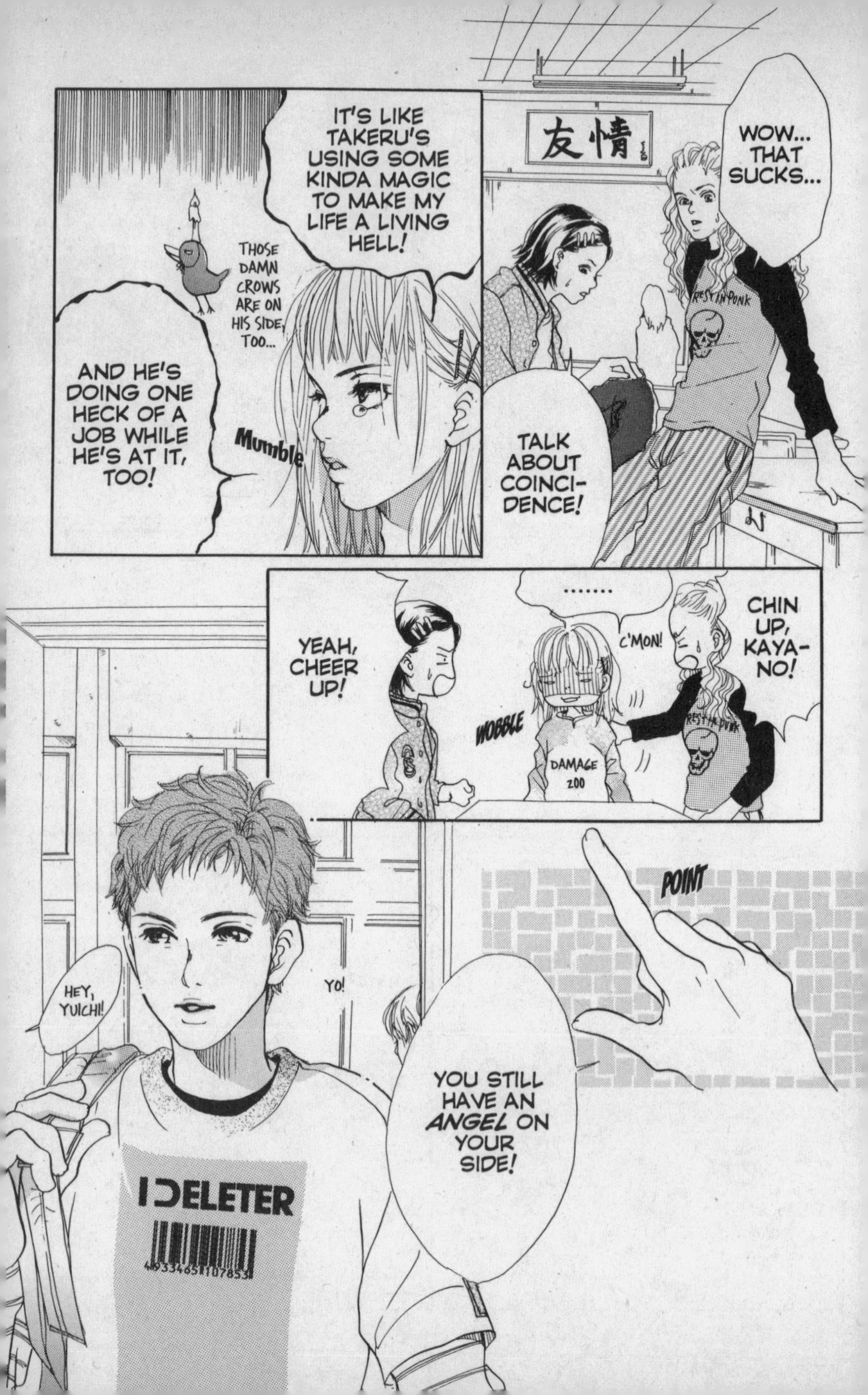

友情
WOW... THAT SUCKS...
TALK ABOUT COINCIDENCE!
IT'S LIKE TAKERU'S USING SOME KINDA MAGIC TO MAKE MY LIFE A LIVING HELL!
THOSE DAMN CROWS ARE ON HIS SIDE, TOO...
AND HE'S DOING ONE HECK OF A JOB WHILE HE'S AT IT, TOO!
Mumble
CHIN UP, KAYA-NO!
C'MON!
....
YEAH, CHEER UP!
WOBBLE
POINT
YOU STILL HAVE AN *ANGEL* ON YOUR SIDE!
YO!
HEY, YUICHI!

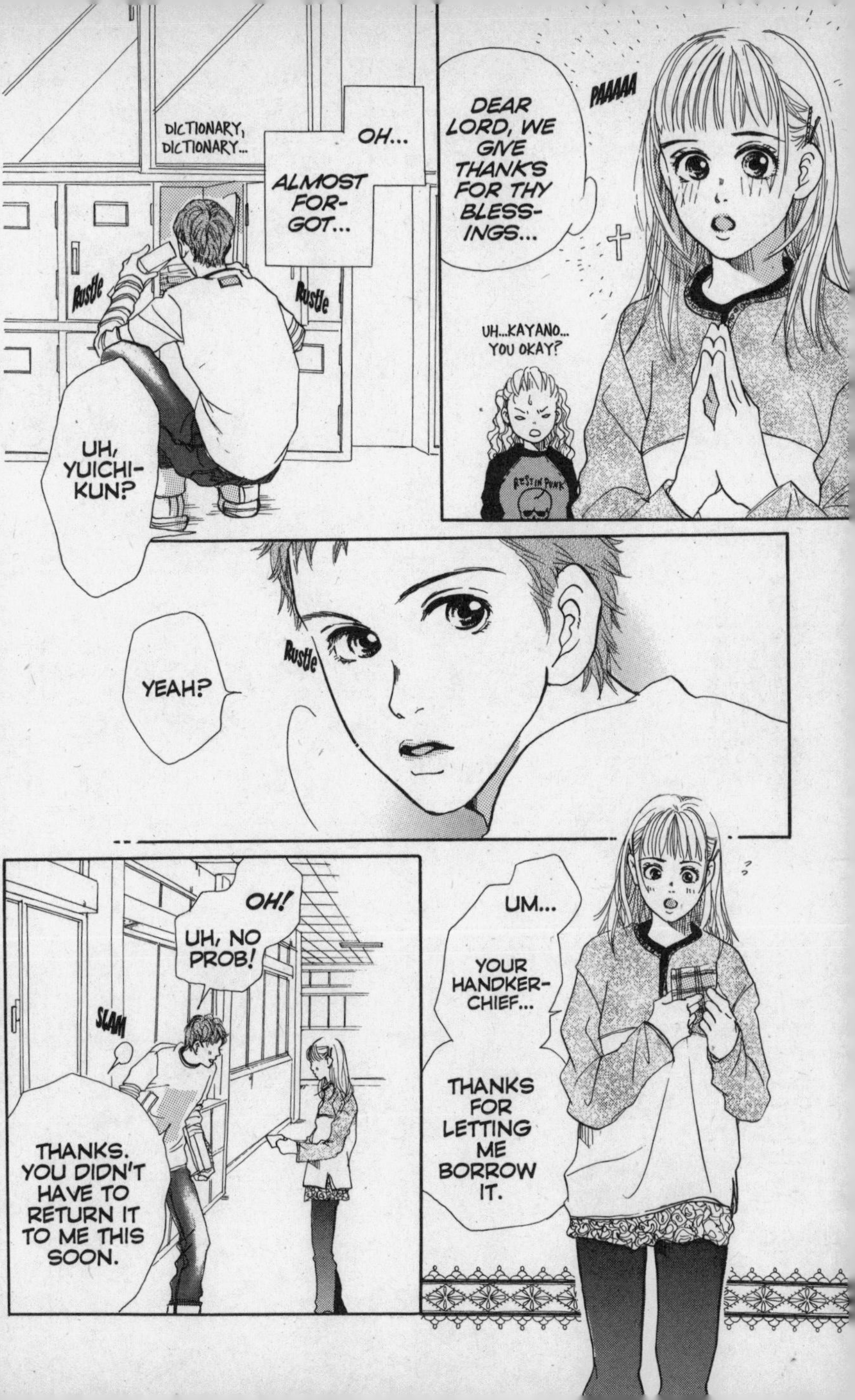
PAAAAA
DEAR LORD, WE GIVE THANKS FOR THY BLESS-INGS...
UH...KAYANO... YOU OKAY?
DICTIONARY, DICTIONARY...
OH...
ALMOST FOR-GOT...
Rustle
Rustle
UH, YUICHI-KUN?
Rustle
YEAH?
UM...
YOUR HANDKER-CHIEF...
THANKS FOR LETTING ME BORROW IT.
OH!
UH, NO PROB!
SLAM
THANKS. YOU DIDN'T HAVE TO RETURN IT TO ME THIS SOON.

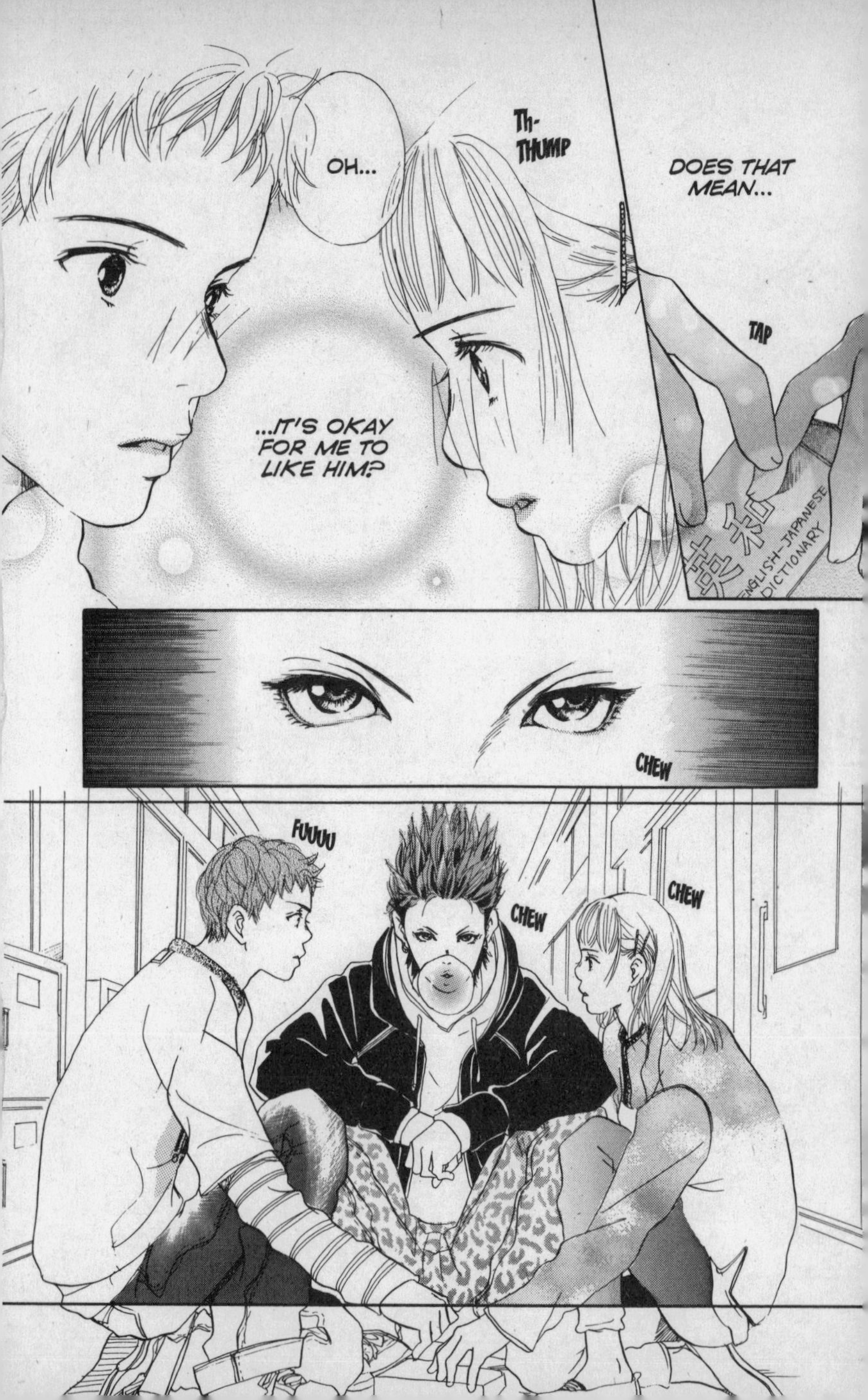
DOES THAT MEAN...
TAP
ENGLISH-JAPANESE DICTIONARY
Th-THUMP
OH...
...IT'S OKAY FOR ME TO LIKE HIM?
CHEW
CHEW
CHEW
FUUUU

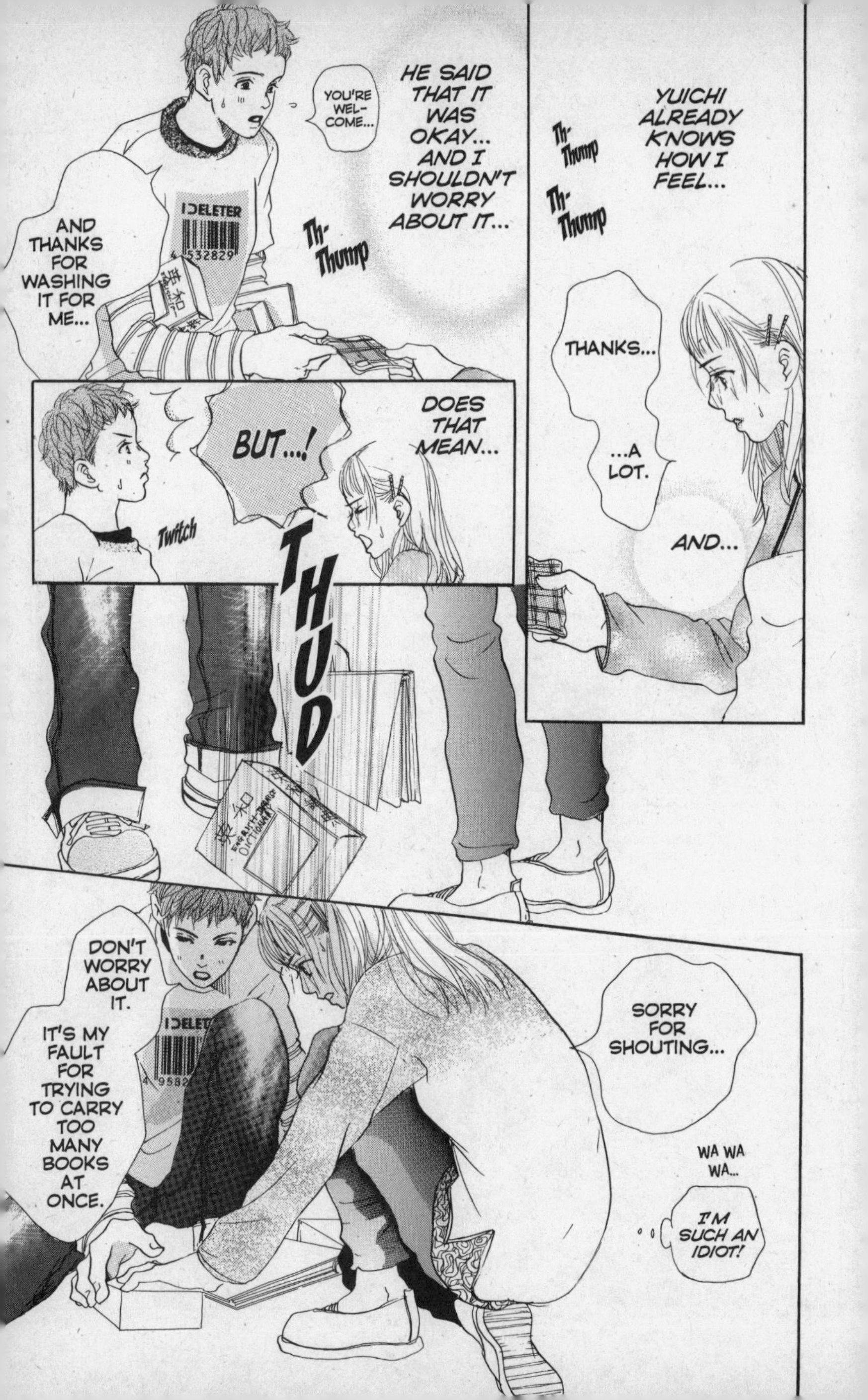
YUICHI ALREADY KNOWS HOW I FEEL...
Th-Thump
Th-Thump
THANKS...
...A LOT.
AND...
HE SAID THAT IT WAS OKAY... AND I SHOULDN'T WORRY ABOUT IT...
YOU'RE WEL-COME...
Th-Thump
AND THANKS FOR WASHING IT FOR ME...
DOES THAT MEAN...
BUT...!
Twitch
THUD
SORRY FOR SHOUTING...
WA WA WA...
I'M SUCH AN IDIOT!
DON'T WORRY ABOUT IT.
IT'S MY FAULT FOR TRYING TO CARRY TOO MANY BOOKS AT ONCE.

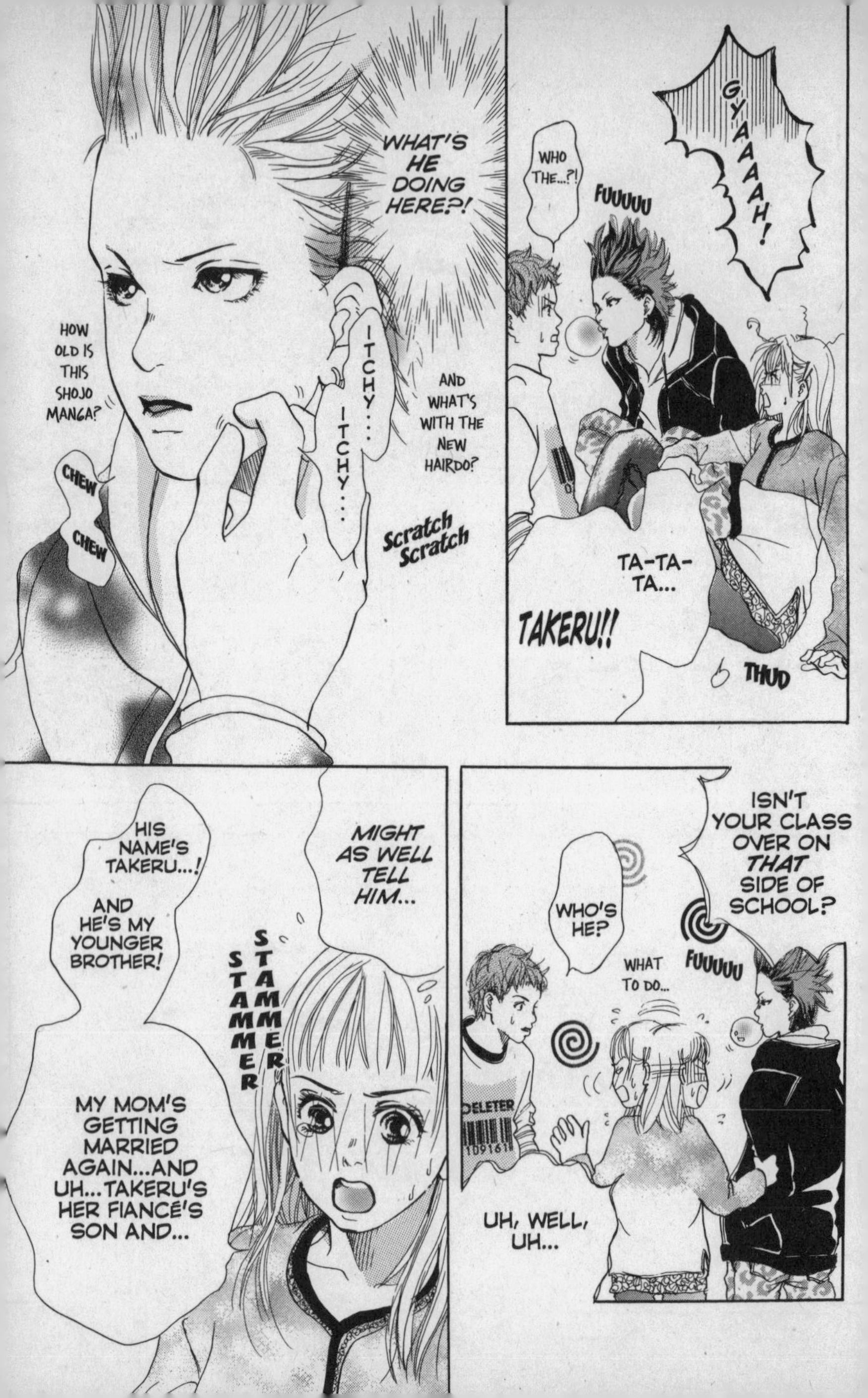
GYAAAAH!
WHO THE...?!
FUUUUU
TA-TA-TA...
TAKERU!!
THUD
WHAT'S HE DOING HERE?!
AND WHAT'S WITH THE NEW HAIRDO?
ITCHY... ITCHY...
Scratch Scratch
HOW OLD IS THIS SHOJO MANGA?
CHEW CHEW
ISN'T YOUR CLASS OVER ON THAT SIDE OF SCHOOL?
WHO'S HE?
FUUUUU
WHAT TO DO...
UH, WELL, UH...
MIGHT AS WELL TELL HIM...
STAMMER STAMMER
HIS NAME'S TAKERU...!
AND HE'S MY YOUNGER BROTHER!
MY MOM'S GETTING MARRIED AGAIN...AND UH...TAKERU'S HER FIANCÉ'S SON AND...

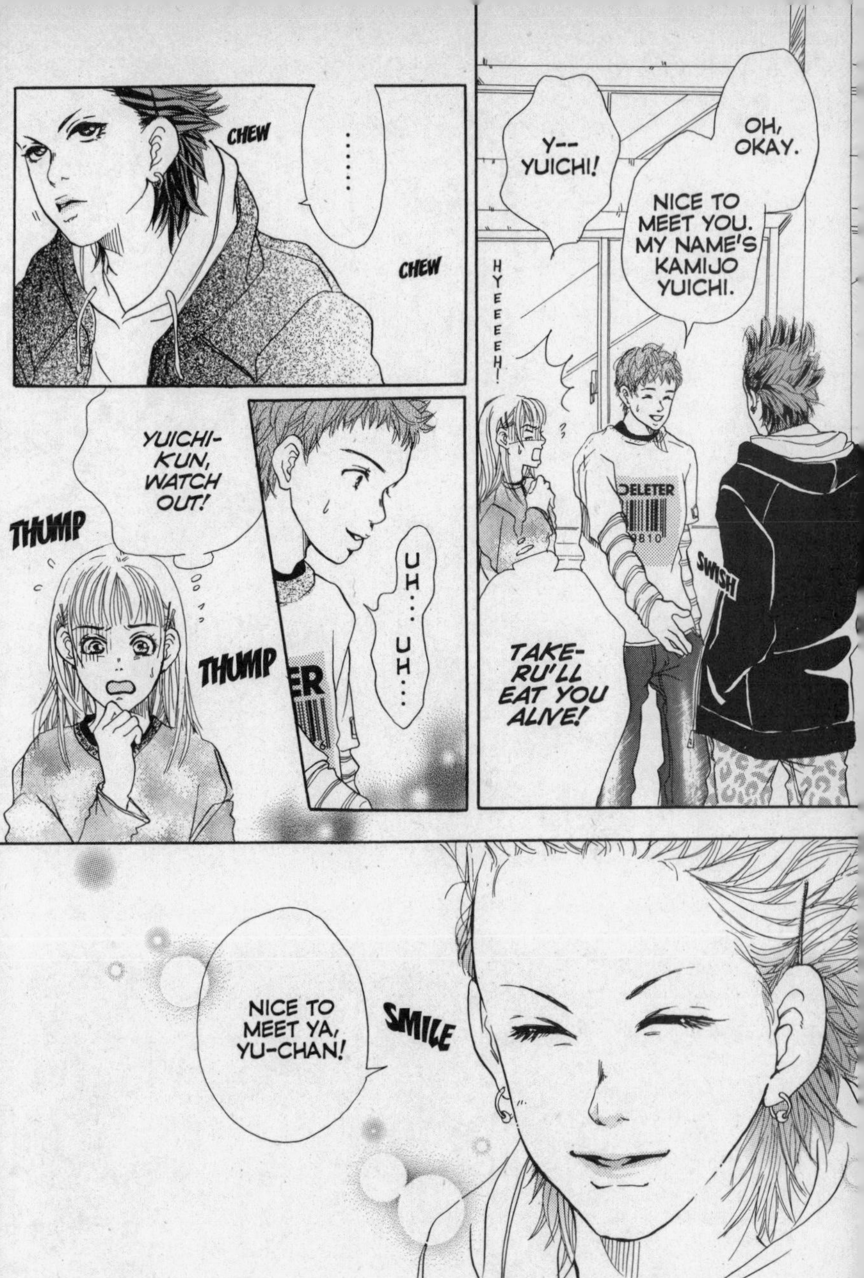
OH, OKAY.
NICE TO MEET YOU. MY NAME'S KAMIJO YUICHI.
Y-- YUICHI!
HYEEEEEH!
SWISH
TAKE-RU'LL EAT YOU ALIVE!
......
CHEW
CHEW
UH... UH...
YUICHI-KUN, WATCH OUT!
THUMP
THUMP
NICE TO MEET YA, YU-CHAN!
SMILE

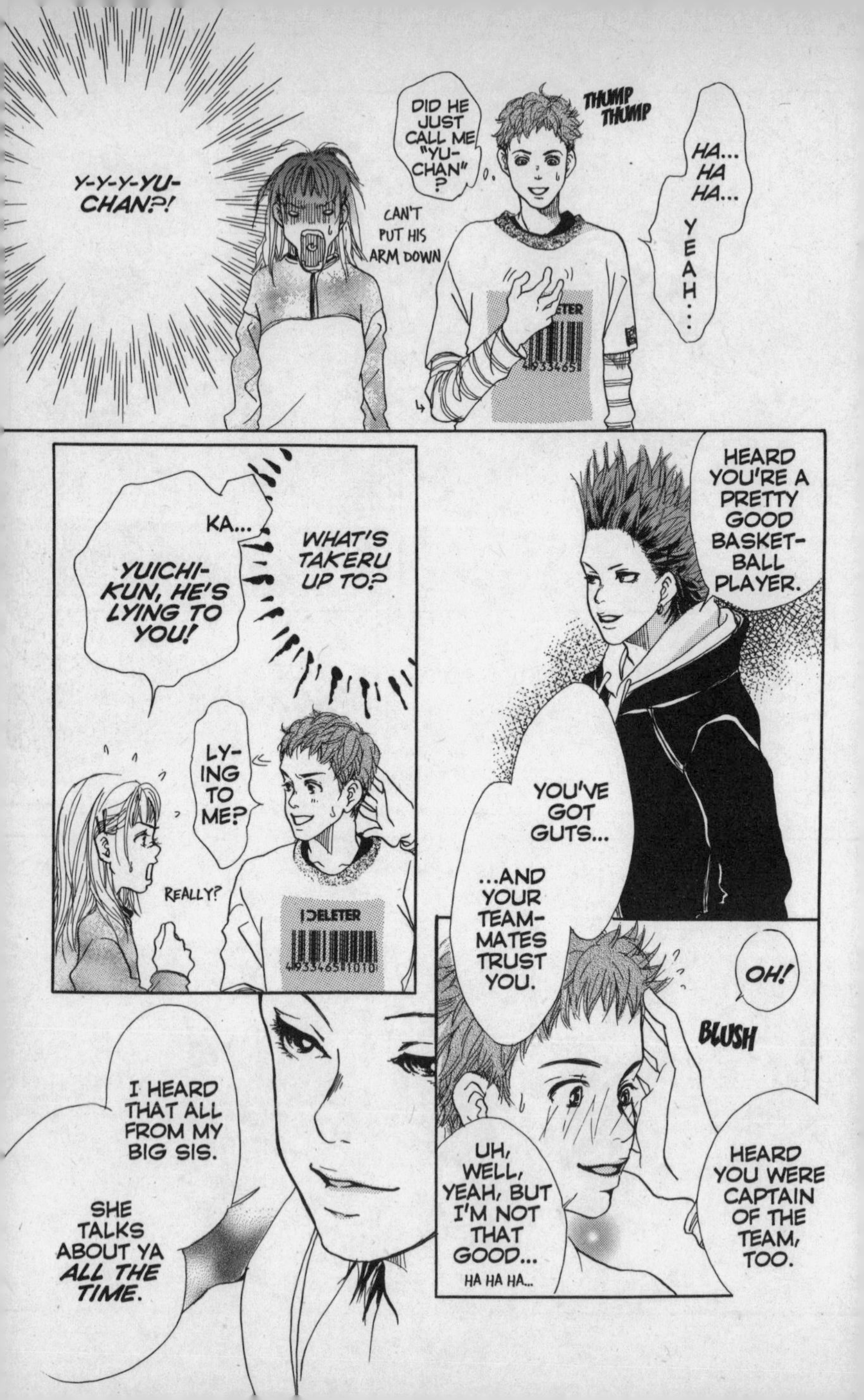

HA... HA HA... YEAH...
THUMP THUMP
DID HE JUST CALL ME "YU-CHAN"?
CAN'T PUT HIS ARM DOWN
Y-Y-Y-YU-CHAN?!
HEARD YOU'RE A PRETTY GOOD BASKETBALL PLAYER.
YOU'VE GOT GUTS...
...AND YOUR TEAMMATES TRUST YOU.
OH!
BLUSH
HEARD YOU WERE CAPTAIN OF THE TEAM, TOO.
UH, WELL, YEAH, BUT I'M NOT THAT GOOD...
HA HA HA...
WHAT'S TAKERU UP TO?
KA...
YUICHI-KUN, HE'S LYING TO YOU!
LYING TO ME?
REALLY?
I HEARD THAT ALL FROM MY BIG SIS.
SHE TALKS ABOUT YA *ALL THE TIME*.

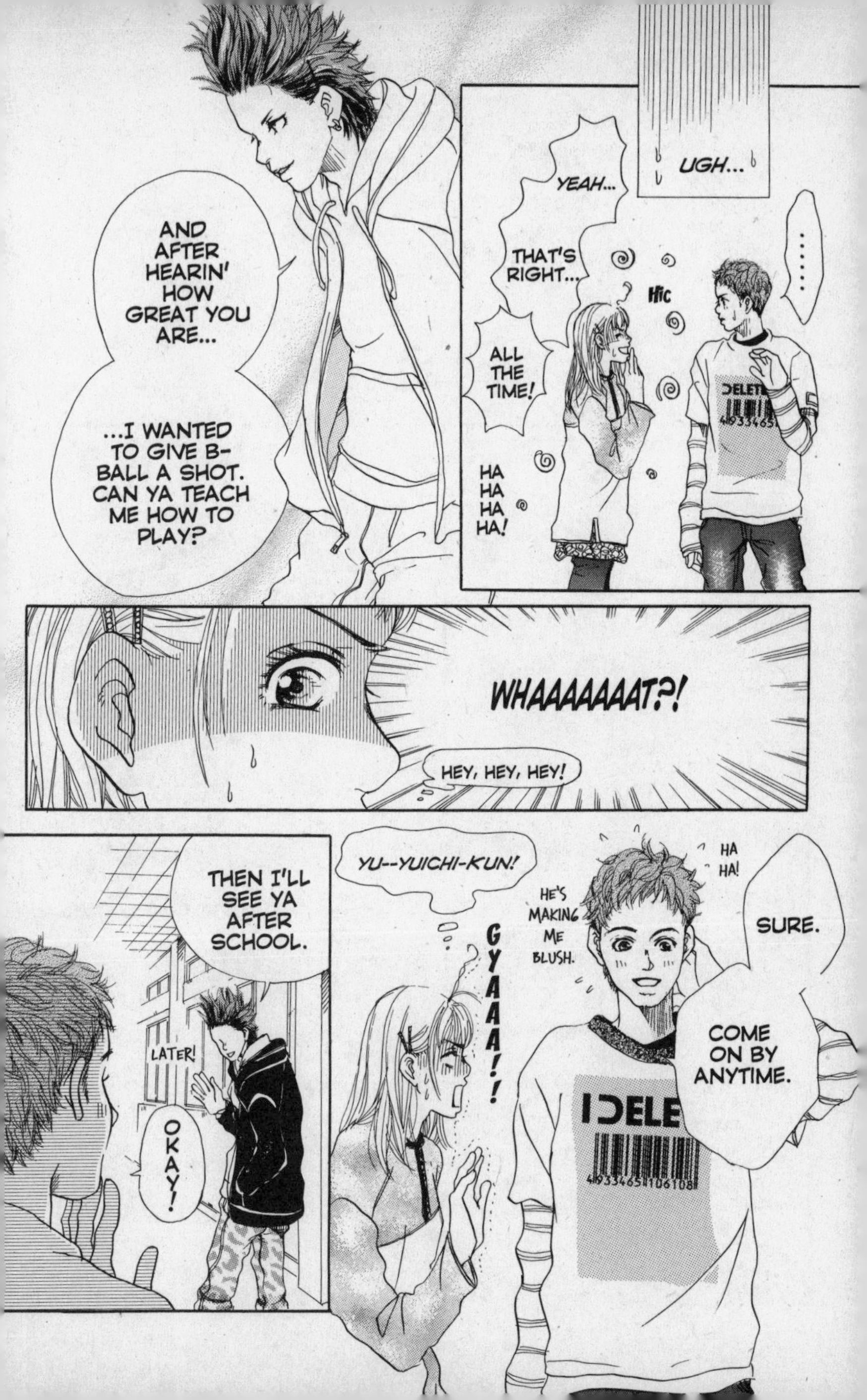
UGH...
......
YEAH...
THAT'S RIGHT...
HIC
ALL THE TIME!
HA HA HA HA!
AND AFTER HEARIN' HOW GREAT YOU ARE...
...I WANTED TO GIVE B-BALL A SHOT. CAN YA TEACH ME HOW TO PLAY?
WHAAAAAAAT?!
HEY, HEY, HEY!
HA HA!
SURE.
COME ON BY ANYTIME.
HE'S MAKING ME BLUSH.
YU--YUICHI-KUN!
GYAAA!!
THEN I'LL SEE YA AFTER SCHOOL.
LATER!
OKAY!

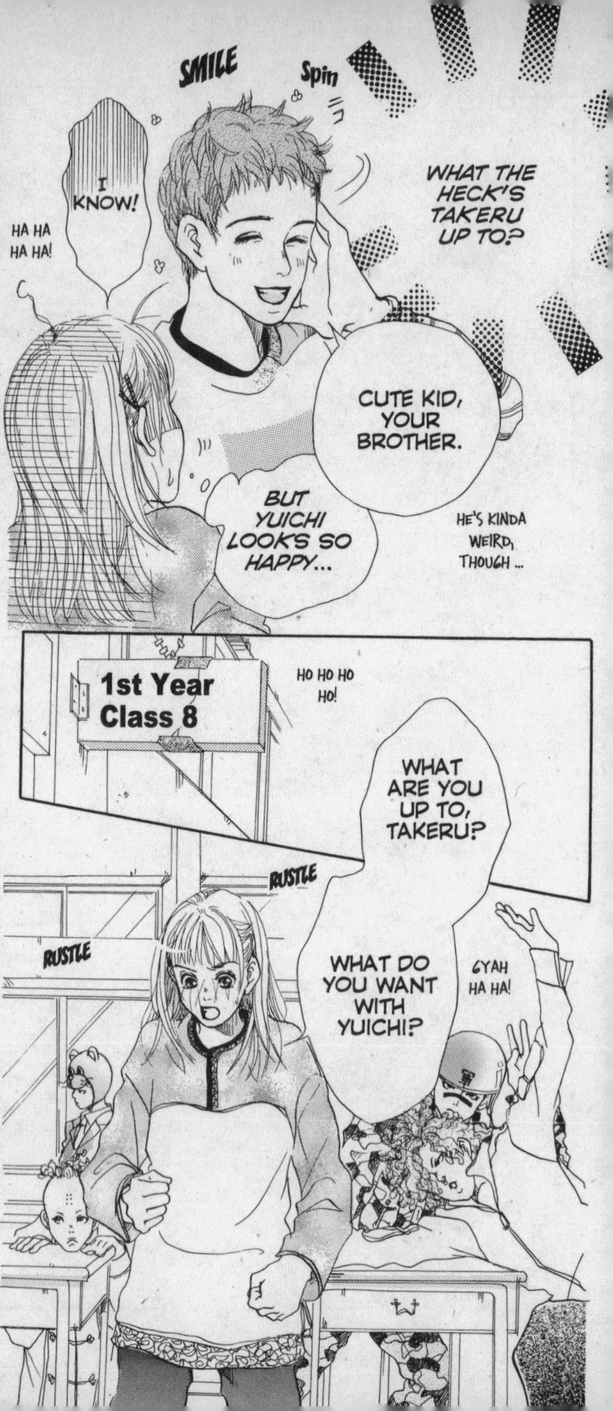
SMILE
Spin
WHAT THE HECK'S TAKERU UP TO?
I KNOW!
HA HA HA HA!
CUTE KID, YOUR BROTHER.
BUT YUICHI LOOKS SO HAPPY...
HE'S KINDA WEIRD, THOUGH...
1st Year Class 8
HO HO HO HO!
WHAT ARE YOU UP TO, TAKERU?
RUSTLE
GYAH HA HA!
WHAT DO YOU WANT WITH YUICHI?
RUSTLE

Mitsuba Club 2

About the cast of characters: from the beginning of this series, in almost all the fan letters, "Is the rock star Hide the model for Takeru? I gotta know!" so wrote many of the letters. I thought I ought to touch on this. To put it directly, that's absolutely RIGHT! So that's it.

As for the rest of the characters, I wanted to make them the coolest, most loveable I could. And for me, that would be someone just like Hide-chan, but expanded into detail. I've molded Hide rather freely here, to suit my own tastes. So I guess I'll have to apologize to Hide for the changes. I feel a little embarrassed admitting I modeled a character after Hide. And I'll bet the Hide fans out there won't be too happy. But either way, I'm glad you the readers are buying the character Takeru.

Continued...

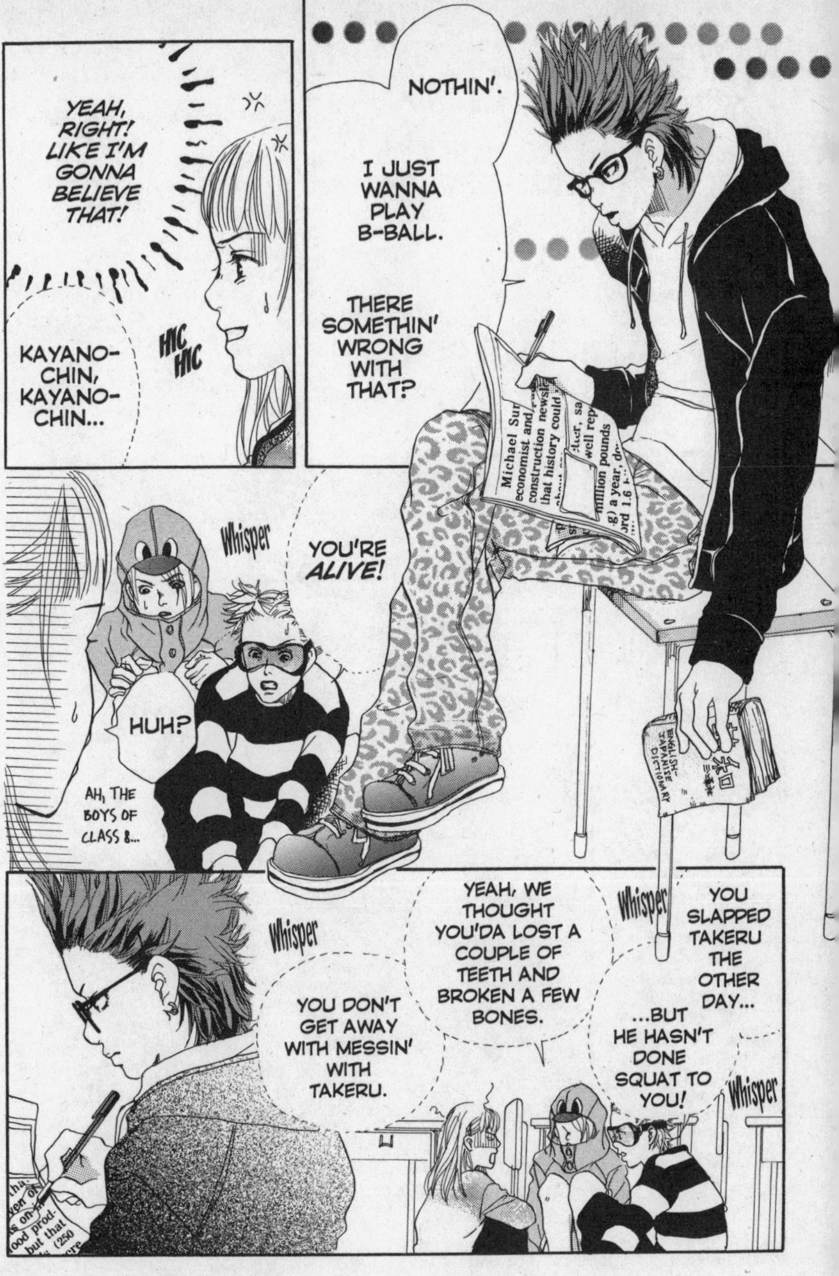
NOTHIN'.
I JUST WANNA PLAY B-BALL.
THERE SOMETHIN' WRONG WITH THAT?
YEAH, RIGHT! LIKE I'M GONNA BELIEVE THAT!
HIC HIC
KAYANO-CHIN, KAYANO-CHIN...
Whisper
YOU'RE *ALIVE*!
HUH?
AH, THE BOYS OF CLASS 8...
ENGLISH-JAPANESE DICTIONARY
YOU SLAPPED TAKERU THE OTHER DAY...
...BUT HE HASN'T DONE SQUAT TO YOU!
Whisper
Whisper
YEAH, WE THOUGHT YOU'DA LOST A COUPLE OF TEETH AND BROKEN A FEW BONES.
YOU DON'T GET AWAY WITH MESSIN' WITH TAKERU.
Whisper

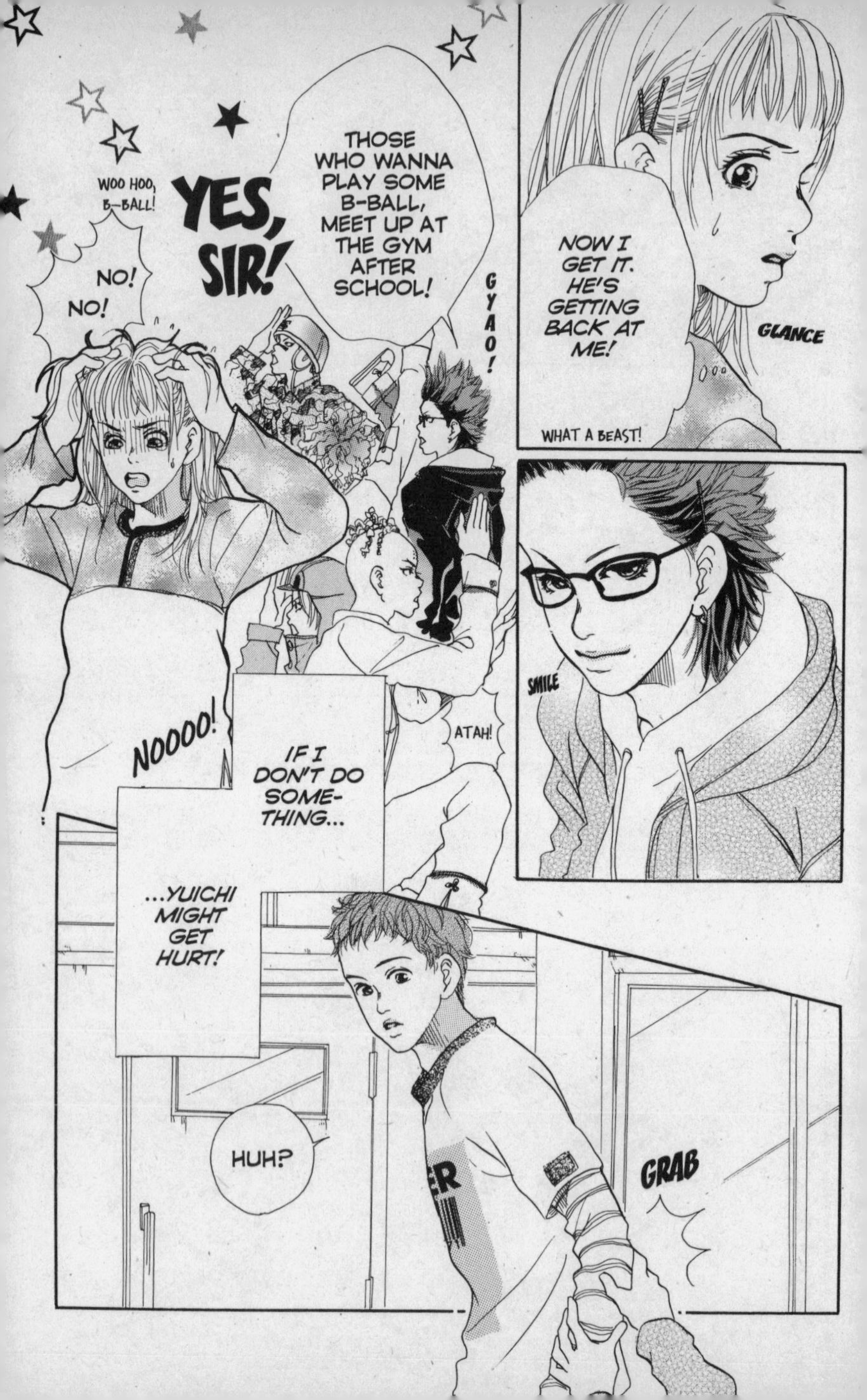
NOW I GET IT. HE'S GETTING BACK AT ME!
GLANCE
WHAT A BEAST!
SMILE
THOSE WHO WANNA PLAY SOME B-BALL, MEET UP AT THE GYM AFTER SCHOOL!
YES, SIR!
GYAO!
WOO HOO, B-BALL!
NO! NO!
ATAH!
NOOOO!
IF I DON'T DO SOME-THING...
...YUICHI MIGHT GET HURT!
GRAB
HUH?

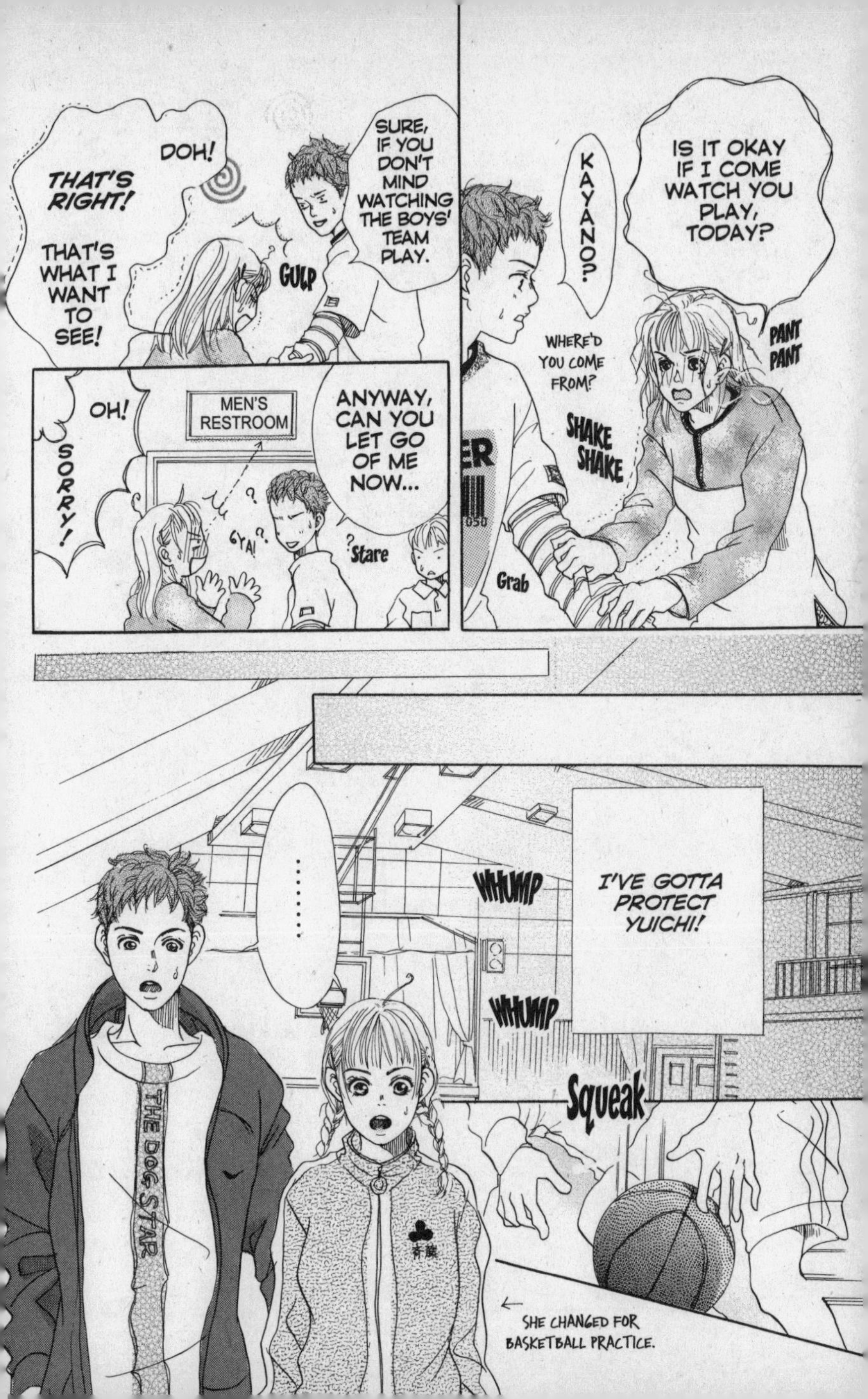
IS IT OKAY IF I COME WATCH YOU PLAY, TODAY?
PANT PANT
KAYANO?
WHERE'D YOU COME FROM?
SHAKE SHAKE
Grab
SURE, IF YOU DON'T MIND WATCHING THE BOYS' TEAM PLAY.
DOH!
THAT'S RIGHT!
THAT'S WHAT I WANT TO SEE!
GULP
ANYWAY, CAN YOU LET GO OF ME NOW...
MEN'S RESTROOM
OH!
SORRY!
GYA!
Stare
I'VE GOTTA PROTECT YUICHI!
WHUMP
WHUMP
Squeak
......
THE DOG STAR
SHE CHANGED FOR BASKETBALL PRACTICE.

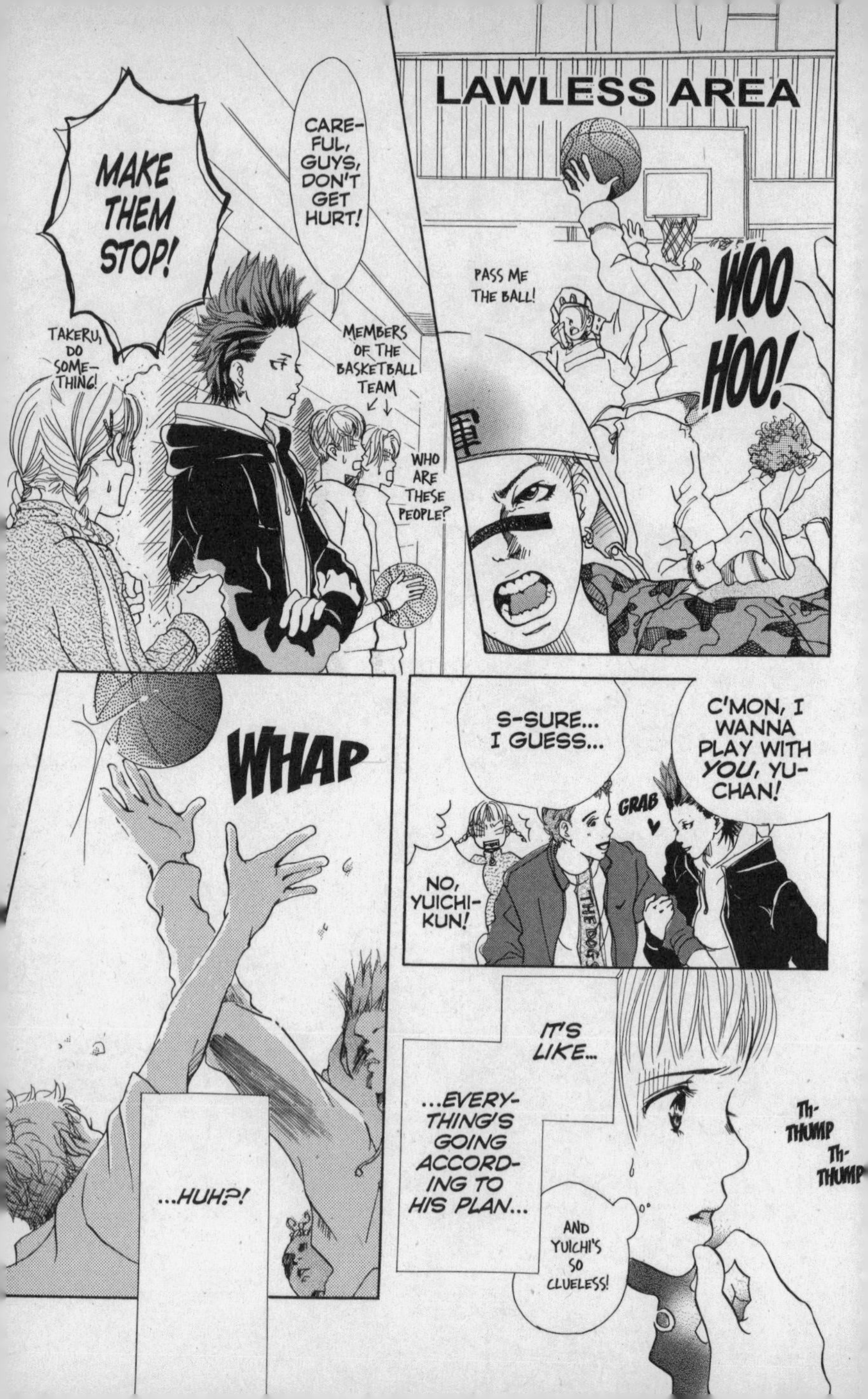
LAWLESS AREA
WOO-HOO!
PASS ME THE BALL!
CARE-FUL, GUYS, DON'T GET HURT!
MAKE THEM STOP!
MEMBERS OF THE BASKETBALL TEAM
TAKERU, DO SOME-THING!
WHO ARE THESE PEOPLE?
C'MON, I WANNA PLAY WITH *YOU*, YU-CHAN!
S-SURE... I GUESS...
GRAB
NO, YUICHI-KUN!
IT'S LIKE...
...EVERY-THING'S GOING ACCORD-ING TO HIS PLAN...
Th-THUMP Th-THUMP
AND YUICHI'S SO CLUELESS!
WHAP
...HUH?!

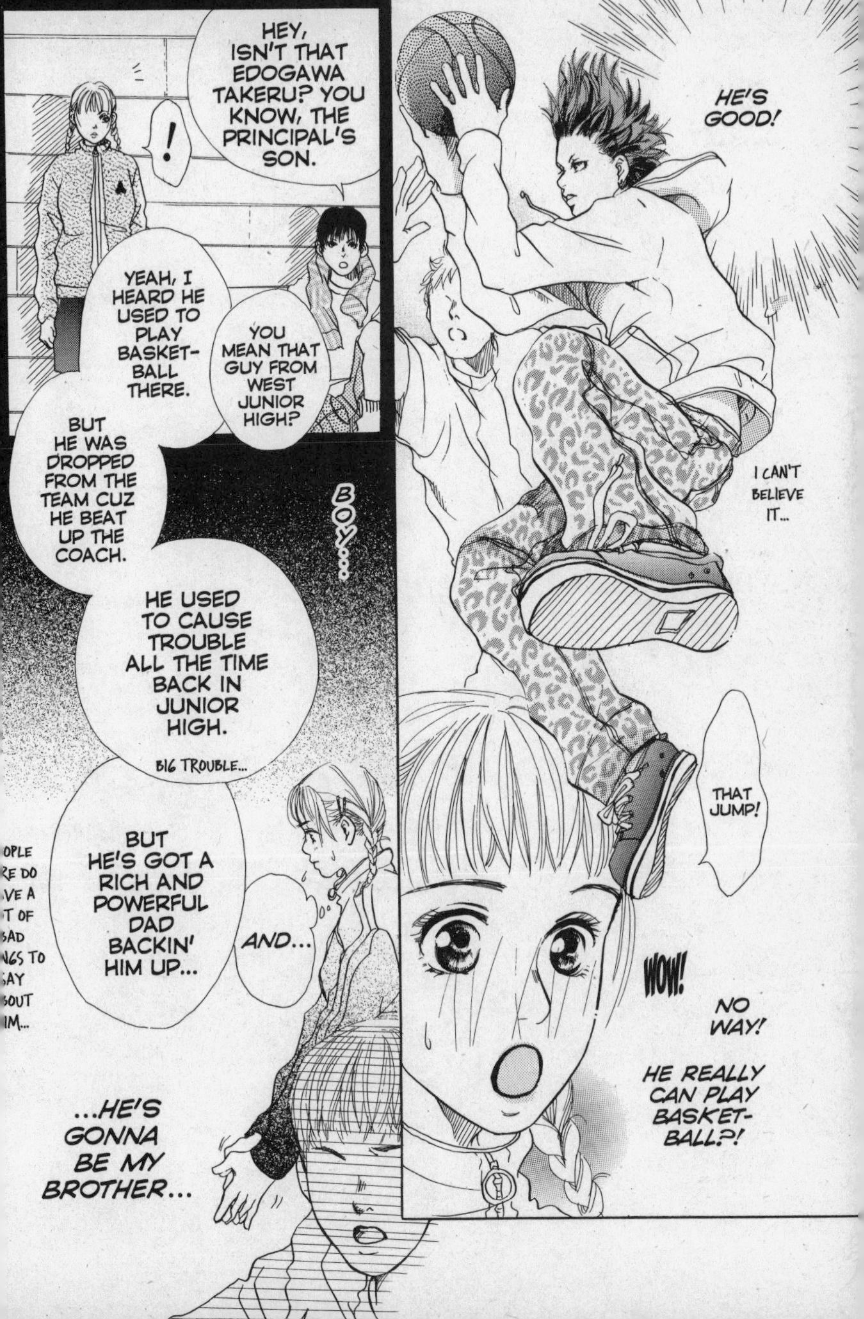
HE'S GOOD!
I CAN'T BELIEVE IT...
THAT JUMP!
WOW!
NO WAY!
HE REALLY CAN PLAY BASKET-BALL?!
HEY, ISN'T THAT EDOGAWA TAKERU? YOU KNOW, THE PRINCIPAL'S SON.
!
YOU MEAN THAT GUY FROM WEST JUNIOR HIGH?
YEAH, I HEARD HE USED TO PLAY BASKET-BALL THERE.
BUT HE WAS DROPPED FROM THE TEAM CUZ HE BEAT UP THE COACH.
BOY...
HE USED TO CAUSE TROUBLE ALL THE TIME BACK IN JUNIOR HIGH.
BIG TROUBLE...
BUT HE'S GOT A RICH AND POWERFUL DAD BACKIN' HIM UP...
AND...
...HE'S GONNA BE MY BROTHER...

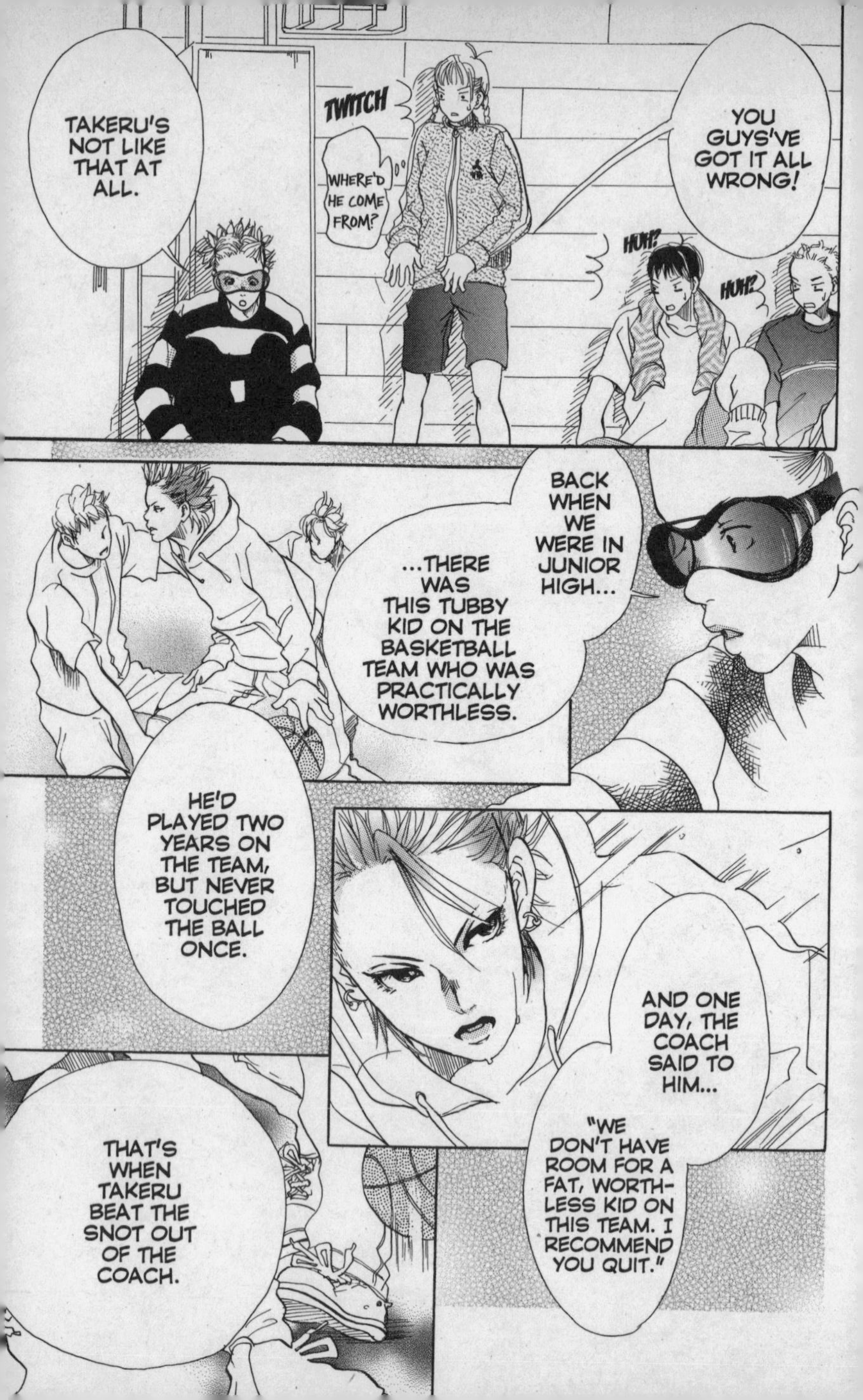
YOU GUYS'VE GOT IT ALL WRONG!
HUH?
HUH?
TWITCH
WHERE'D HE COME FROM?
TAKERU'S NOT LIKE THAT AT ALL.
BACK WHEN WE WERE IN JUNIOR HIGH...
...THERE WAS THIS TUBBY KID ON THE BASKETBALL TEAM WHO WAS PRACTICALLY WORTHLESS.
AND ONE DAY, THE COACH SAID TO HIM...
"WE DON'T HAVE ROOM FOR A FAT, WORTH-LESS KID ON THIS TEAM. I RECOMMEND YOU QUIT."
HE'D PLAYED TWO YEARS ON THE TEAM, BUT NEVER TOUCHED THE BALL ONCE.
THAT'S WHEN TAKERU BEAT THE SNOT OUT OF THE COACH.

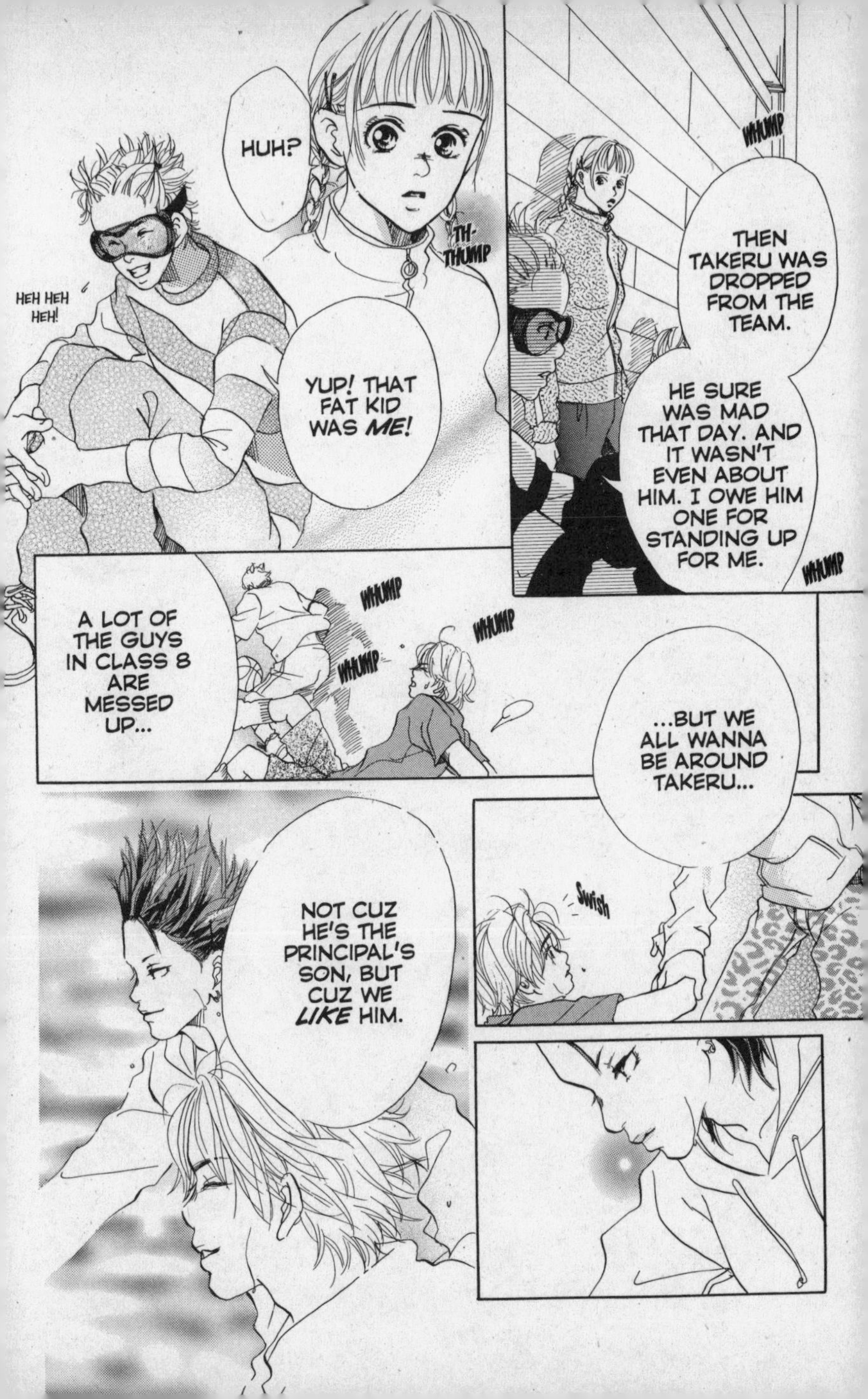
WHUMP
THEN TAKERU WAS DROPPED FROM THE TEAM.
HE SURE WAS MAD THAT DAY. AND IT WASN'T EVEN ABOUT HIM. I OWE HIM ONE FOR STANDING UP FOR ME.
WHUMP
HUH?
TH-THUMP
YUP! THAT FAT KID WAS *ME!*
HEH HEH HEH!
WHUMP
WHUMP
WHUMP
A LOT OF THE GUYS IN CLASS 8 ARE MESSED UP...
...BUT WE ALL WANNA BE AROUND TAKERU...
Swish
NOT CUZ HE'S THE PRINCIPAL'S SON, BUT CUZ WE *LIKE* HIM.

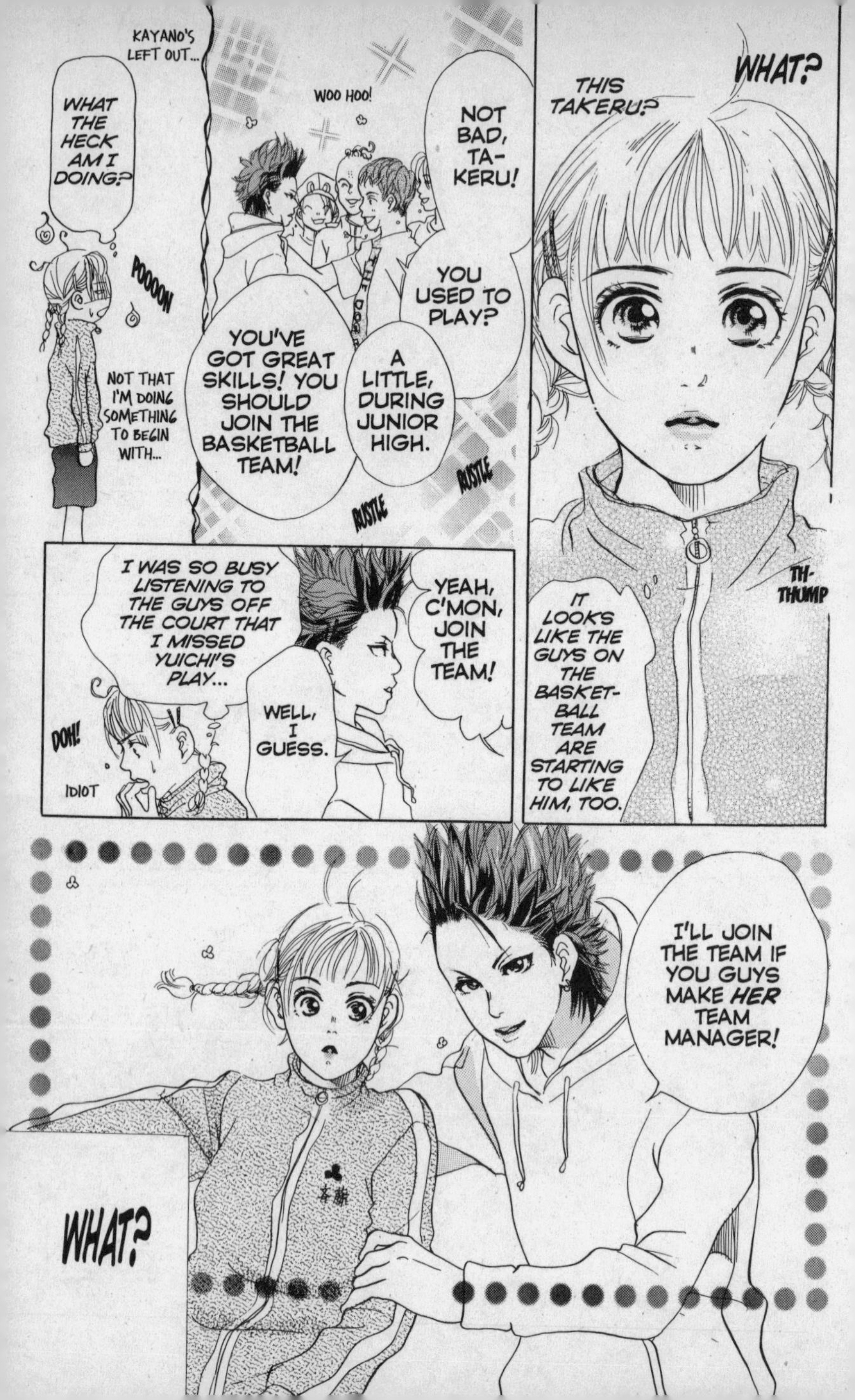
WHAT?
THIS TAKERU?
TH-THUMP
IT LOOKS LIKE THE GUYS ON THE BASKETBALL TEAM ARE STARTING TO LIKE HIM, TOO.
NOT BAD, TAKERU!
WOO HOO!
YOU USED TO PLAY?
A LITTLE, DURING JUNIOR HIGH.
YOU'VE GOT GREAT SKILLS! YOU SHOULD JOIN THE BASKETBALL TEAM!
RUSTLE
RUSTLE
KAYANO'S LEFT OUT...
WHAT THE HECK AM I DOING?
POOOON
NOT THAT I'M DOING SOMETHING TO BEGIN WITH...
YEAH, C'MON, JOIN THE TEAM!
WELL, I GUESS.
I WAS SO BUSY LISTENING TO THE GUYS OFF THE COURT THAT I MISSED YUICHI'S PLAY...
DOH!
IDIOT
I'LL JOIN THE TEAM IF YOU GUYS MAKE *HER* TEAM MANAGER!
WHAT?

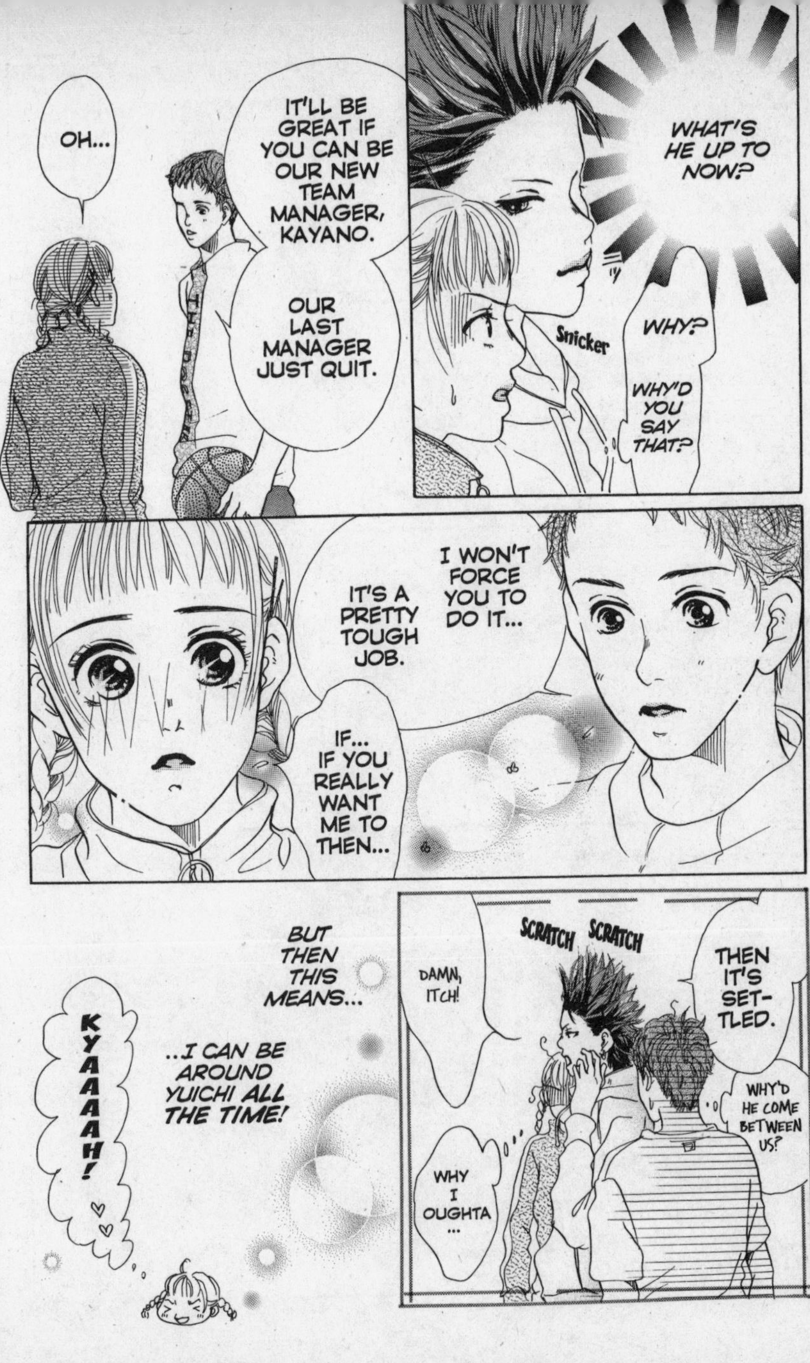
WHAT'S HE UP TO NOW?
Snicker
WHY?
WHY'D YOU SAY THAT?
IT'LL BE GREAT IF YOU CAN BE OUR NEW TEAM MANAGER, KAYANO.
OUR LAST MANAGER JUST QUIT.
OH...
I WON'T FORCE YOU TO DO IT...
IT'S A PRETTY TOUGH JOB.
IF... IF YOU REALLY WANT ME TO THEN...
THEN IT'S SET-TLED.
SCRATCH SCRATCH
WHY'D HE COME BETWEEN US?
DAMN, ITCH!
WHY I OUGHTA ...
BUT THEN THIS MEANS...
...I CAN BE AROUND YUICHI ALL THE TIME!
KYAAAAH!

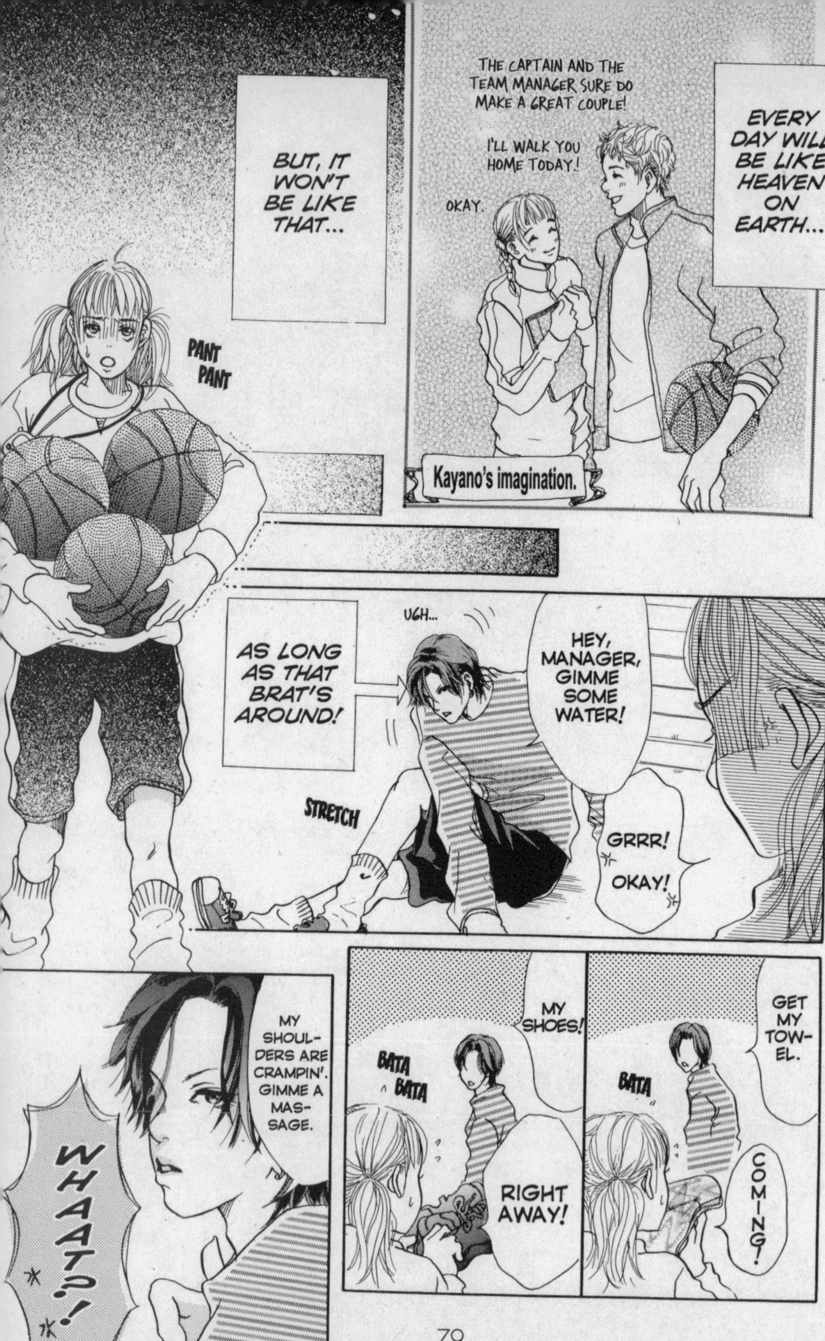
EVERY DAY WILL BE LIKE HEAVEN ON EARTH...
THE CAPTAIN AND THE TEAM MANAGER SURE DO MAKE A GREAT COUPLE!
I'LL WALK YOU HOME TODAY!
OKAY.
Kayano's imagination.
BUT, IT WON'T BE LIKE THAT...
PANT PANT
HEY, MANAGER, GIMME SOME WATER!
UGH...
AS LONG AS THAT BRAT'S AROUND!
STRETCH
GRRR!
OKAY!
GET MY TOW-EL.
BATA
COMING!
MY SHOES!
BATA BATA
RIGHT AWAY!
MY SHOUL-DERS ARE CRAMPIN'. GIMME A MAS-SAGE.
WHAAT?!!

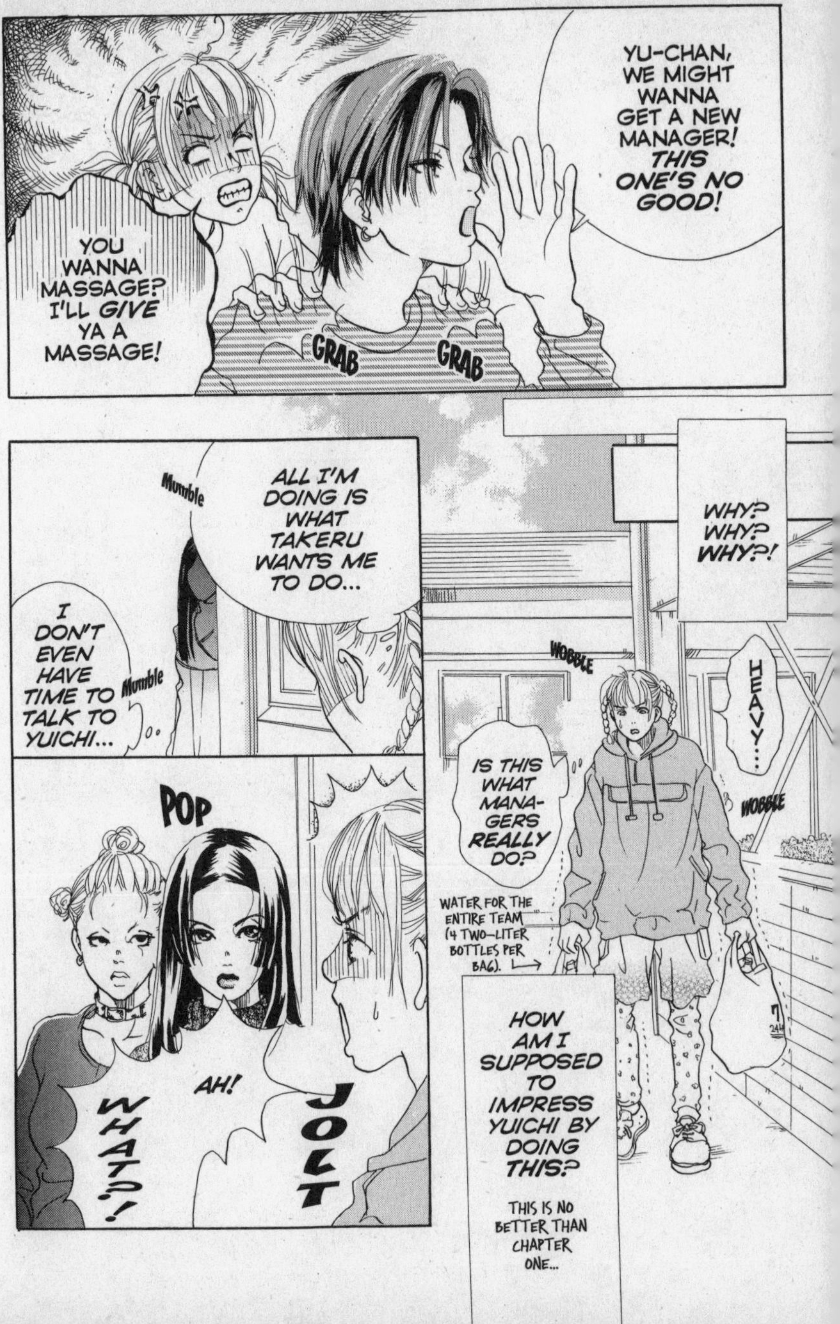

YU-CHAN, WE MIGHT WANNA GET A NEW MANAGER! THIS ONE'S NO GOOD!
GRAB
GRAB
YOU WANNA MASSAGE? I'LL GIVE YA A MASSAGE!
WHY? WHY? WHY?!
HEAVY...
WOBBLE
WOBBLE
IS THIS WHAT MANAGERS REALLY DO?
WATER FOR THE ENTIRE TEAM (4 TWO-LITER BOTTLES PER BAG).
HOW AM I SUPPOSED TO IMPRESS YUICHI BY DOING THIS?
THIS IS NO BETTER THAN CHAPTER ONE...
ALL I'M DOING IS WHAT TAKERU WANTS ME TO DO...
Mumble
I DON'T EVEN HAVE TIME TO TALK TO YUICHI...
Mumble
POP
JOLT
AH!
WHAT?!

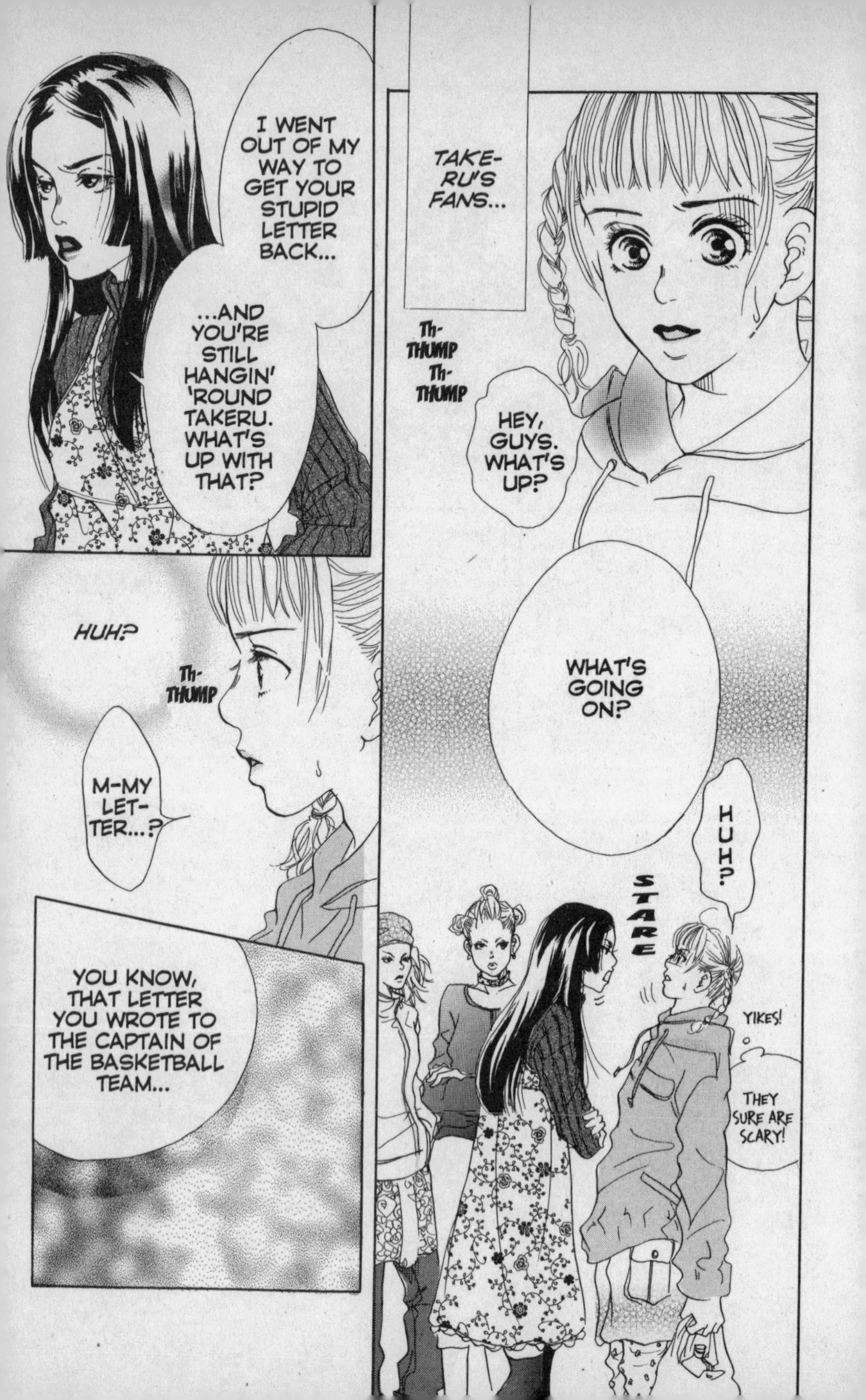
TAKE-RU'S FANS...
Th-THUMP Th-THUMP
HEY, GUYS. WHAT'S UP?
WHAT'S GOING ON?
STARE
HUH?
YIKES!
THEY SURE ARE SCARY!
I WENT OUT OF MY WAY TO GET YOUR STUPID LETTER BACK...
...AND YOU'RE STILL HANGIN' 'ROUND TAKERU. WHAT'S UP WITH THAT?
HUH?
Th-THUMP
M-MY LET-TER...?
YOU KNOW, THAT LETTER YOU WROTE TO THE CAPTAIN OF THE BASKETBALL TEAM...

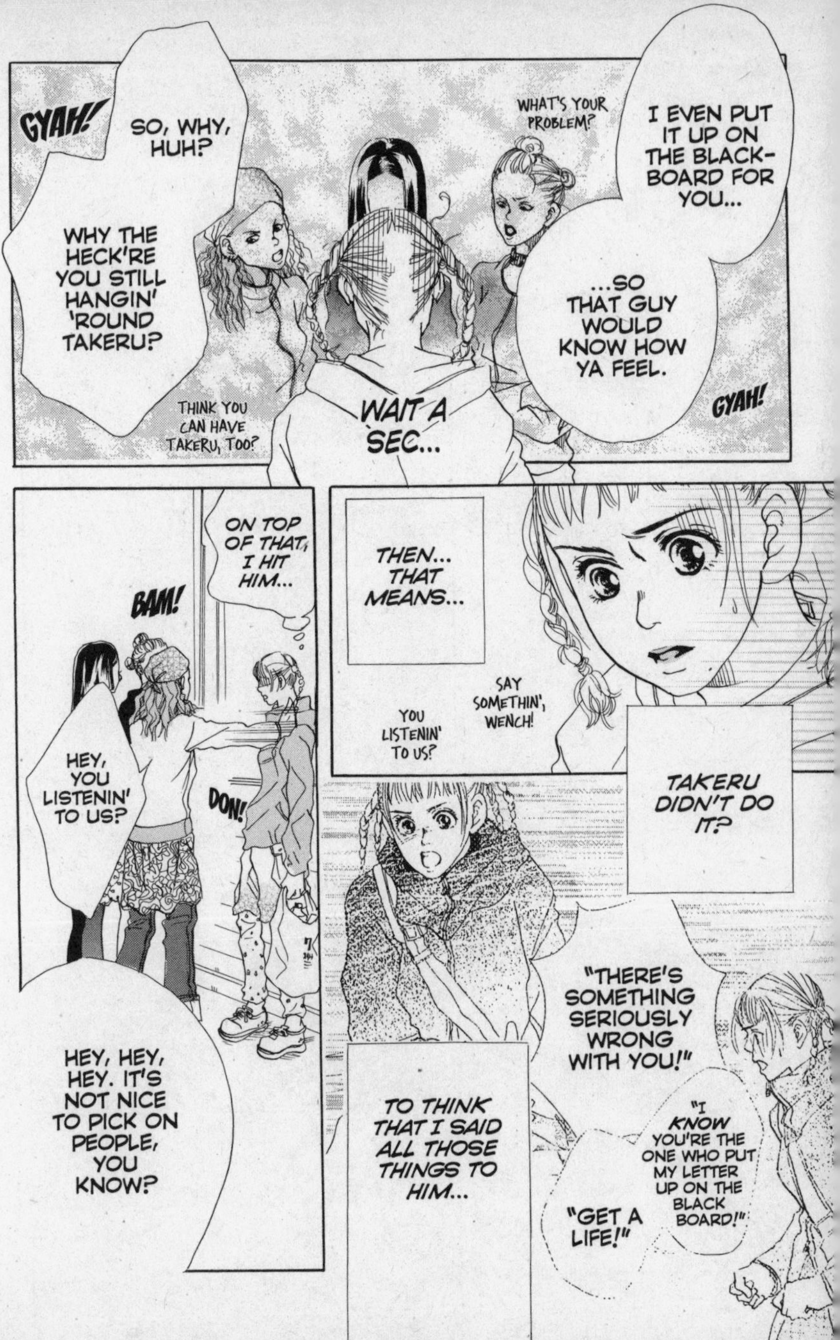
I EVEN PUT IT UP ON THE BLACK-BOARD FOR YOU...
WHAT'S YOUR PROBLEM?
...SO THAT GUY WOULD KNOW HOW YA FEEL.
GYAH!
WAIT A SEC...
SO, WHY, HUH?
GYAH!
WHY THE HECK'RE YOU STILL HANGIN' 'ROUND TAKERU?
THINK YOU CAN HAVE TAKERU, TOO?
THEN... THAT MEANS...
SAY SOMETHIN', WENCH!
YOU LISTENIN' TO US?
TAKERU DIDN'T DO IT?
"THERE'S SOMETHING SERIOUSLY WRONG WITH YOU!"
"I KNOW YOU'RE THE ONE WHO PUT MY LETTER UP ON THE BLACK BOARD!"
"GET A LIFE!"
TO THINK THAT I SAID ALL THOSE THINGS TO HIM...
ON TOP OF THAT, I HIT HIM...
BAM!
HEY, YOU LISTENIN' TO US?
DON!
HEY, HEY, HEY. IT'S NOT NICE TO PICK ON PEOPLE, YOU KNOW?

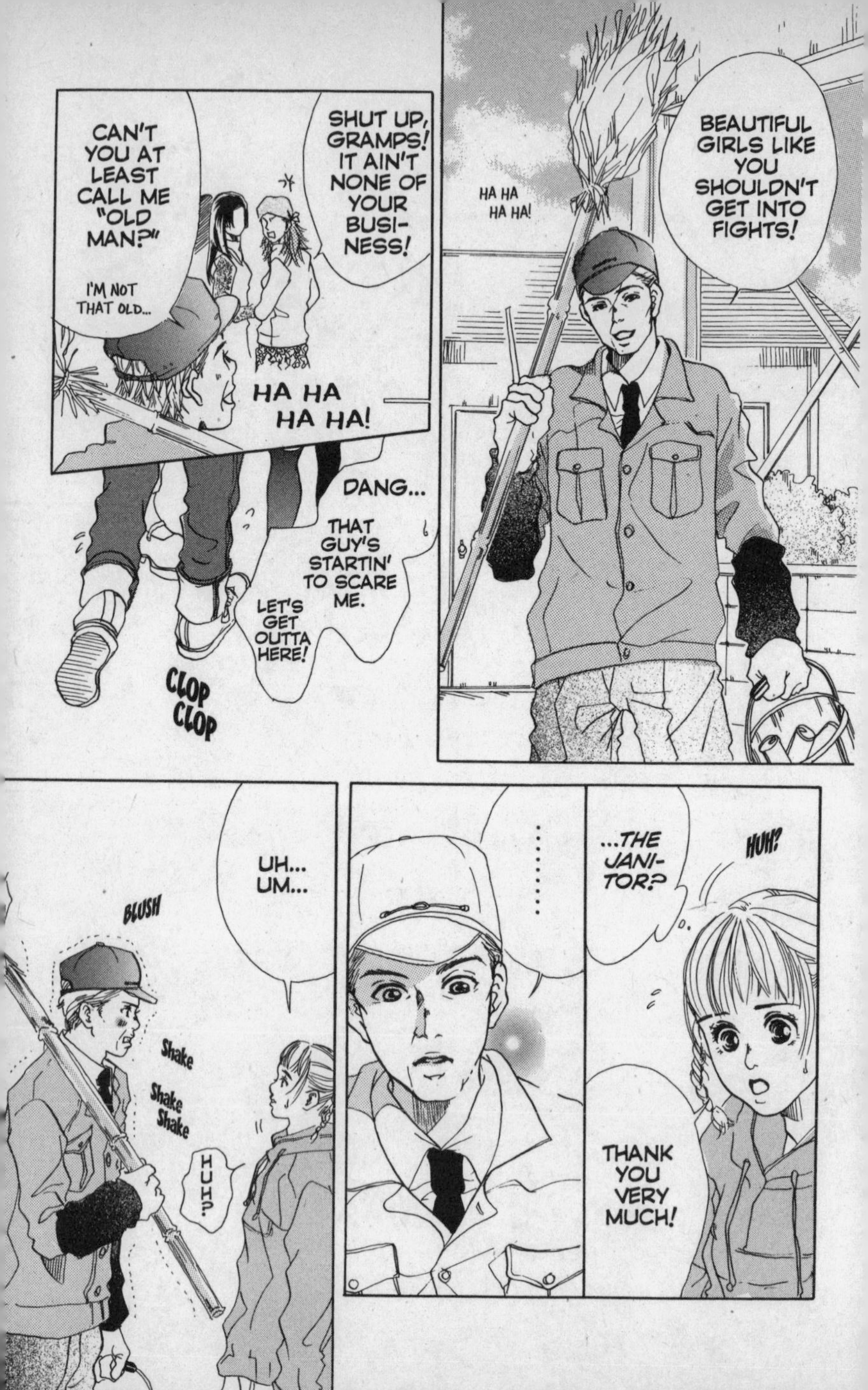
BEAUTIFUL GIRLS LIKE YOU SHOULDN'T GET INTO FIGHTS!
HA HA HA HA!
SHUT UP, GRAMPS! IT AIN'T NONE OF YOUR BUSI- NESS!
CAN'T YOU AT LEAST CALL ME "OLD MAN?"
I'M NOT THAT OLD...
HA HA HA HA!
DANG...
THAT GUY'S STARTIN' TO SCARE ME.
LET'S GET OUTTA HERE!
CLOP CLOP
...THE JANI- TOR?
HUH?
THANK YOU VERY MUCH!
....
UH... UM...
BLUSH
Shake
Shake Shake
HUH?

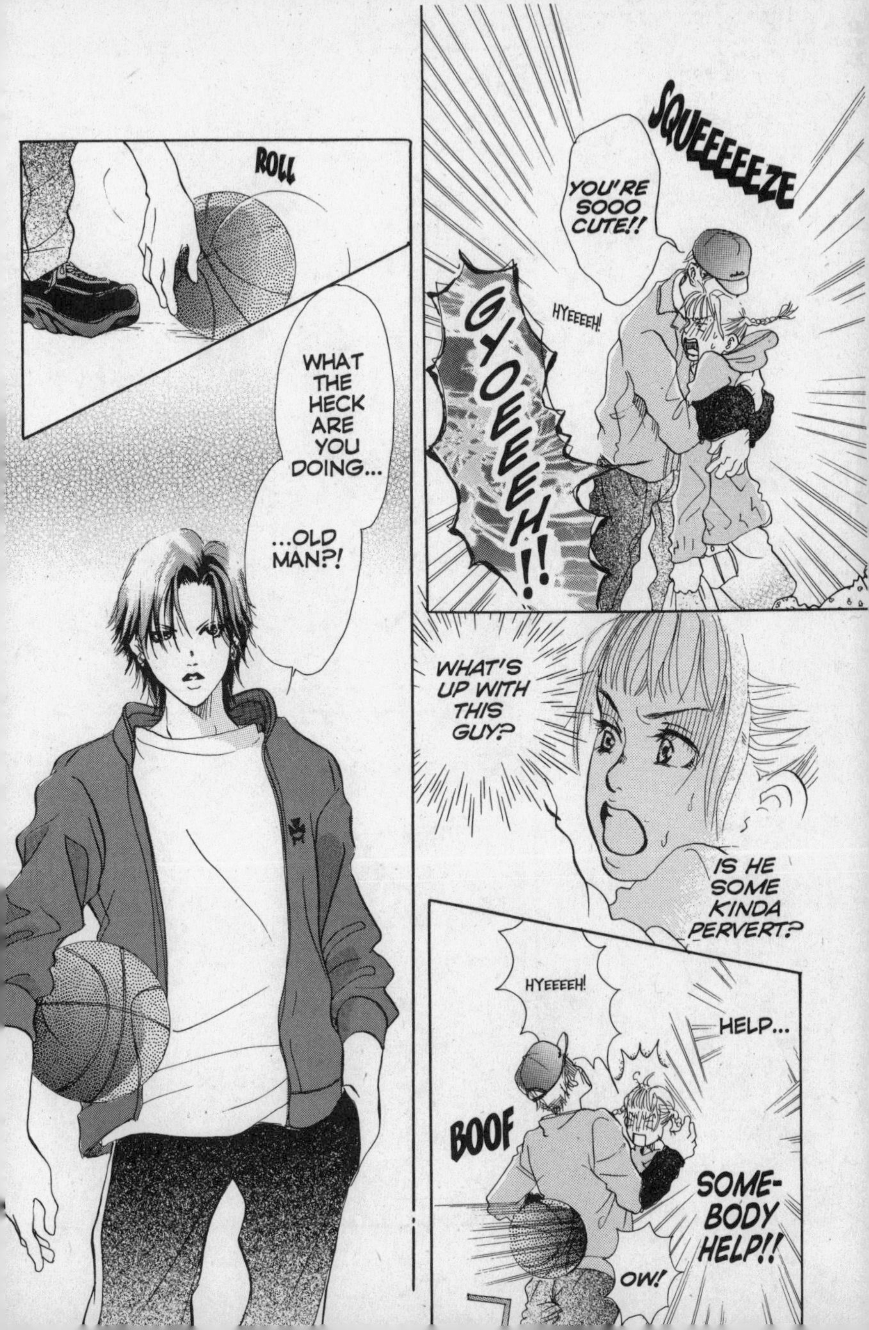
SQUEEEEEEZE
YOU'RE SOOO CUTE!!
HYEEEEH!
GYOEEEEH!!
WHAT'S UP WITH THIS GUY?
IS HE SOME KINDA PERVERT?
HYEEEEH!
HELP...
SOME-BODY HELP!!
BOOF
OW!
ROLL
WHAT THE HECK ARE YOU DOING...
...OLD MAN?!

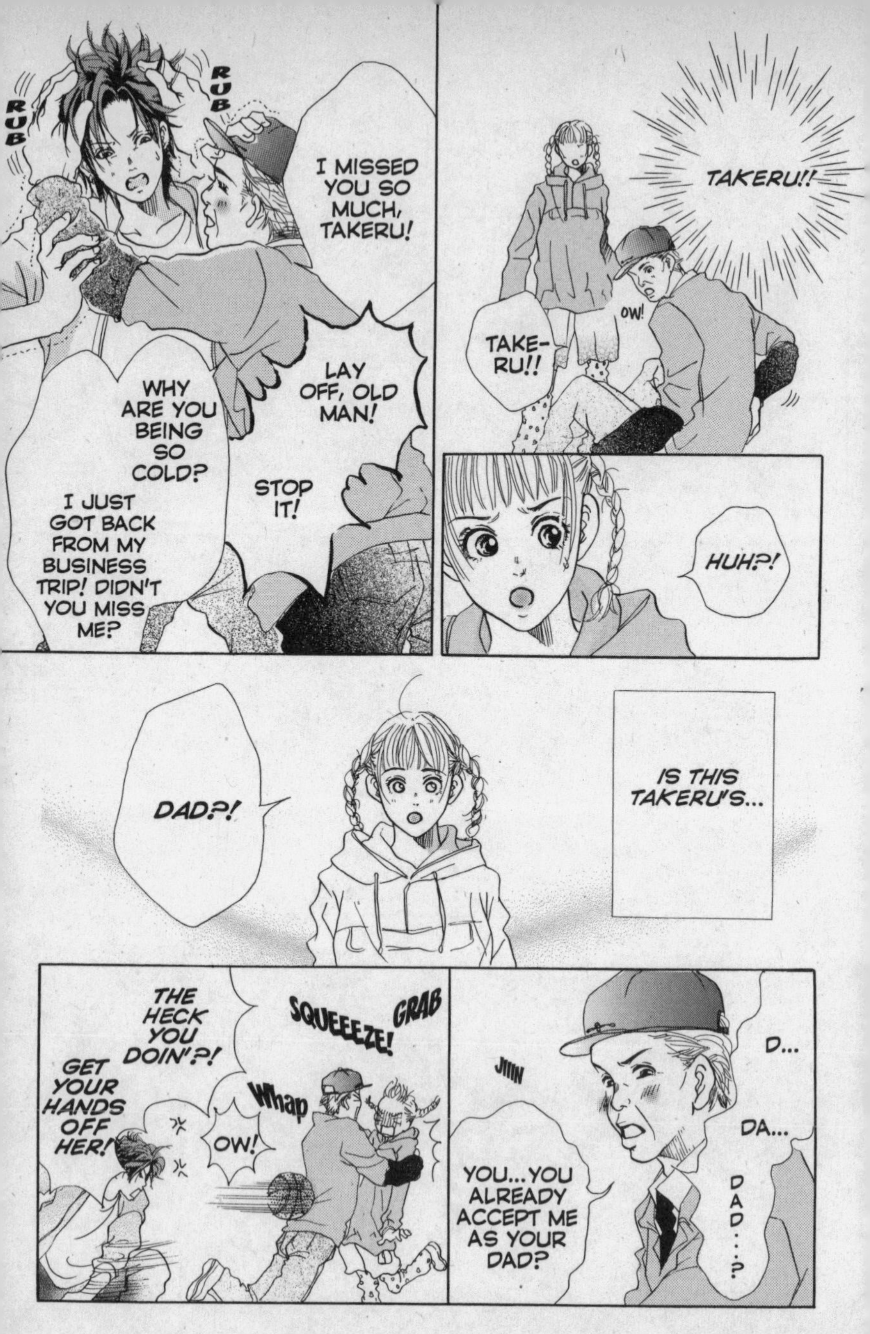
TAKERU!!
OW!
TAKE-RU!!
HUH?!
RUB
I MISSED YOU SO MUCH, TAKERU!
LAY OFF, OLD MAN!
WHY ARE YOU BEING SO COLD? I JUST GOT BACK FROM MY BUSINESS TRIP! DIDN'T YOU MISS ME?
STOP IT!
RUB
IS THIS TAKERU'S...
DAD?!
D...
DA...
DAD...?
JIIIN
YOU...YOU ALREADY ACCEPT ME AS YOUR DAD?
GRAB
SQUEEEEZE!
THE HECK YOU DOIN'?!
Whap
OW!
GET YOUR HANDS OFF HER!

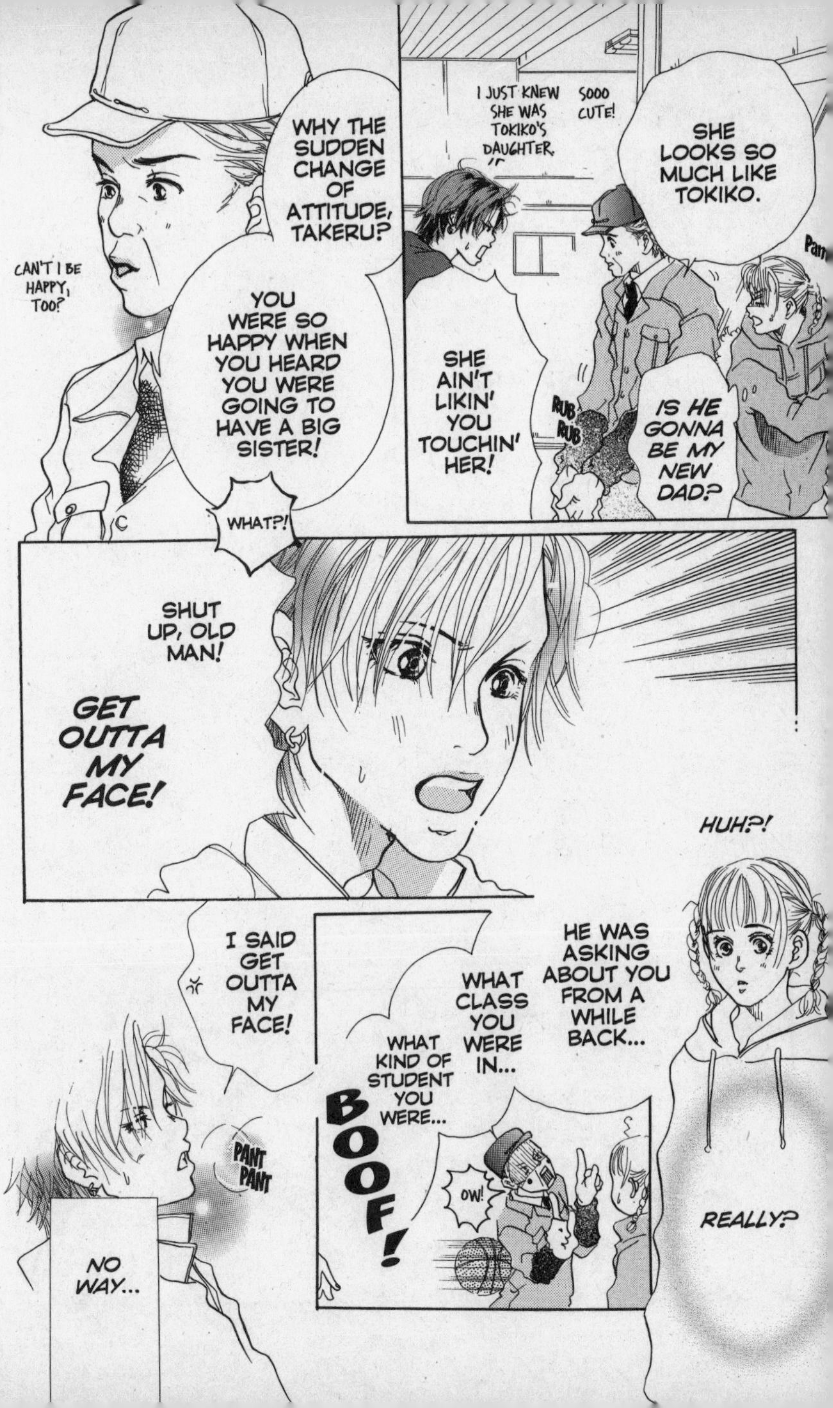
SHE LOOKS SO MUCH LIKE TOKIKO.
SOOO CUTE!
I JUST KNEW SHE WAS TOKIKO'S DAUGHTER.
IS HE GONNA BE MY NEW DAD?
RUB RUB
SHE AIN'T LIKIN' YOU TOUCHIN' HER!
WHY THE SUDDEN CHANGE OF ATTITUDE, TAKERU?
YOU WERE SO HAPPY WHEN YOU HEARD YOU WERE GOING TO HAVE A BIG SISTER!
CAN'T I BE HAPPY, TOO?
WHAT?!
SHUT UP, OLD MAN!
GET OUTTA MY FACE!
HUH?!
HE WAS ASKING ABOUT YOU FROM A WHILE BACK...
WHAT CLASS YOU WERE IN...
WHAT KIND OF STUDENT YOU WERE...
REALLY?
BOOF!
OW!
I SAID GET OUTTA MY FACE!
PANT PANT
NO WAY...

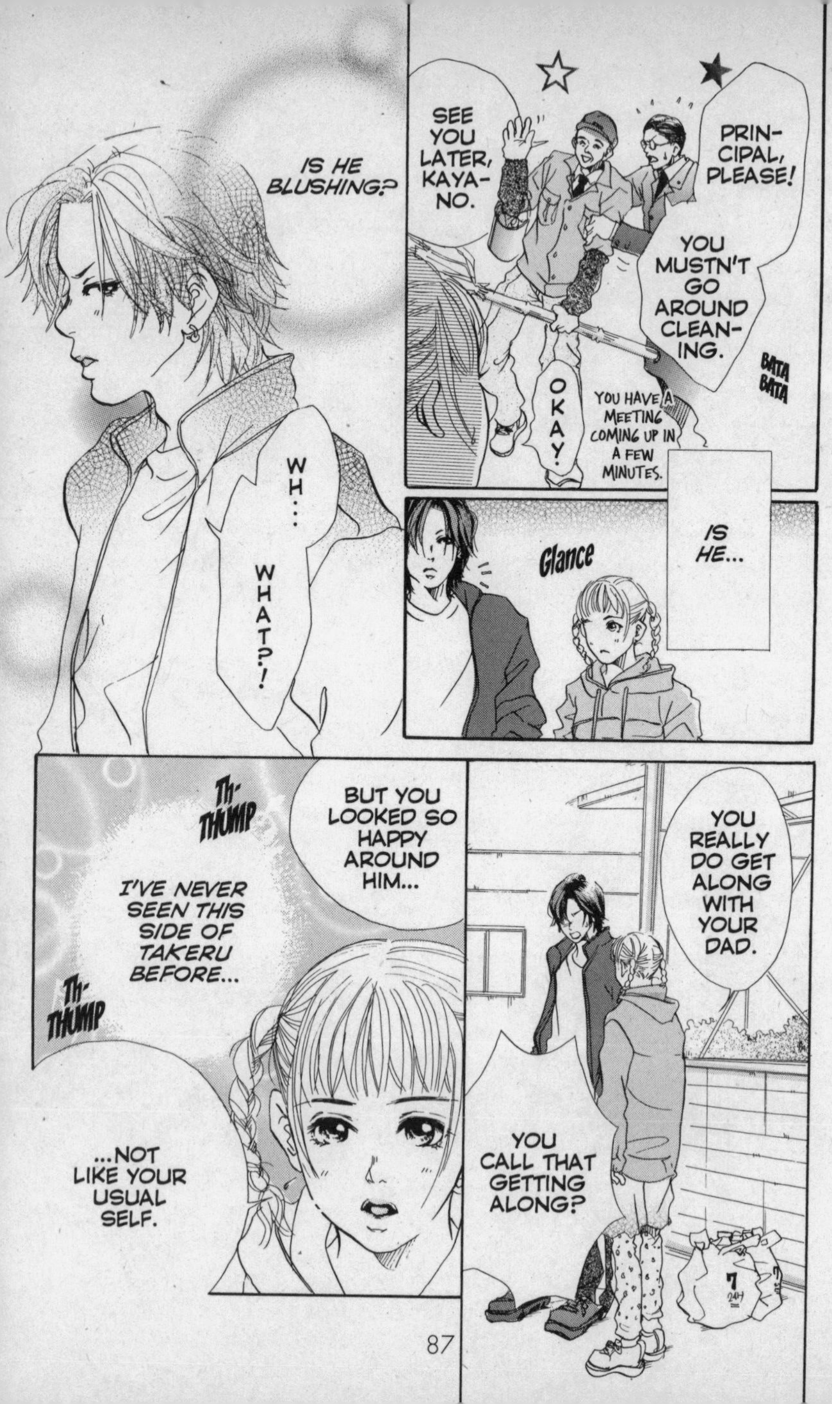
PRIN-CIPAL, PLEASE!
SEE YOU LATER, KAYA-NO.
YOU MUSTN'T GO AROUND CLEAN-ING.
BATA BATA
YOU HAVE A MEETING COMING UP IN A FEW MINUTES.
OKAY.
IS HE...
Glance
IS HE BLUSHING?
WH...
WHAT?!
YOU REALLY DO GET ALONG WITH YOUR DAD.
YOU CALL THAT GETTING ALONG?
BUT YOU LOOKED SO HAPPY AROUND HIM...
Th-THUMP
I'VE NEVER SEEN THIS SIDE OF TAKERU BEFORE...
Th-THUMP
...NOT LIKE YOUR USUAL SELF.

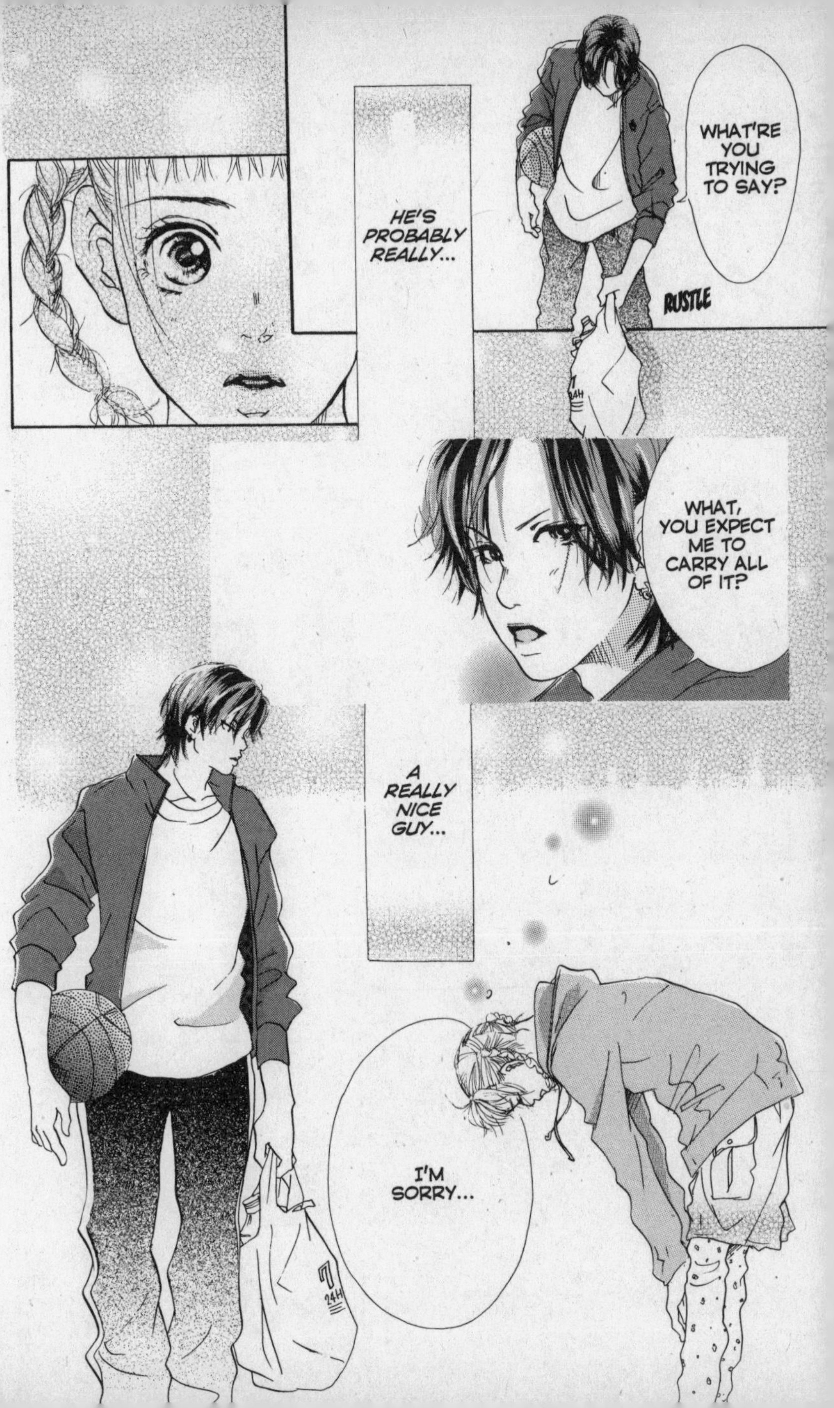
WHAT'RE YOU TRYING TO SAY?
RUSTLE
HE'S PROBABLY REALLY...
WHAT, YOU EXPECT ME TO CARRY ALL OF IT?
A REALLY NICE GUY...
I'M SORRY...

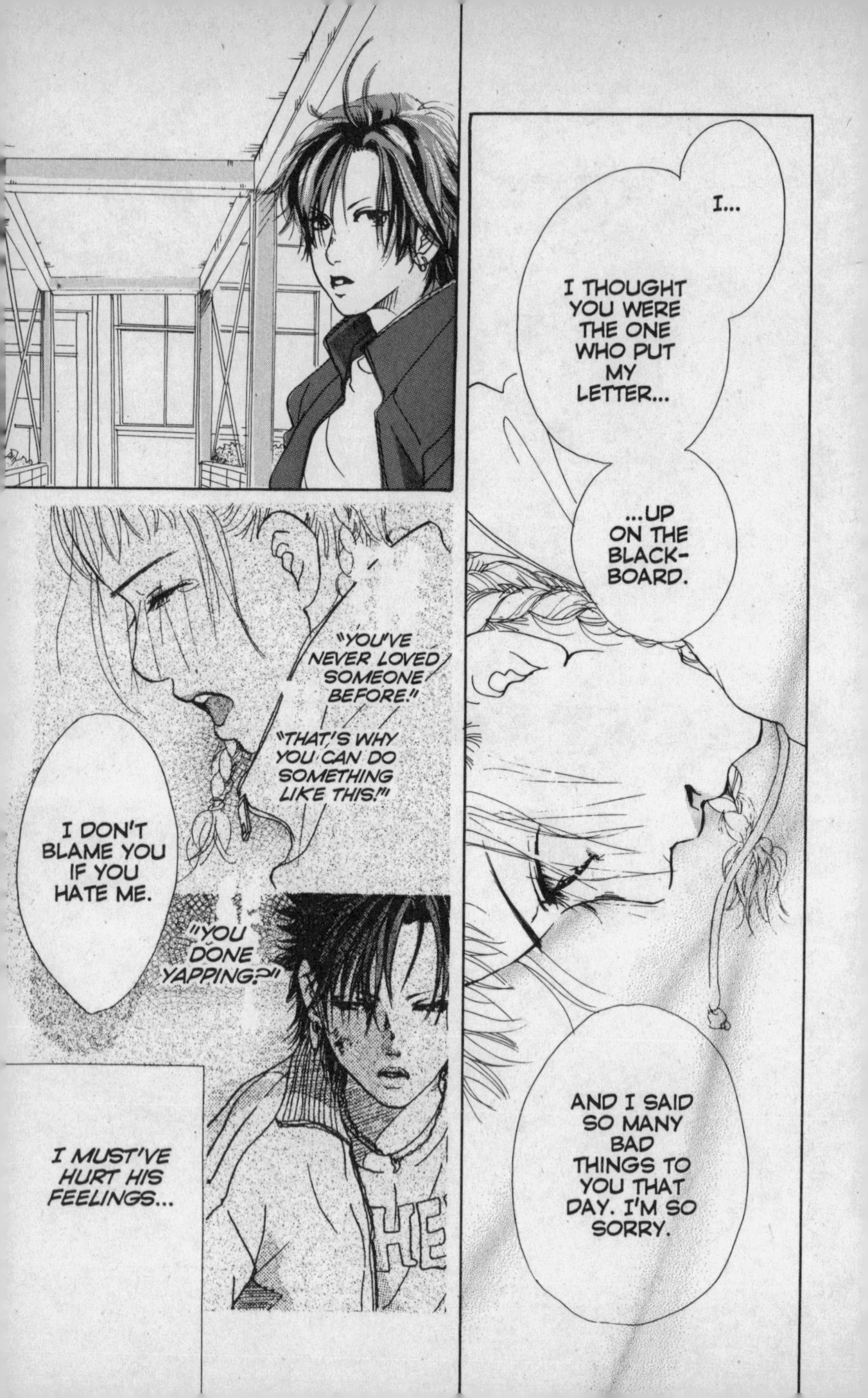
I...
I THOUGHT YOU WERE THE ONE WHO PUT MY LETTER...
...UP ON THE BLACK-BOARD.
AND I SAID SO MANY BAD THINGS TO YOU THAT DAY. I'M SO SORRY.
"YOU'VE NEVER LOVED SOMEONE BEFORE."
"THAT'S WHY YOU CAN DO SOMETHING LIKE THIS!"
I DON'T BLAME YOU IF YOU HATE ME.
"YOU DONE YAPPING?"
I MUST'VE HURT HIS FEELINGS...

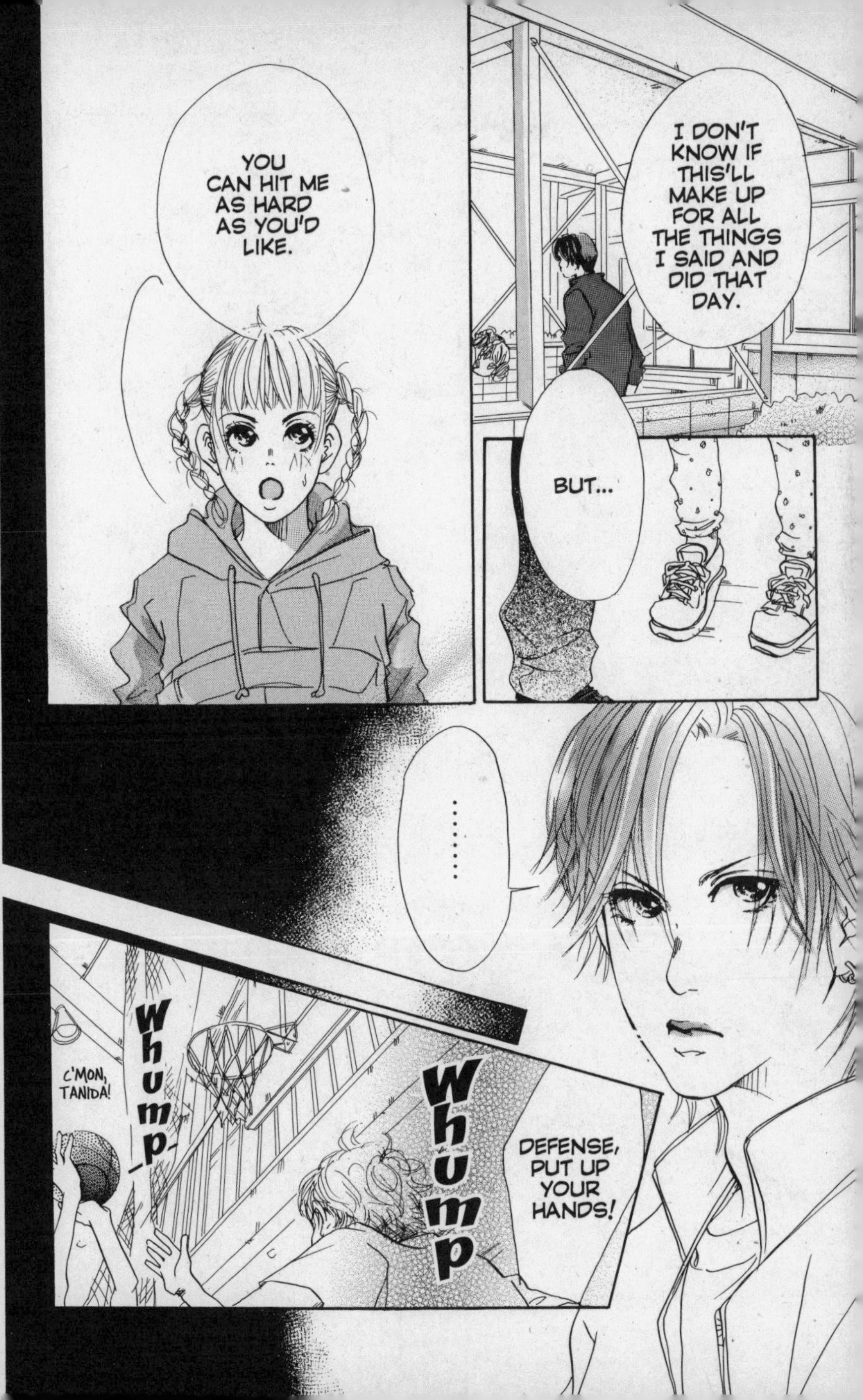
I DON'T KNOW IF THIS'LL MAKE UP FOR ALL THE THINGS I SAID AND DID THAT DAY.
BUT...
YOU CAN HIT ME AS HARD AS YOU'D LIKE.
......
Whump
DEFENSE, PUT UP YOUR HANDS!
Whump
C'MON, TANIDA!

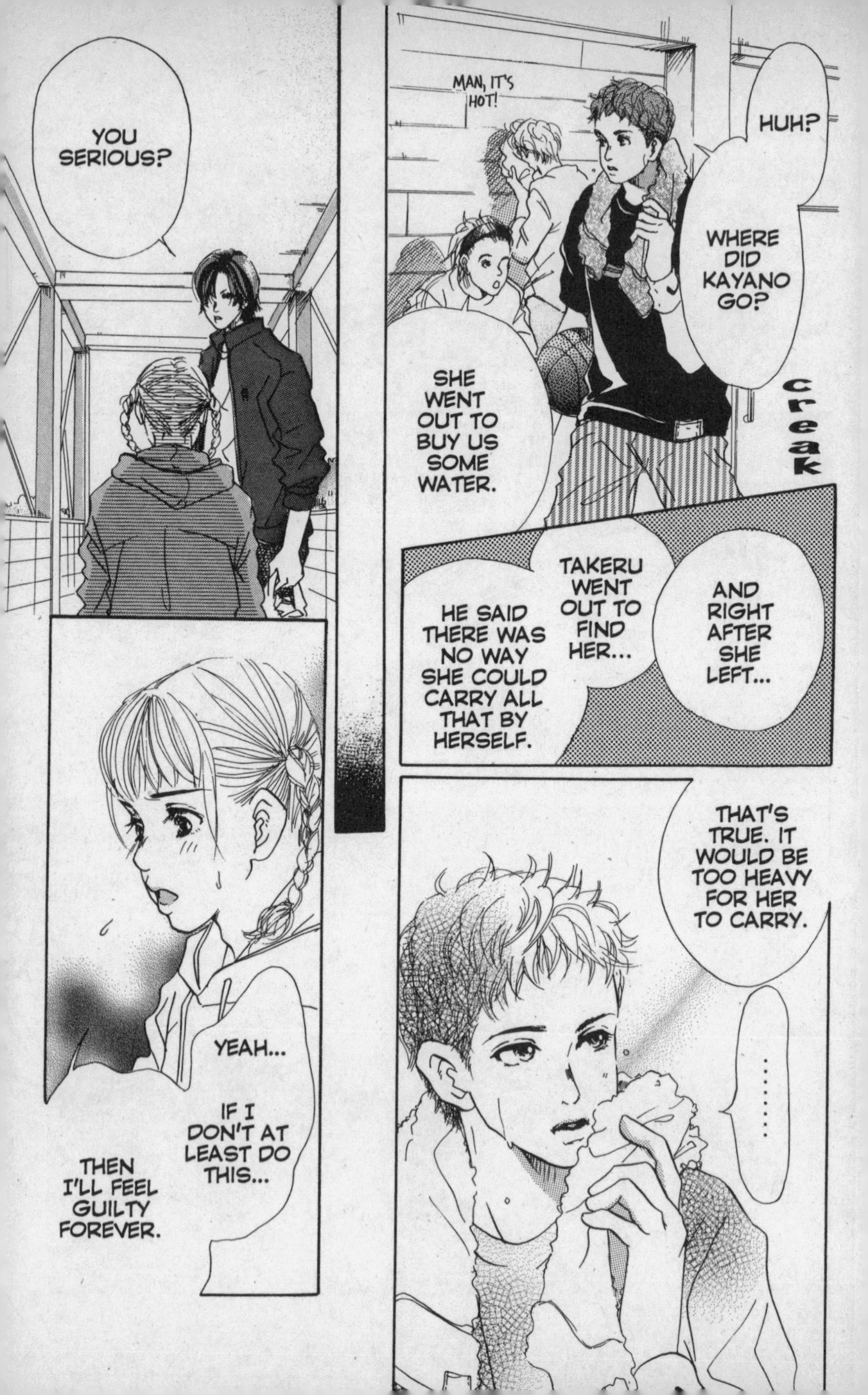
HUH?
WHERE DID KAYANO GO?
MAN, IT'S HOT!
creak
SHE WENT OUT TO BUY US SOME WATER.
AND RIGHT AFTER SHE LEFT...
TAKERU WENT OUT TO FIND HER...
HE SAID THERE WAS NO WAY SHE COULD CARRY ALL THAT BY HERSELF.
THAT'S TRUE. IT WOULD BE TOO HEAVY FOR HER TO CARRY.
......
YOU SERIOUS?
YEAH...
IF I DON'T AT LEAST DO THIS...
THEN I'LL FEEL GUILTY FOREVER.

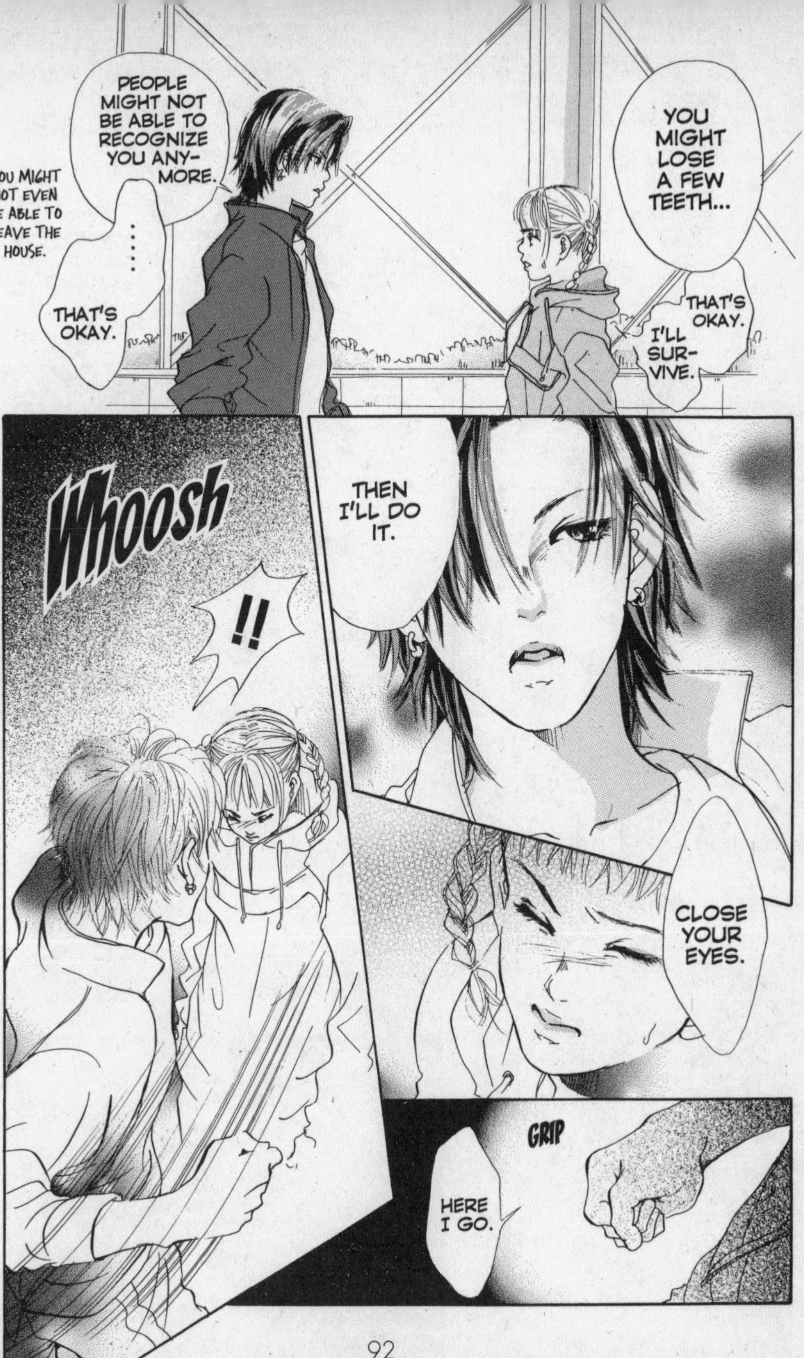
YOU MIGHT LOSE A FEW TEETH...
THAT'S OKAY. I'LL SURVIVE.
PEOPLE MIGHT NOT BE ABLE TO RECOGNIZE YOU ANYMORE.
YOU MIGHT NOT EVEN BE ABLE TO LEAVE THE HOUSE.
...... THAT'S OKAY.
THEN I'LL DO IT.
CLOSE YOUR EYES.
GRIP
HERE I GO.
Whoosh
!!

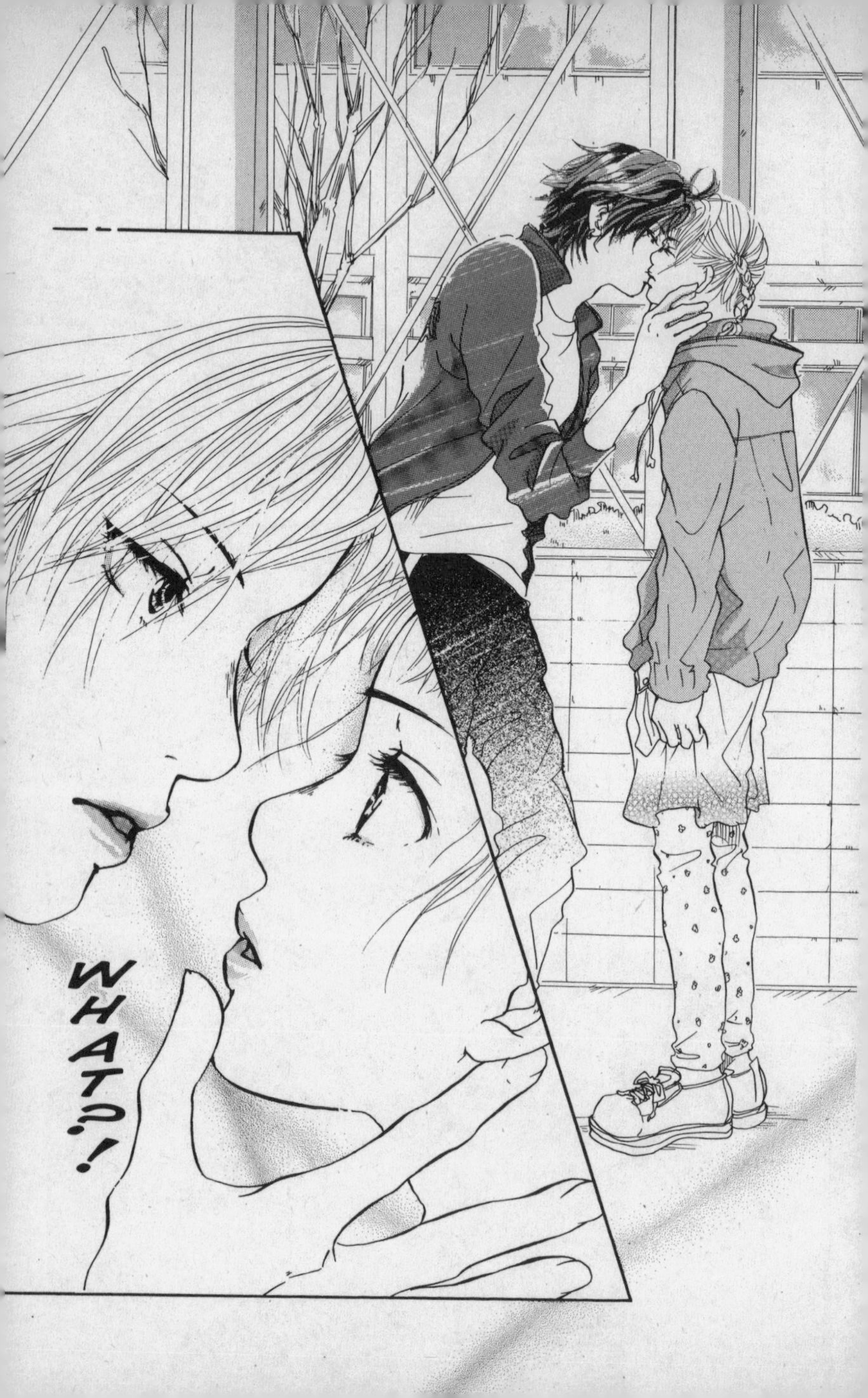
WHAT?!

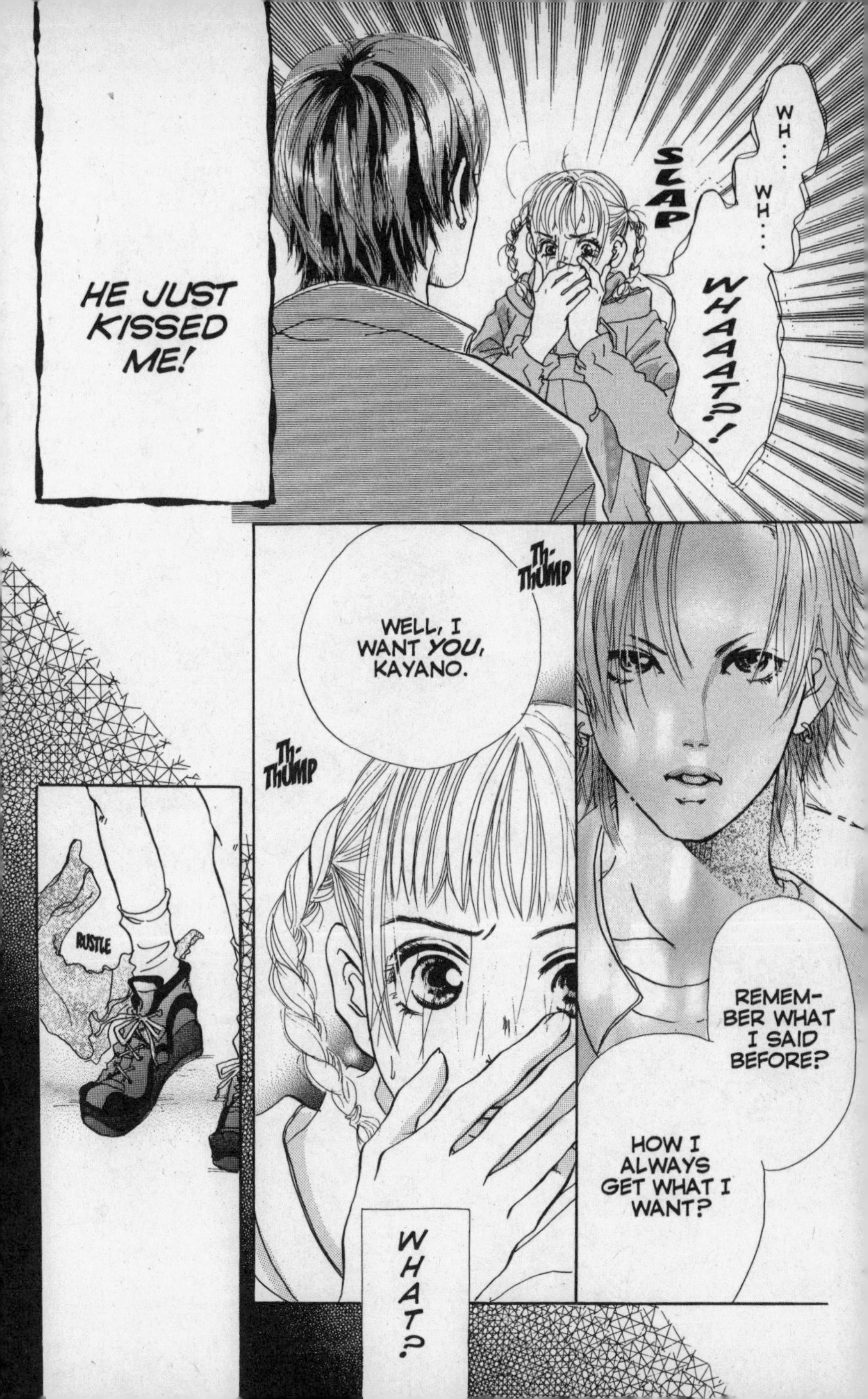

WH... WH... WHAAAT?!
SLAP
HE JUST KISSED ME!
REMEM-BER WHAT I SAID BEFORE?
HOW I ALWAYS GET WHAT I WANT?
Th-THUMP
WELL, I WANT YOU, KAYANO.
Th-THUMP
WHAT?
RUSTLE

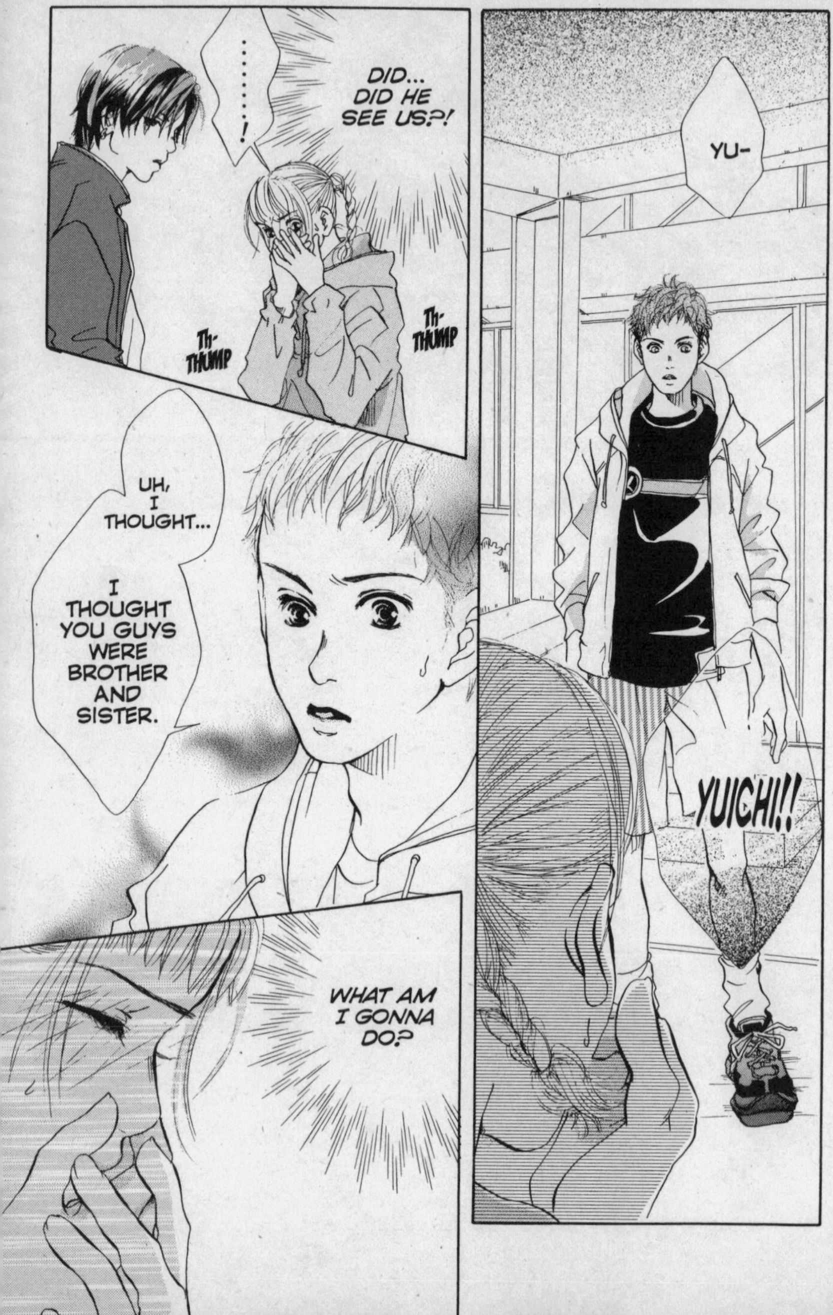
YU-
YUICHI!!
......!
DID... DID HE SEE US?!
Th-THUMP
Th-THUMP
UH, I THOUGHT...
I THOUGHT YOU GUYS WERE BROTHER AND SISTER.
WHAT AM I GONNA DO?

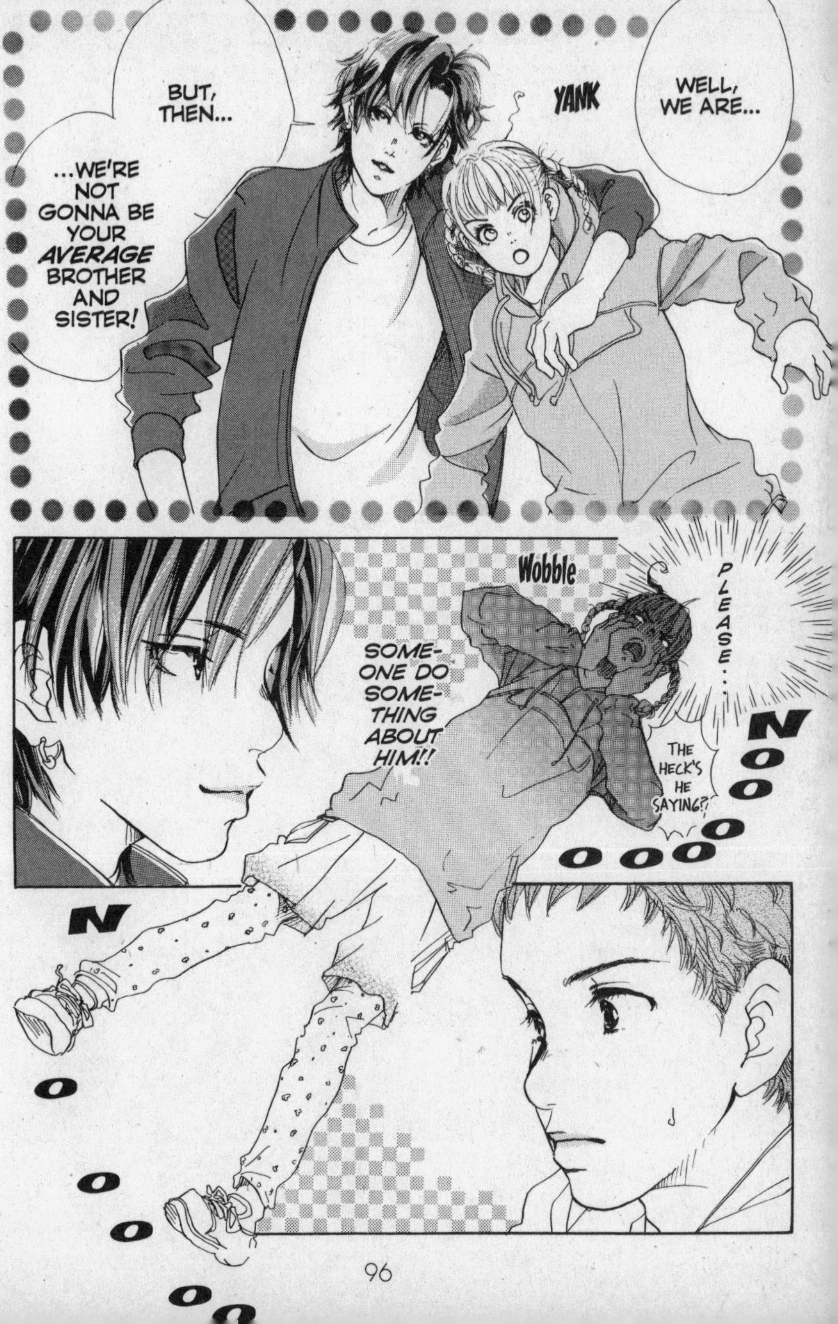
WELL, WE ARE...
YANK
BUT, THEN...
...WE'RE NOT GONNA BE YOUR *AVERAGE* BROTHER AND SISTER!
PLEASE...
Wobble
THE HECK'S HE SAYING?!
SOME-ONE DO SOME-THING ABOUT HIM!!
NOOOOOO
NOOOOOO

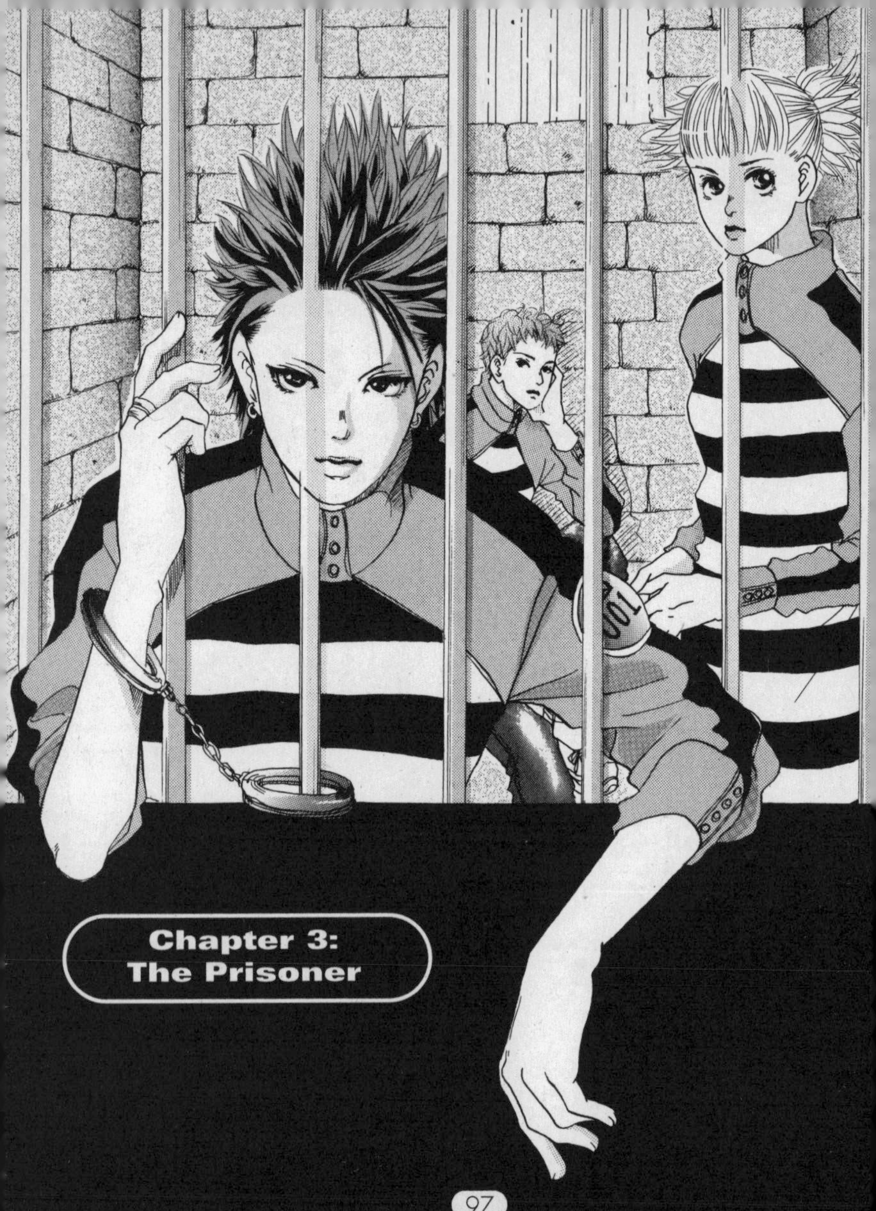
Chapter 3:
The Prisoner

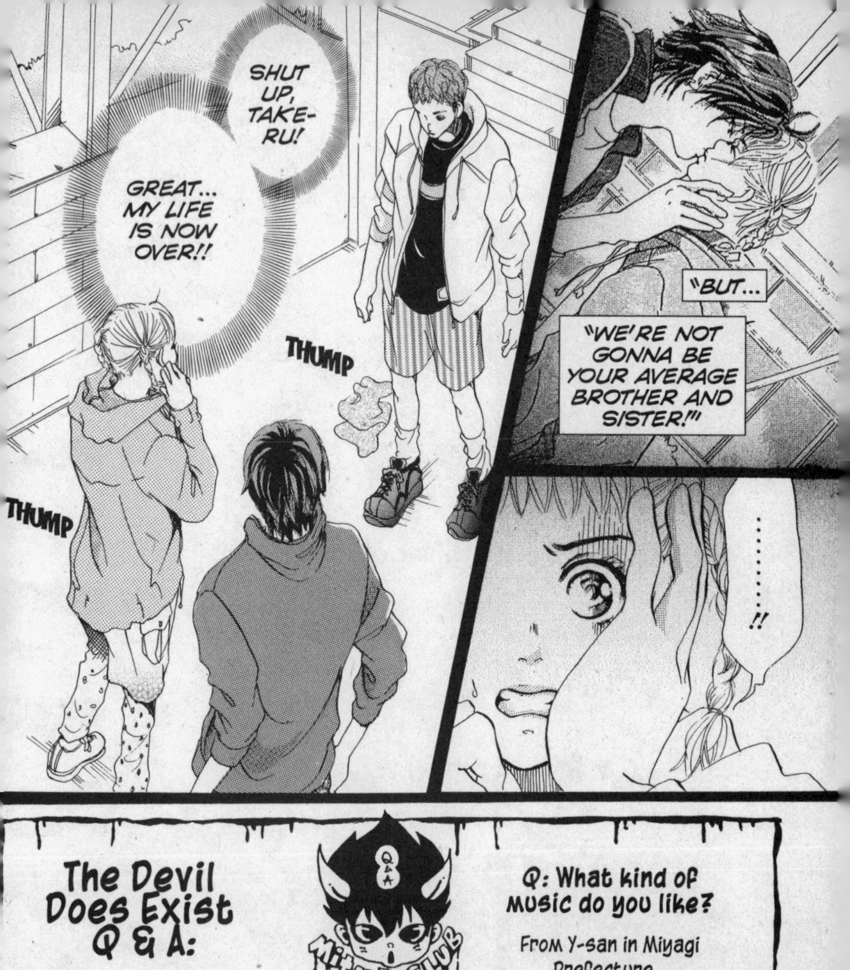
"BUT...
"WE'RE NOT GONNA BE YOUR AVERAGE BROTHER AND SISTER!"
......!!
SHUT UP, TAKE-RU!
GREAT... MY LIFE IS NOW OVER!!
THUMP
THUMP

The Devil Does Exist Q & A:

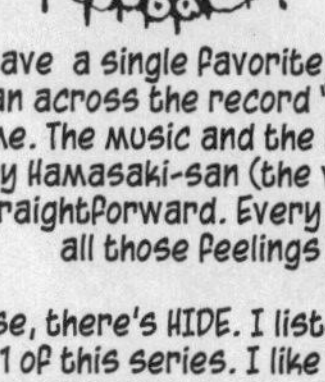
Q&A
MitsuBa CLUB

Q: What kind of music do you like?

From Y-san in Miyagi Prefecture.

A: I don't really have a single favorite, but when I was a third-year in middle school, I ran across the record "Be Happy" by the Flying Kids, and it really rocked me. The music and the lyrics are awesome! I especially liked the lyrics by Hamasaki-san (the vocalist), "this is youth!" It's so nostalgic and straightforward. Every now and then I play the CD, and all those feelings come back.

And then, of course, there's HIDE. I listened to him the whole time I was writing episode 1 of this series. I like The Yellow Monkey, Sakura, and Brahman. It's all music that makes me feel really happy. I also really like listening to Jazz and Blues music too. I'll dance to it no matter where I am.

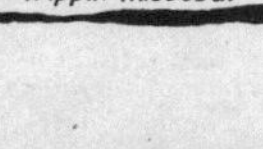

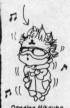

Dancing Mitsuba, Trippin' Mitsuba.

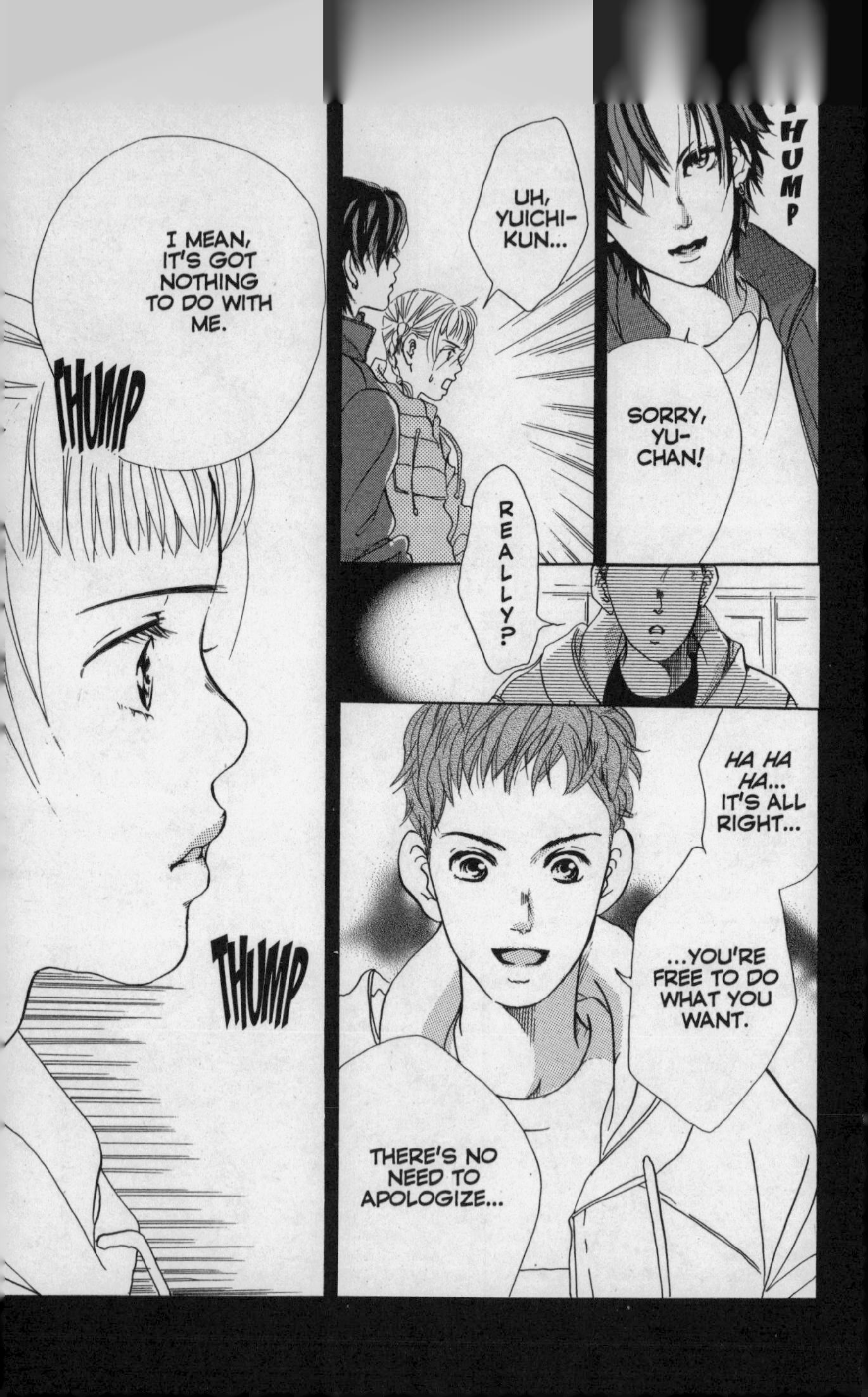
THUMP
SORRY, YU-CHAN!
UH, YUICHI-KUN...
REALLY?
HA HA HA... IT'S ALL RIGHT...
...YOU'RE FREE TO DO WHAT YOU WANT.
THERE'S NO NEED TO APOLOGIZE...
I MEAN, IT'S GOT NOTHING TO DO WITH ME.
THUMP
THUMP

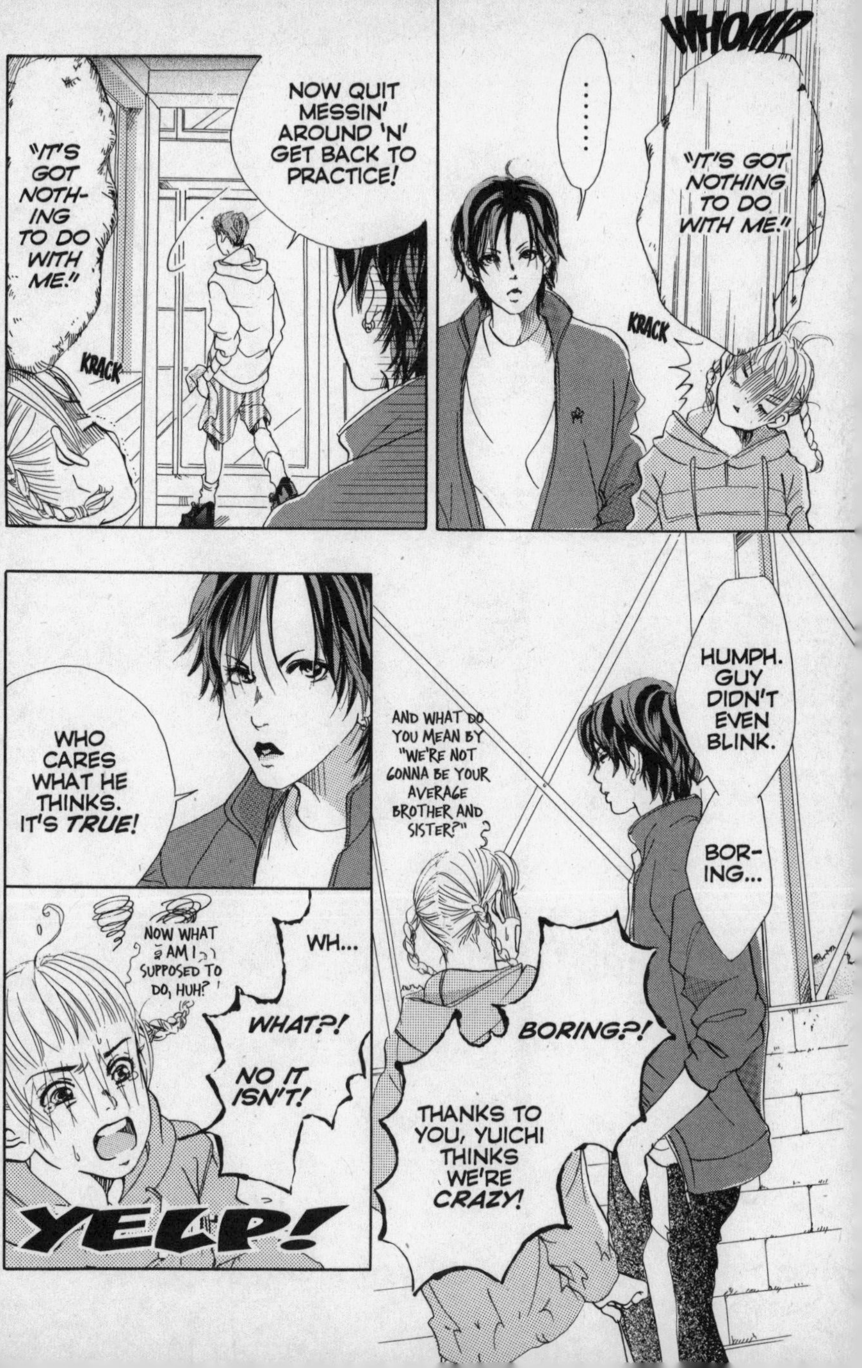
WHOMP
......
"IT'S GOT NOTHING TO DO WITH ME."
KRACK
NOW QUIT MESSIN' AROUND 'N' GET BACK TO PRACTICE!
"IT'S GOT NOTHING TO DO WITH ME."
KRACK
HUMPH. GUY DIDN'T EVEN BLINK.
BOR-ING...
AND WHAT DO YOU MEAN BY "WE'RE NOT GONNA BE YOUR AVERAGE BROTHER AND SISTER?"
BORING?!
THANKS TO YOU, YUICHI THINKS WE'RE CRAZY!
WHO CARES WHAT HE THINKS. IT'S TRUE!
WH...
WHAT?!
NO IT ISN'T!
NOW WHAT AM I SUPPOSED TO DO, HUH?
YELP!

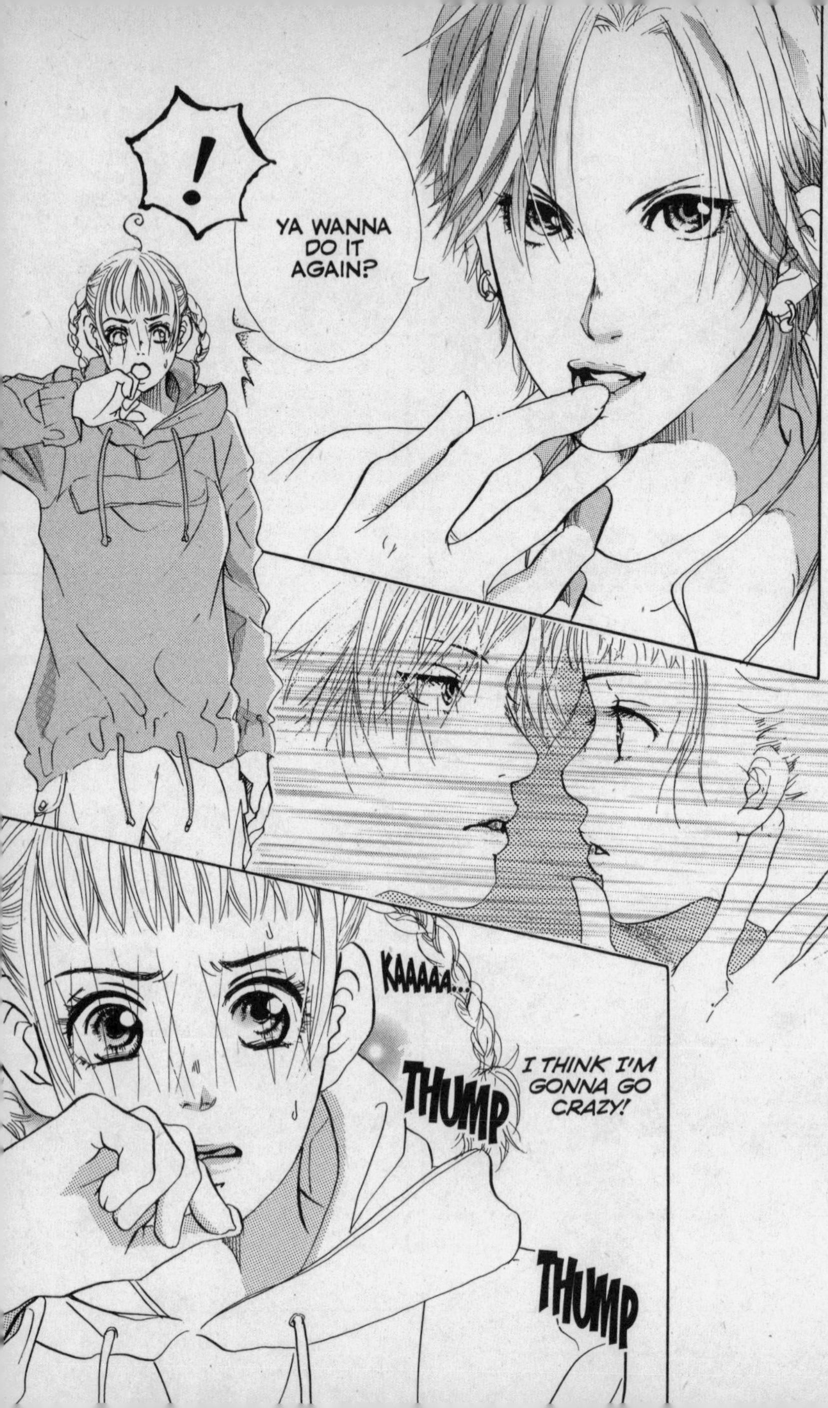
YA WANNA DO IT AGAIN?
!
KAAAAA...
THUMP
I THINK I'M GONNA GO CRAZY!
THUMP

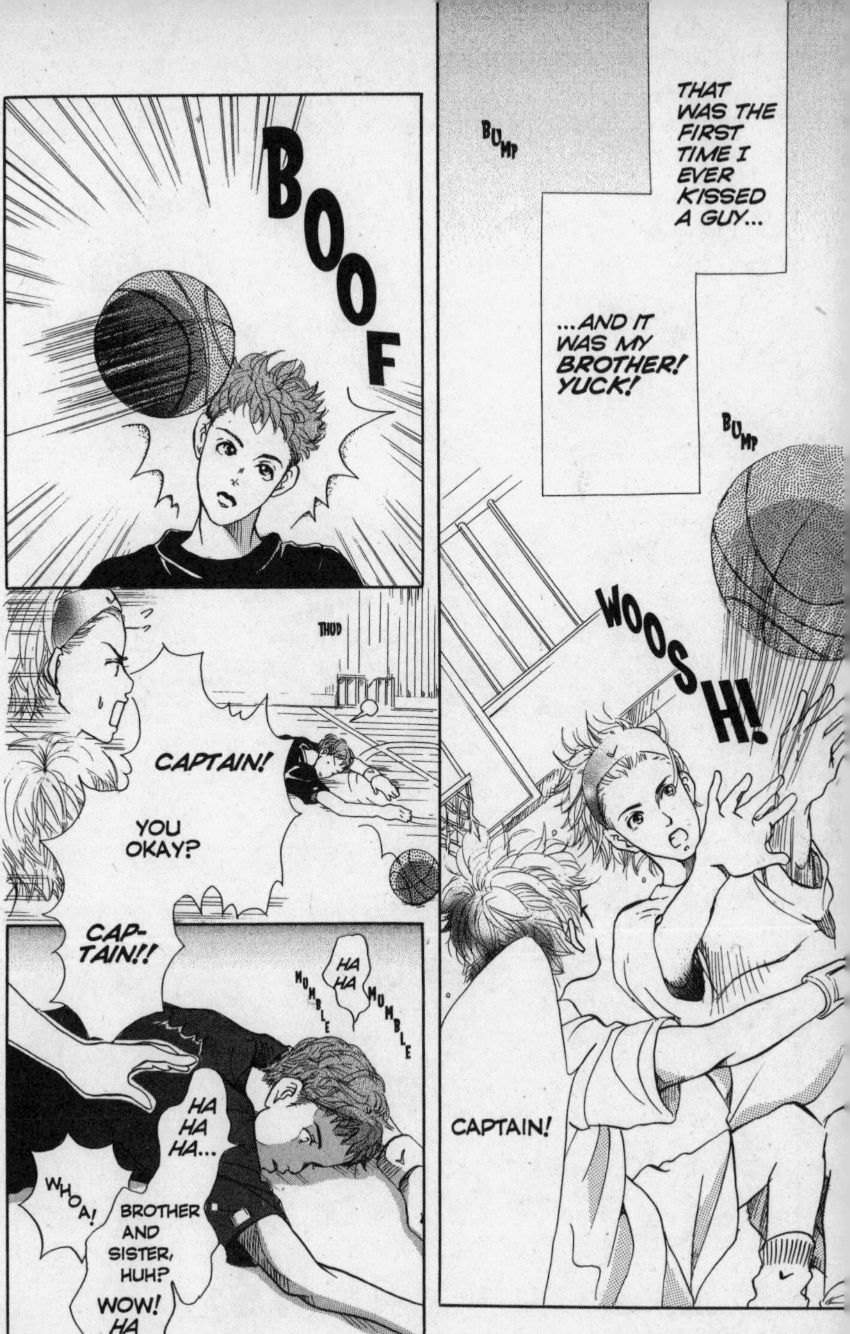
THAT WAS THE FIRST TIME I EVER KISSED A GUY...
BUMP
...AND IT WAS MY BROTHER! YUCK!
BUMP
WOOSH!
CAPTAIN!
BOOF
THUD
CAPTAIN!
YOU OKAY?
CAP-TAIN!!
HA HA
MUMBLE MUMBLE
HA HA HA...
WHOA!
BROTHER AND SISTER, HUH?
WOW! HA HA...

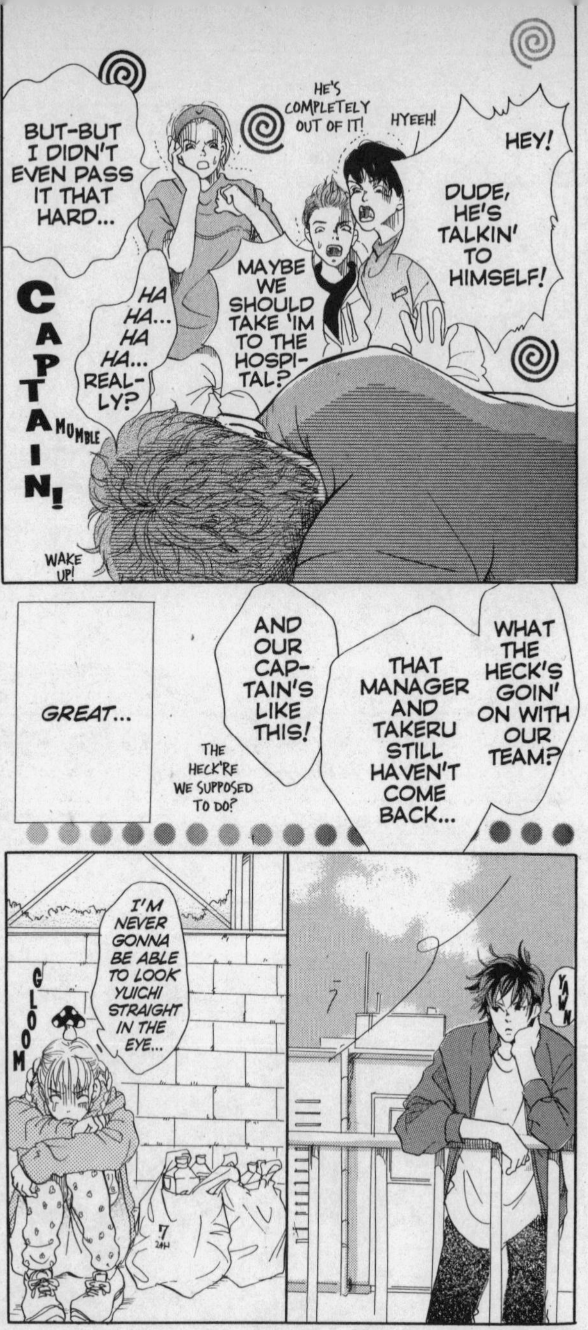
HEY!
DUDE, HE'S TALKIN' TO HIMSELF!
HYEEH!
HE'S COMPLETELY OUT OF IT!
MAYBE WE SHOULD TAKE 'IM TO THE HOSPITAL?
BUT-BUT I DIDN'T EVEN PASS IT THAT HARD...
HA HA... HA HA... REAL-LY?
CAPTAIN!
MUMBLE
WAKE UP!
WHAT THE HECK'S GOIN' ON WITH OUR TEAM?
THAT MANAGER AND TAKERU STILL HAVEN'T COME BACK...
AND OUR CAP-TAIN'S LIKE THIS!
THE HECK'RE WE SUPPOSED TO DO?
GREAT...
YAWN
I'M NEVER GONNA BE ABLE TO LOOK YUICHI STRAIGHT IN THE EYE...
GLOOM
7 24H

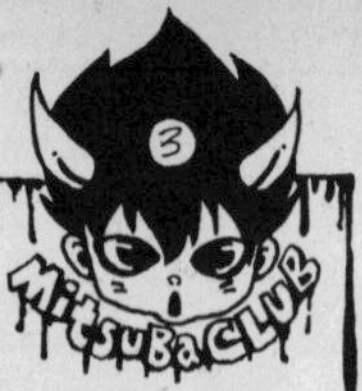
MitsuBa CLUB

This is the very first time one of my works has been serialized. So, for the first time, the deadlines keep coming, month after month! Before, I didn't worry about the future, and just tried to get it out each month. Every time I was writing the last page, I thought, "Wow. What will happen next episode? What'll I do?" I'd slap my head and wonder. Even though I was the author, I didn't know! When people asked what the next story was, I couldn't just tell them I didn't know. It was really scary to write every month like that. Then I would get the feeling like I wanted to turn into a lion. Really!

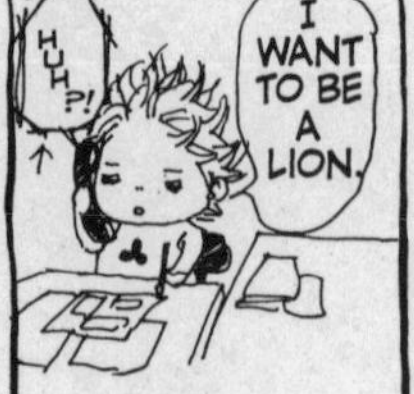
HUH?!
I WANT TO BE A LION.

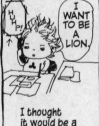

I thought it would be a great way to escape.

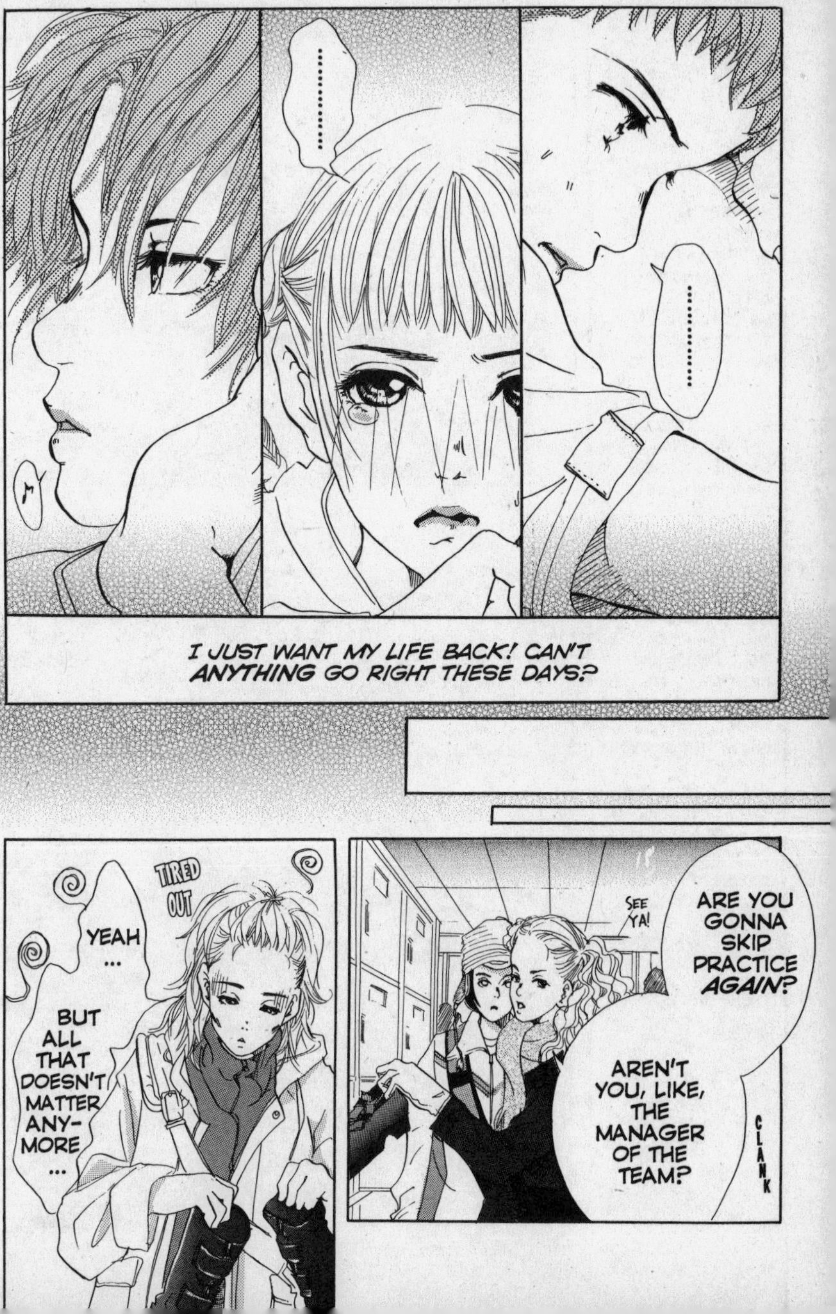
......
......
I JUST WANT MY LIFE BACK! CAN'T ANYTHING GO RIGHT THESE DAYS?
SEE YA!
ARE YOU GONNA SKIP PRACTICE AGAIN?
AREN'T YOU, LIKE, THE MANAGER OF THE TEAM?
CLANK
TIRED OUT
YEAH ...
BUT ALL THAT DOESN'T MATTER ANY-MORE ...

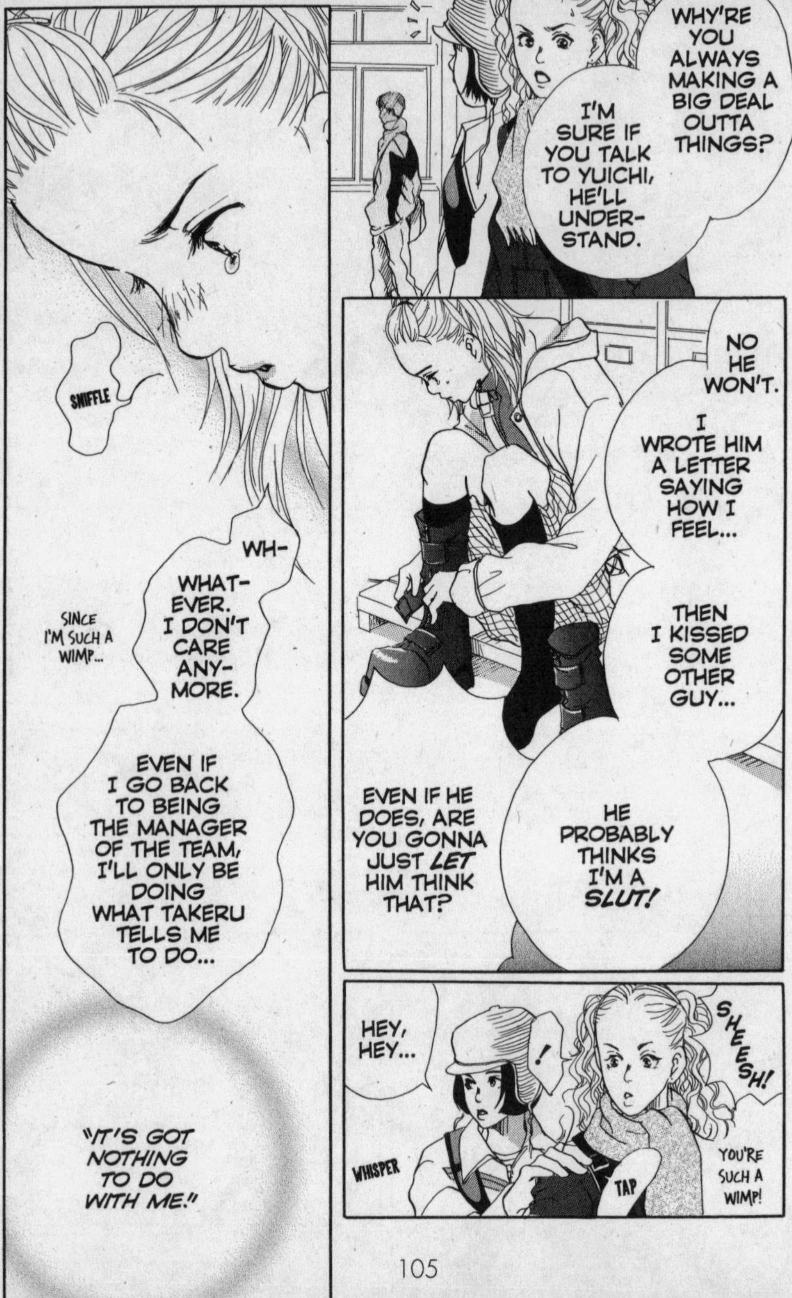
WHY'RE YOU ALWAYS MAKING A BIG DEAL OUTTA THINGS?
I'M SURE IF YOU TALK TO YUICHI, HE'LL UNDER-STAND.
NO HE WON'T.
I WROTE HIM A LETTER SAYING HOW I FEEL...
THEN I KISSED SOME OTHER GUY...
HE PROBABLY THINKS I'M A *SLUT!*
EVEN IF HE DOES, ARE YOU GONNA JUST *LET* HIM THINK THAT?
SHEESH!
YOU'RE SUCH A WIMP!
TAP
HEY, HEY...
WHISPER
SNIFFLE
WH- WHAT-EVER. I DON'T CARE ANY-MORE.
SINCE I'M SUCH A WIMP...
EVEN IF I GO BACK TO BEING THE MANAGER OF THE TEAM, I'LL ONLY BE DOING WHAT TAKERU TELLS ME TO DO...
"IT'S GOT NOTHING TO DO WITH ME."

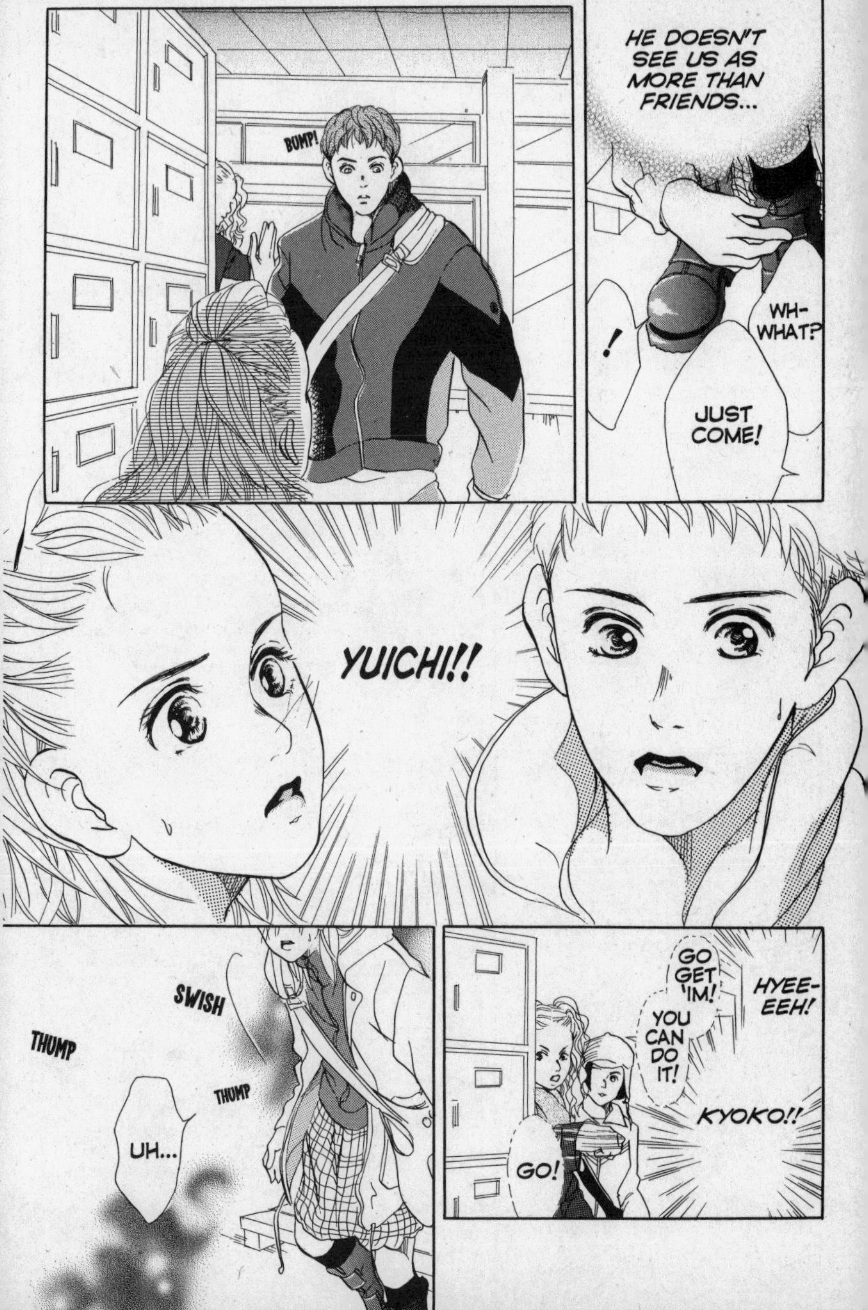
HE DOESN'T SEE US AS MORE THAN FRIENDS...
WH- WHAT?
!
JUST COME!
BUMP!
YUICHI!!
HYEEE-EEH!
GO GET 'IM!
YOU CAN DO IT!
KYOKO!!
GO!
SWISH
THUMP
THUMP
UH...

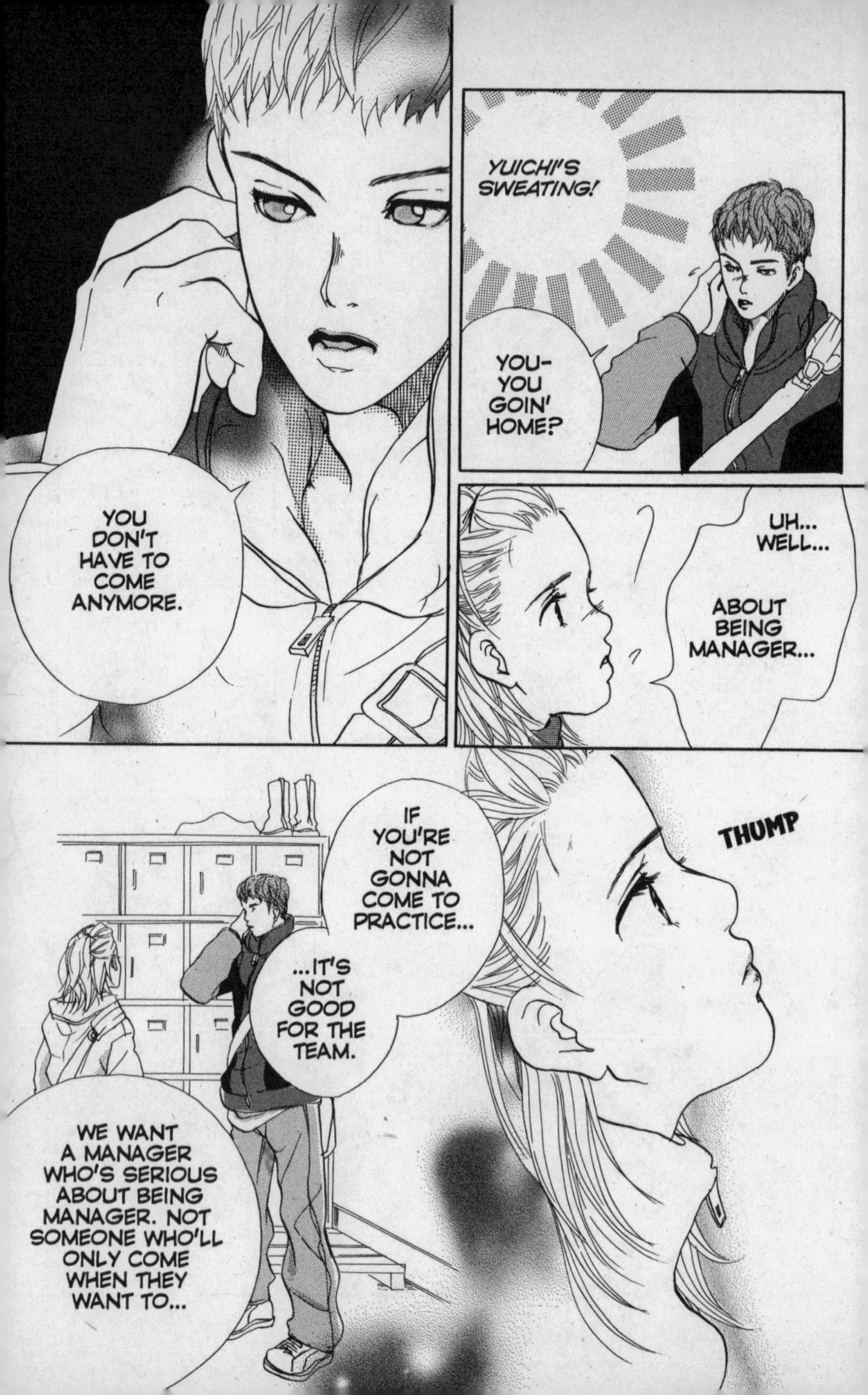
YUICHI'S SWEATING!
YOU- YOU GOIN' HOME?
UH... WELL...
ABOUT BEING MANAGER...
YOU DON'T HAVE TO COME ANYMORE.
THUMP
IF YOU'RE NOT GONNA COME TO PRACTICE...
...IT'S NOT GOOD FOR THE TEAM.
WE WANT A MANAGER WHO'S SERIOUS ABOUT BEING MANAGER. NOT SOMEONE WHO'LL ONLY COME WHEN THEY WANT TO...

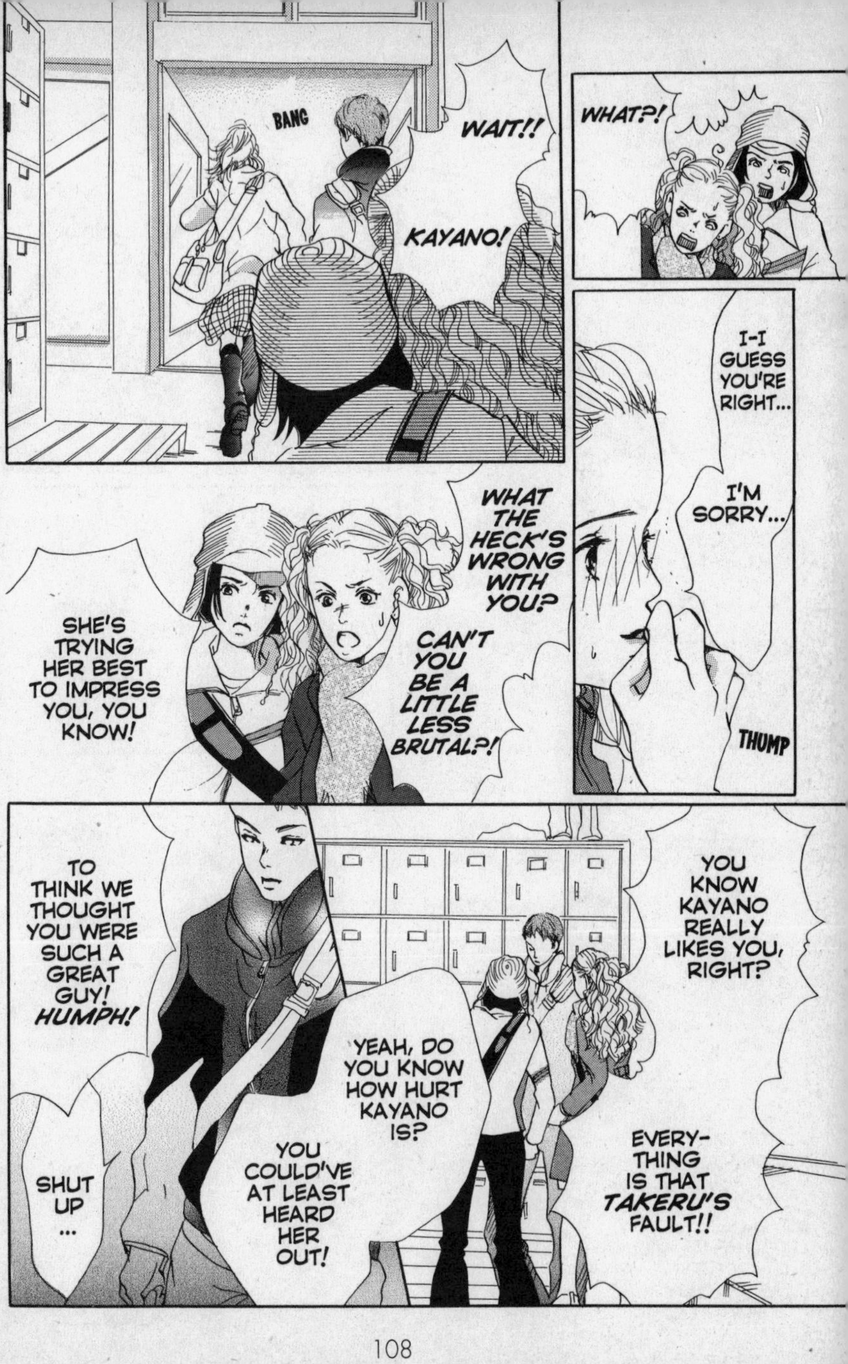
BANG
WAIT!!
KAYANO!
WHAT?!
WHAT THE HECK'S WRONG WITH YOU?
CAN'T YOU BE A LITTLE LESS BRUTAL?!
SHE'S TRYING HER BEST TO IMPRESS YOU, YOU KNOW!
I-I GUESS YOU'RE RIGHT...
I'M SORRY...
THUMP
YOU KNOW KAYANO REALLY LIKES YOU, RIGHT?
EVERYTHING IS THAT TAKERU'S FAULT!!
YEAH, DO YOU KNOW HOW HURT KAYANO IS?
YOU COULD'VE AT LEAST HEARD HER OUT!
TO THINK WE THOUGHT YOU WERE SUCH A GREAT GUY! HUMPH!
SHUT UP ...

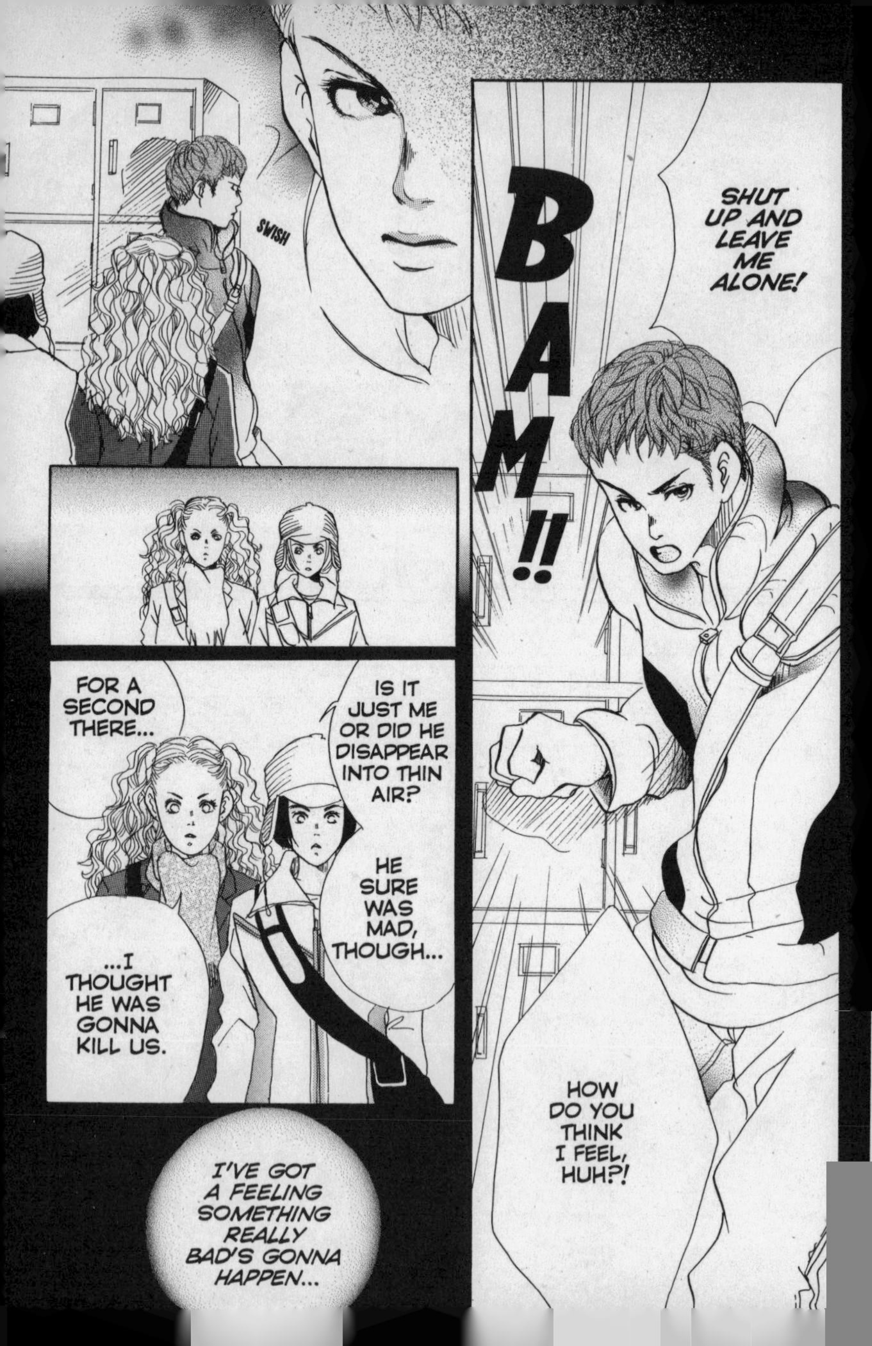
SHUT UP AND LEAVE ME ALONE!
BAM!!
HOW DO YOU THINK I FEEL, HUH?!
SWISH
IS IT JUST ME OR DID HE DISAPPEAR INTO THIN AIR?
FOR A SECOND THERE...
HE SURE WAS MAD, THOUGH...
...I THOUGHT HE WAS GONNA KILL US.
I'VE GOT A FEELING SOMETHING REALLY BAD'S GONNA HAPPEN...

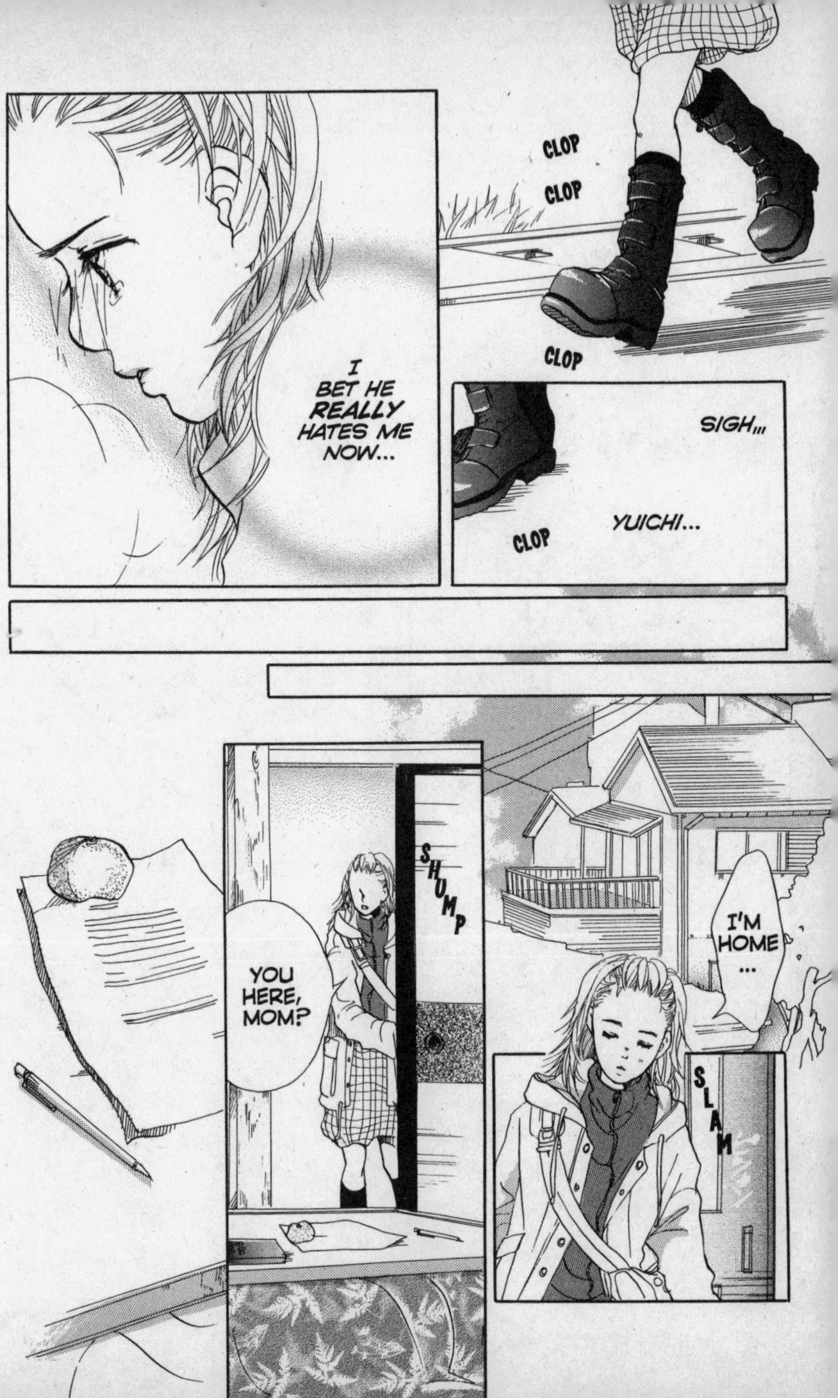
CLOP
CLOP
CLOP
SIGH...
YUICHI...
CLOP
I BET HE REALLY HATES ME NOW...
I'M HOME ...
SLAM
SHUMP
YOU HERE, MOM?

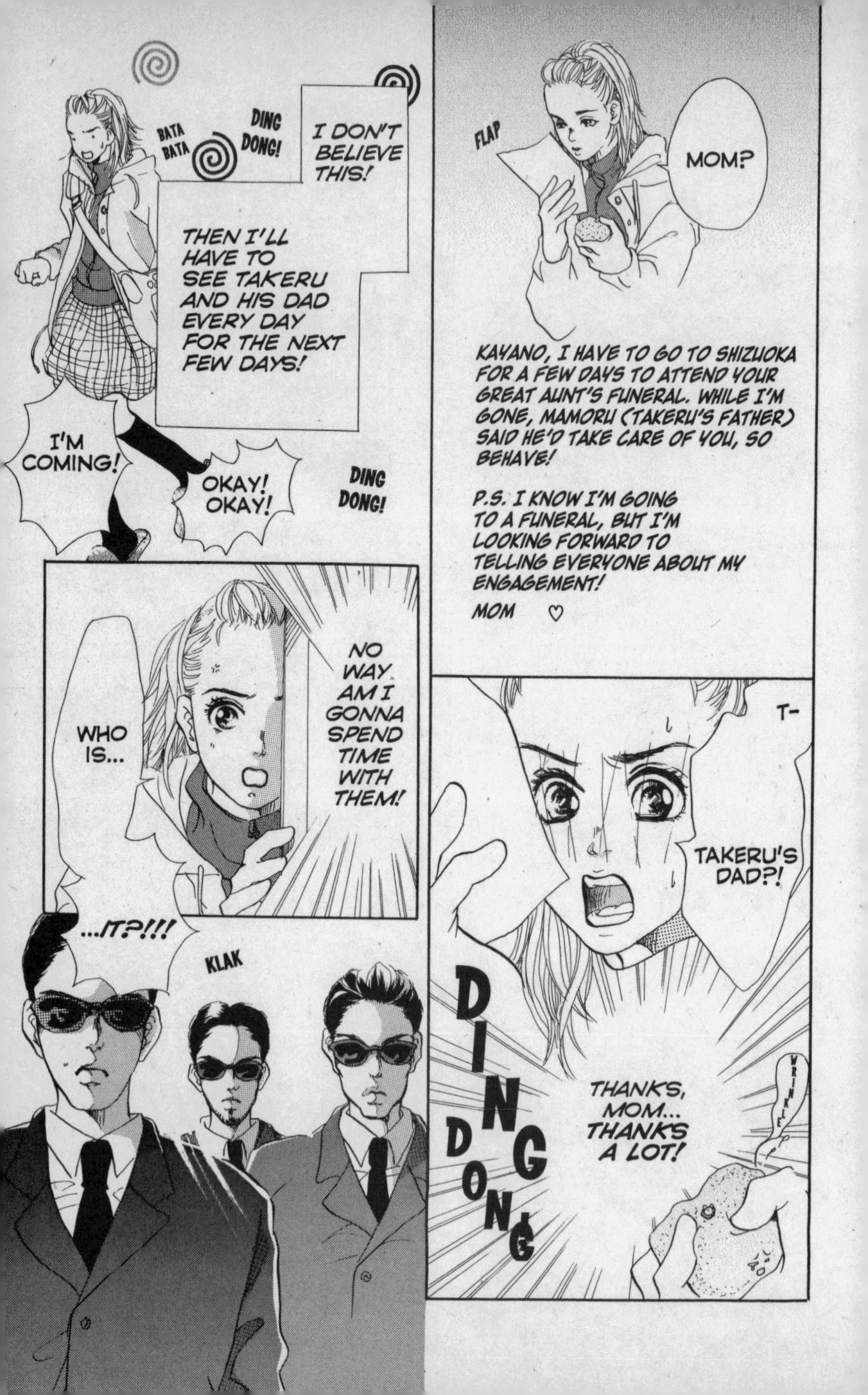
FLAP
MOM?
KAYANO, I HAVE TO GO TO SHIZUOKA FOR A FEW DAYS TO ATTEND YOUR GREAT AUNT'S FUNERAL. WHILE I'M GONE, MAMORU (TAKERU'S FATHER) SAID HE'D TAKE CARE OF YOU, SO BEHAVE!
P.S. I KNOW I'M GOING TO A FUNERAL, BUT I'M LOOKING FORWARD TO TELLING EVERYONE ABOUT MY ENGAGEMENT!
MOM ♡
T-
TAKERU'S DAD?!
DING DONG
THANKS, MOM... THANKS A LOT!
WRINKLE
I DON'T BELIEVE THIS!
DING DONG!
BATA BATA
THEN I'LL HAVE TO SEE TAKERU AND HIS DAD EVERY DAY FOR THE NEXT FEW DAYS!
DING DONG!
OKAY! OKAY!
I'M COMING!
NO WAY AM I GONNA SPEND TIME WITH THEM!
WHO IS...
KLAK
...IT?!!!

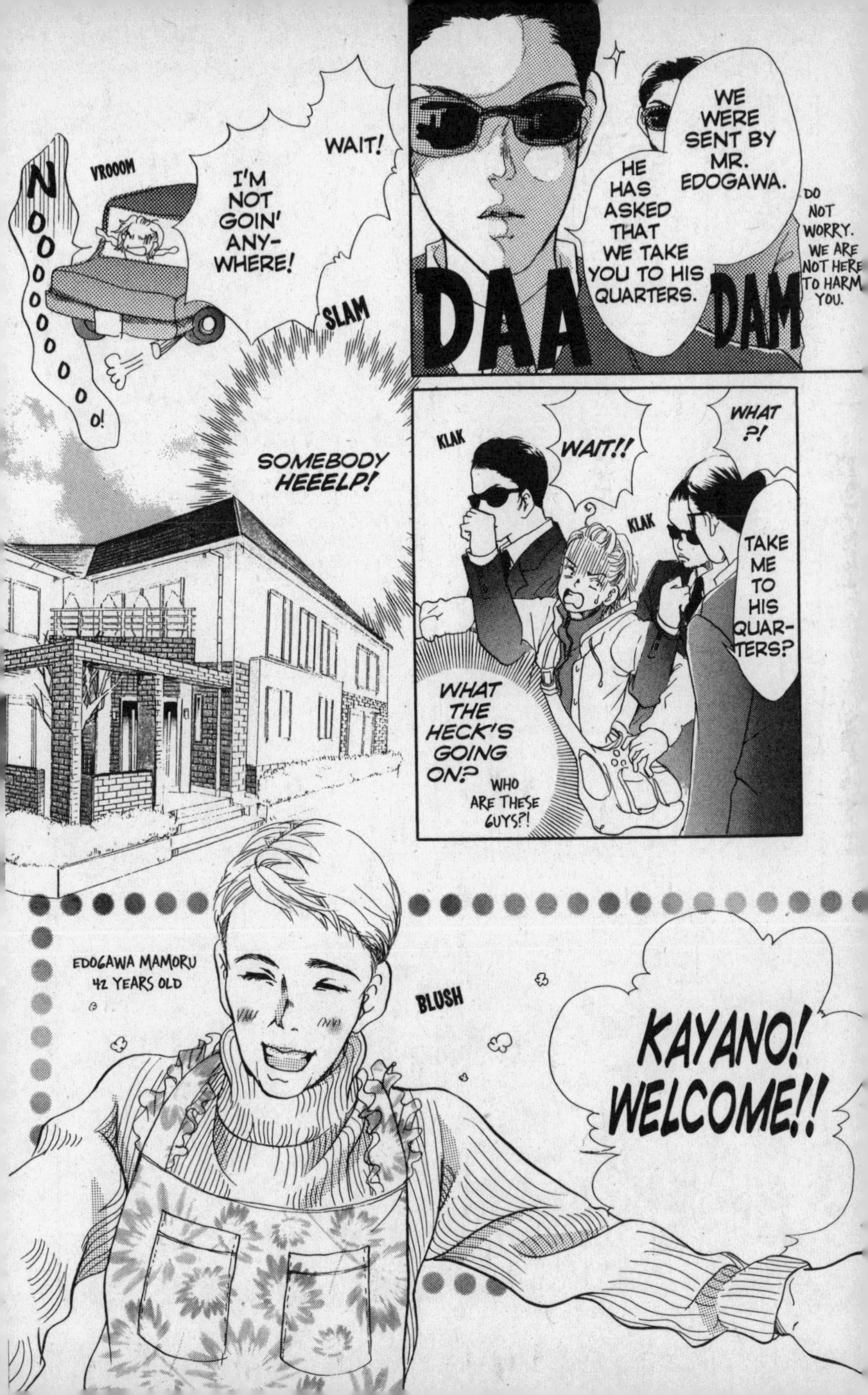
WE WERE SENT BY MR. EDOGAWA.
HE HAS ASKED THAT WE TAKE YOU TO HIS QUARTERS.
DO NOT WORRY. WE ARE NOT HERE TO HARM YOU.
DAA DAM
WHAT?!
WAIT!!
KLAK
TAKE ME TO HIS QUARTERS?
KLAK
WHAT THE HECK'S GOING ON?
WHO ARE THESE GUYS?!
WAIT!
I'M NOT GOIN' ANYWHERE!
SLAM
VROOOM
NOOOOOOOOOO!
SOMEBODY HEEELP!
KAYANO! WELCOME!!
BLUSH
EDOGAWA MAMORU 42 YEARS OLD

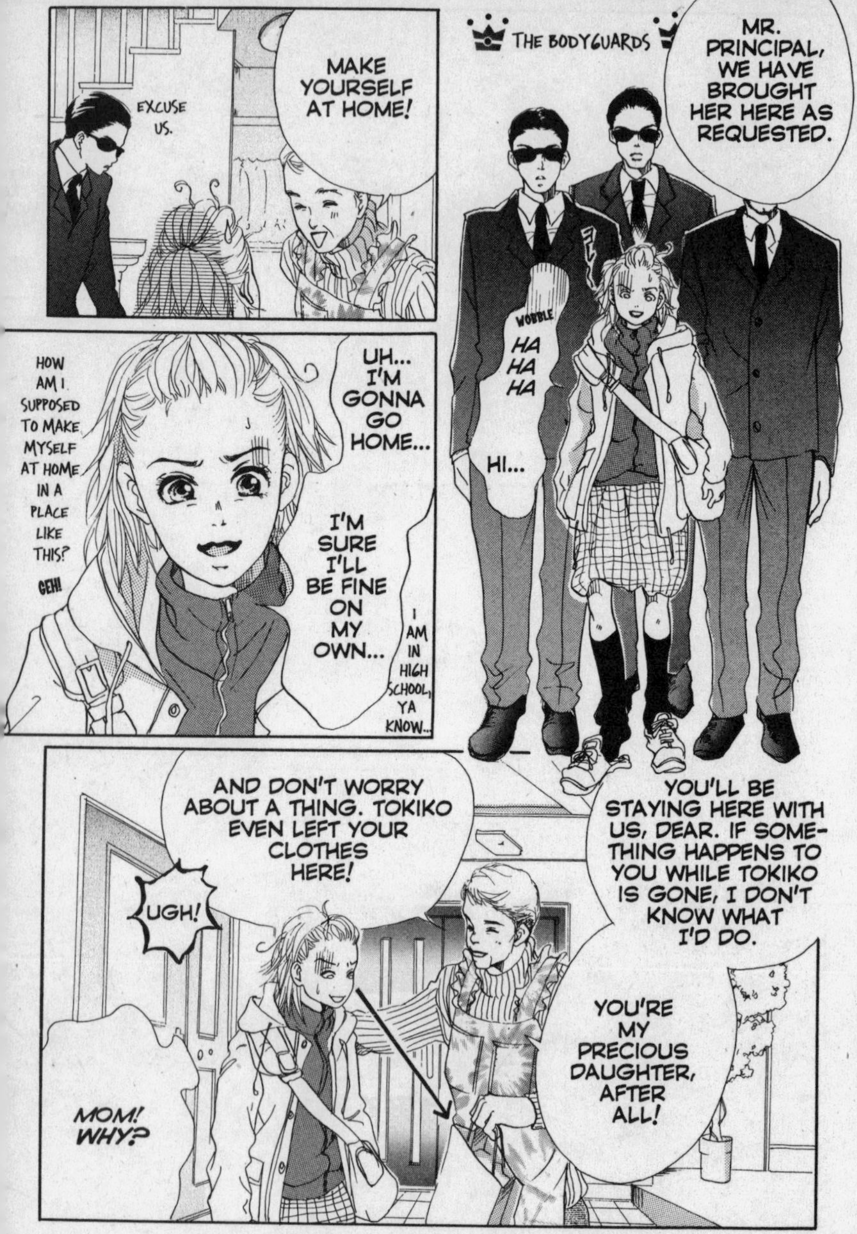
THE BODYGUARDS
MR. PRINCIPAL, WE HAVE BROUGHT HER HERE AS REQUESTED.
WOBBLE
HA HA HA
HI...
MAKE YOURSELF AT HOME!
EXCUSE US.
UH... I'M GONNA GO HOME...
I'M SURE I'LL BE FINE ON MY OWN...
I AM IN HIGH SCHOOL, YA KNOW...
HOW AM I SUPPOSED TO MAKE MYSELF AT HOME IN A PLACE LIKE THIS?
GEH!
YOU'LL BE STAYING HERE WITH US, DEAR. IF SOMETHING HAPPENS TO YOU WHILE TOKIKO IS GONE, I DON'T KNOW WHAT I'D DO.
YOU'RE MY PRECIOUS DAUGHTER, AFTER ALL!
AND DON'T WORRY ABOUT A THING. TOKIKO EVEN LEFT YOUR CLOTHES HERE!
UGH!
MOM! WHY?

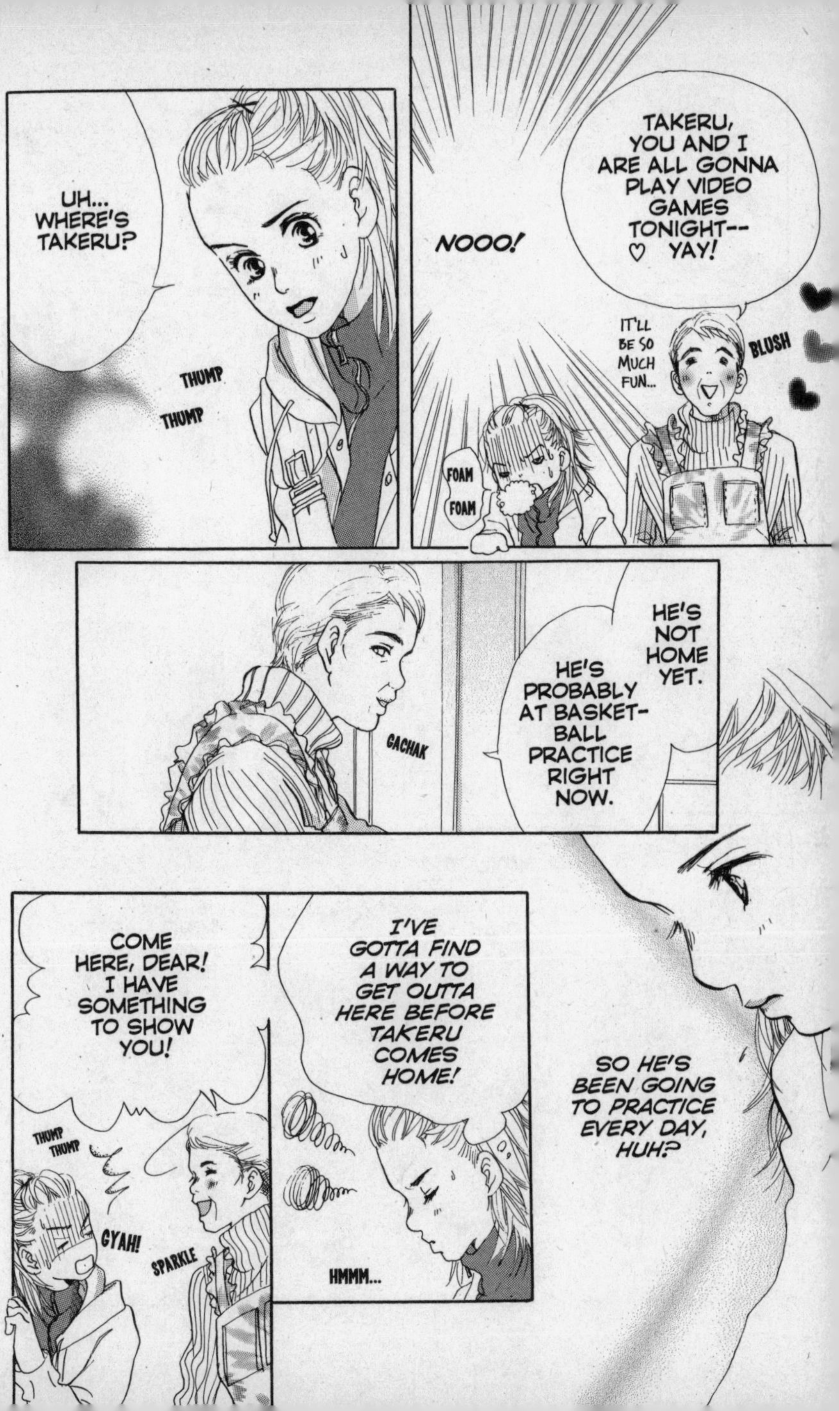
TAKERU, YOU AND I ARE ALL GONNA PLAY VIDEO GAMES TONIGHT-- ♡ YAY!
IT'LL BE SO MUCH FUN...
BLUSH
NOOO!
FOAM FOAM
UH... WHERE'S TAKERU?
THUMP THUMP
HE'S NOT HOME YET.
HE'S PROBABLY AT BASKETBALL PRACTICE RIGHT NOW.
GACHAK
SO HE'S BEEN GOING TO PRACTICE EVERY DAY, HUH?
I'VE GOTTA FIND A WAY TO GET OUTTA HERE BEFORE TAKERU COMES HOME!
HMMM...
COME HERE, DEAR! I HAVE SOMETHING TO SHOW YOU!
THUMP THUMP
GYAH!
SPARKLE

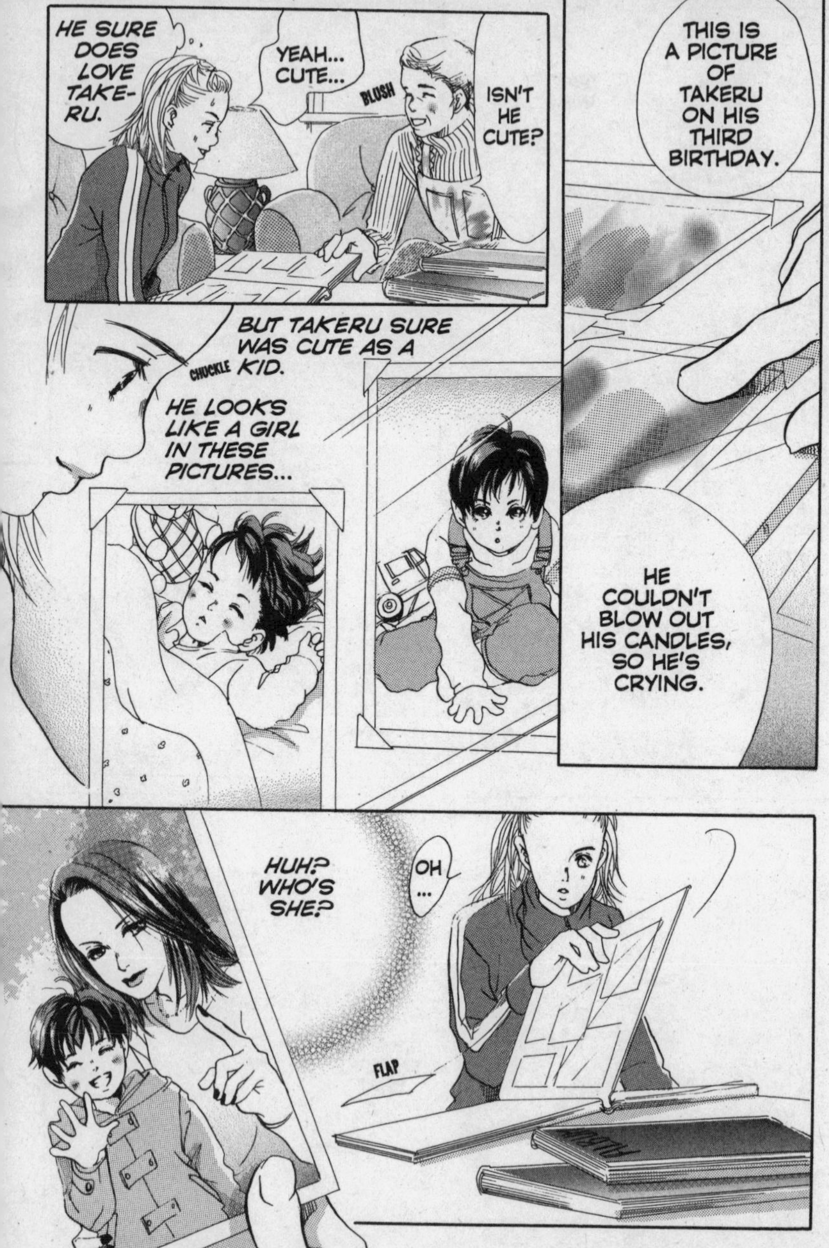
THIS IS A PICTURE OF TAKERU ON HIS THIRD BIRTHDAY.
HE COULDN'T BLOW OUT HIS CANDLES, SO HE'S CRYING.
ISN'T HE CUTE?
BLUSH
YEAH... CUTE...
HE SURE DOES LOVE TAKE-RU.
BUT TAKERU SURE WAS CUTE AS A KID.
CHUCKLE
HE LOOKS LIKE A GIRL IN THESE PICTURES...
OH...
HUH? WHO'S SHE?
FLAP

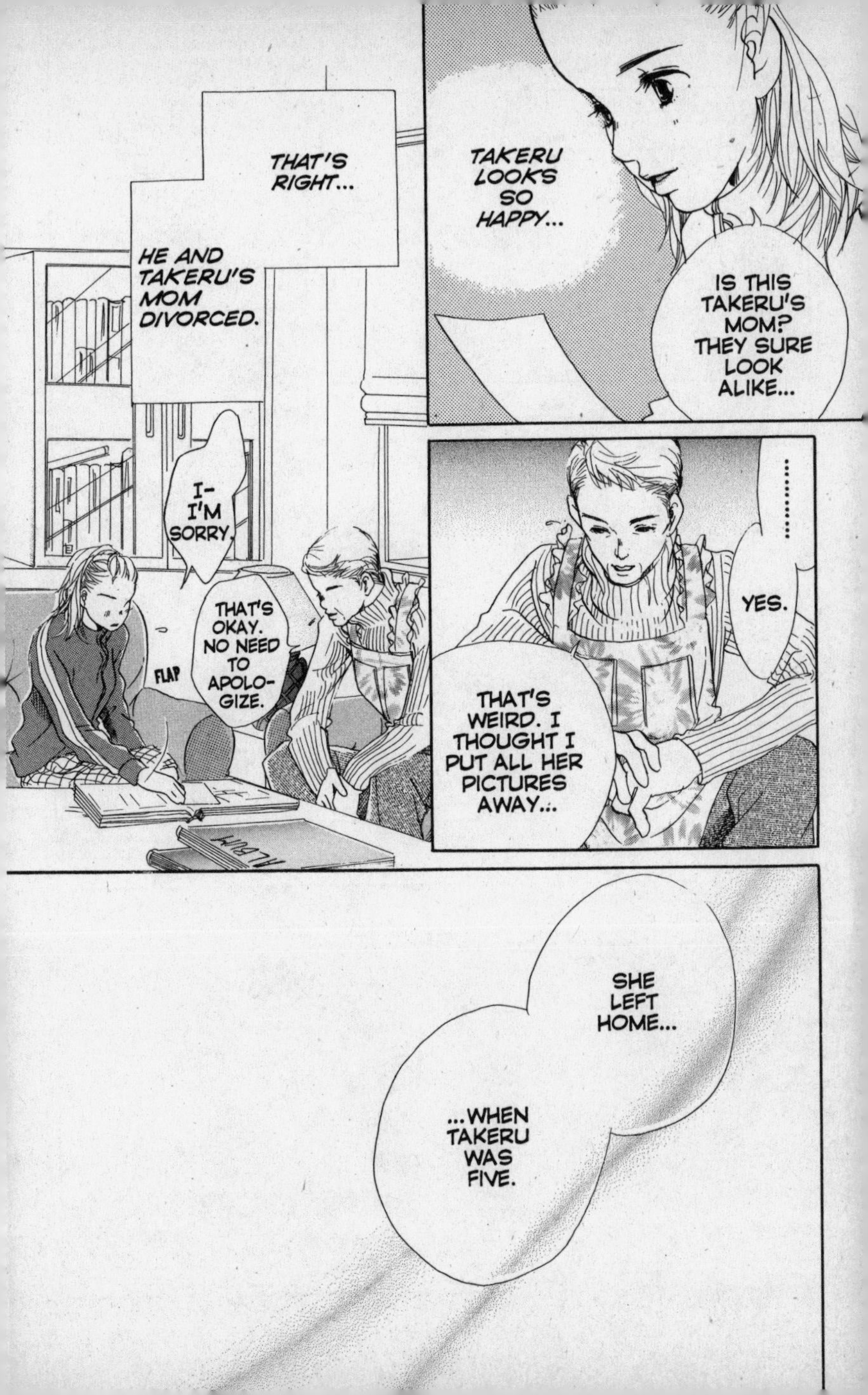
TAKERU LOOKS SO HAPPY...
IS THIS TAKERU'S MOM? THEY SURE LOOK ALIKE...
......
YES.
THAT'S WEIRD. I THOUGHT I PUT ALL HER PICTURES AWAY...
THAT'S RIGHT...
HE AND TAKERU'S MOM DIVORCED.
I- I'M SORRY.
THAT'S OKAY. NO NEED TO APOLOGIZE.
FLAP
ALBUM
SHE LEFT HOME...
...WHEN TAKERU WAS FIVE.

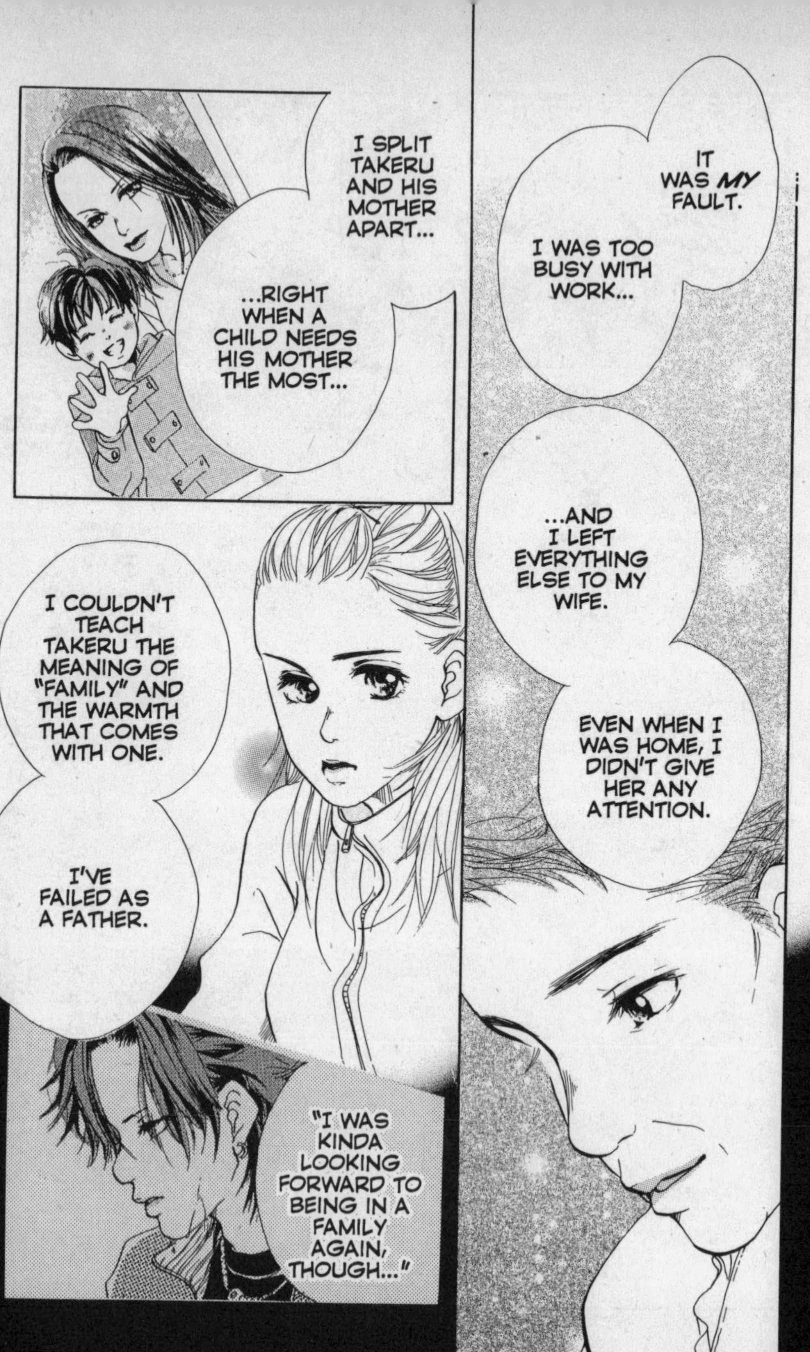
IT WAS MY FAULT.
I WAS TOO BUSY WITH WORK...
...AND I LEFT EVERYTHING ELSE TO MY WIFE.
EVEN WHEN I WAS HOME, I DIDN'T GIVE HER ANY ATTENTION.
I SPLIT TAKERU AND HIS MOTHER APART...
...RIGHT WHEN A CHILD NEEDS HIS MOTHER THE MOST...
I COULDN'T TEACH TAKERU THE MEANING OF "FAMILY" AND THE WARMTH THAT COMES WITH ONE.
I'VE FAILED AS A FATHER.
"I WAS KINDA LOOKING FORWARD TO BEING IN A FAMILY AGAIN, THOUGH..."

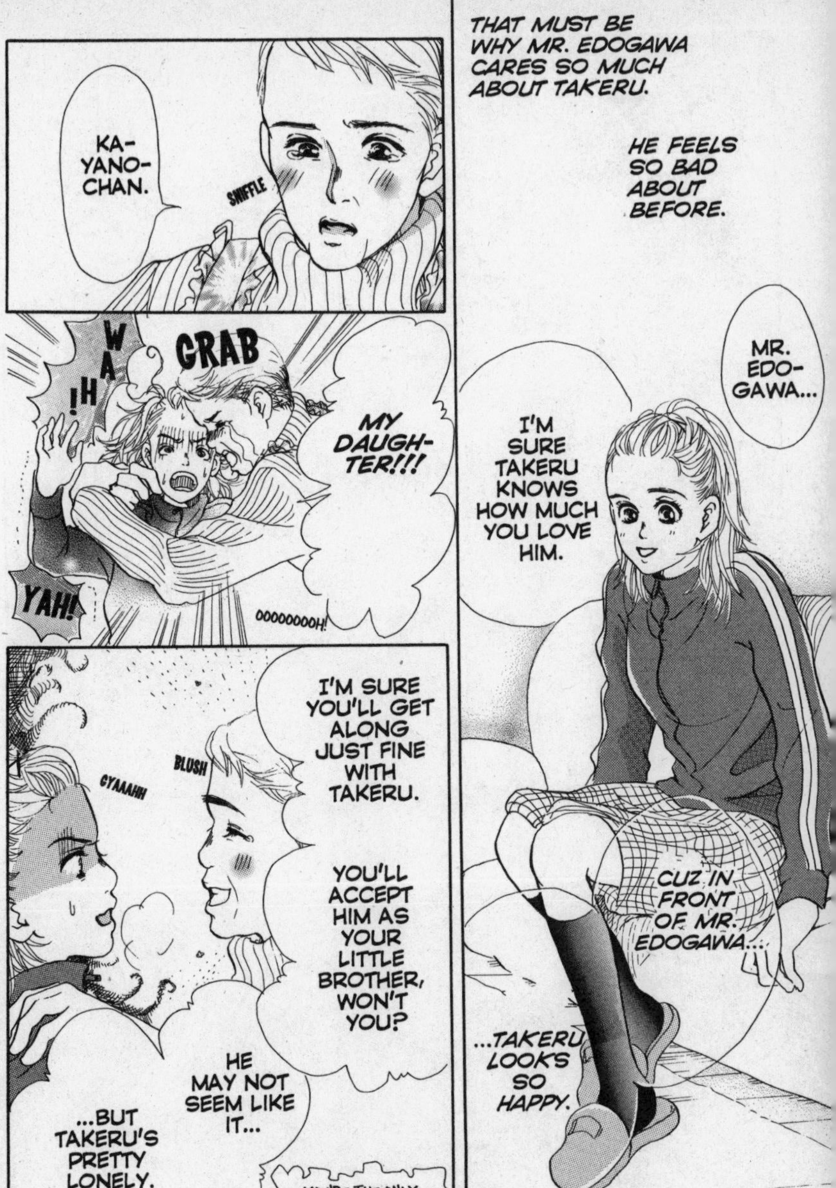
THAT MUST BE WHY MR. EDOGAWA CARES SO MUCH ABOUT TAKERU.
HE FEELS SO BAD ABOUT BEFORE.
MR. EDOGAWA...
I'M SURE TAKERU KNOWS HOW MUCH YOU LOVE HIM.
CUZ IN FRONT OF MR. EDOGAWA...
...TAKERU LOOKS SO HAPPY.
SNIFFLE
KA-YANO-CHAN.
MY DAUGHTER!!!
GRAB
WAH!
OOOOOOOOH!
YAH!
I'M SURE YOU'LL GET ALONG JUST FINE WITH TAKERU.
YOU'LL ACCEPT HIM AS YOUR LITTLE BROTHER, WON'T YOU?
BLUSH
GYAAAHH
HE MAY NOT SEEM LIKE IT...
YOU'RE THE ONLY ONE WHO CAN!
...BUT TAKERU'S PRETTY LONELY.

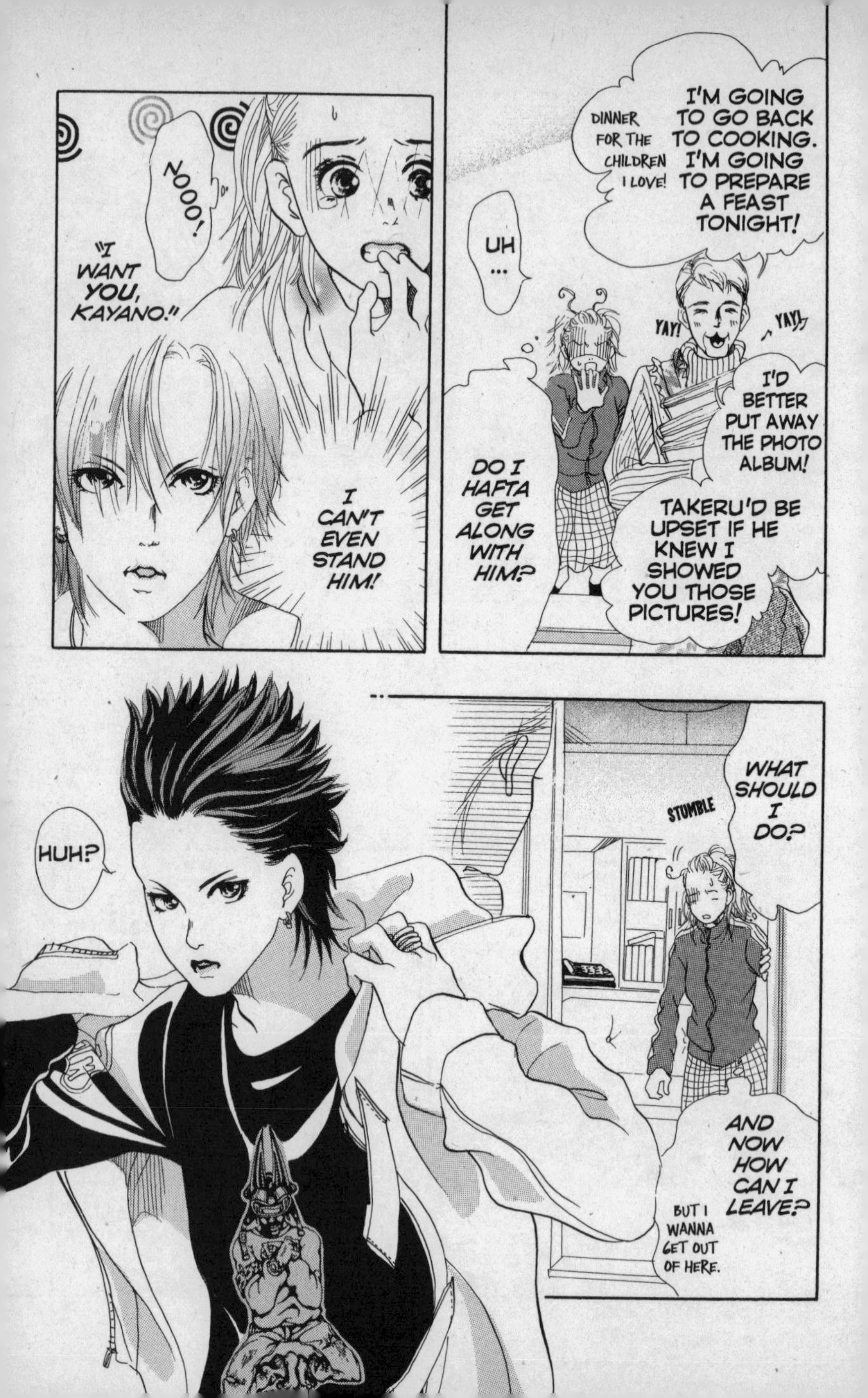
DINNER FOR THE CHILDREN I LOVE!
I'M GOING TO GO BACK TO COOKING. I'M GOING TO PREPARE A FEAST TONIGHT!
UH ...
YAY!
YAY!
I'D BETTER PUT AWAY THE PHOTO ALBUM!
DO I HAFTA GET ALONG WITH HIM?
TAKERU'D BE UPSET IF HE KNEW I SHOWED YOU THOSE PICTURES!
NOOO!
"I WANT YOU, KAYANO."
I CAN'T EVEN STAND HIM!
WHAT SHOULD I DO?
STUMBLE
AND NOW HOW CAN I LEAVE?
BUT I WANNA GET OUT OF HERE.
HUH?

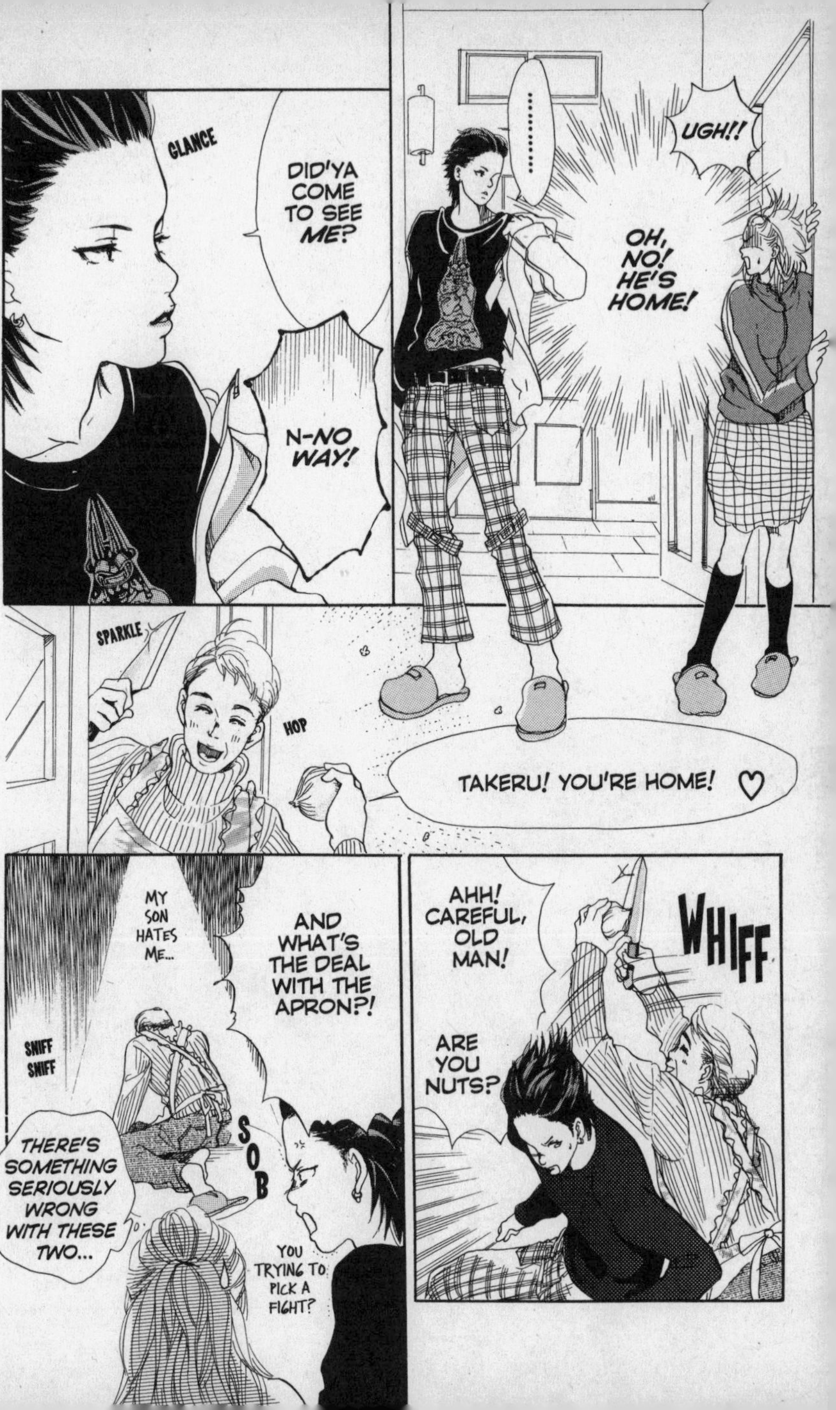

UGH!!
OH, NO! HE'S HOME!
......
GLANCE
DID'YA COME TO SEE ME?
N-NO WAY!
SPARKLE
HOP
TAKERU! YOU'RE HOME! ♡
AHH! CAREFUL, OLD MAN!
WHIFF
ARE YOU NUTS?
AND WHAT'S THE DEAL WITH THE APRON?!
MY SON HATES ME...
SNIFF SNIFF
SOB
YOU TRYING TO PICK A FIGHT?
THERE'S SOMETHING SERIOUSLY WRONG WITH THESE TWO...

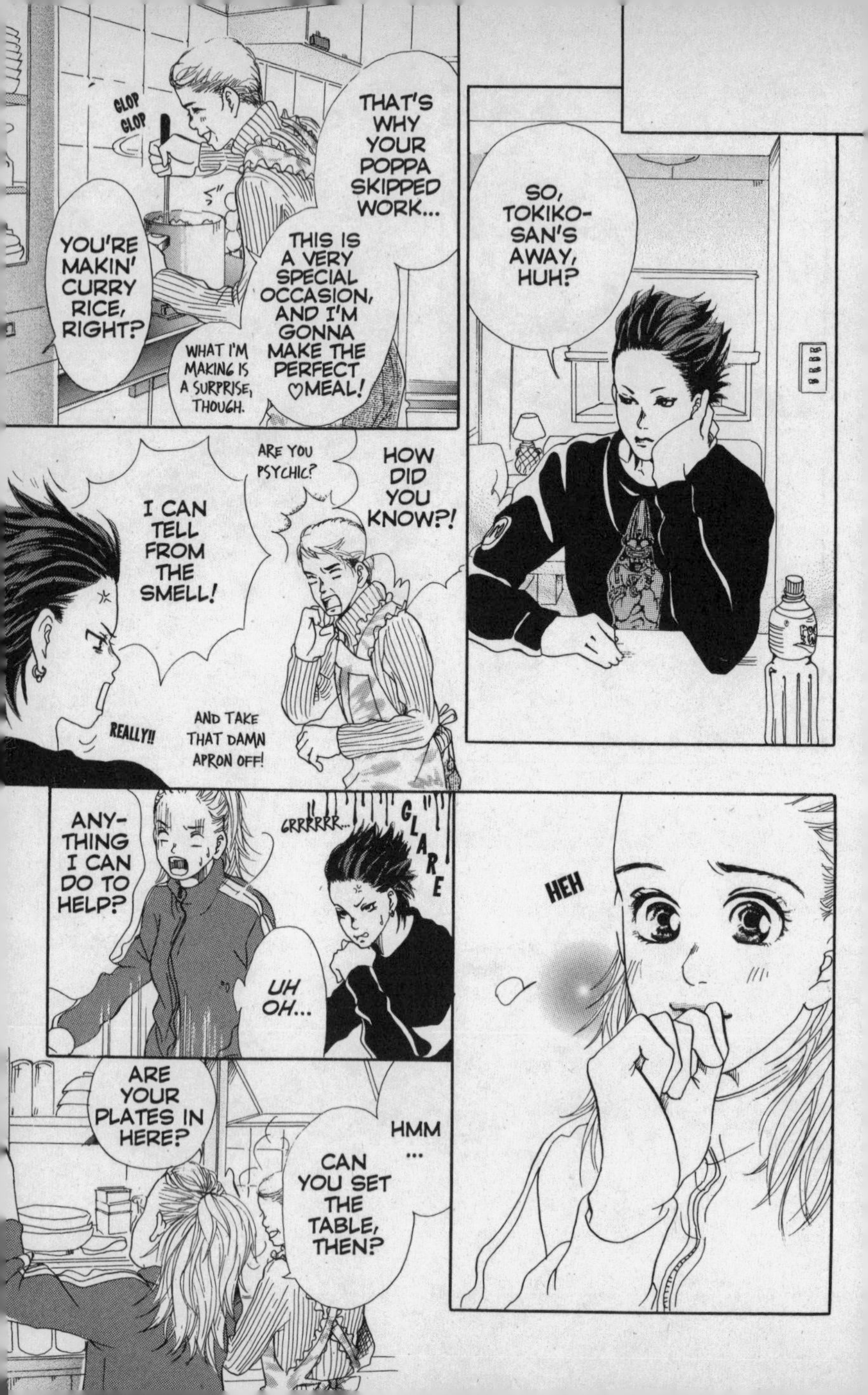
SO, TOKIKO-SAN'S AWAY, HUH?
THAT'S WHY YOUR POPPA SKIPPED WORK...
GLOP GLOP
THIS IS A VERY SPECIAL OCCASION, AND I'M GONNA MAKE THE PERFECT ♡MEAL!
YOU'RE MAKIN' CURRY RICE, RIGHT?
WHAT I'M MAKING IS A SURPRISE, THOUGH.
HOW DID YOU KNOW?!
ARE YOU PSYCHIC?
I CAN TELL FROM THE SMELL!
REALLY!!
AND TAKE THAT DAMN APRON OFF!
HEH
ANY-THING I CAN DO TO HELP?
GLARE
GRRRRRR...
UH OH...
HMM ...
CAN YOU SET THE TABLE, THEN?
ARE YOUR PLATES IN HERE?

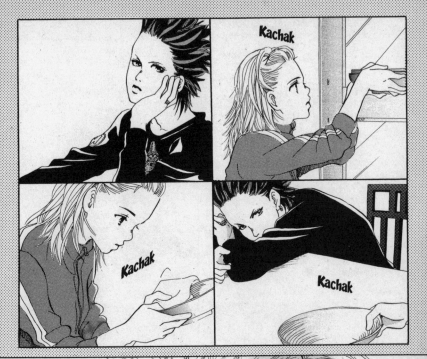

Kachak

Kachak

Kachak

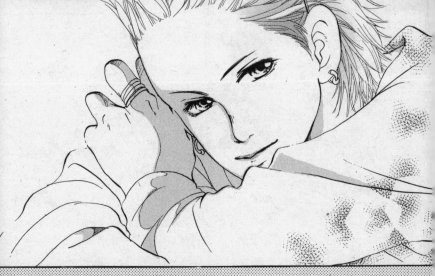

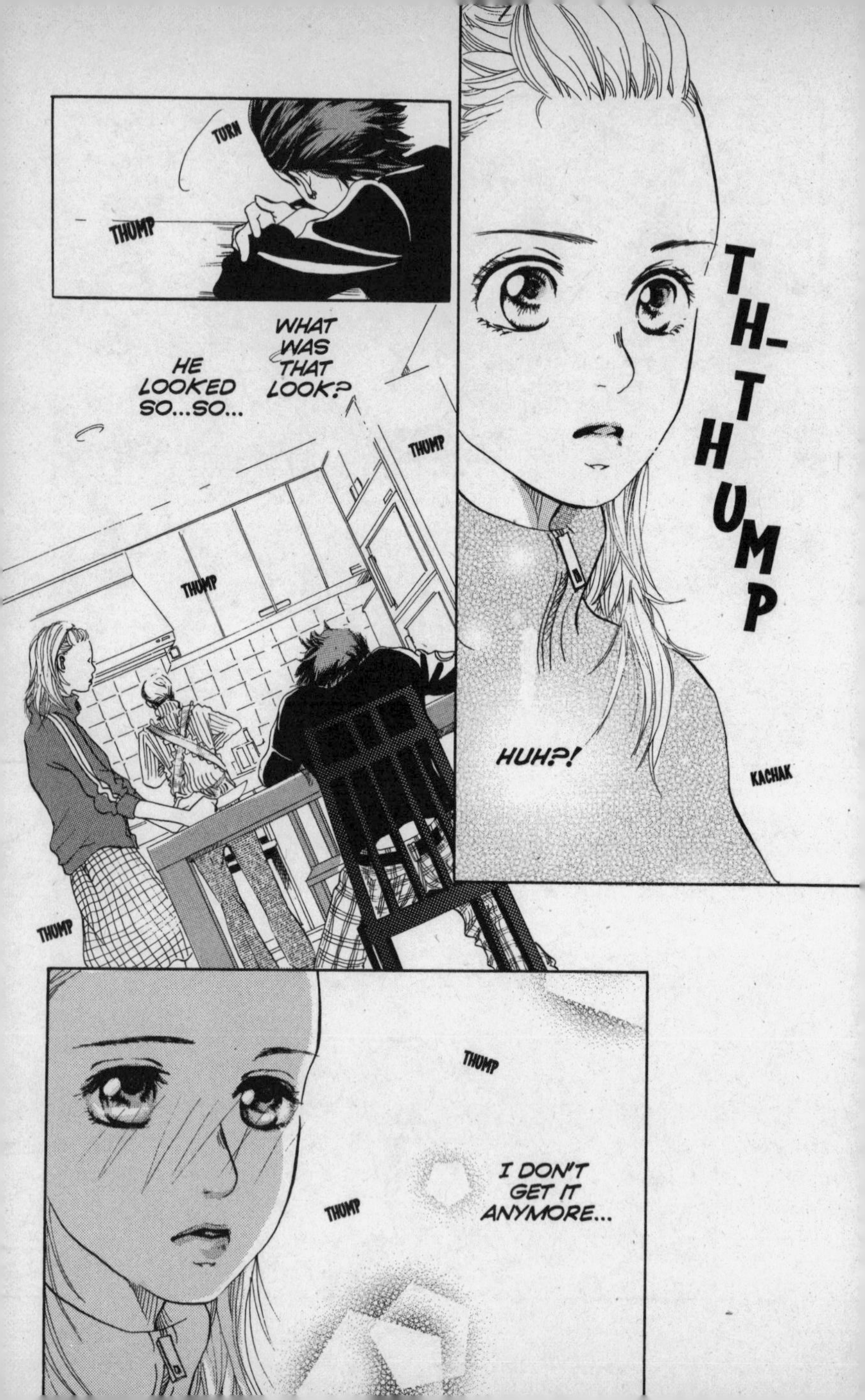
TH-THUMP
HUH?!
KACHAK
TURN
THUMP
WHAT WAS THAT LOOK?
HE LOOKED SO...SO...
THUMP
THUMP
THUMP
THUMP
I DON'T GET IT ANYMORE...
THUMP

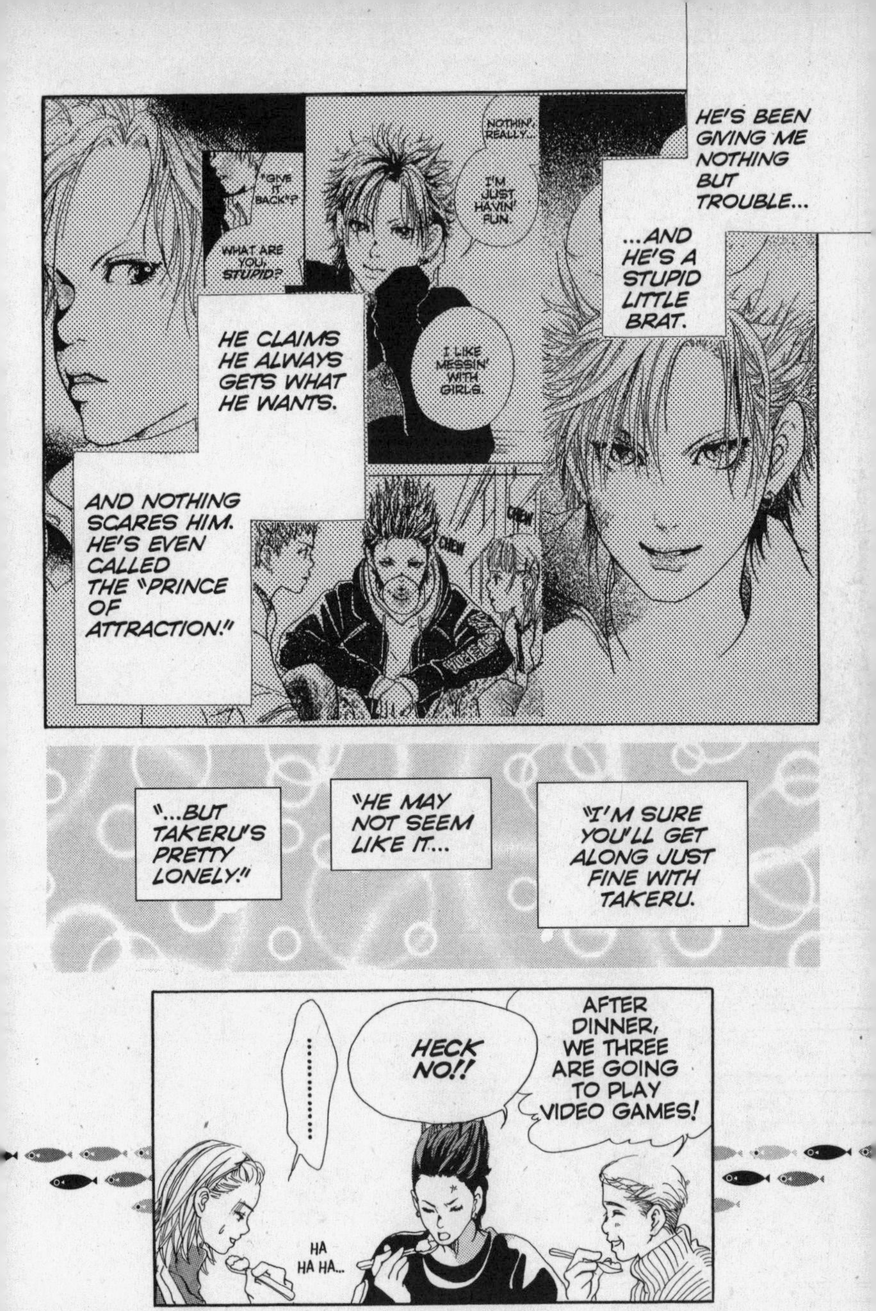
HE'S BEEN GIVING ME NOTHING BUT TROUBLE...
...AND HE'S A STUPID LITTLE BRAT.
NOTHIN', REALLY...
I'M JUST HAVIN' FUN.
I LIKE MESSIN' WITH GIRLS.
"GIVE IT BACK"?
WHAT ARE YOU, STUPID?
HE CLAIMS HE ALWAYS GETS WHAT HE WANTS.
CHEW
CHEW
AND NOTHING SCARES HIM. HE'S EVEN CALLED THE "PRINCE OF ATTRACTION."
"I'M SURE YOU'LL GET ALONG JUST FINE WITH TAKERU.
"HE MAY NOT SEEM LIKE IT...
"...BUT TAKERU'S PRETTY LONELY!"
AFTER DINNER, WE THREE ARE GOING TO PLAY VIDEO GAMES!
HECK NO!!
....
HA HA HA...

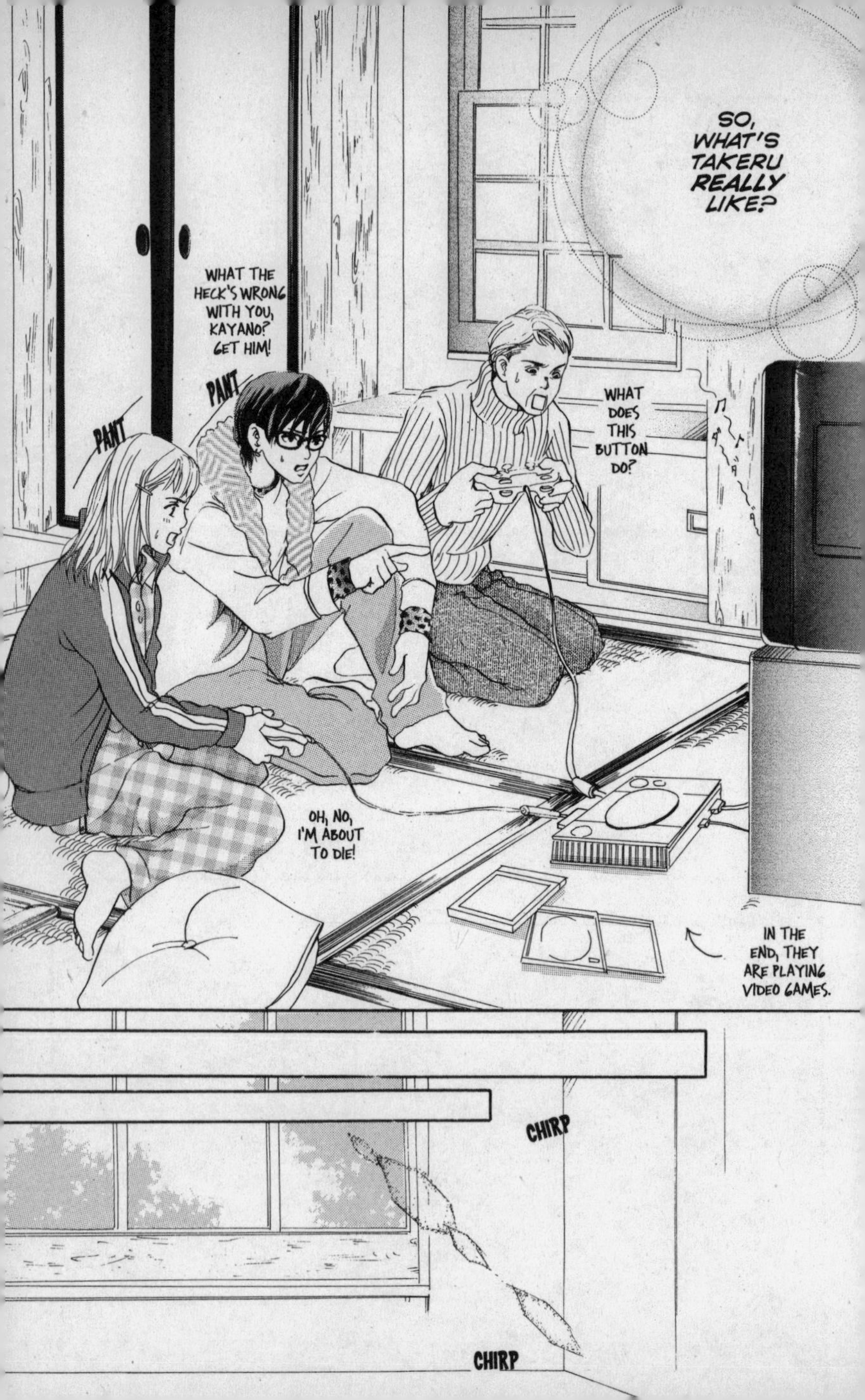
SO, WHAT'S TAKERU REALLY LIKE?
WHAT DOES THIS BUTTON DO?
WHAT THE HECK'S WRONG WITH YOU, KAYANO? GET HIM!
PANT
PANT
OH, NO, I'M ABOUT TO DIE!
IN THE END, THEY ARE PLAYING VIDEO GAMES.
CHIRP
CHIRP

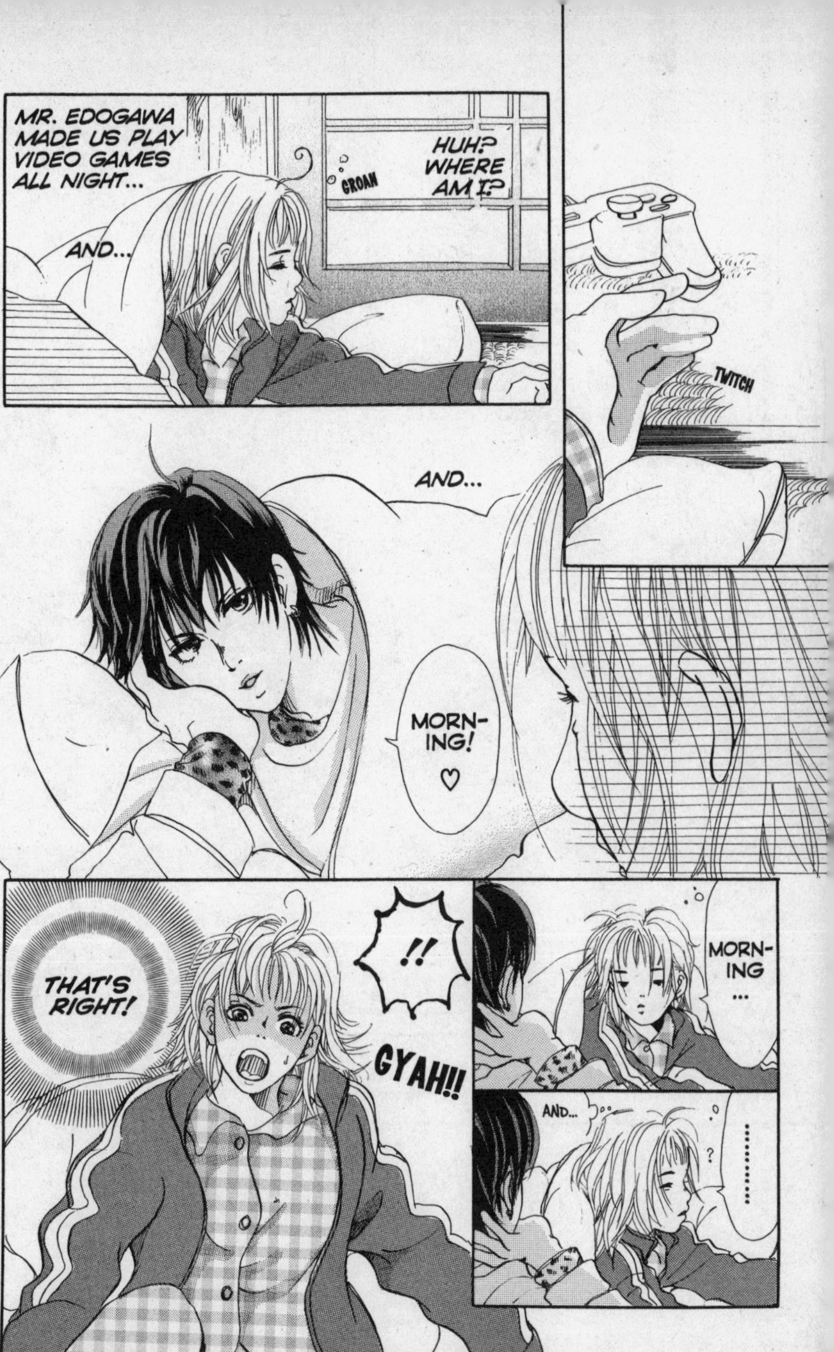
TWITCH
HUH? WHERE AM I?
GROAN
MR. EDOGAWA MADE US PLAY VIDEO GAMES ALL NIGHT...
AND...
AND...
MORNING! ♡
MORNING ...
....
?
AND...
!!
GYAH!!
THAT'S RIGHT!

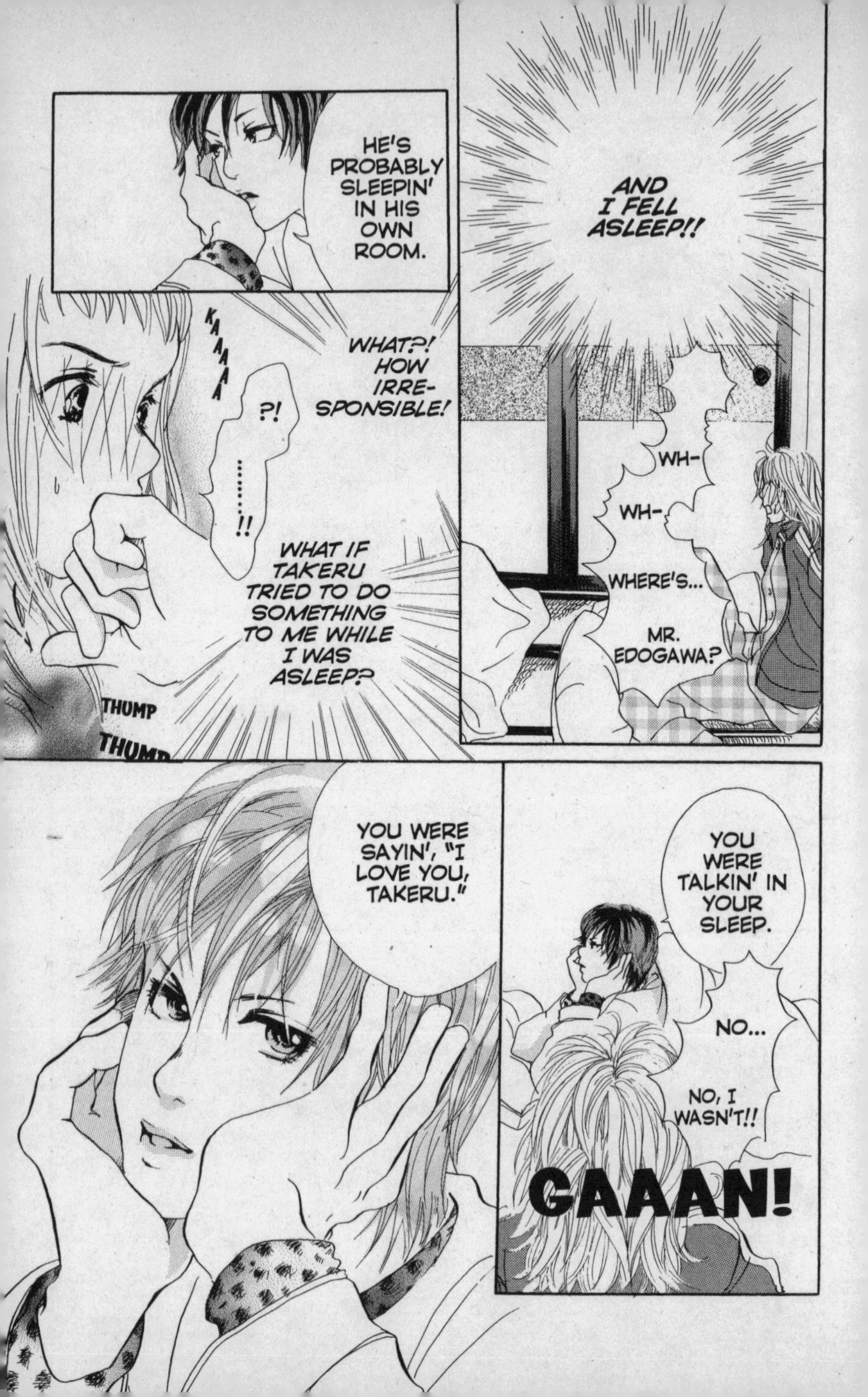
AND I FELL ASLEEP!!
WH-
WH-
WHERE'S...
MR. EDOGAWA?
HE'S PROBABLY SLEEPIN' IN HIS OWN ROOM.
KAAAAA
WHAT?! HOW IRRE-SPONSIBLE!
?!
......!!
WHAT IF TAKERU TRIED TO DO SOMETHING TO ME WHILE I WAS ASLEEP?
THUMP
THUMP
YOU WERE TALKIN' IN YOUR SLEEP.
NO...
NO, I WASN'T!!
GAAAN!
YOU WERE SAYIN', "I LOVE YOU, TAKERU."

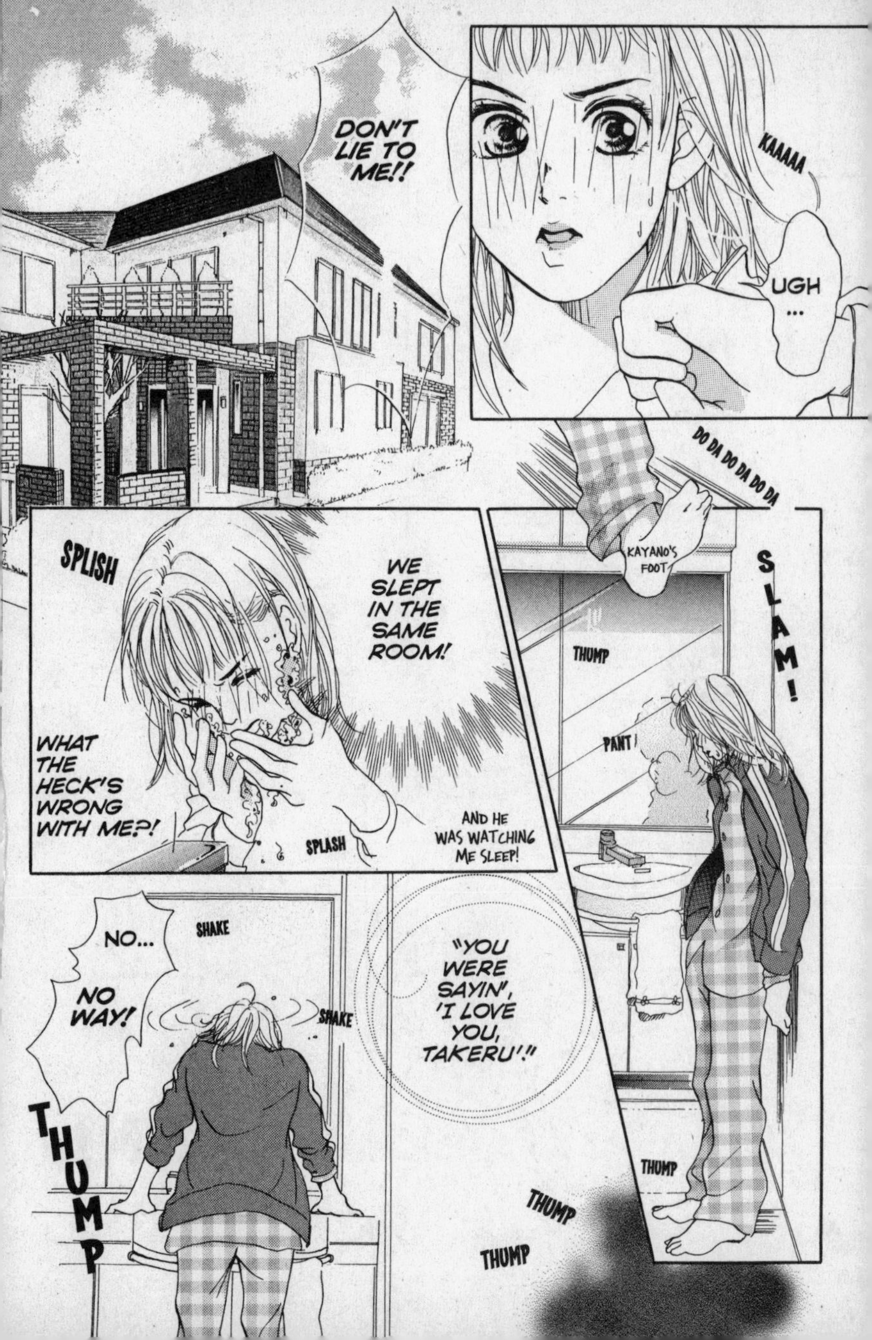

KAAAAA
UGH ...
DON'T LIE TO ME!!
DO DA DO DA DO DA
KAYANO'S FOOT
SLAM!
THUMP
PANT
WE SLEPT IN THE SAME ROOM!
SPLISH
AND HE WAS WATCHING ME SLEEP!
WHAT THE HECK'S WRONG WITH ME?!
SPLASH
THUMP
THUMP
THUMP
"YOU WERE SAYIN', 'I LOVE YOU, TAKERU'."
SHAKE
SHAKE
NO...
NO WAY!
THUMP

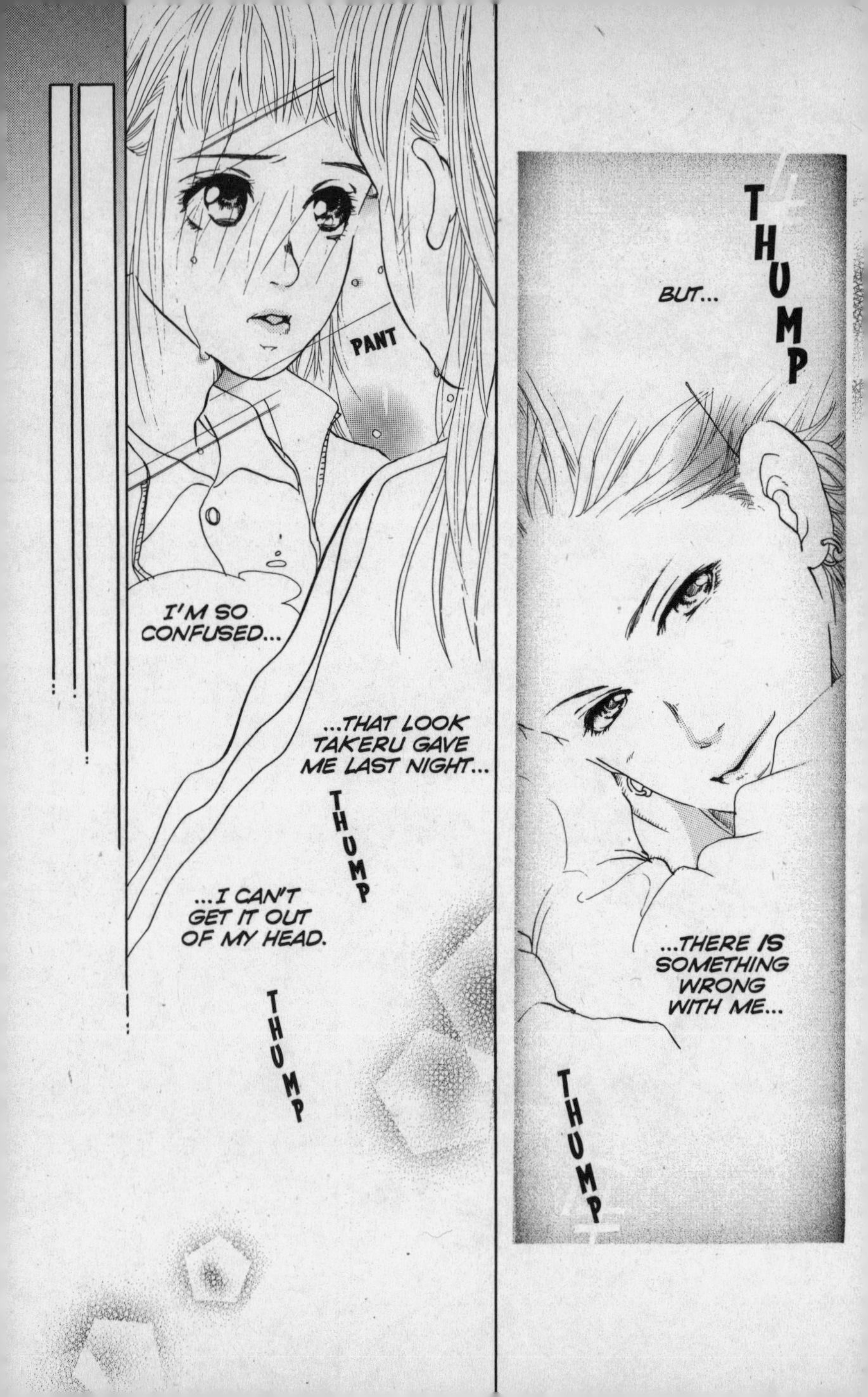
THUMP
BUT...
...THERE IS SOMETHING WRONG WITH ME...
THUMP
PANT
I'M SO CONFUSED...
...THAT LOOK TAKERU GAVE ME LAST NIGHT...
THUMP
...I CAN'T GET IT OUT OF MY HEAD.
THUMP

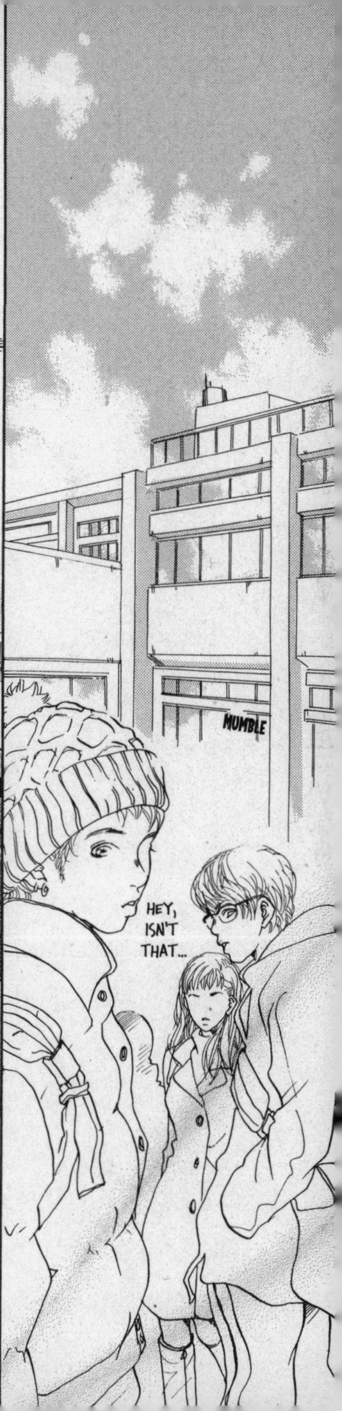
MUMBLE
HEY, ISN'T THAT...
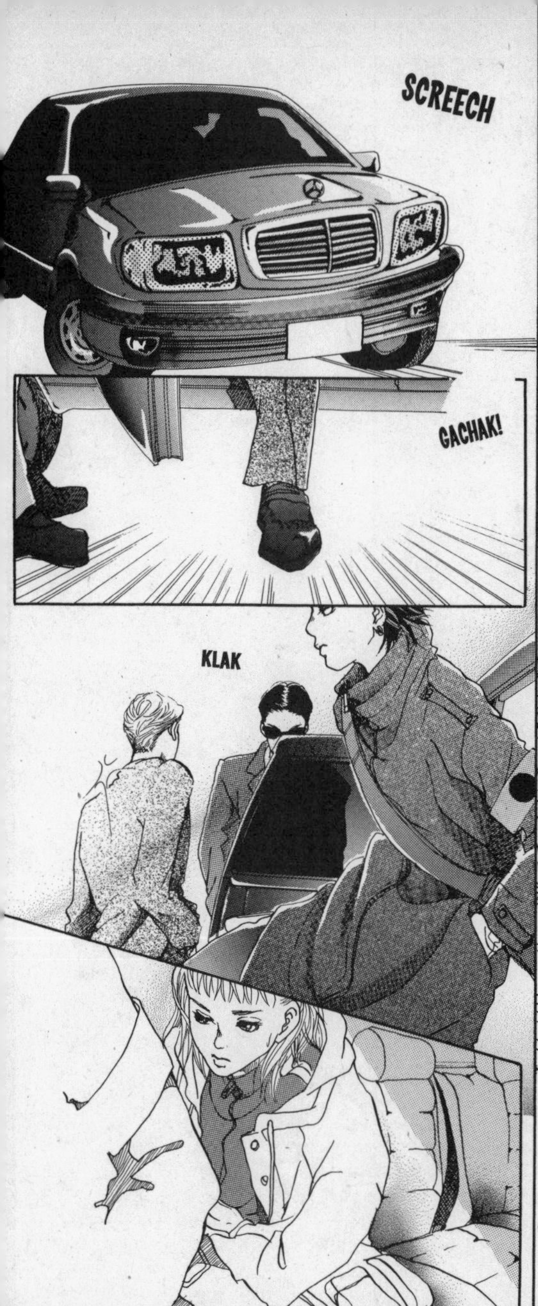
SCREECH
GACHAK!
KLAK

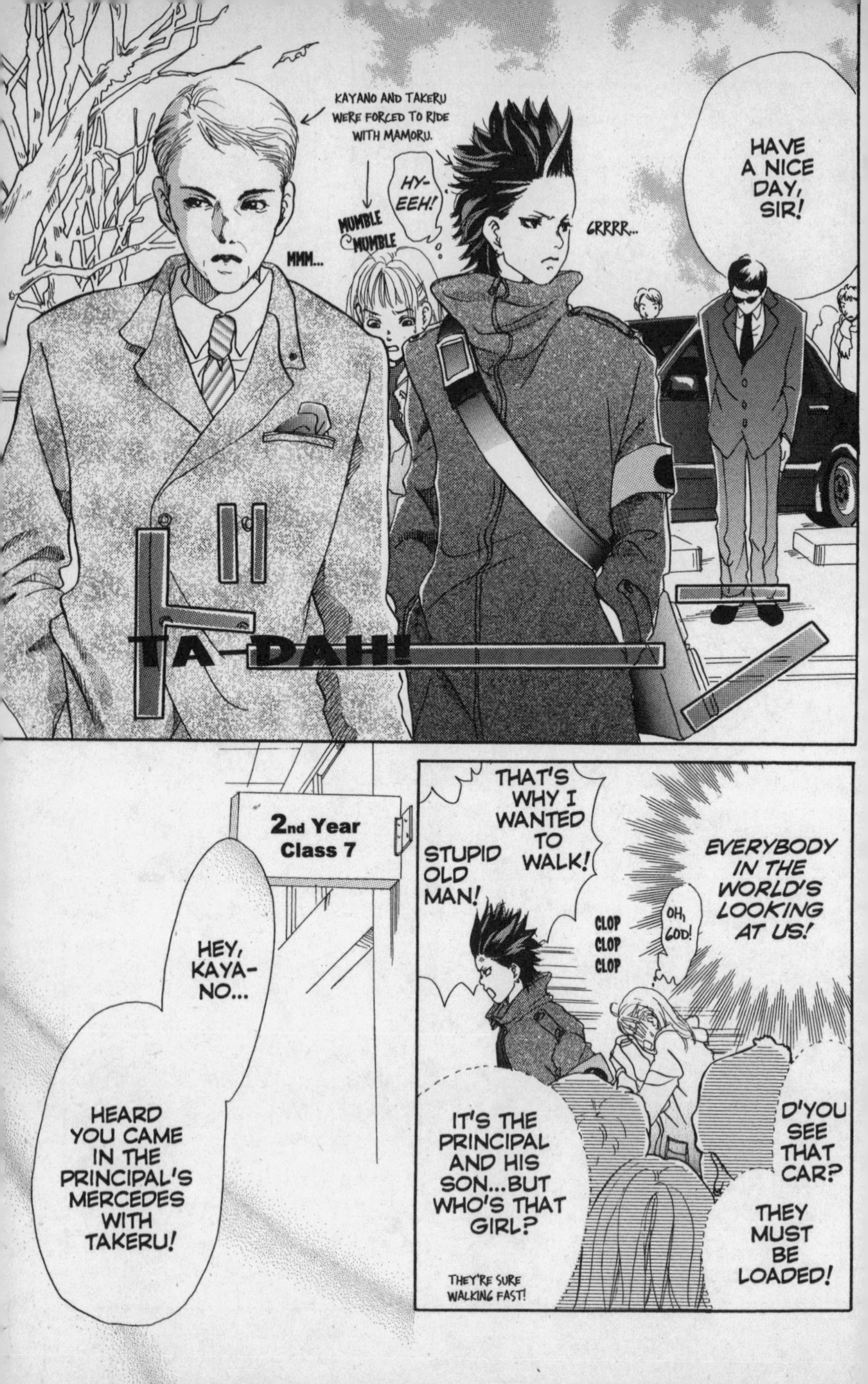
HAVE A NICE DAY, SIR!
GRRRR...
HY-EEH!
MUMBLE MUMBLE
KAYANO AND TAKERU WERE FORCED TO RIDE WITH MAMORU.
MMM...
TA-DAH!
EVERYBODY IN THE WORLD'S LOOKING AT US!
THAT'S WHY I WANTED TO WALK!
STUPID OLD MAN!
OH, GOD!
CLOP CLOP CLOP
D'YOU SEE THAT CAR?
THEY MUST BE LOADED!
IT'S THE PRINCIPAL AND HIS SON...BUT WHO'S THAT GIRL?
THEY'RE SURE WALKING FAST!
2nd Year Class 7
HEY, KAYA-NO...
HEARD YOU CAME IN THE PRINCIPAL'S MERCEDES WITH TAKERU!

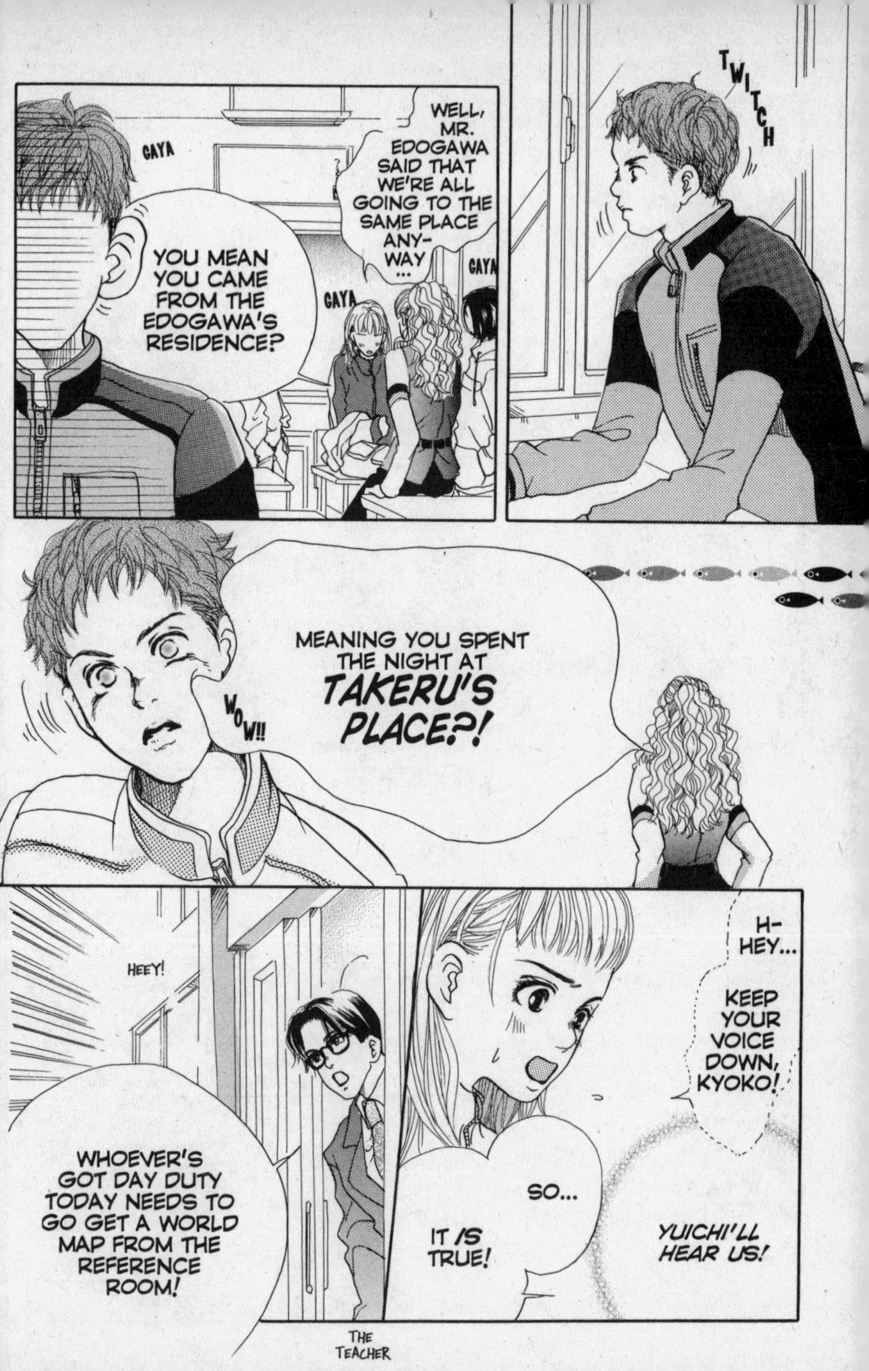
TWITCH
WELL, MR. EDOGAWA SAID THAT WE'RE ALL GOING TO THE SAME PLACE ANYWAY...
GAYA
GAYA
YOU MEAN YOU CAME FROM THE EDOGAWA'S RESIDENCE?
GAYA
MEANING YOU SPENT THE NIGHT AT *TAKERU'S PLACE?!*
WOW!!
H-HEY... KEEP YOUR VOICE DOWN, KYOKO!
SO...
YUICHI'LL HEAR US!
IT *IS* TRUE!
HEEY!
WHOEVER'S GOT DAY DUTY TODAY NEEDS TO GO GET A WORLD MAP FROM THE REFERENCE ROOM!
THE TEACHER

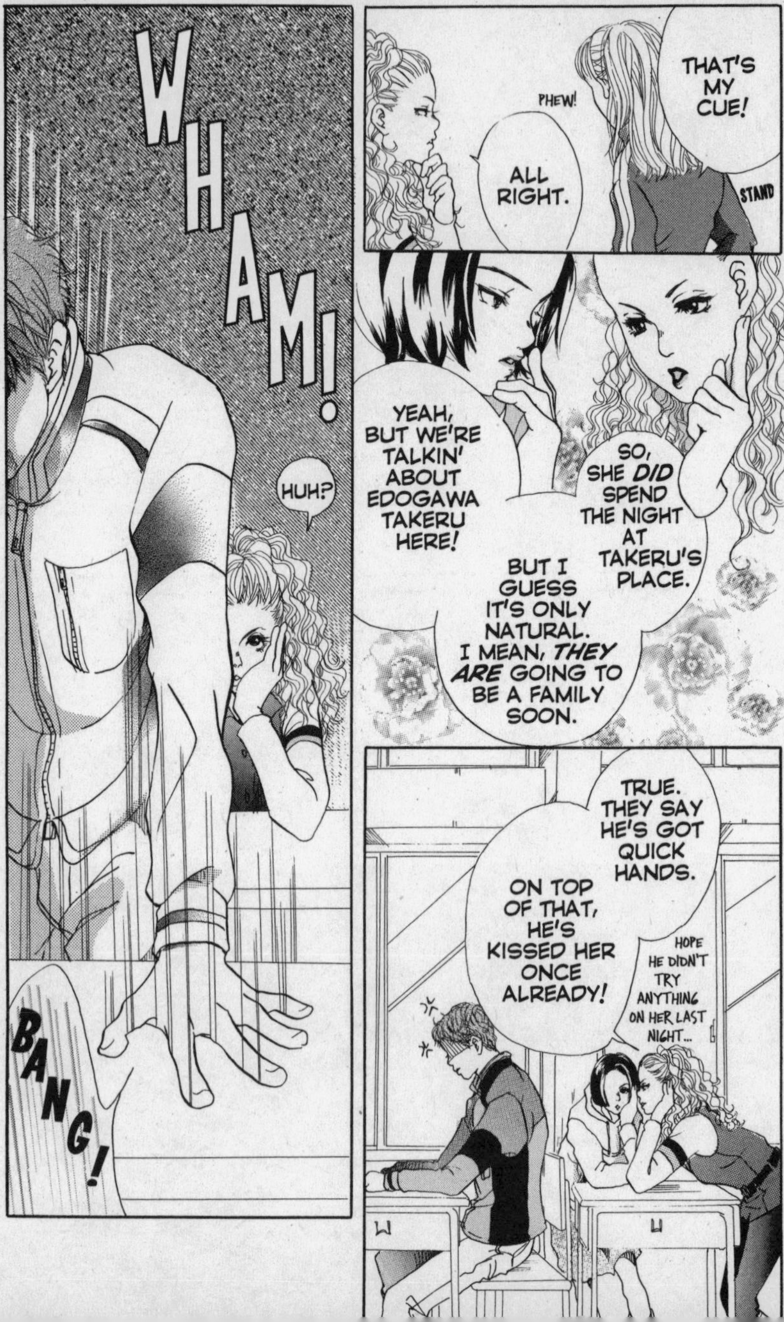
THAT'S MY CUE!
PHEW!
STAND
ALL RIGHT.
SO, SHE *DID* SPEND THE NIGHT AT TAKERU'S PLACE.
BUT I GUESS IT'S ONLY NATURAL. I MEAN, *THEY ARE* GOING TO BE A FAMILY SOON.
YEAH, BUT WE'RE TALKIN' ABOUT EDOGAWA TAKERU HERE!
TRUE. THEY SAY HE'S GOT QUICK HANDS.
HOPE HE DIDN'T TRY ANYTHING ON HER LAST NIGHT...
ON TOP OF THAT, HE'S KISSED HER ONCE ALREADY!
WHAM!
HUH?
BANG!

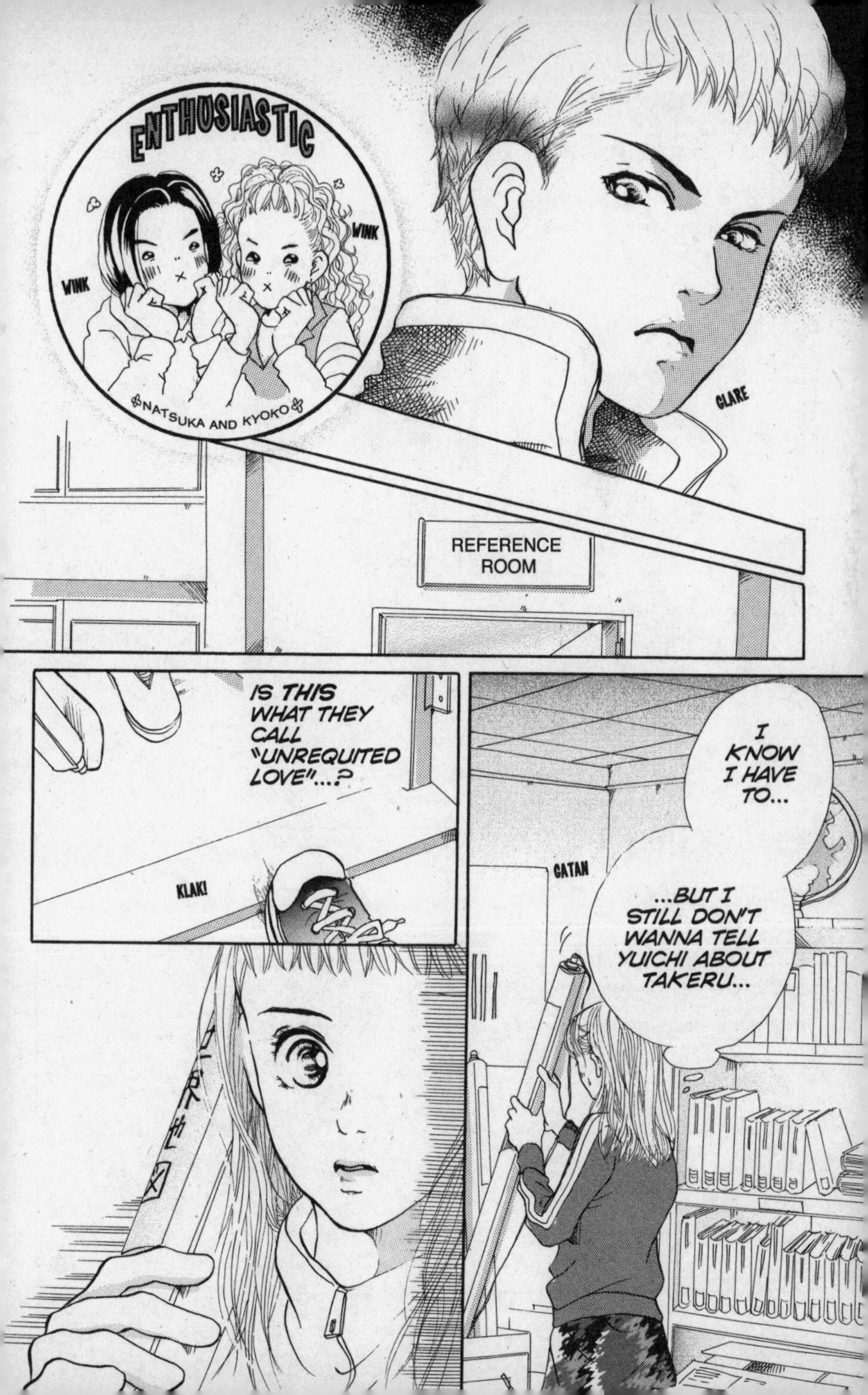
ENTHUSIASTIC
WINK
WINK
NATSUKA AND KYOKO
GLARE
REFERENCE ROOM
I KNOW I HAVE TO...
GATAN
...BUT I STILL DON'T WANNA TELL YUICHI ABOUT TAKERU...
IS THIS WHAT THEY CALL "UNREQUITED LOVE"...?
KLAK!

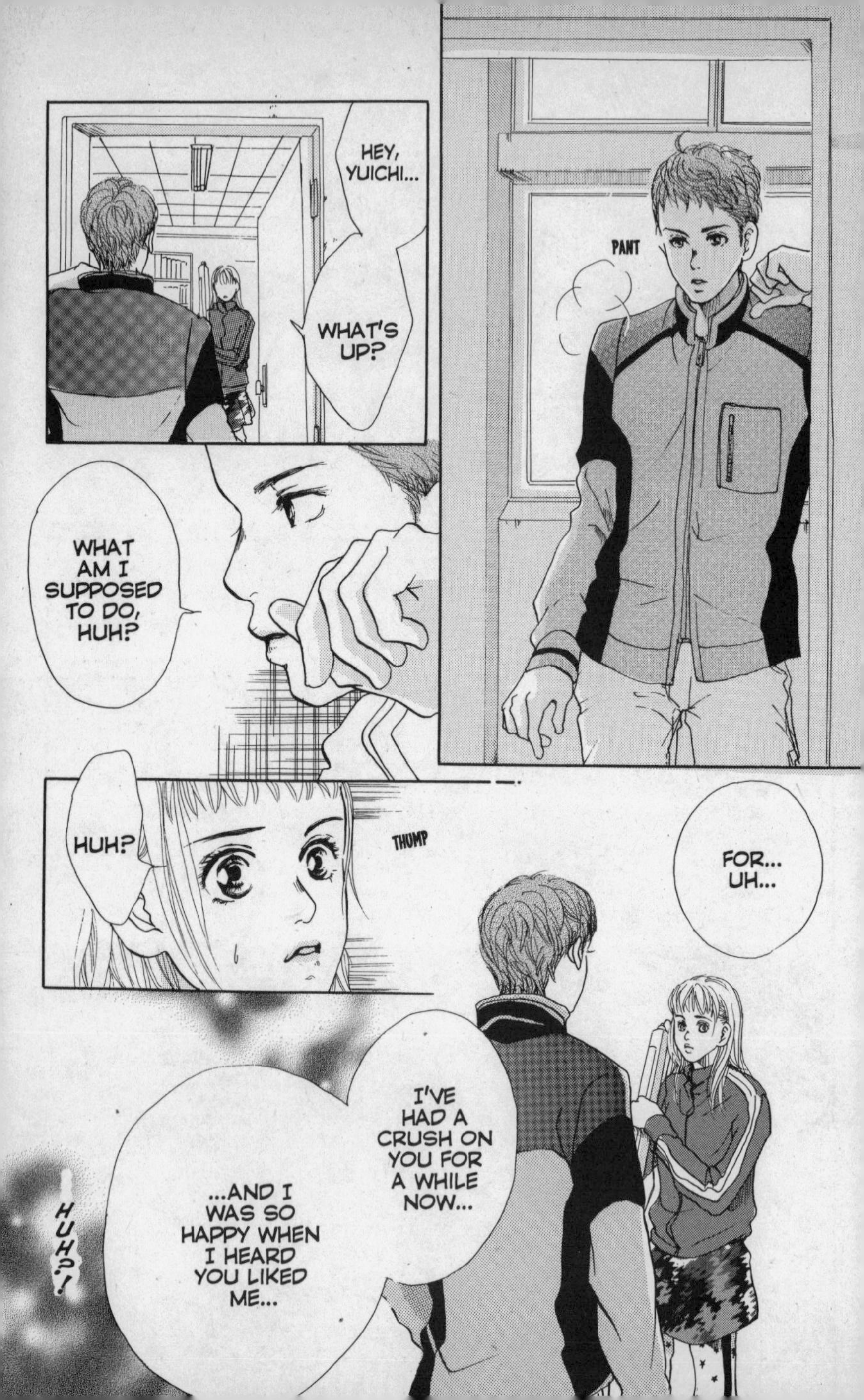
PANT
HEY, YUICHI...
WHAT'S UP?
WHAT AM I SUPPOSED TO DO, HUH?
HUH?
THUMP
FOR... UH...
I'VE HAD A CRUSH ON YOU FOR A WHILE NOW...
...AND I WAS SO HAPPY WHEN I HEARD YOU LIKED ME...
HUH?!

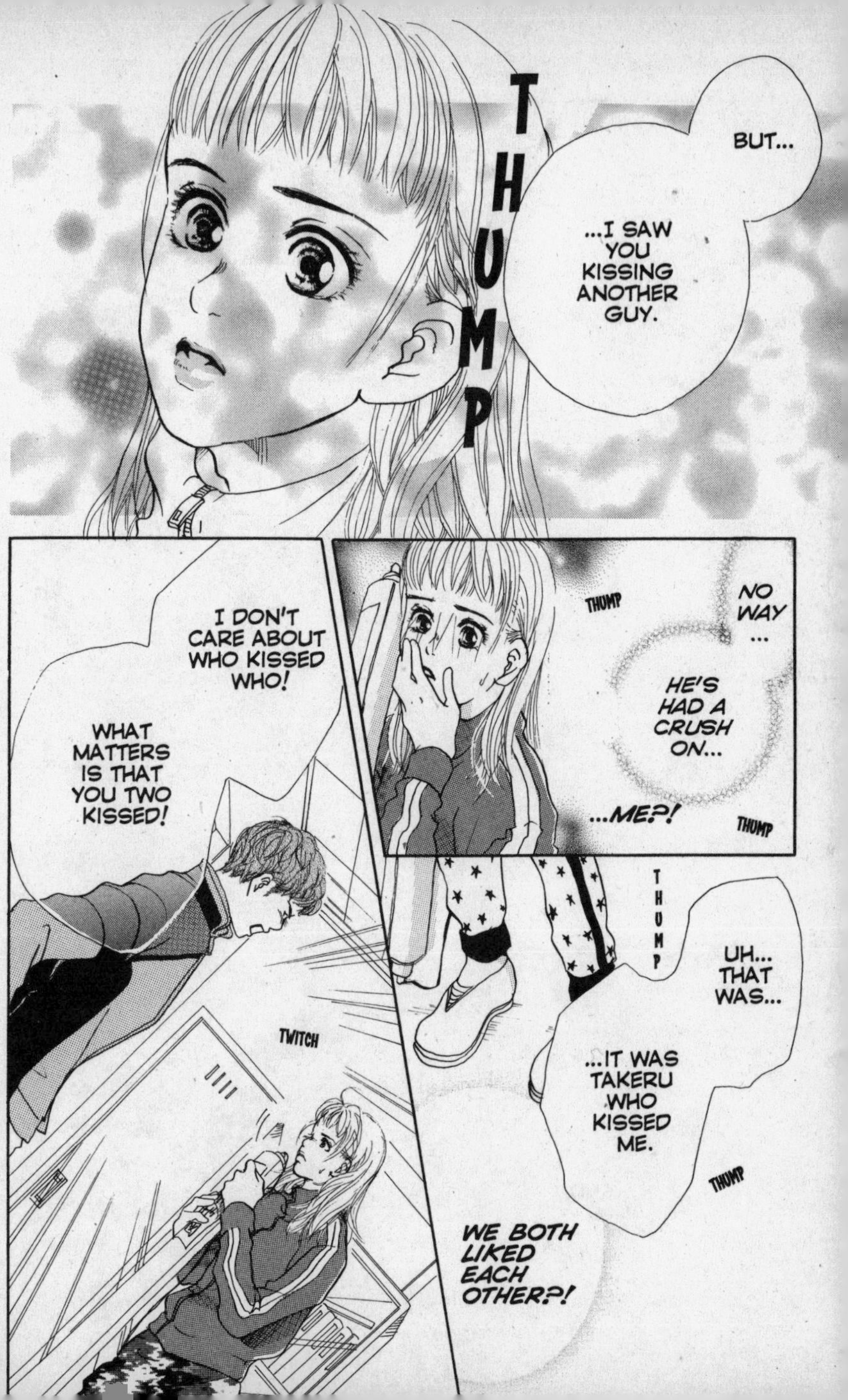
THUMP
BUT...
...I SAW YOU KISSING ANOTHER GUY.
THUMP
NO WAY...
HE'S HAD A CRUSH ON...
...ME?!
THUMP
THUMP
UH... THAT WAS...
...IT WAS TAKERU WHO KISSED ME.
THUMP
WE BOTH LIKED EACH OTHER?!
I DON'T CARE ABOUT WHO KISSED WHO!
WHAT MATTERS IS THAT YOU TWO KISSED!
TWITCH

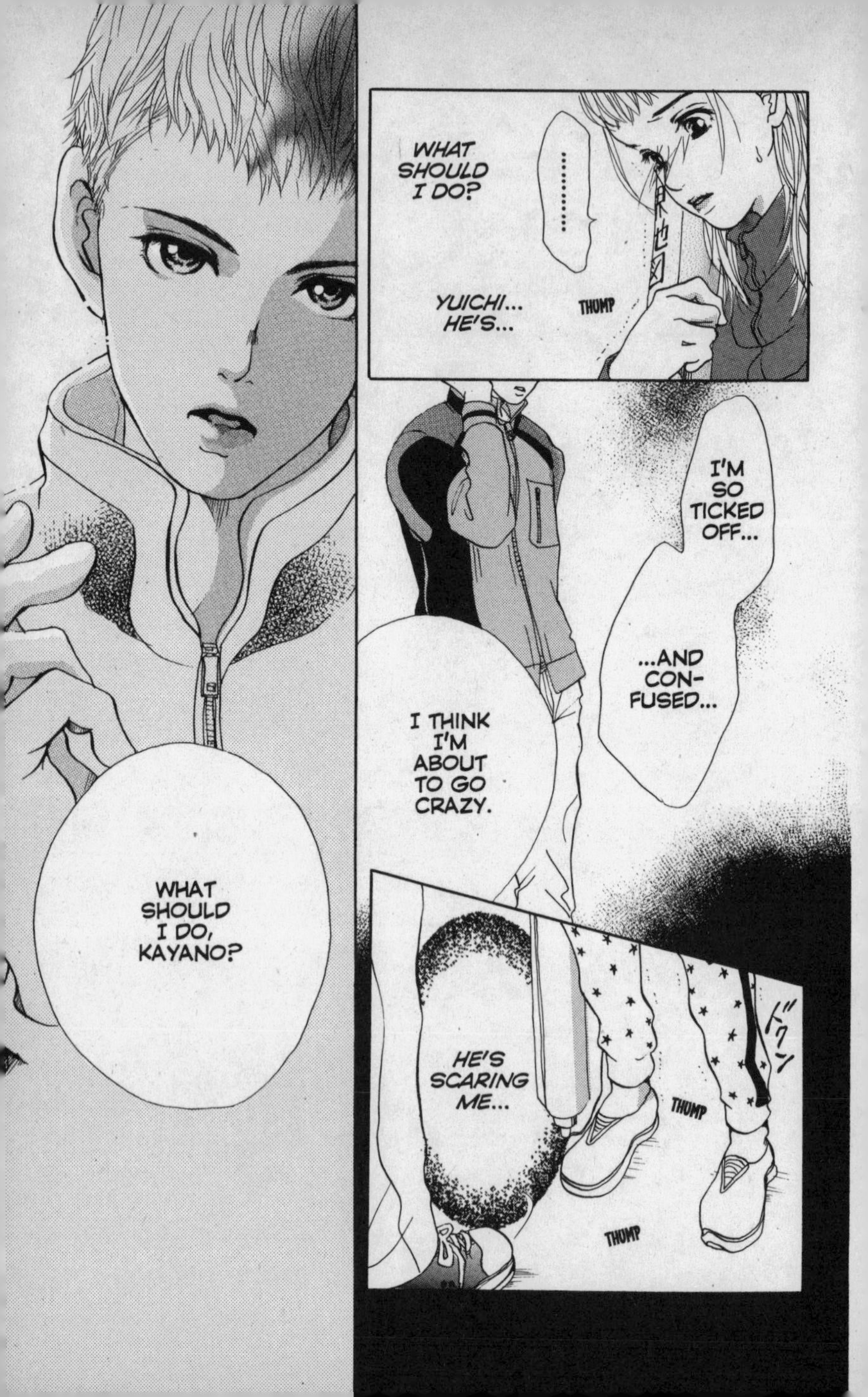
......
WHAT SHOULD I DO?
THUMP
YUICHI... HE'S...
I'M SO TICKED OFF...
...AND CON-FUSED...
I THINK I'M ABOUT TO GO CRAZY.
ドクン
THUMP
HE'S SCARING ME...
THUMP
WHAT SHOULD I DO, KAYANO?

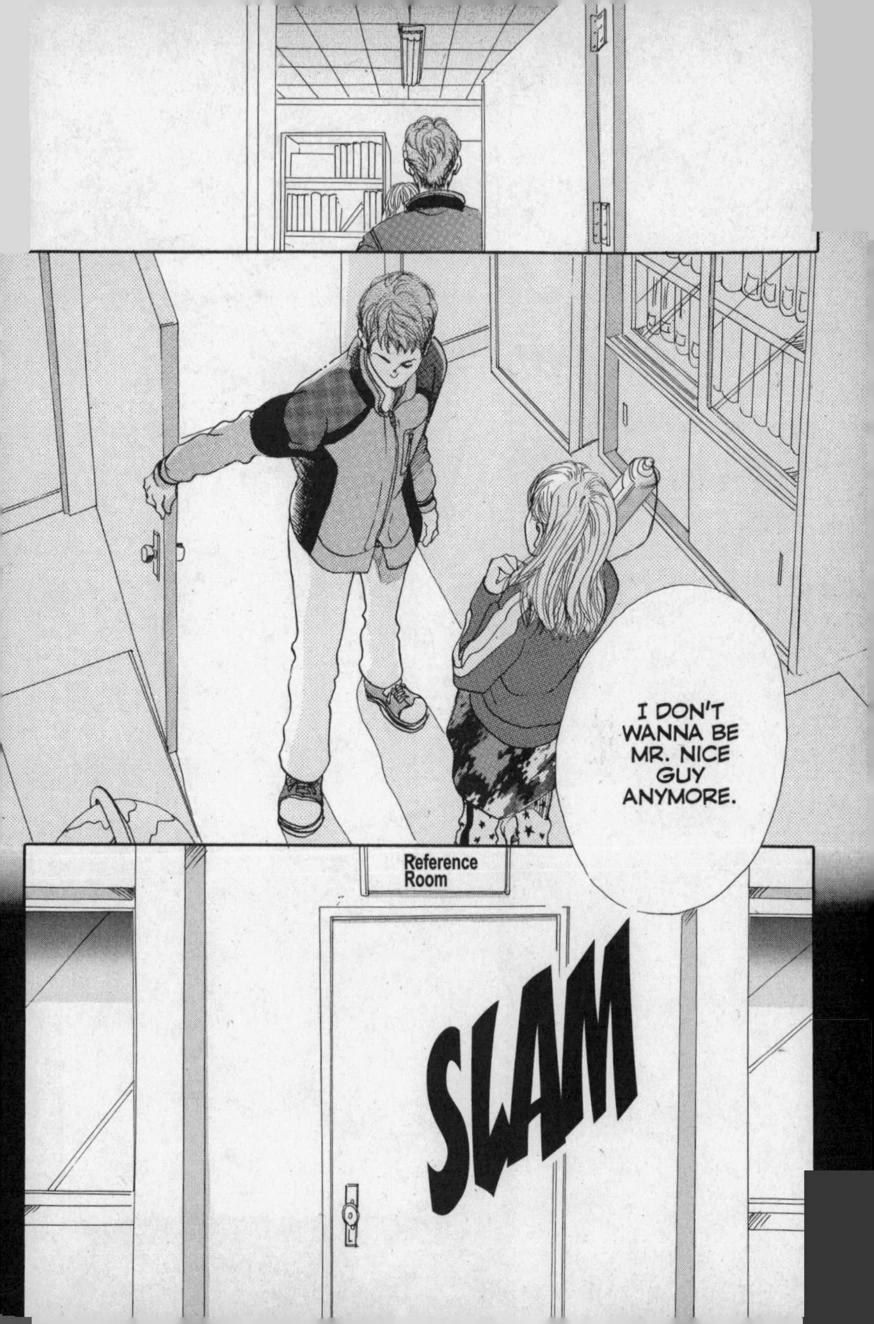
I DON'T WANNA BE MR. NICE GUY ANYMORE.
Reference Room
SLAM

Chapter 4: Wandering

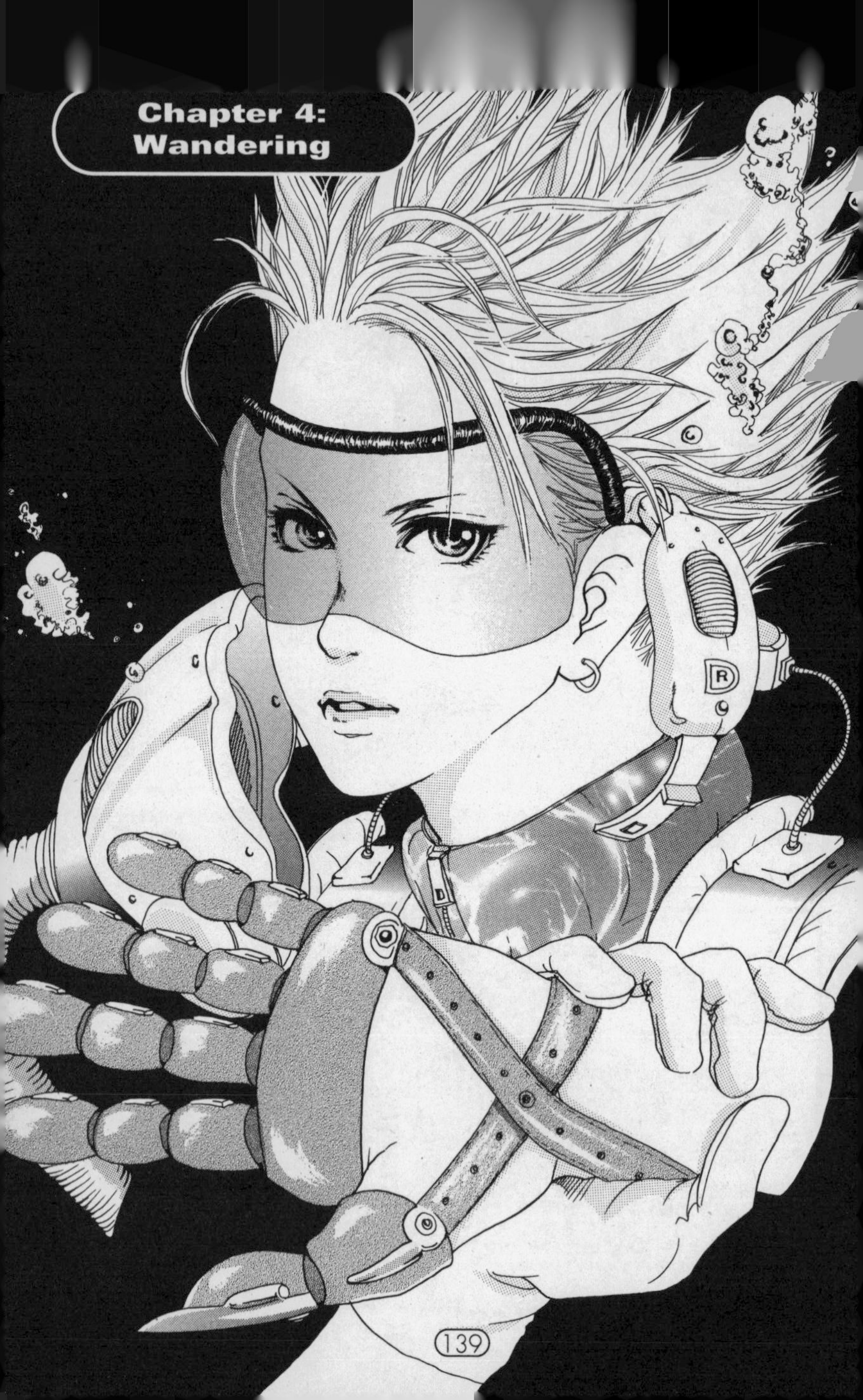

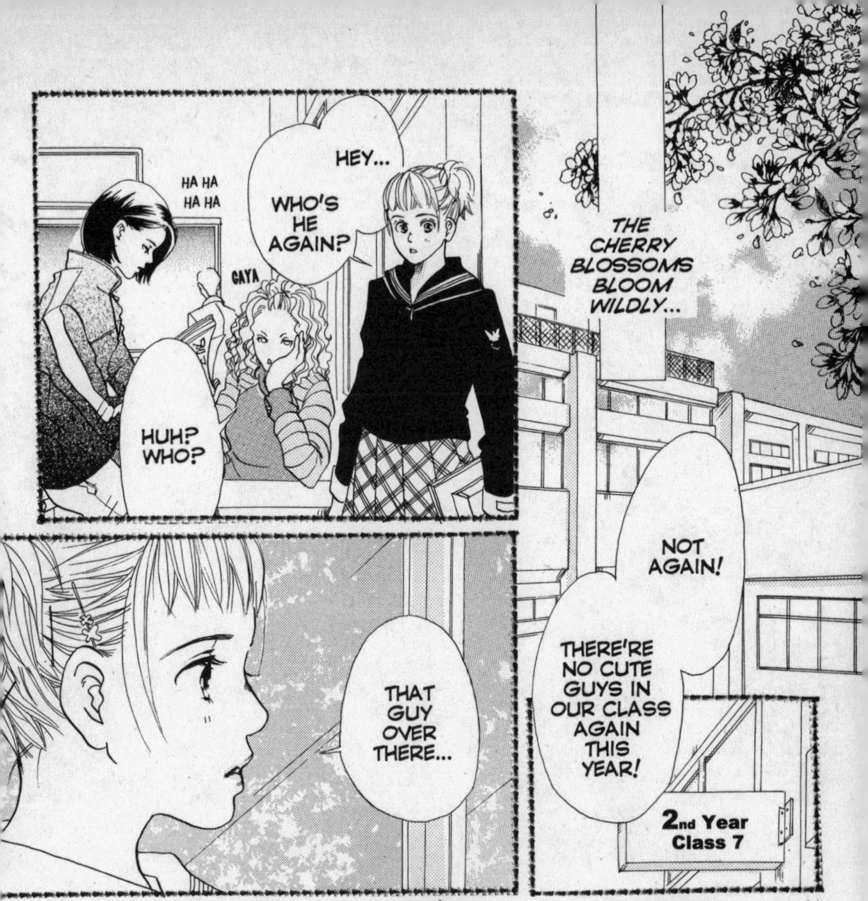
THE CHERRY BLOSSOMS BLOOM WILDLY...
NOT AGAIN!
THERE'RE NO CUTE GUYS IN OUR CLASS AGAIN THIS YEAR!
2nd Year Class 7
HEY... WHO'S HE AGAIN?
HA HA HA HA
GAYA
HUH? WHO?
THAT GUY OVER THERE...

THE DEVIL DOES EXIST Q & A

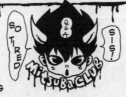

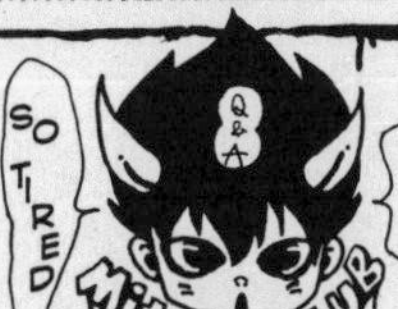
SIS!
Q&A
SO TIRED
MitsuBa CLUB

Q: IS IT OKAY IF I CALL YOU "MITSUBA-CHI?" FROM S IN AICHI-KEN

A: OKAY!! CALL ME ANYTHING YOU WANT!

Q: IS IT OKAY IF I CALL YOU *BIG SIS?* FROM A IN SHIZUOKA-KEN.

A: UH...NO. I'M SORRY, BUT I'M AFRAID I'LL HAVE TO DRAW THE LINE THERE.

Q: HOW COME YOU WANT TO TURN INTO A LION? FROM R IN TOKYO.

A: HOW COME I WANT TO BE A LION?? WELL...UM...*IT'S BECAUSE I WANT TO EAT YOU!!* THAT'S WHY. IT'S GETTING TO THE END OF THE BOOK, AND I'M TIRED, SO I BELIEVE THIS IS THE END OF Q & A TIME. I'M SORRY THAT I WASN'T ABLE TO ANSWER ALL OF YOUR LETTERS. INSTEAD, I CREATED THIS Q & A CORNER. SORRY I COULDN'T DO MORE!

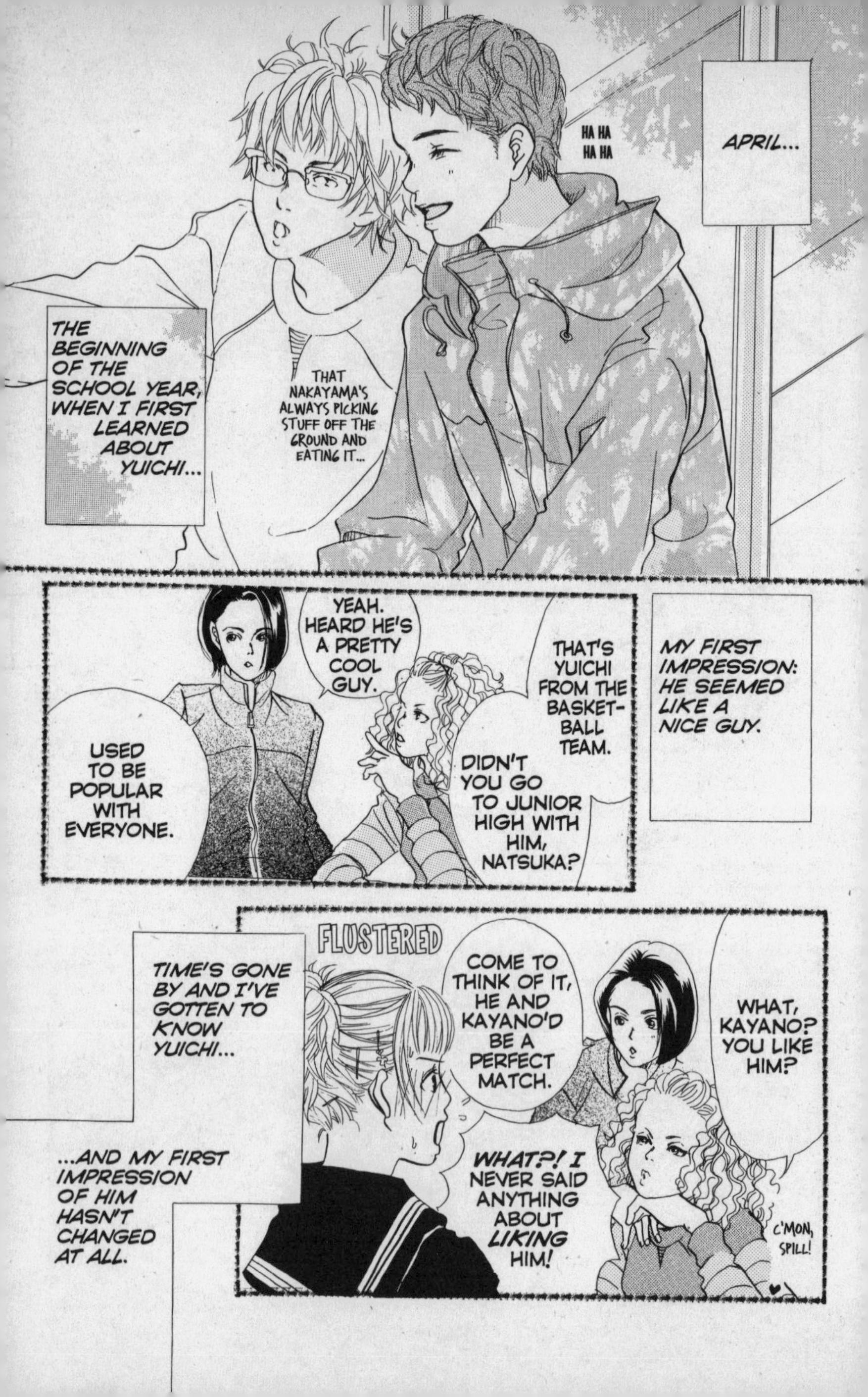
APRIL...
HA HA HA HA
THAT NAKAYAMA'S ALWAYS PICKING STUFF OFF THE GROUND AND EATING IT...
THE BEGINNING OF THE SCHOOL YEAR, WHEN I FIRST LEARNED ABOUT YUICHI...
MY FIRST IMPRESSION: HE SEEMED LIKE A NICE GUY.
THAT'S YUICHI FROM THE BASKET-BALL TEAM.
DIDN'T YOU GO TO JUNIOR HIGH WITH HIM, NATSUKA?
YEAH. HEARD HE'S A PRETTY COOL GUY.
USED TO BE POPULAR WITH EVERYONE.
WHAT, KAYANO? YOU LIKE HIM?
COME TO THINK OF IT, HE AND KAYANO'D BE A PERFECT MATCH.
FLUSTERED
C'MON, SPILL!
WHAT?! I NEVER SAID ANYTHING ABOUT LIKING HIM!
TIME'S GONE BY AND I'VE GOTTEN TO KNOW YUICHI...
...AND MY FIRST IMPRESSION OF HIM HASN'T CHANGED AT ALL.

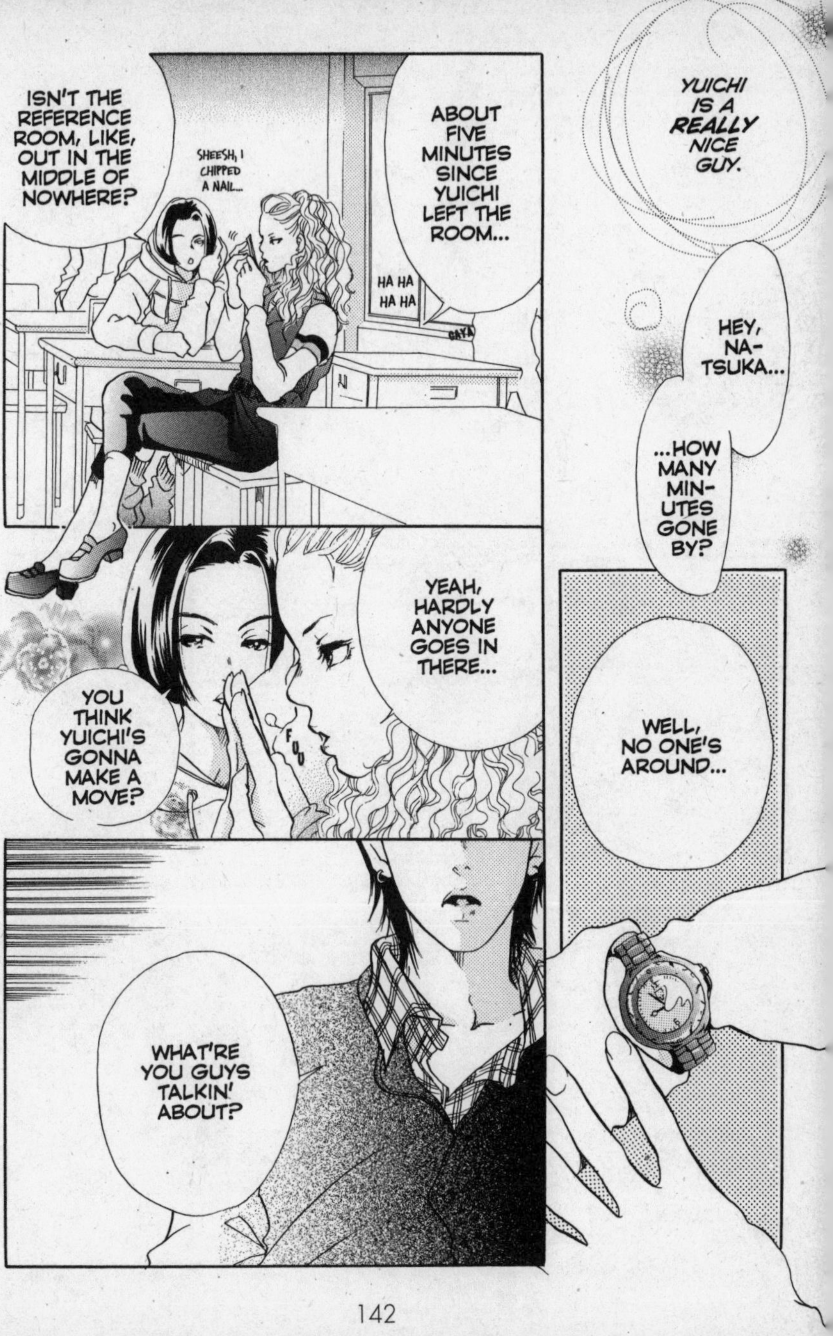
YUICHI IS A REALLY NICE GUY.
HEY, NA-TSUKA...
...HOW MANY MIN-UTES GONE BY?
WELL, NO ONE'S AROUND...
ABOUT FIVE MINUTES SINCE YUICHI LEFT THE ROOM...
GAYA
HA HA HA HA
SHEESH, I CHIPPED A NAIL...
ISN'T THE REFERENCE ROOM, LIKE, OUT IN THE MIDDLE OF NOWHERE?
YEAH, HARDLY ANYONE GOES IN THERE...
FUU
YOU THINK YUICHI'S GONNA MAKE A MOVE?
WHAT'RE YOU GUYS TALKIN' ABOUT?

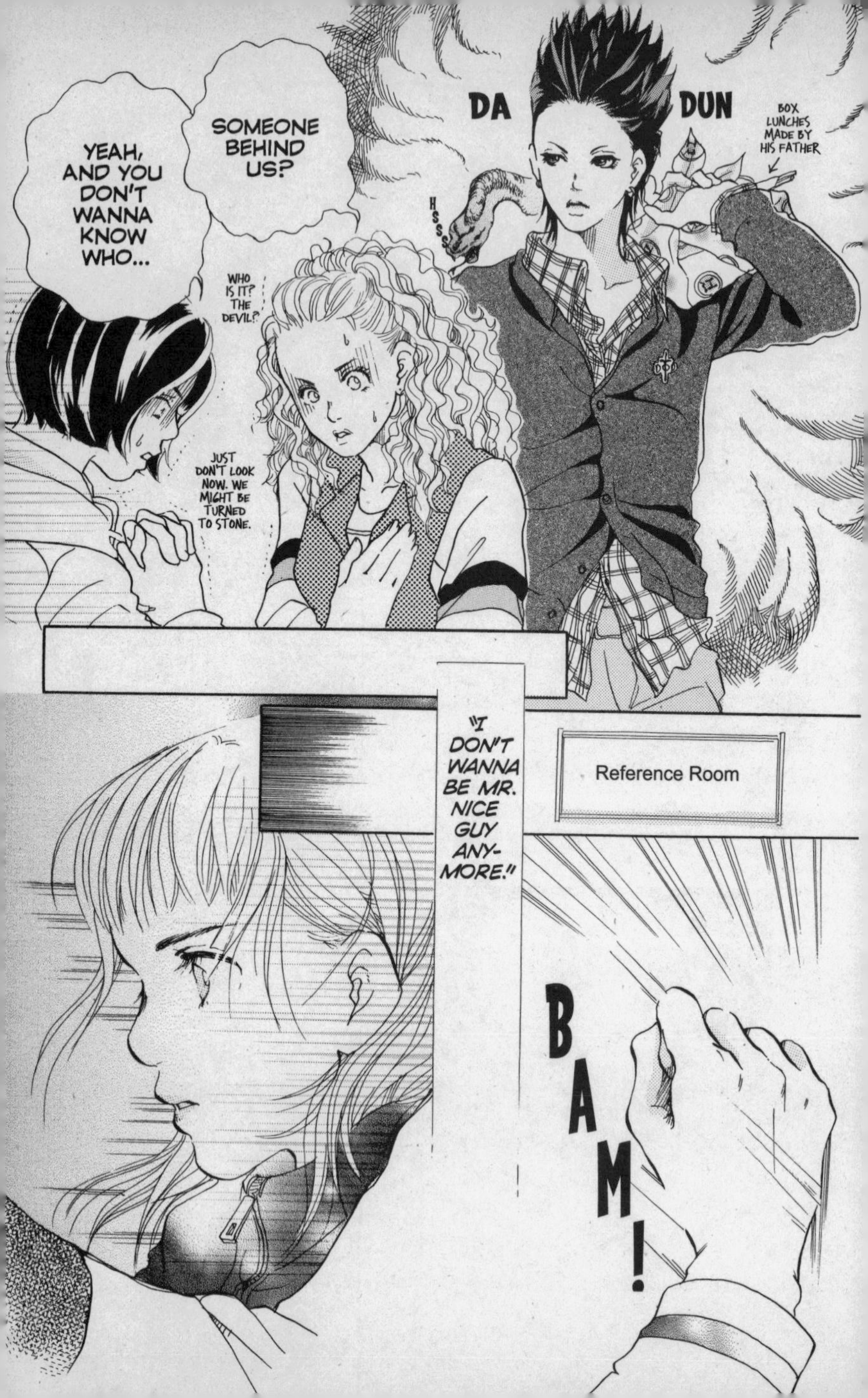
DA DUN
BOX LUNCHES MADE BY HIS FATHER
HSSS
SOMEONE BEHIND US?
YEAH, AND YOU DON'T WANNA KNOW WHO...
WHO IS IT? THE DEVIL?
JUST DON'T LOOK NOW. WE MIGHT BE TURNED TO STONE.
Reference Room
BAM!
"I DON'T WANNA BE MR. NICE GUY ANYMORE."

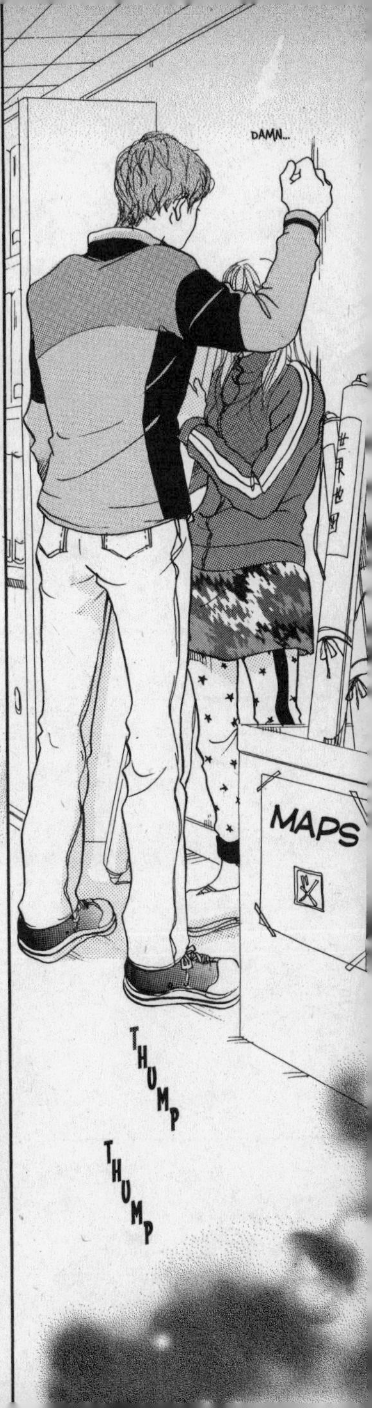
DAMN...
MAPS
THUMP
THUMP
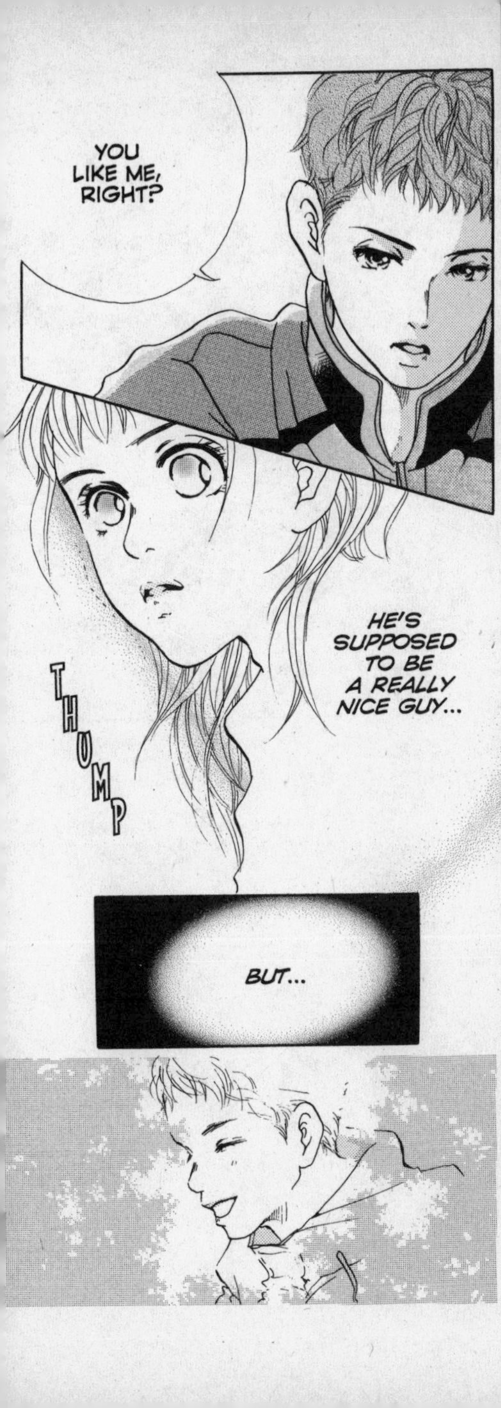
YOU LIKE ME, RIGHT?
HE'S SUPPOSED TO BE A REALLY NICE GUY...
THUMP
BUT...

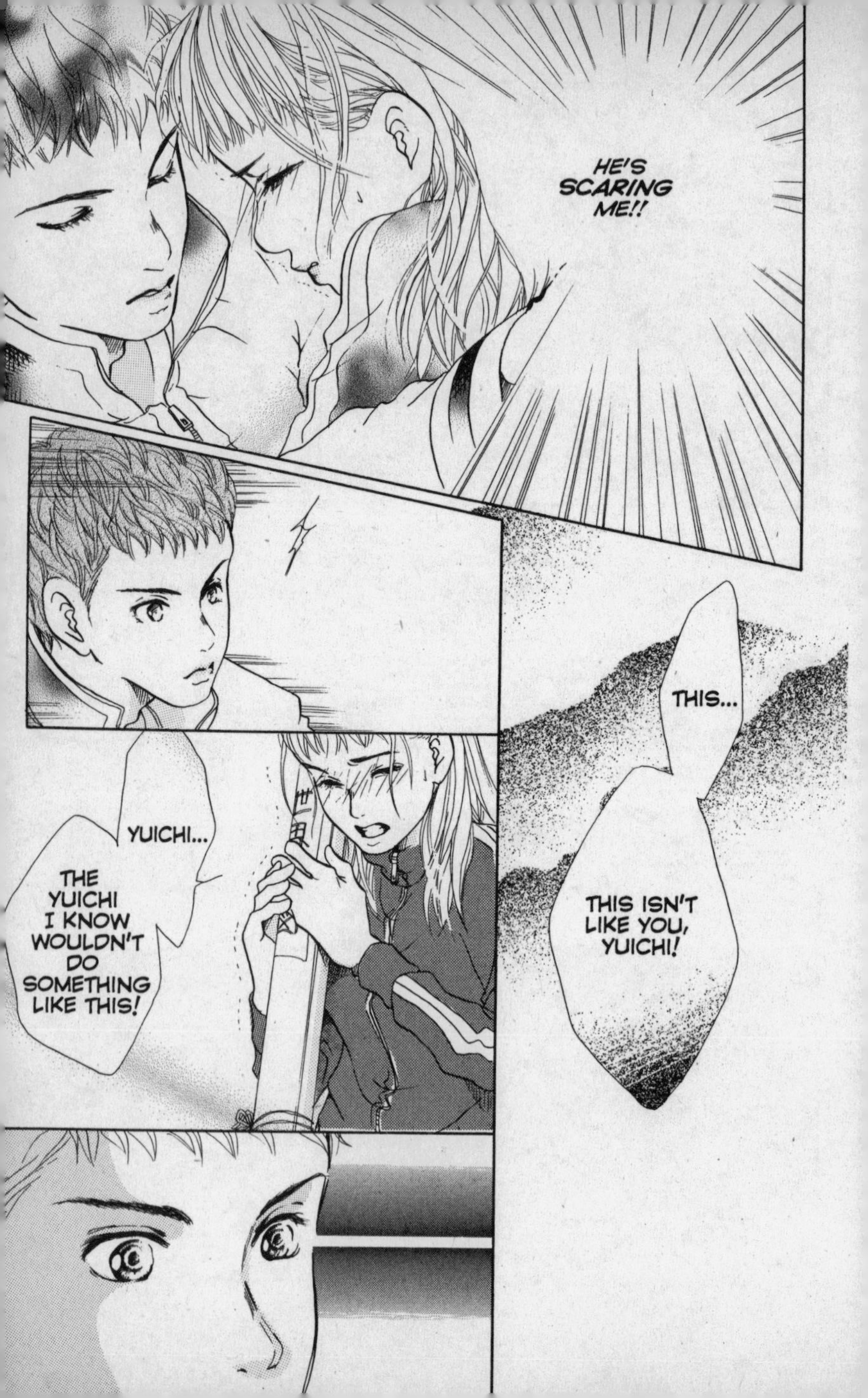
HE'S SCARING ME!!
THIS...
THIS ISN'T LIKE YOU, YUICHI!
YUICHI...
THE YUICHI I KNOW WOULDN'T DO SOMETHING LIKE THIS!

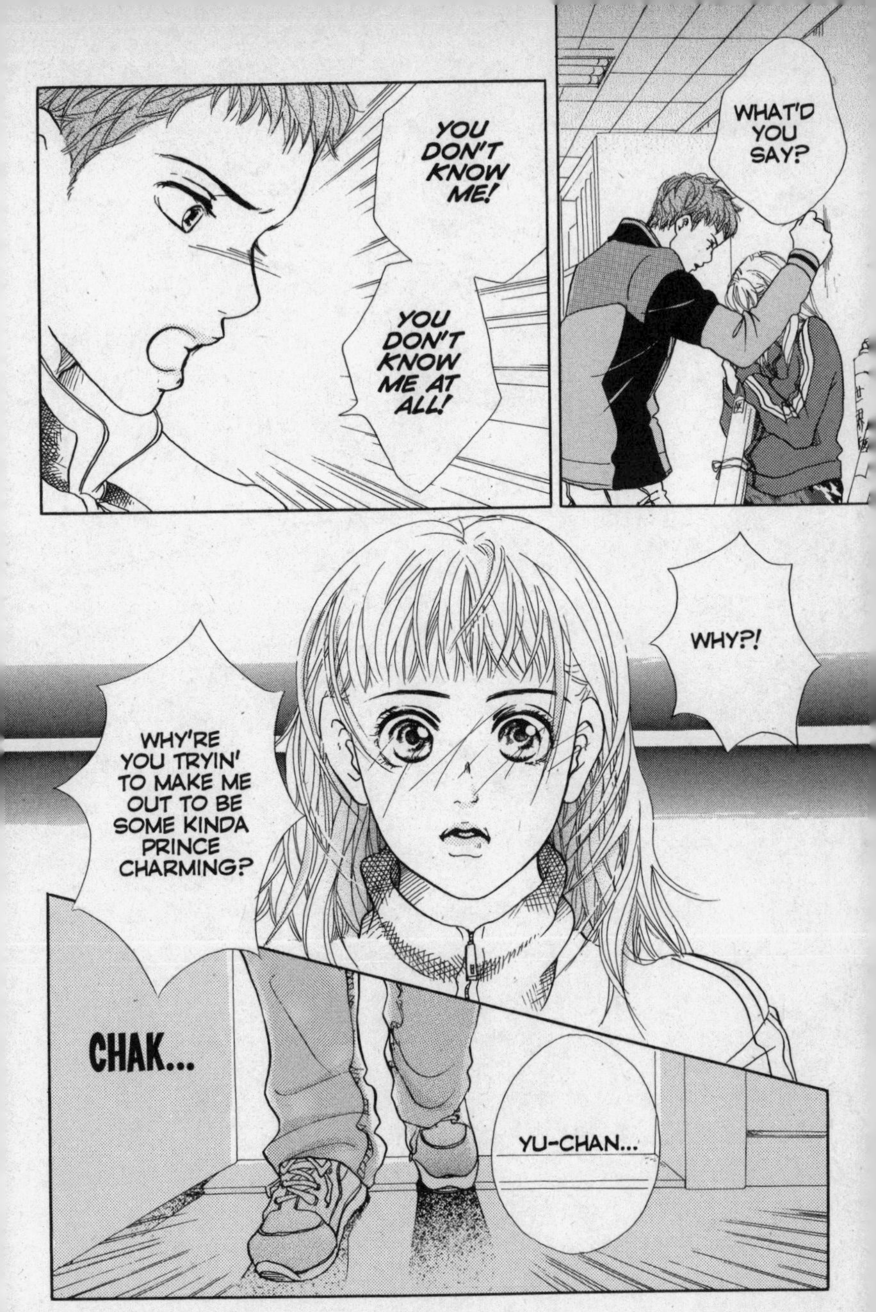
WHAT'D YOU SAY?
YOU DON'T KNOW ME!
YOU DON'T KNOW ME AT ALL!
WHY?!
WHY'RE YOU TRYIN' TO MAKE ME OUT TO BE SOME KINDA PRINCE CHARMING?
YU-CHAN...
CHAK...

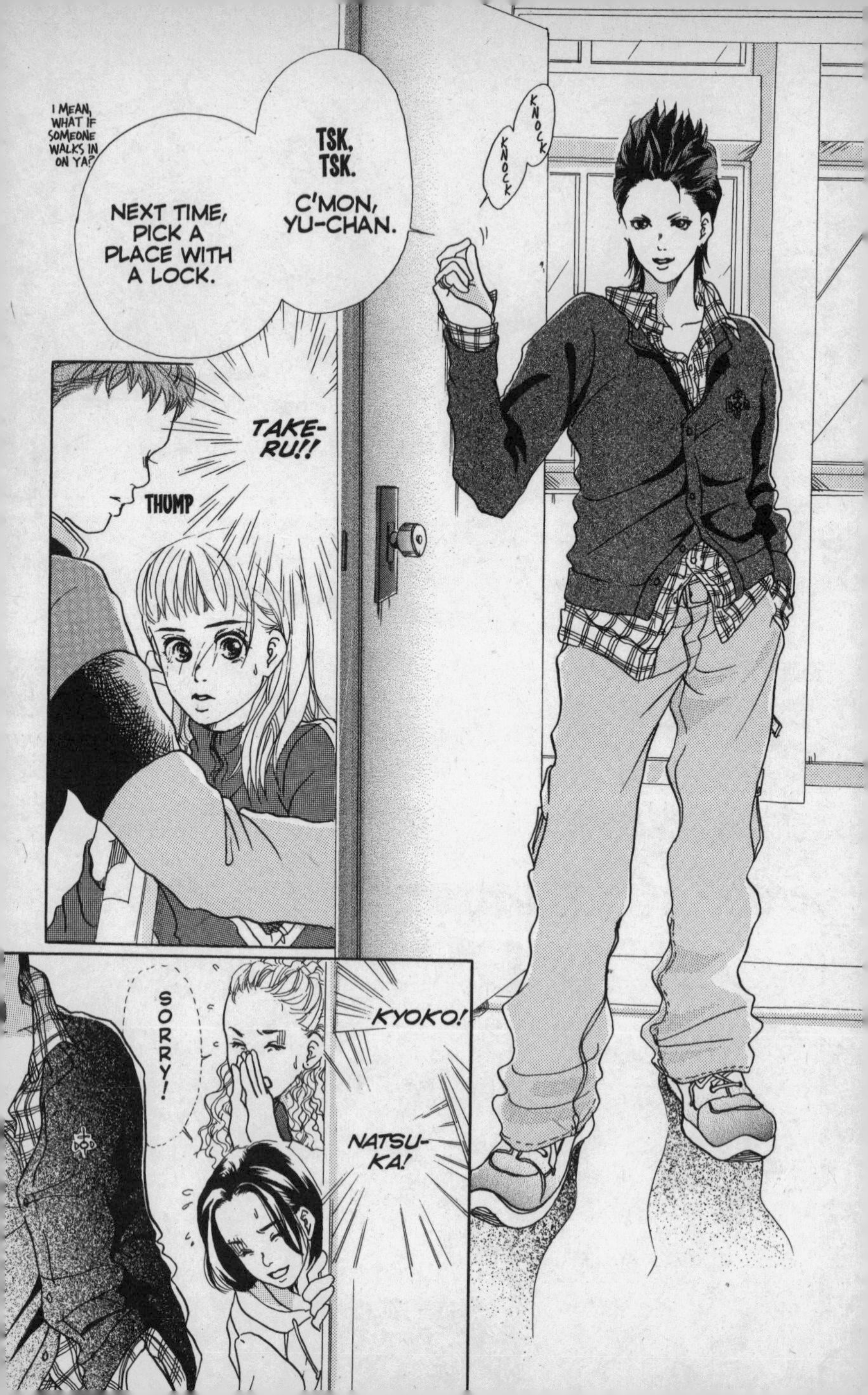
KNOCK KNOCK
TSK, TSK. C'MON, YU-CHAN.
NEXT TIME, PICK A PLACE WITH A LOCK.
I MEAN, WHAT IF SOMEONE WALKS IN ON YA?
TAKE-RU!!
THUMP
KYOKO!
SORRY!
NATSU-KA!

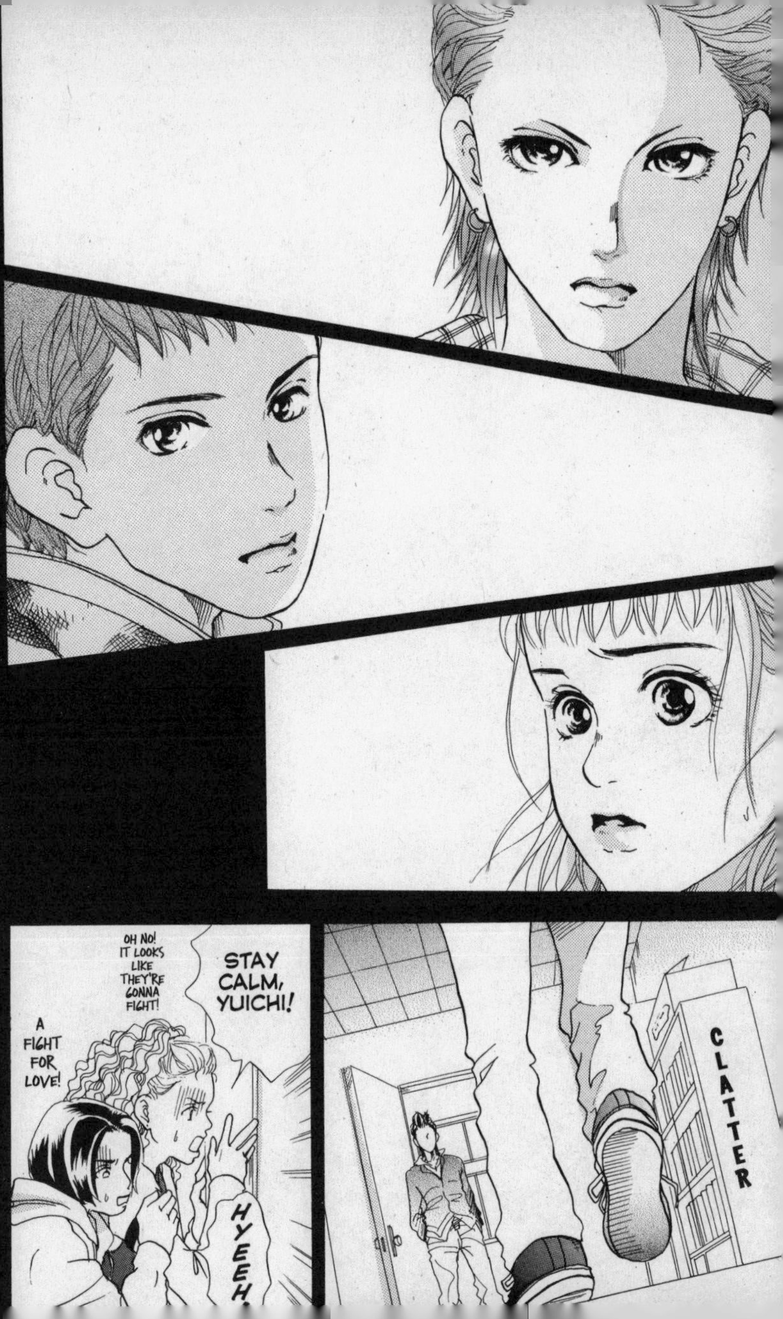

CLATTER
STAY CALM, YUICHI!
OH NO! IT LOOKS LIKE THEY'RE GONNA FIGHT!
A FIGHT FOR LOVE!
HYEEH

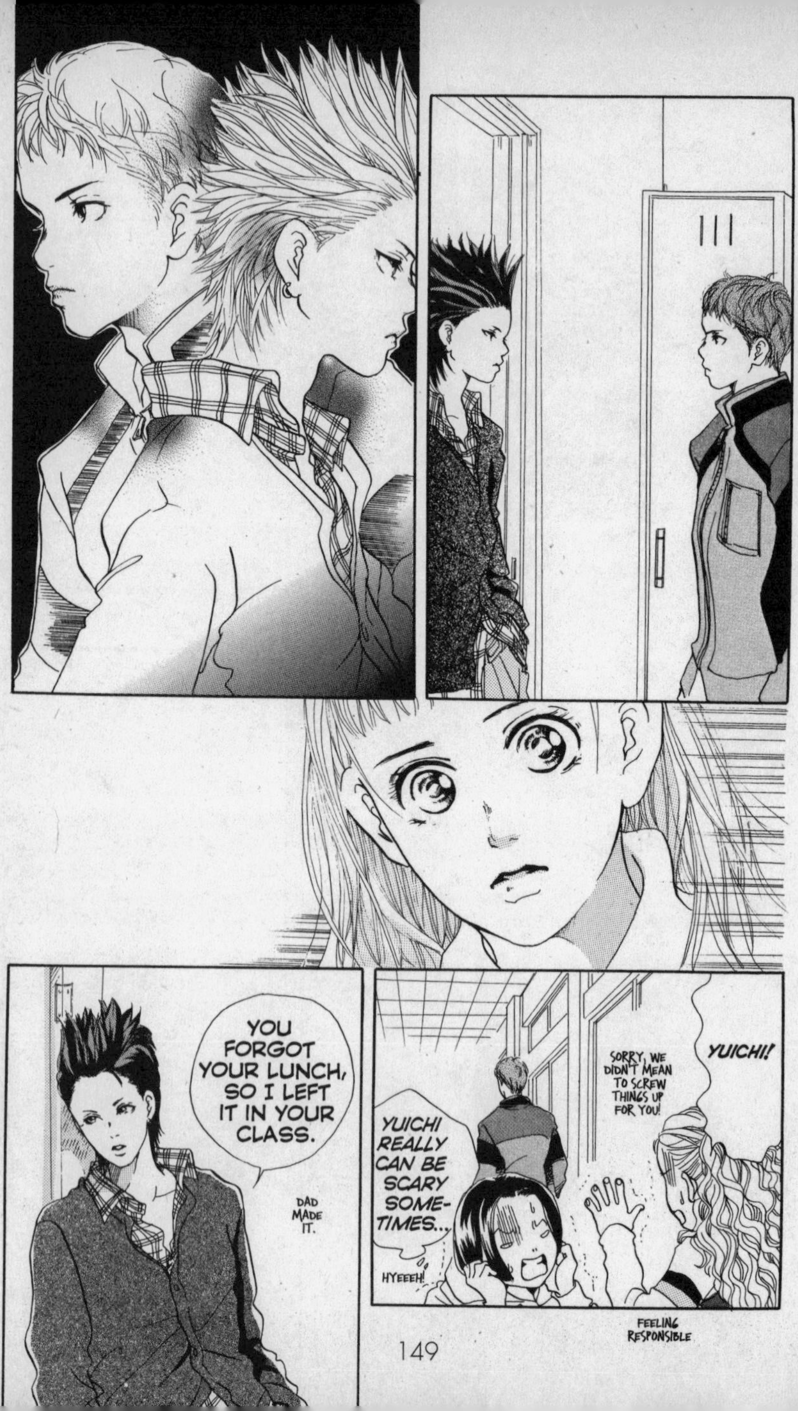
YUICHI!
SORRY, WE DIDN'T MEAN TO SCREW THINGS UP FOR YOU!
YUICHI REALLY CAN BE SCARY SOME-TIMES...
HYEEEH!
FEELING RESPONSIBLE
YOU FORGOT YOUR LUNCH, SO I LEFT IT IN YOUR CLASS.
DAD MADE IT.

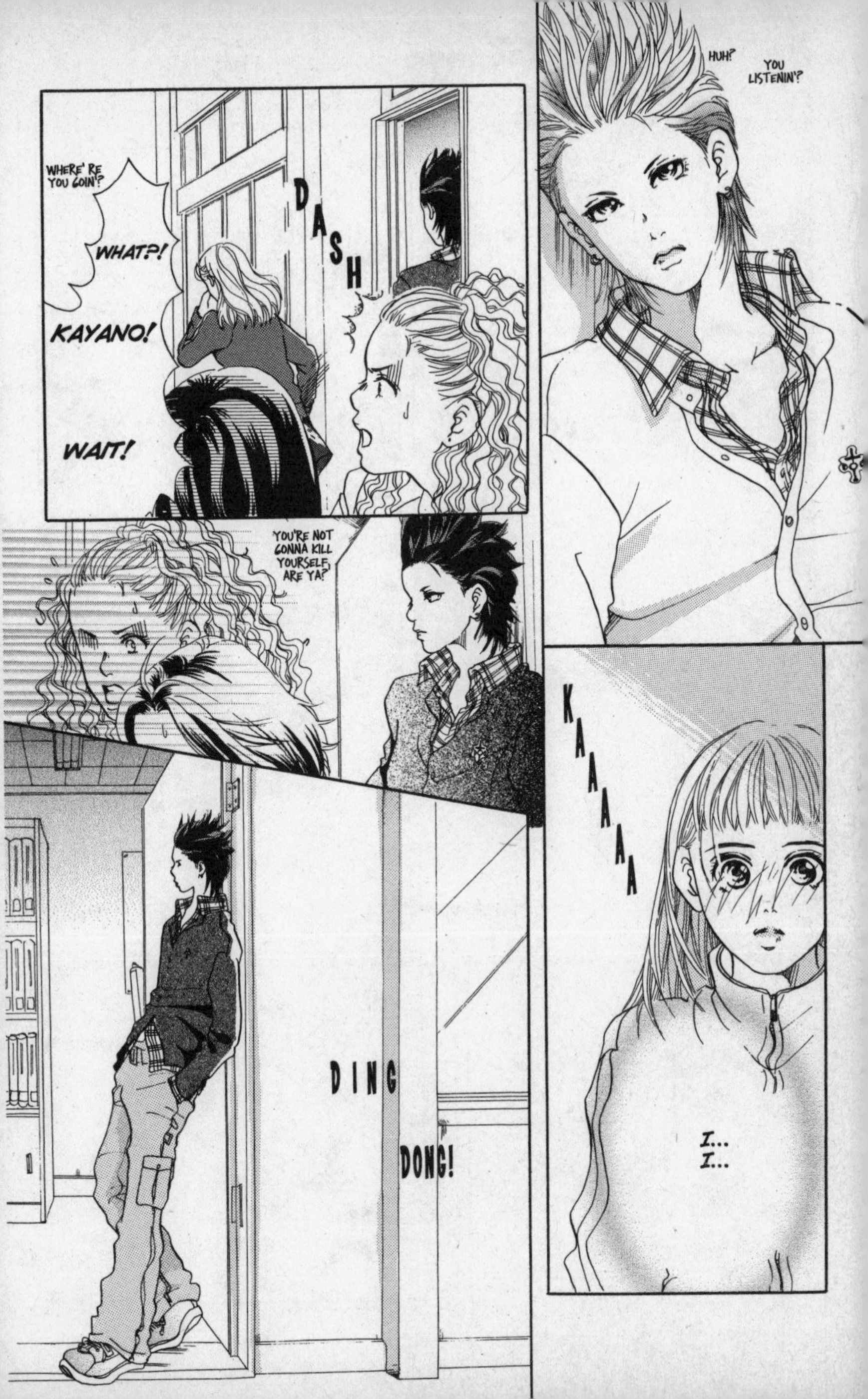
YOU LISTENIN'?
HUH?
KAAAAAA
I...
I...
DASH
WHERE'RE YOU GOIN'?
WHAT?!
KAYANO!
WAIT!
YOU'RE NOT GONNA KILL YOURSELF, ARE YA?
DING
DONG!

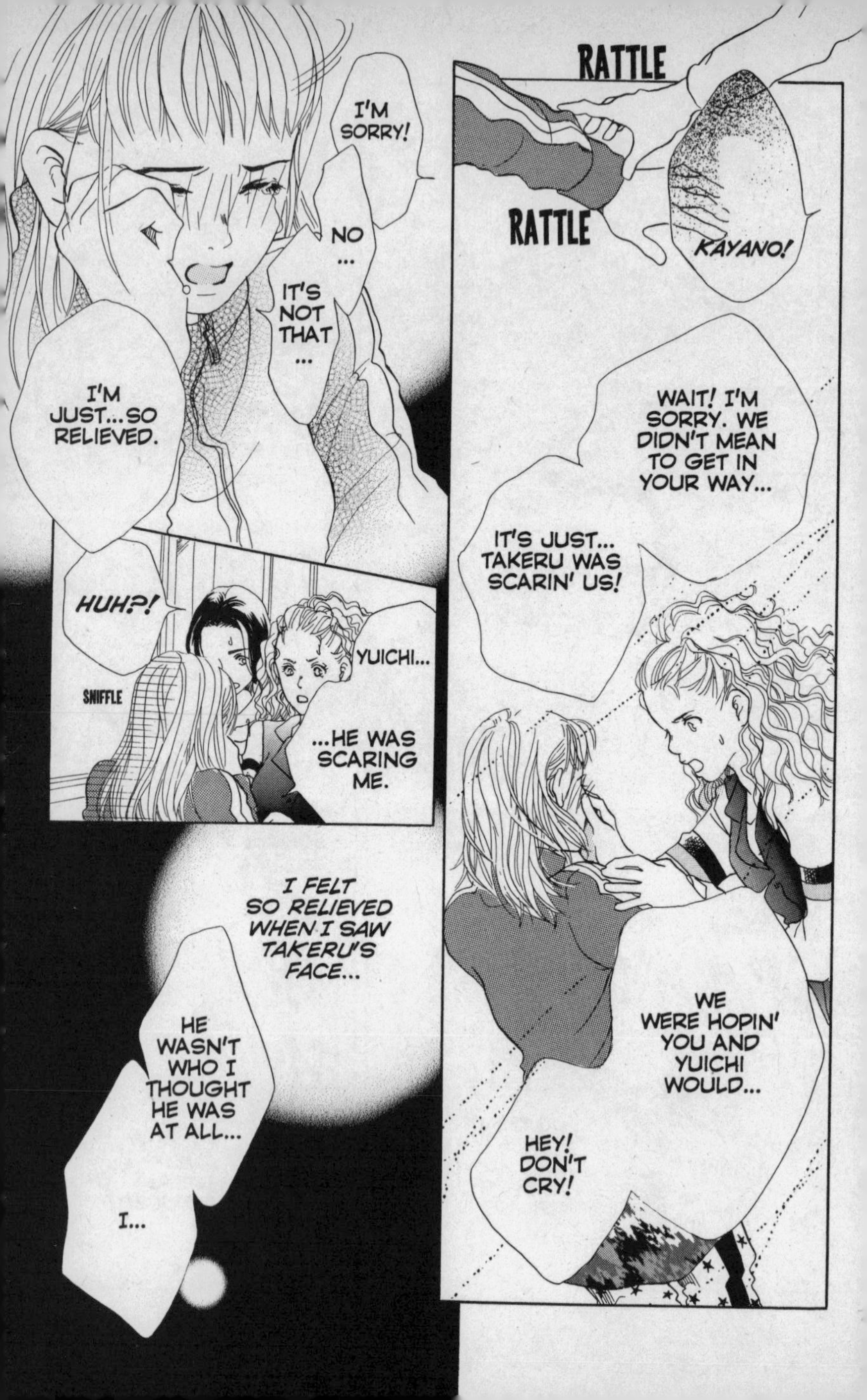
RATTLE
RATTLE
KAYANO!
WAIT! I'M SORRY. WE DIDN'T MEAN TO GET IN YOUR WAY...
IT'S JUST... TAKERU WAS SCARIN' US!
WE WERE HOPIN' YOU AND YUICHI WOULD...
HEY! DON'T CRY!
I'M SORRY!
NO ... IT'S NOT THAT ...
I'M JUST...SO RELIEVED.
YUICHI...
...HE WAS SCARING ME.
HUH?!
SNIFFLE
I FELT SO RELIEVED WHEN I SAW TAKERU'S FACE...
HE WASN'T WHO I THOUGHT HE WAS AT ALL...
I...

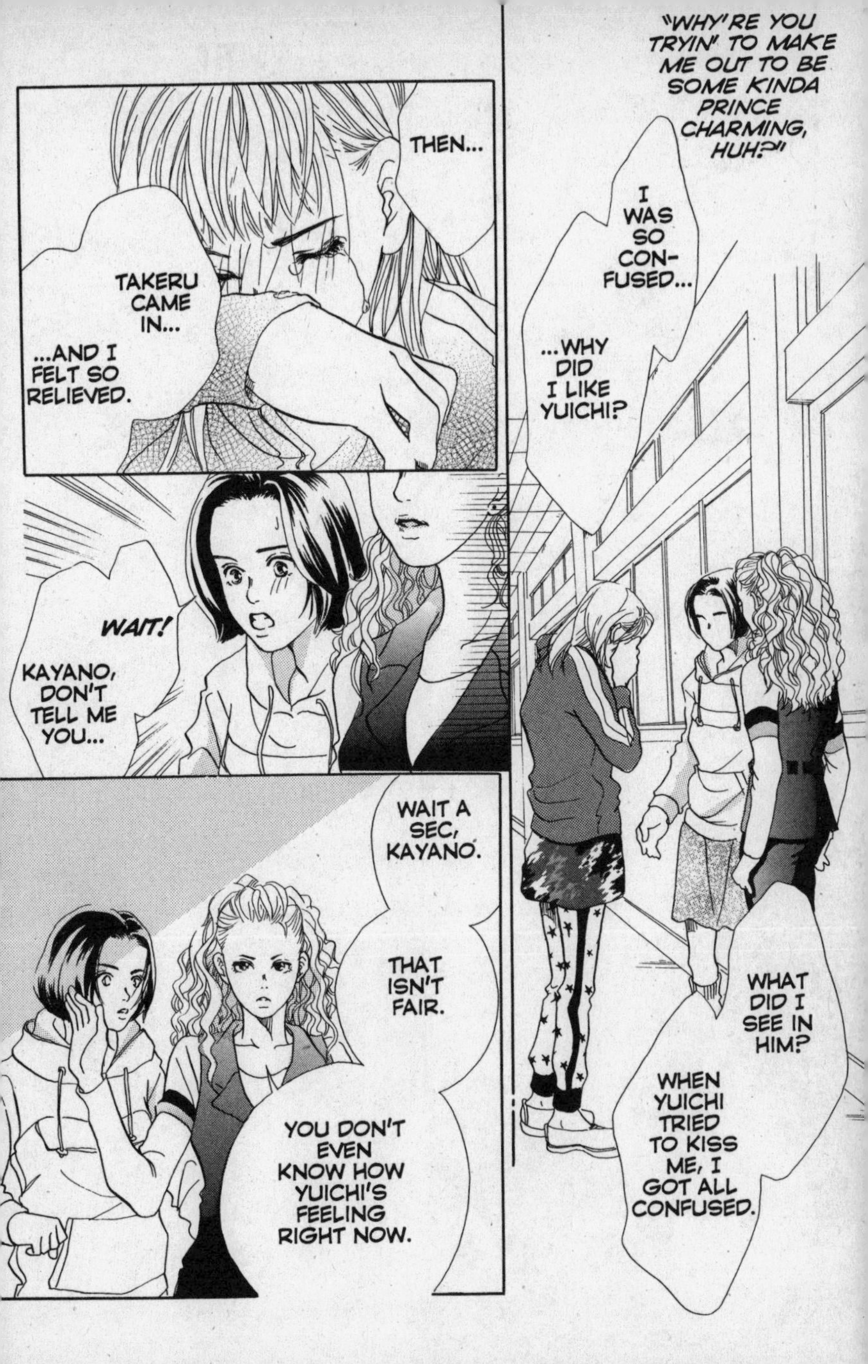
"WHY'RE YOU TRYIN' TO MAKE ME OUT TO BE SOME KINDA PRINCE CHARMING, HUH?"
I WAS SO CON-FUSED...
...WHY DID I LIKE YUICHI?
WHAT DID I SEE IN HIM?
WHEN YUICHI TRIED TO KISS ME, I GOT ALL CONFUSED.
THEN...
TAKERU CAME IN...
...AND I FELT SO RELIEVED.
WAIT!
KAYANO, DON'T TELL ME YOU...
WAIT A SEC, KAYANO.
THAT ISN'T FAIR.
YOU DON'T EVEN KNOW HOW YUICHI'S FEELING RIGHT NOW.

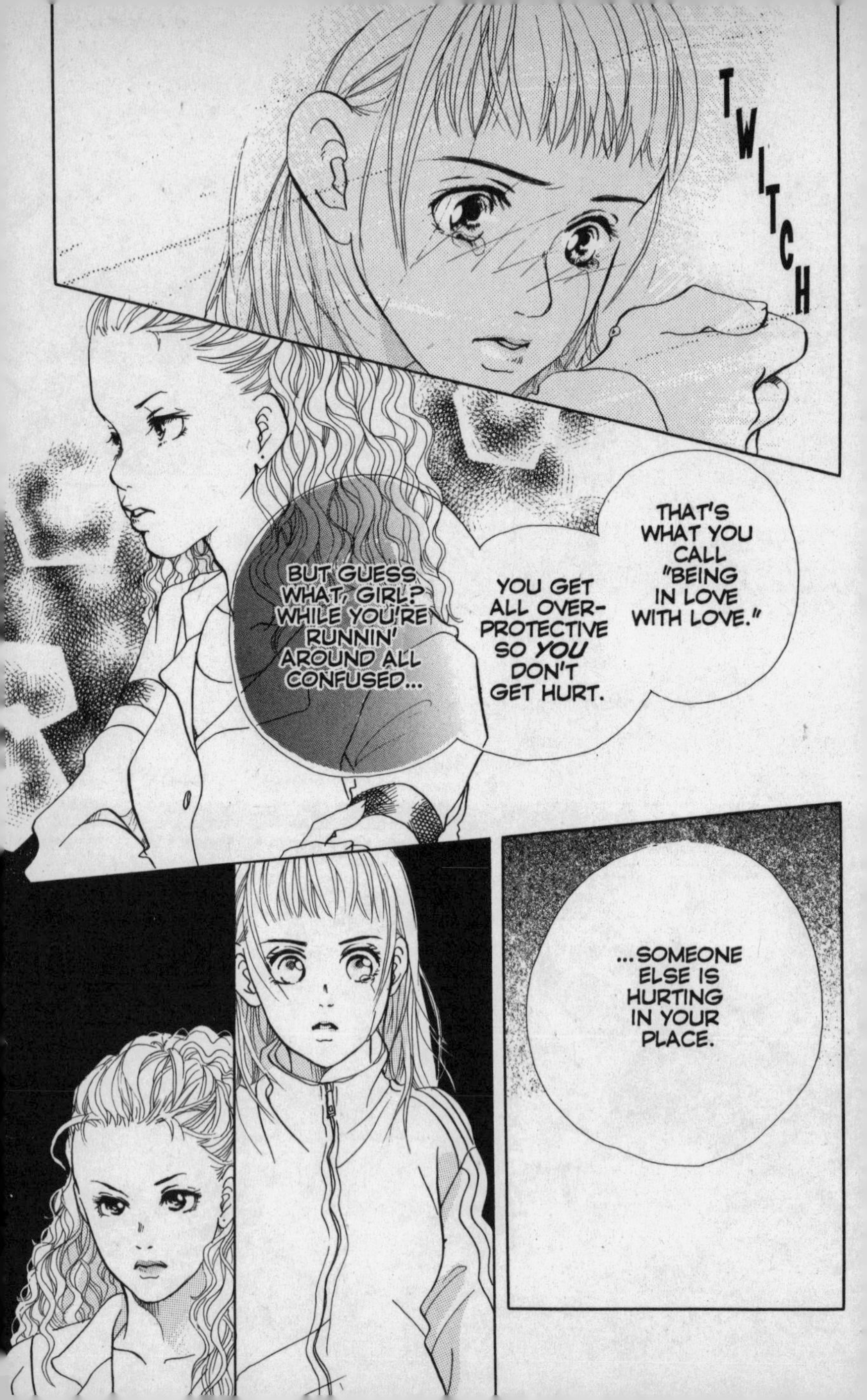
TWITCH
THAT'S WHAT YOU CALL "BEING IN LOVE WITH LOVE."
YOU GET ALL OVER-PROTECTIVE SO *YOU* DON'T GET HURT.
BUT GUESS WHAT, GIRL? WHILE YOU'RE RUNNIN' AROUND ALL CONFUSED...
...SOMEONE ELSE IS HURTING IN YOUR PLACE.

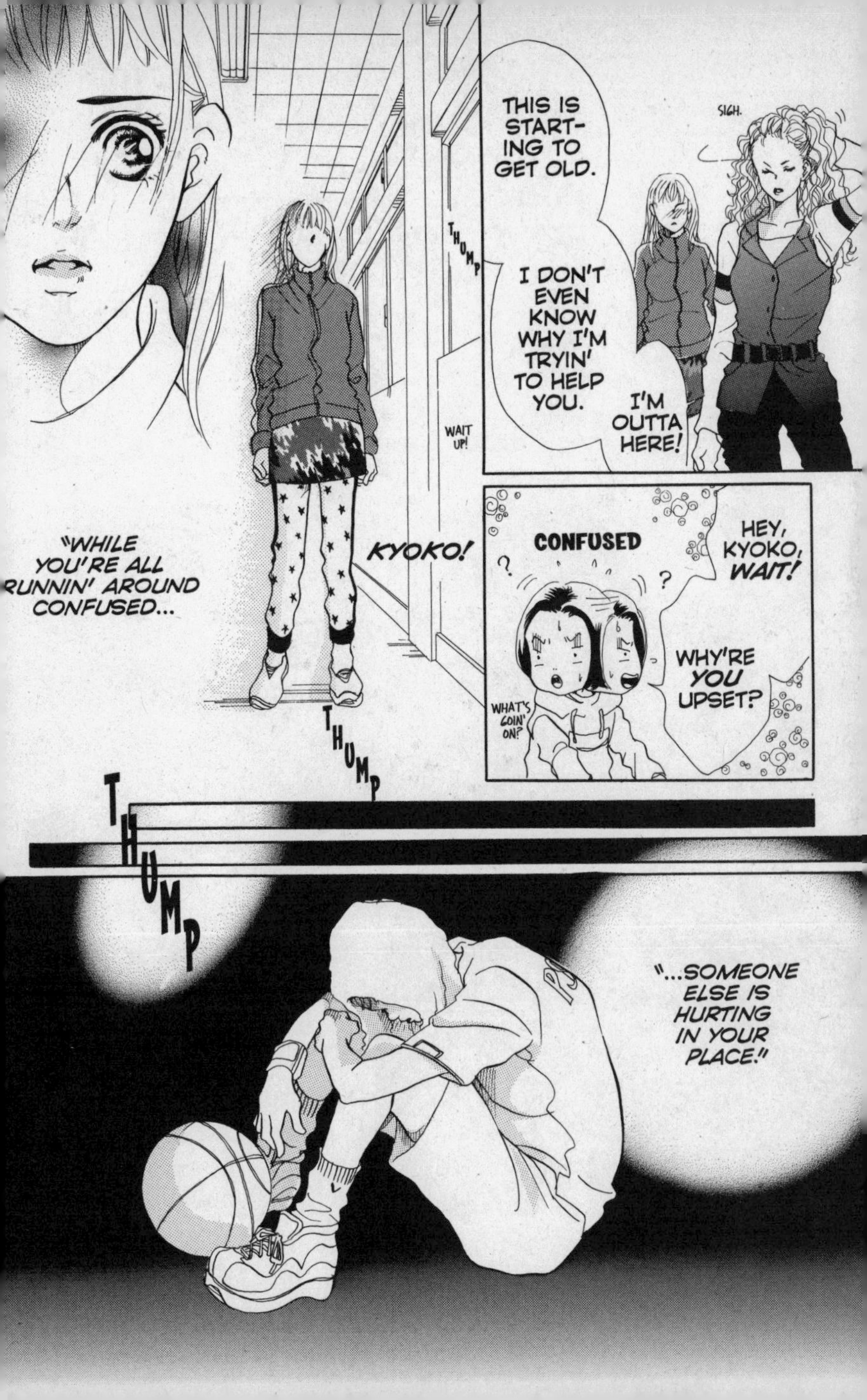

SIGH.
THIS IS STARTING-ING TO GET OLD.
I DON'T EVEN KNOW WHY I'M TRYIN' TO HELP YOU.
I'M OUTTA HERE!
HEY, KYOKO, WAIT!
CONFUSED
WHY'RE YOU UPSET?
WHAT'S GOIN' ON?
THUMP
WAIT UP!
KYOKO!
"WHILE YOU'RE ALL RUNNIN' AROUND CONFUSED...
THUMP
THUMP
"...SOMEONE ELSE IS HURTING IN YOUR PLACE."

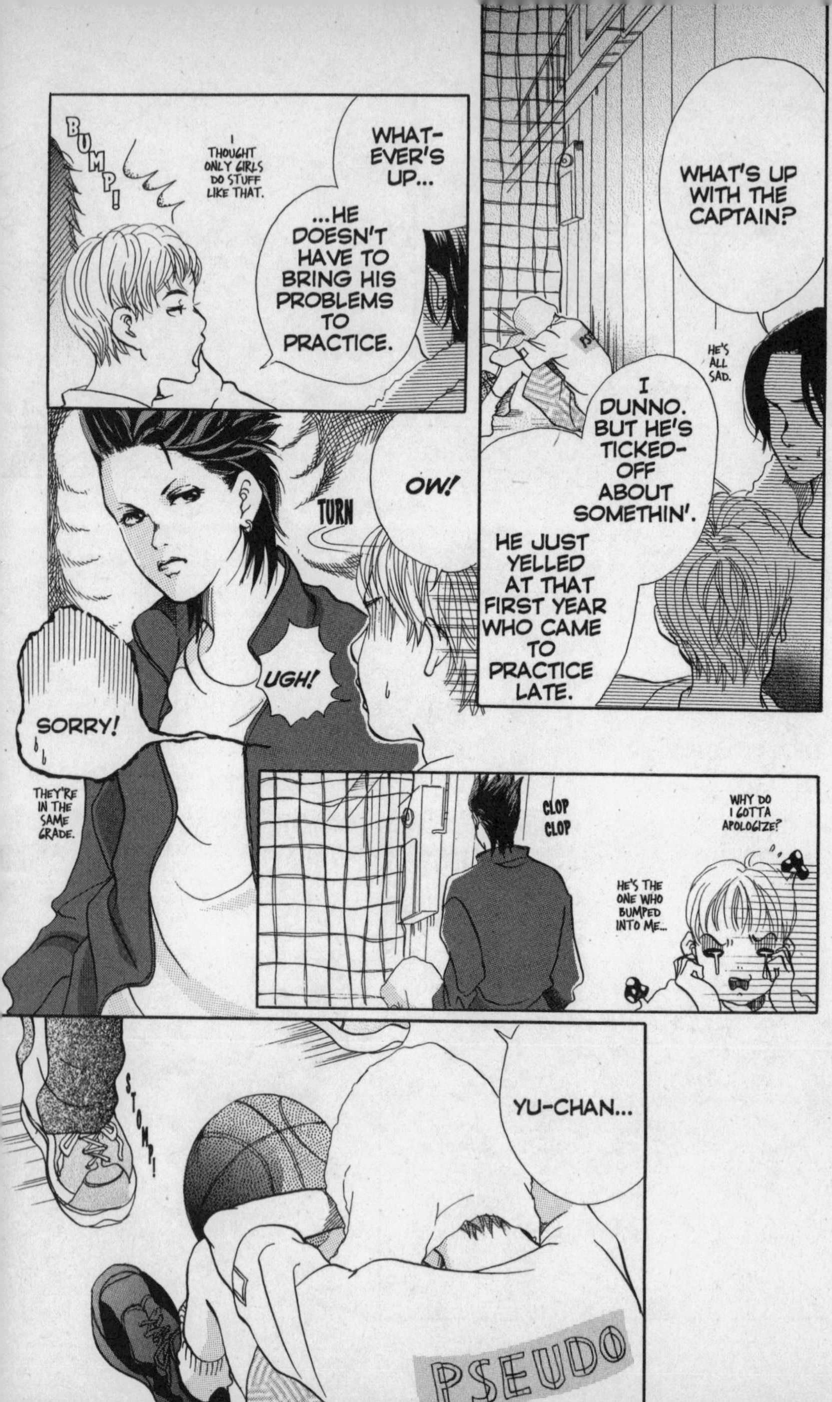
WHAT'S UP WITH THE CAPTAIN?
HE'S ALL SAD.
I DUNNO. BUT HE'S TICKED-OFF ABOUT SOMETHIN'.
HE JUST YELLED AT THAT FIRST YEAR WHO CAME TO PRACTICE LATE.
WHAT-EVER'S UP...
...HE DOESN'T HAVE TO BRING HIS PROBLEMS TO PRACTICE.
I THOUGHT ONLY GIRLS DO STUFF LIKE THAT.
BUMP!
OW!
TURN
UGH!
SORRY!
THEY'RE IN THE SAME GRADE.
WHY DO I GOTTA APOLOGIZE?
HE'S THE ONE WHO BUMPED INTO ME...
CLOP CLOP
YU-CHAN...
STOMP!
PSEUDO

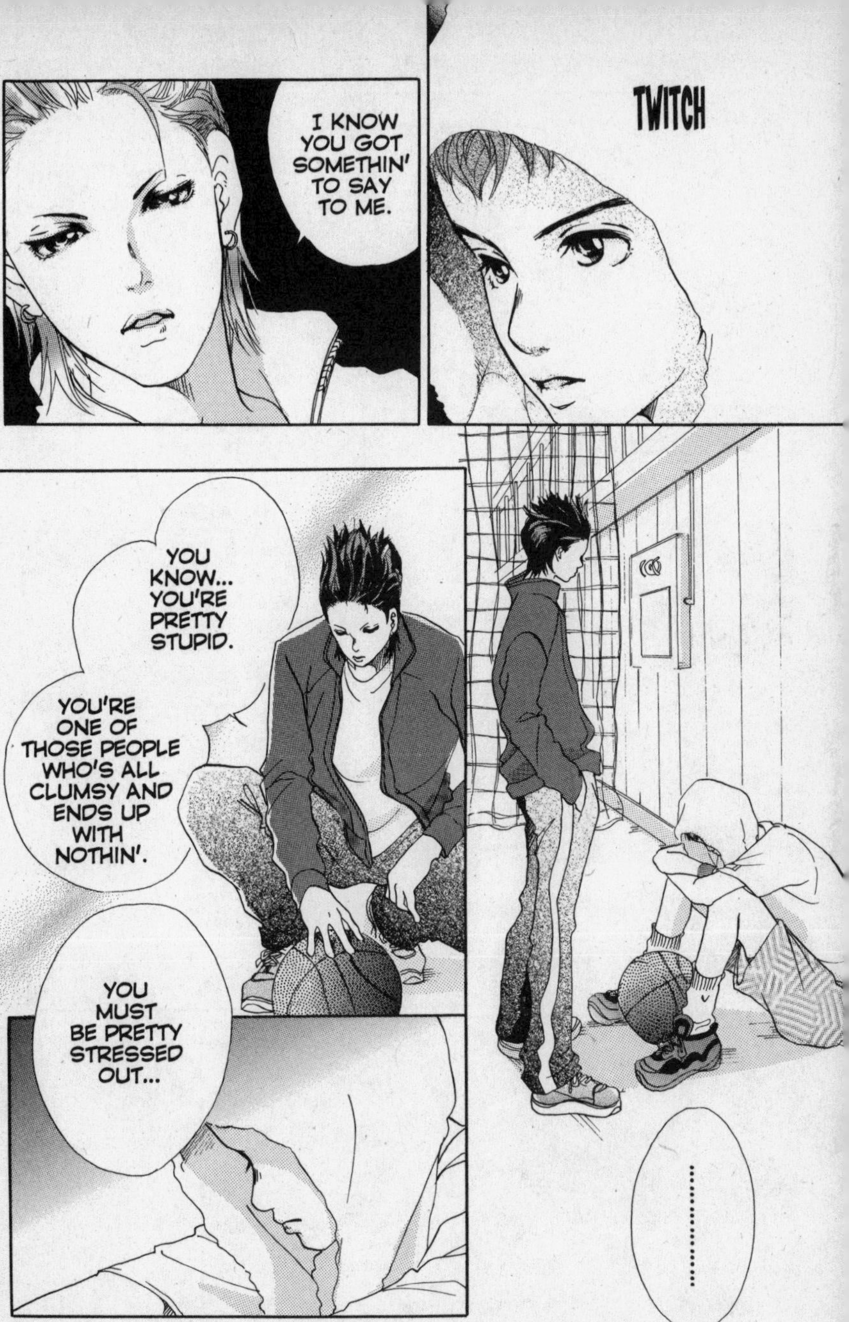
TWITCH
I KNOW YOU GOT SOMETHIN' TO SAY TO ME.
....
YOU KNOW... YOU'RE PRETTY STUPID.
YOU'RE ONE OF THOSE PEOPLE WHO'S ALL CLUMSY AND ENDS UP WITH NOTHIN'.
YOU MUST BE PRETTY STRESSED OUT...

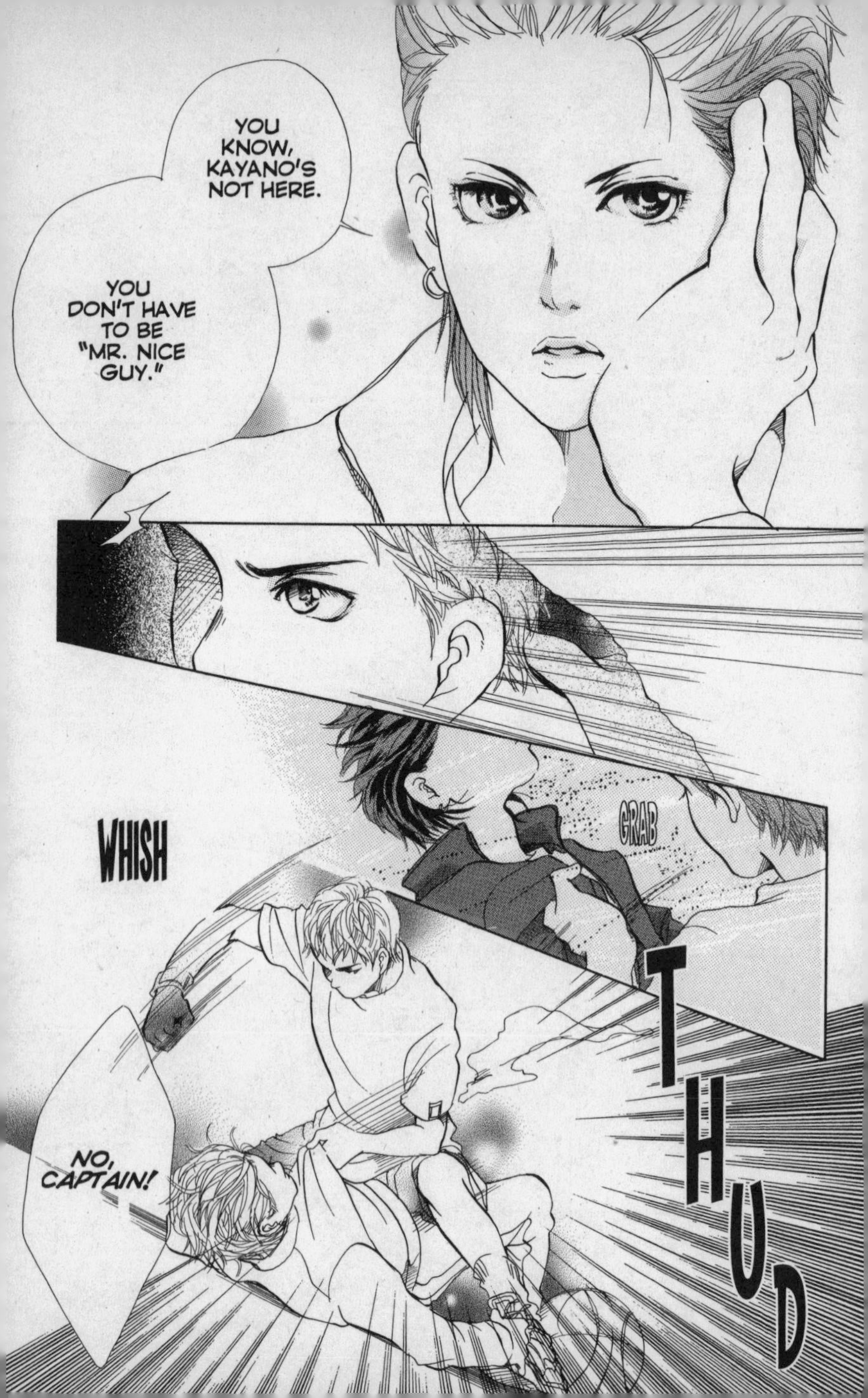
YOU KNOW, KAYANO'S NOT HERE.
YOU DON'T HAVE TO BE "MR. NICE GUY."
GRAB
WHISH
THUD
NO, CAPTAIN!

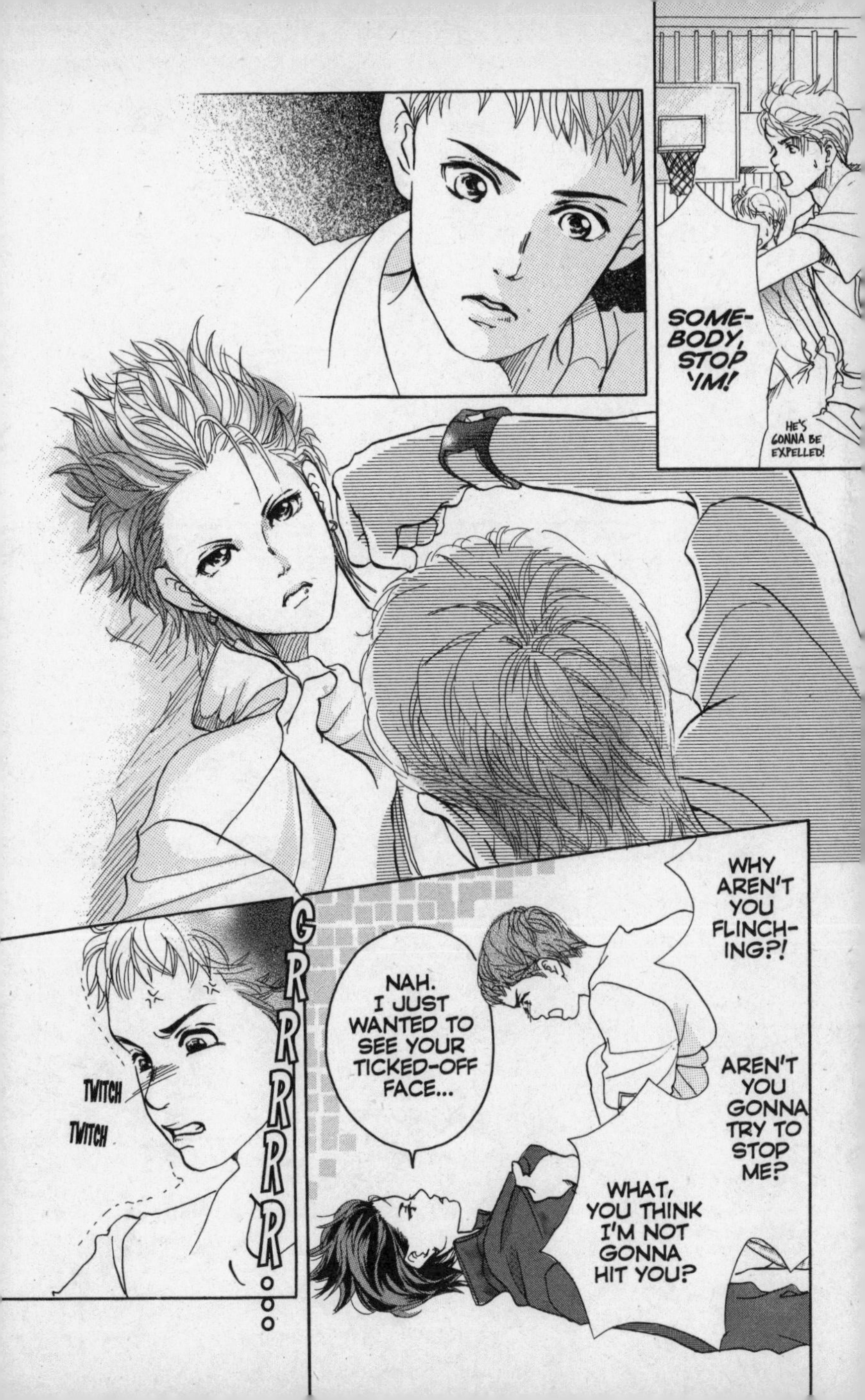
SOME-BODY, STOP 'IM!
HE'S GONNA BE EXPELLED!
WHY AREN'T YOU FLINCH-ING?!
AREN'T YOU GONNA TRY TO STOP ME?
WHAT, YOU THINK I'M NOT GONNA HIT YOU?
NAH. I JUST WANTED TO SEE YOUR TICKED-OFF FACE...
GRRRRRR...
TWITCH
TWITCH

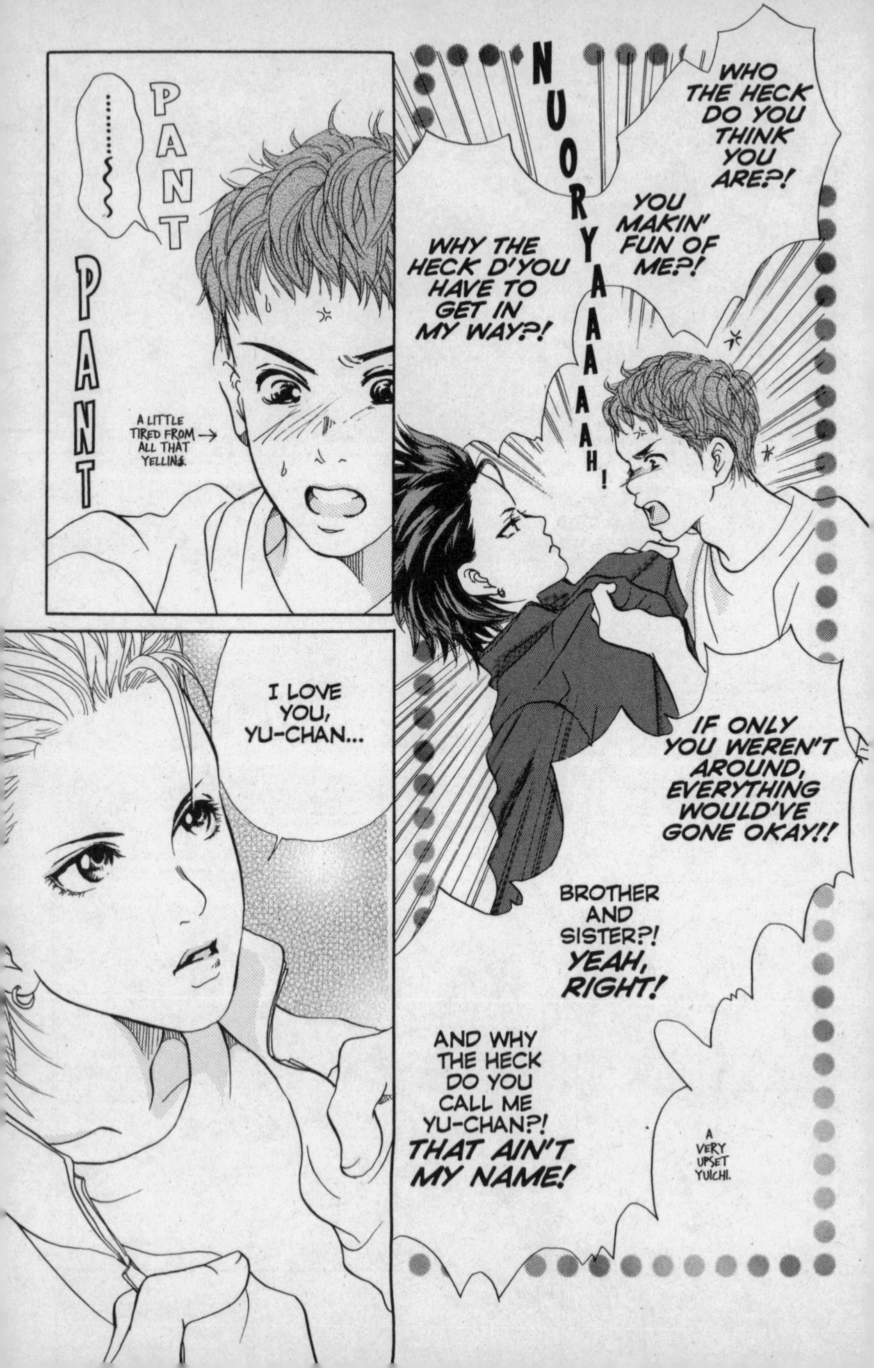
NUORYAAAAAH!
WHO THE HECK DO YOU THINK YOU ARE?!
YOU MAKIN' FUN OF ME?!
WHY THE HECK D'YOU HAVE TO GET IN MY WAY?!
IF ONLY YOU WEREN'T AROUND, EVERYTHING WOULD'VE GONE OKAY!!
BROTHER AND SISTER?! YEAH, RIGHT!
AND WHY THE HECK DO YOU CALL ME YU-CHAN?! THAT AIN'T MY NAME!
A VERY UPSET YUICHI.
......
PANT
PANT
A LITTLE TIRED FROM ALL THAT YELLING.
I LOVE YOU, YU-CHAN...

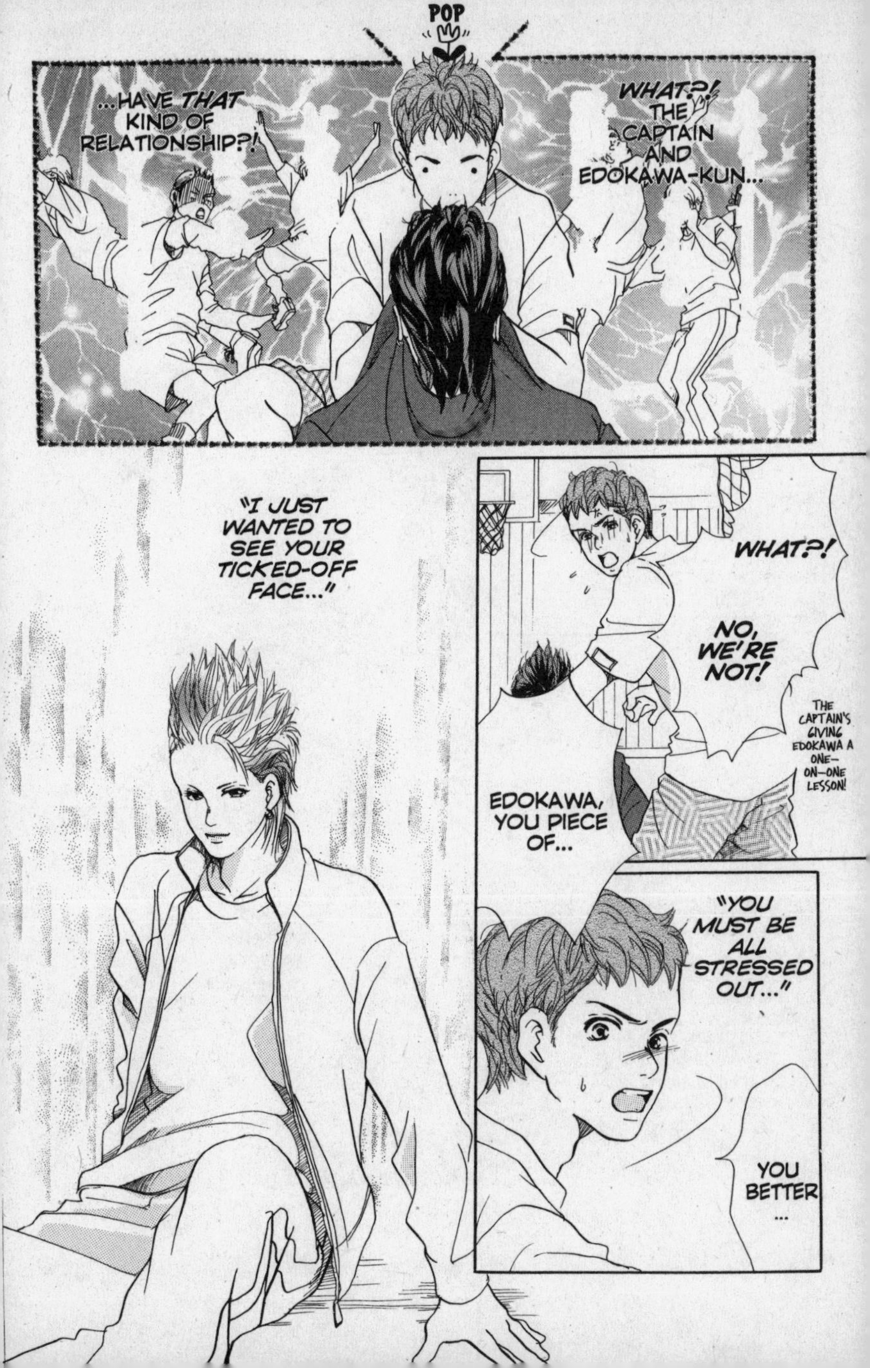
POP
WHAT?! THE CAPTAIN AND EDOKAWA-KUN...
...HAVE THAT KIND OF RELATIONSHIP?!
WHAT?!
NO, WE'RE NOT!
THE CAPTAIN'S GIVING EDOKAWA A ONE-ON-ONE LESSON!
EDOKAWA, YOU PIECE OF...
"YOU MUST BE ALL STRESSED OUT..."
YOU BETTER ...
"I JUST WANTED TO SEE YOUR TICKED-OFF FACE..."

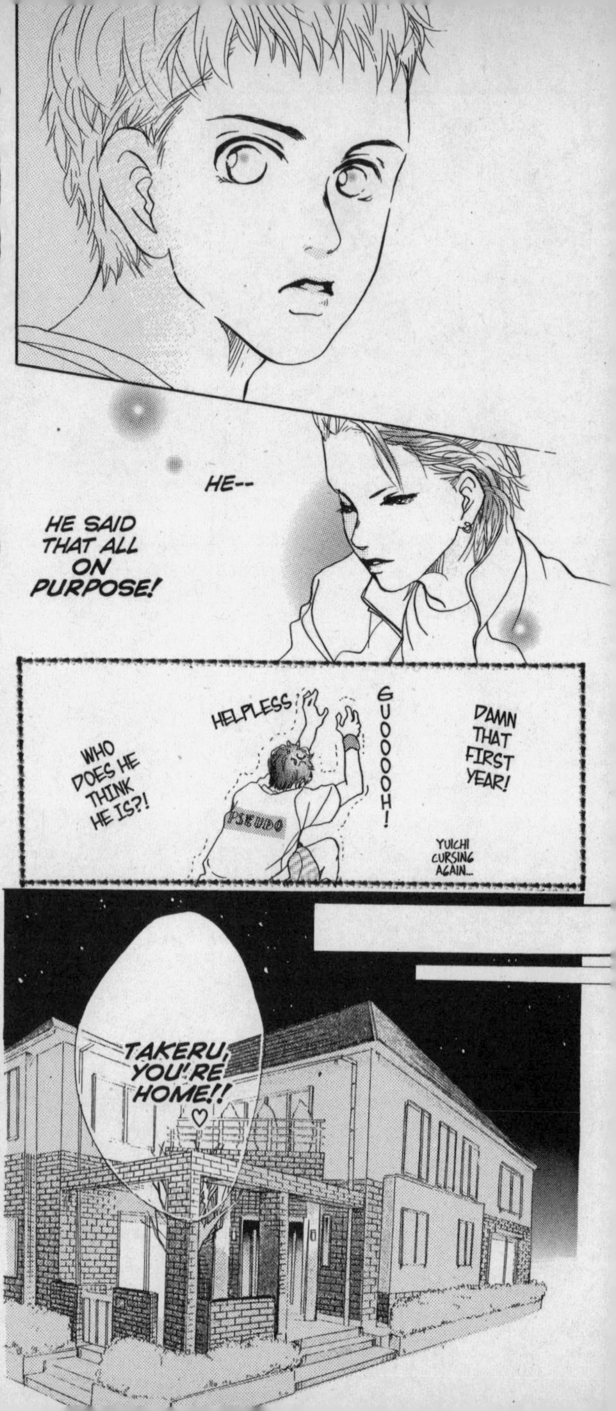
HE--
HE SAID THAT ALL ON PURPOSE!
DAMN THAT FIRST YEAR!
GUOOOOOH!
HELPLESS
WHO DOES HE THINK HE IS?!
YUICHI CURSING AGAIN...
TAKERU, YOU'RE HOME!!

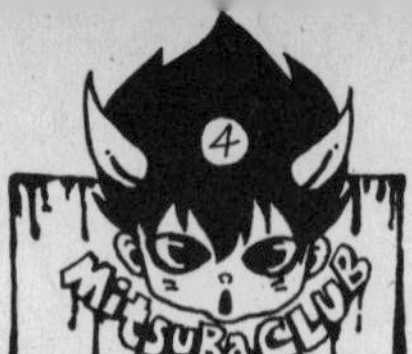
4
MITSUBA CLUB

Scary Mitsuba, right before a deadline.

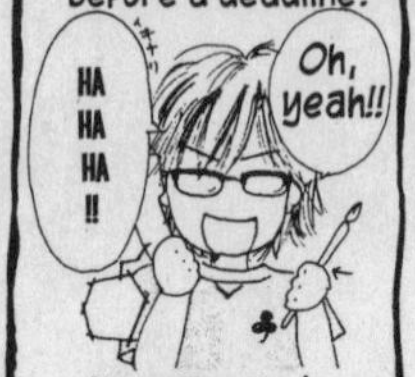
Oh, yeah!!
HA HA HA !!

Usually, she's a pretty young girl. Really!

This is a picture that Aikawa Yabe-Chan drew of me right before a deadline. If I don't get, like this, I can't do "Devil Does Exist." I want to thank her for helping me out at those times. Sorry, I'm such a meanie,

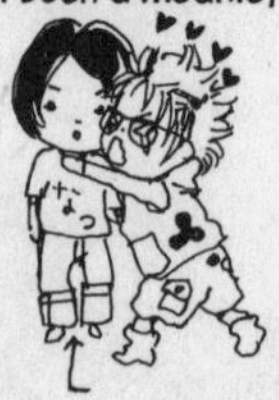

This is how we get then. I get support from a lot of people (of course the fans and editors), and that's how I can do "Devil Does Exist." With your help, I'll keep drawing even if I become a lion. See you in volume 2.

Special Thanks
HAL, NATSU, RYOKO xxx

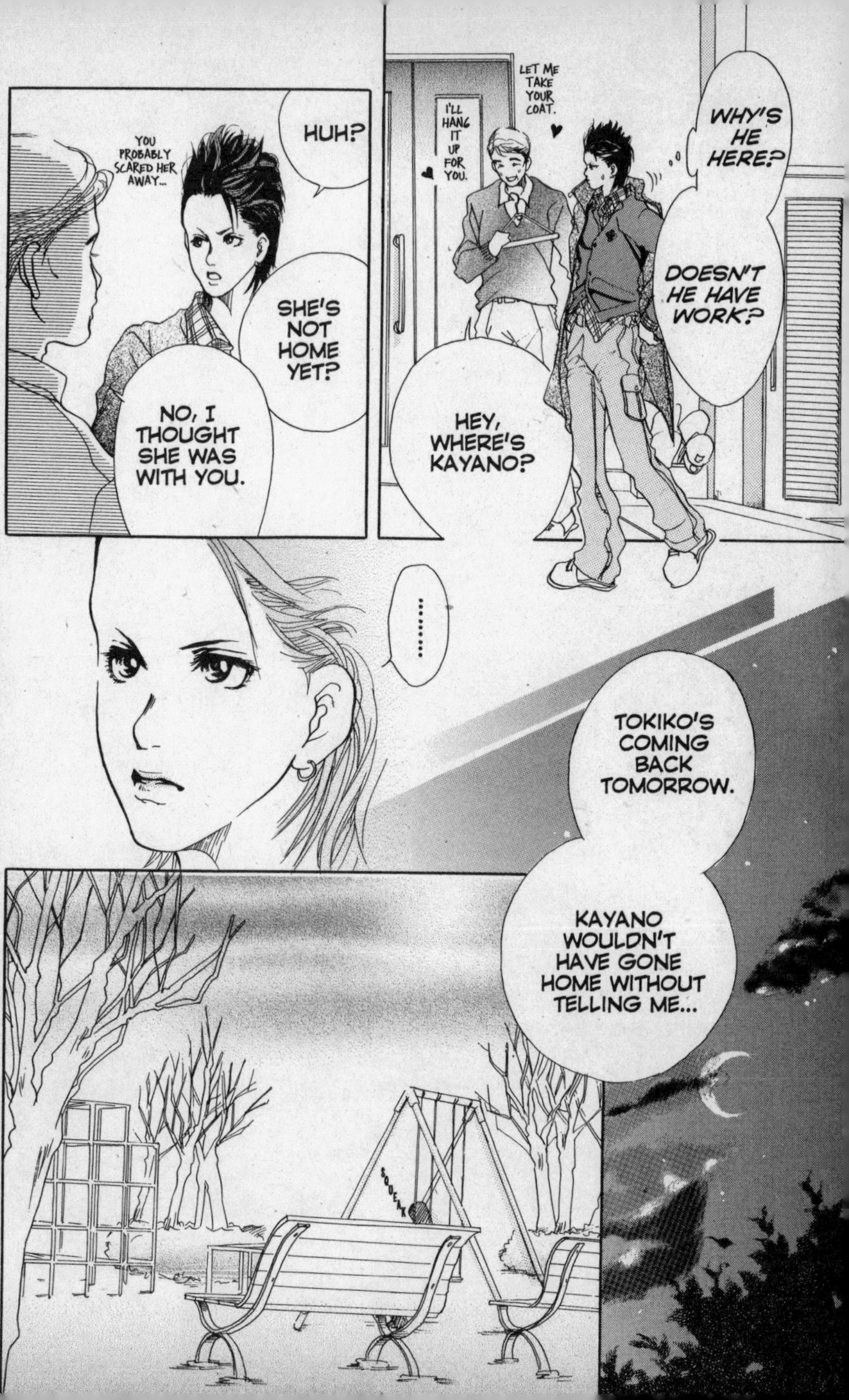
WHY'S HE HERE?
LET ME TAKE YOUR COAT.
I'LL HANG IT UP FOR YOU.
DOESN'T HE HAVE WORK?
HEY, WHERE'S KAYANO?
HUH?
YOU PROBABLY SCARED HER AWAY...
SHE'S NOT HOME YET?
NO, I THOUGHT SHE WAS WITH YOU.
....
TOKIKO'S COMING BACK TOMORROW.
KAYANO WOULDN'T HAVE GONE HOME WITHOUT TELLING ME...
SQUEAK

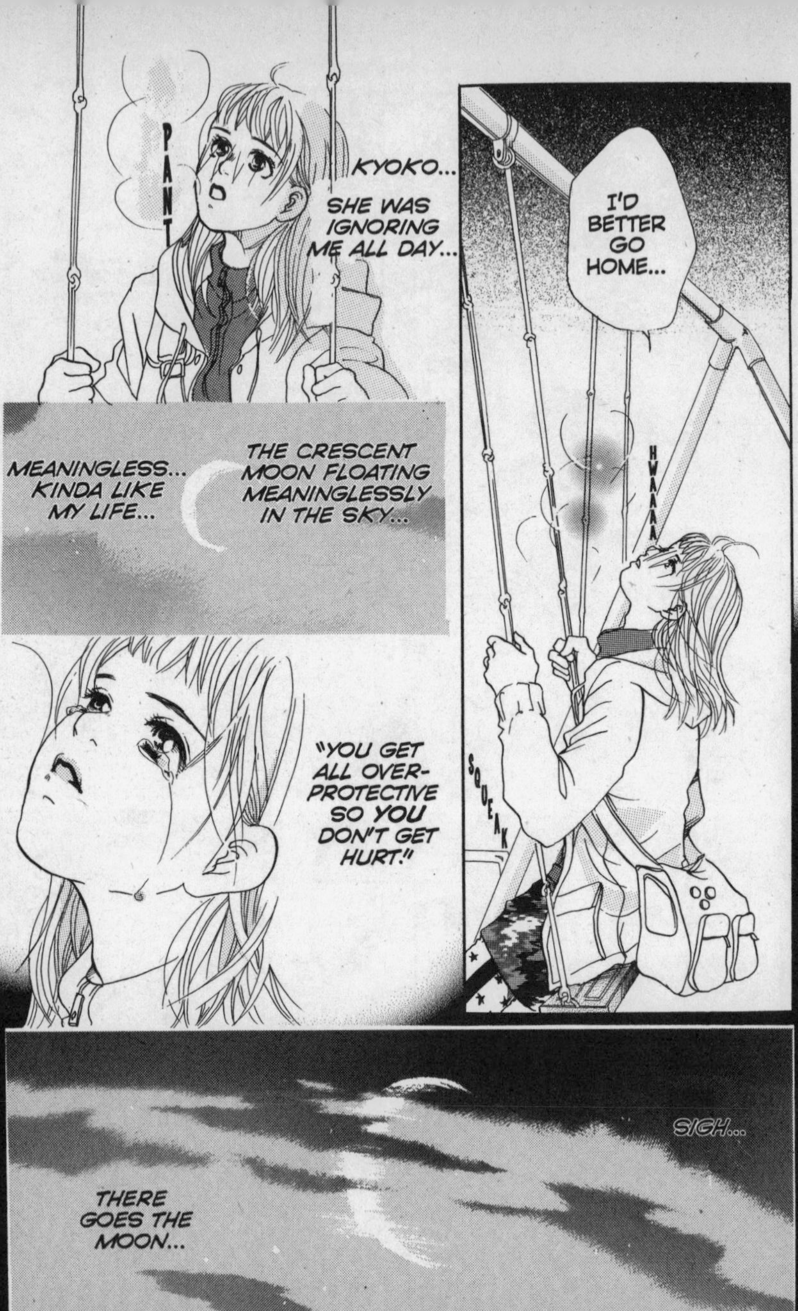
I'D BETTER GO HOME...
HWAAAA
SQUEAK
KYOKO...
SHE WAS IGNORING ME ALL DAY...
PANT
THE CRESCENT MOON FLOATING MEANINGLESSLY IN THE SKY...
MEANINGLESS... KINDA LIKE MY LIFE...
"YOU GET ALL OVER-PROTECTIVE SO YOU DON'T GET HURT."
SIGH...
THERE GOES THE MOON...

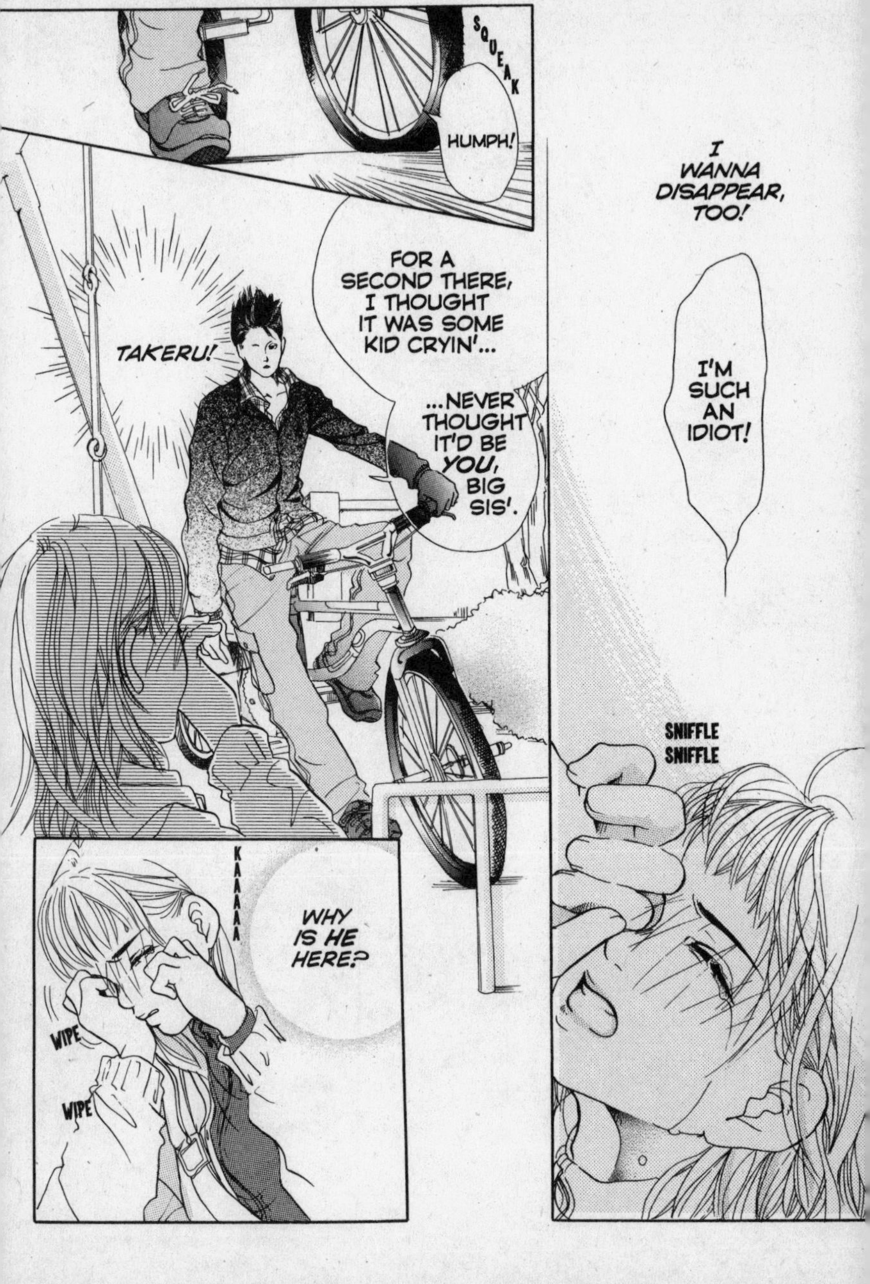
I WANNA DISAPPEAR, TOO!
I'M SUCH AN IDIOT!
SNIFFLE SNIFFLE
SQUEAK
HUMPH!
TAKERU!
FOR A SECOND THERE, I THOUGHT IT WAS SOME KID CRYIN'...
...NEVER THOUGHT IT'D BE *YOU*, BIG SIS'.
KAAAAA
WHY IS HE HERE?
WIPE
WIPE

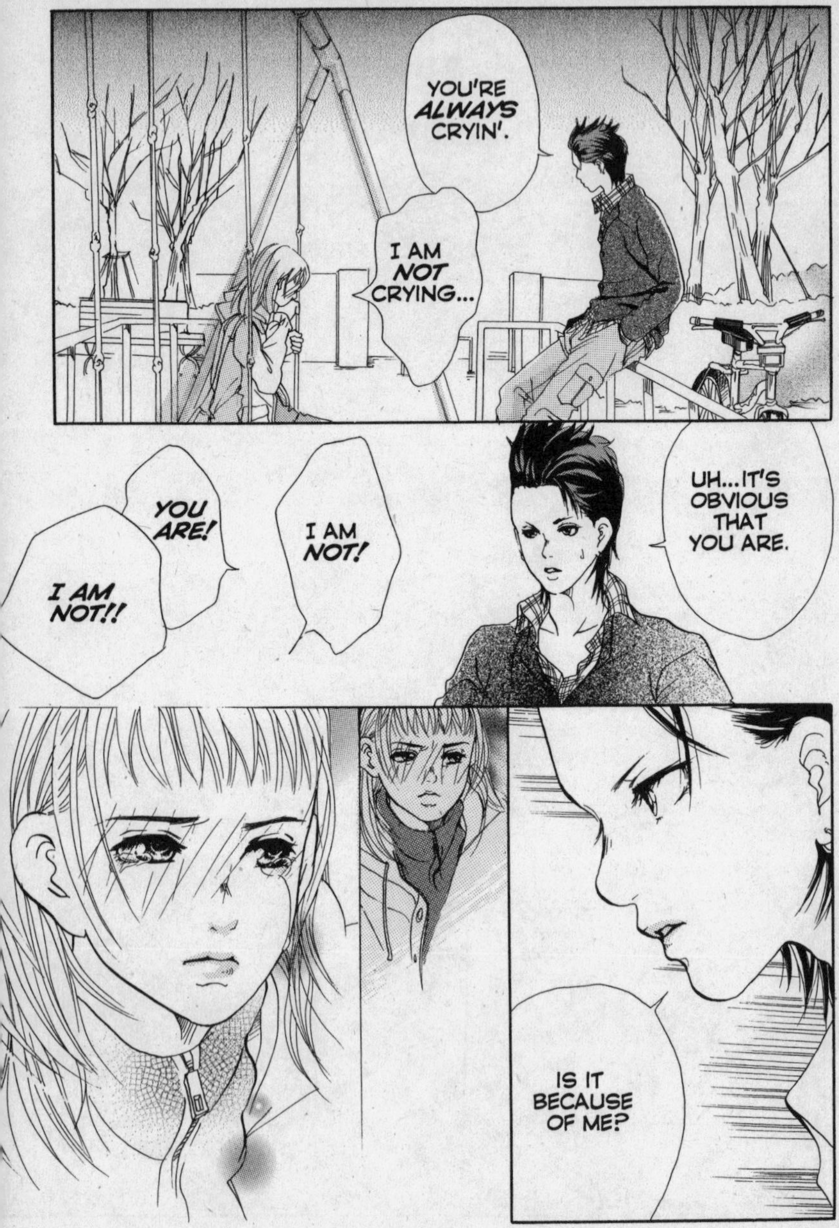
YOU'RE *ALWAYS* CRYIN'.
I AM *NOT* CRYING...
UH...IT'S OBVIOUS THAT YOU ARE.
I AM *NOT!*
YOU ARE!
I AM NOT!!
IS IT BECAUSE OF ME?

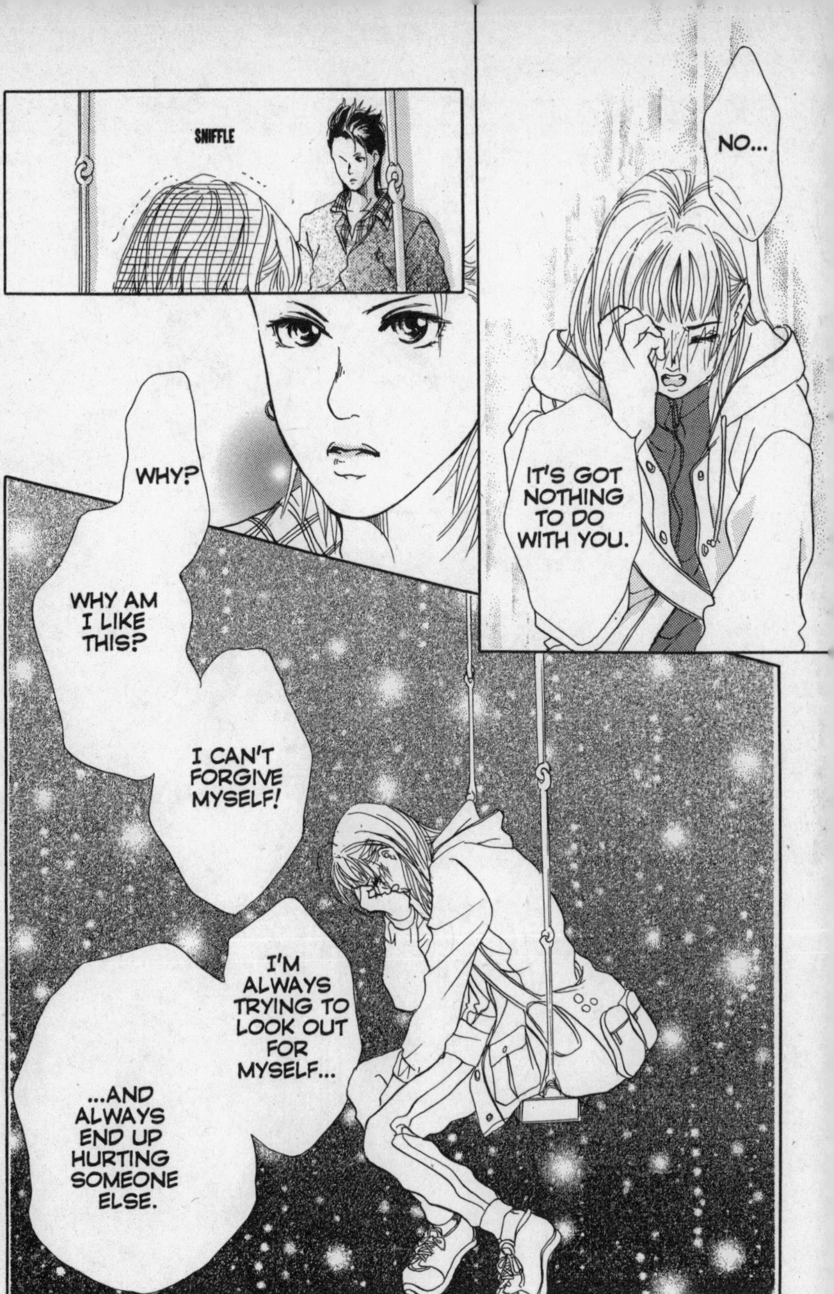
NO...
IT'S GOT NOTHING TO DO WITH YOU.
SNIFFLE
WHY?
WHY AM I LIKE THIS?
I CAN'T FORGIVE MYSELF!
I'M ALWAYS TRYING TO LOOK OUT FOR MYSELF...
...AND ALWAYS END UP HURTING SOMEONE ELSE.

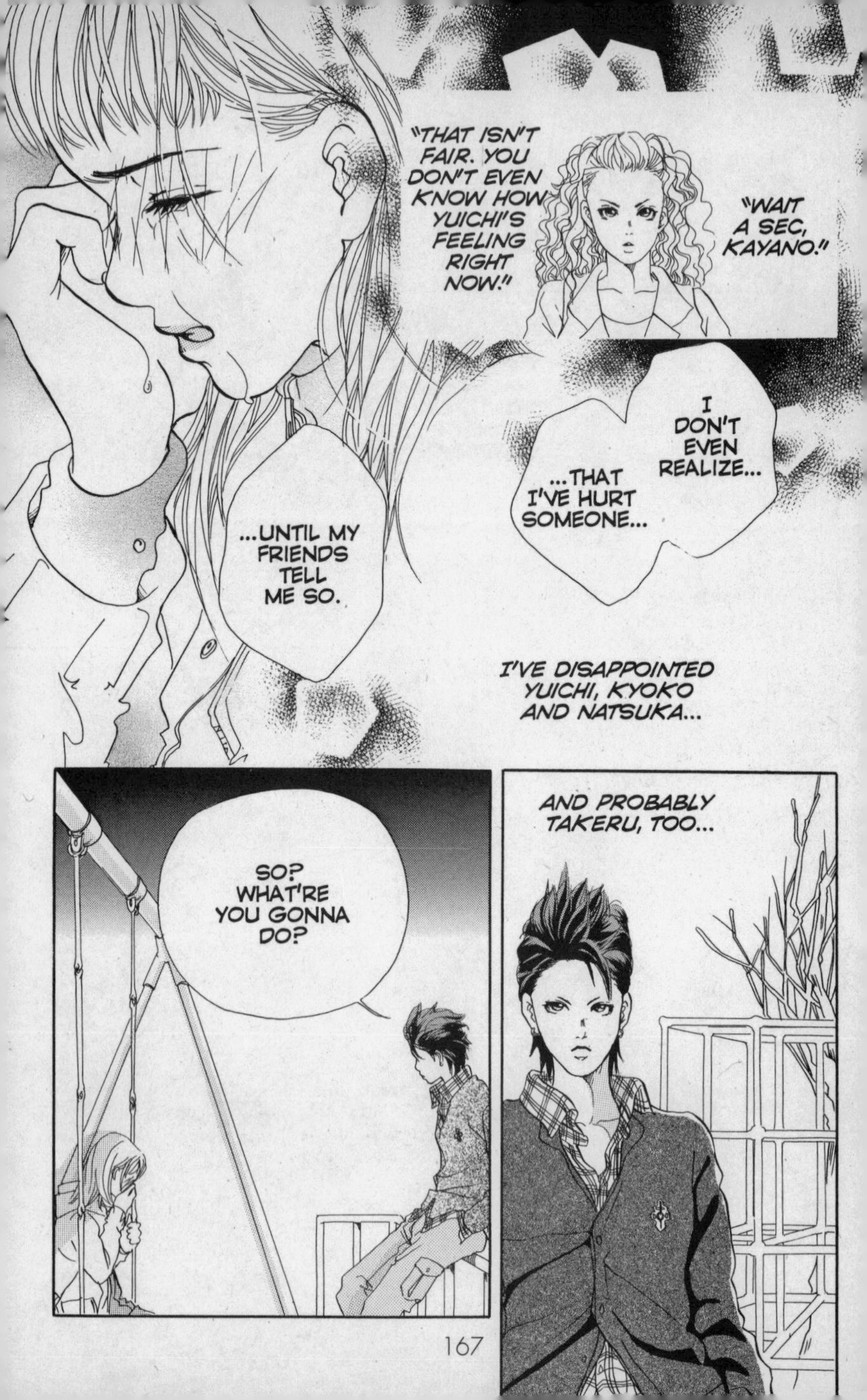
"WAIT A SEC, KAYANO."
"THAT ISN'T FAIR. YOU DON'T EVEN KNOW HOW YUICHI'S FEELING RIGHT NOW."
I DON'T EVEN REALIZE...
...THAT I'VE HURT SOMEONE...
...UNTIL MY FRIENDS TELL ME SO.
I'VE DISAPPOINTED YUICHI, KYOKO AND NATSUKA...
AND PROBABLY TAKERU, TOO...
SO? WHAT'RE YOU GONNA DO?

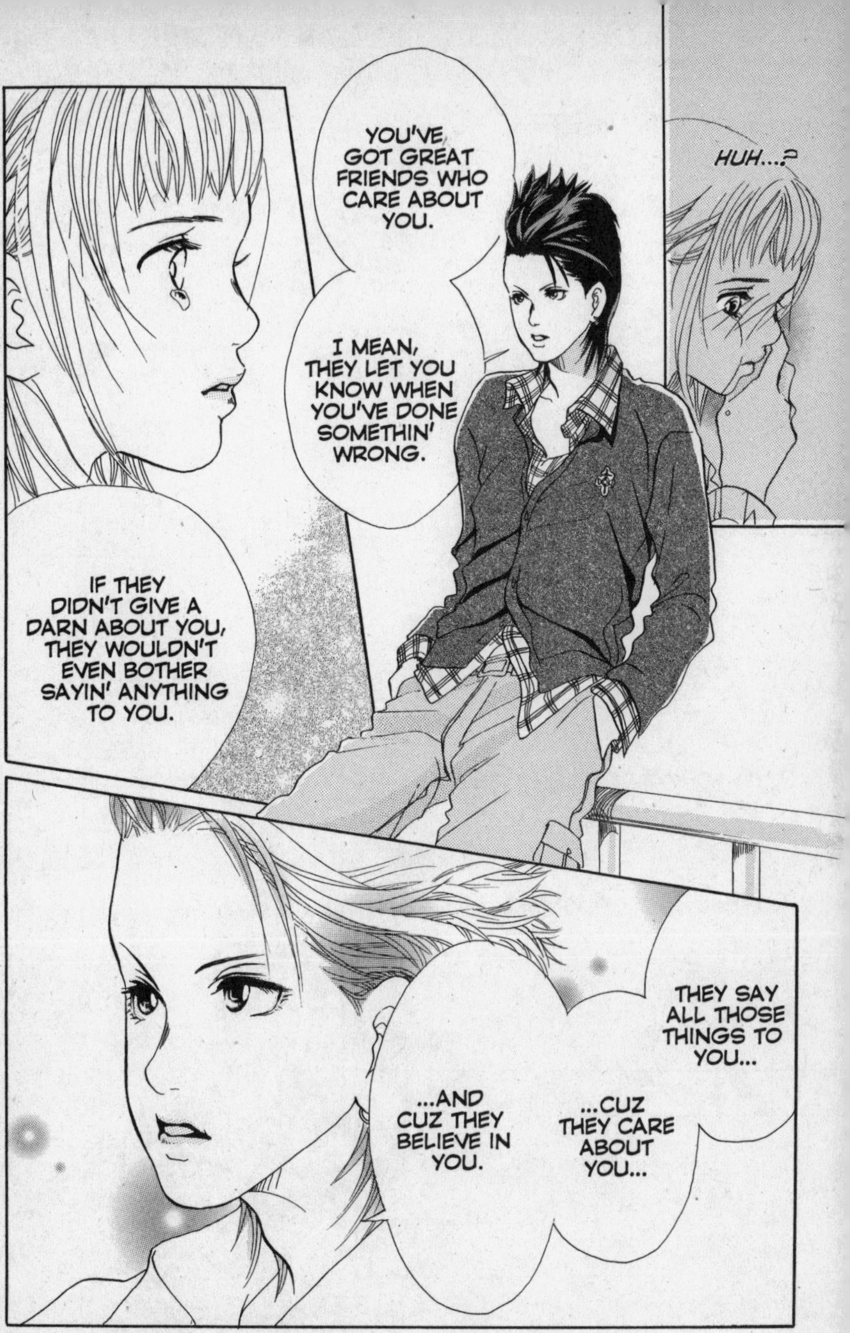
HUH...?
YOU'VE GOT GREAT FRIENDS WHO CARE ABOUT YOU.
I MEAN, THEY LET YOU KNOW WHEN YOU'VE DONE SOMETHIN' WRONG.
IF THEY DIDN'T GIVE A DARN ABOUT YOU, THEY WOULDN'T EVEN BOTHER SAYIN' ANYTHING TO YOU.
THEY SAY ALL THOSE THINGS TO YOU...
...CUZ THEY CARE ABOUT YOU...
...AND CUZ THEY BELIEVE IN YOU.

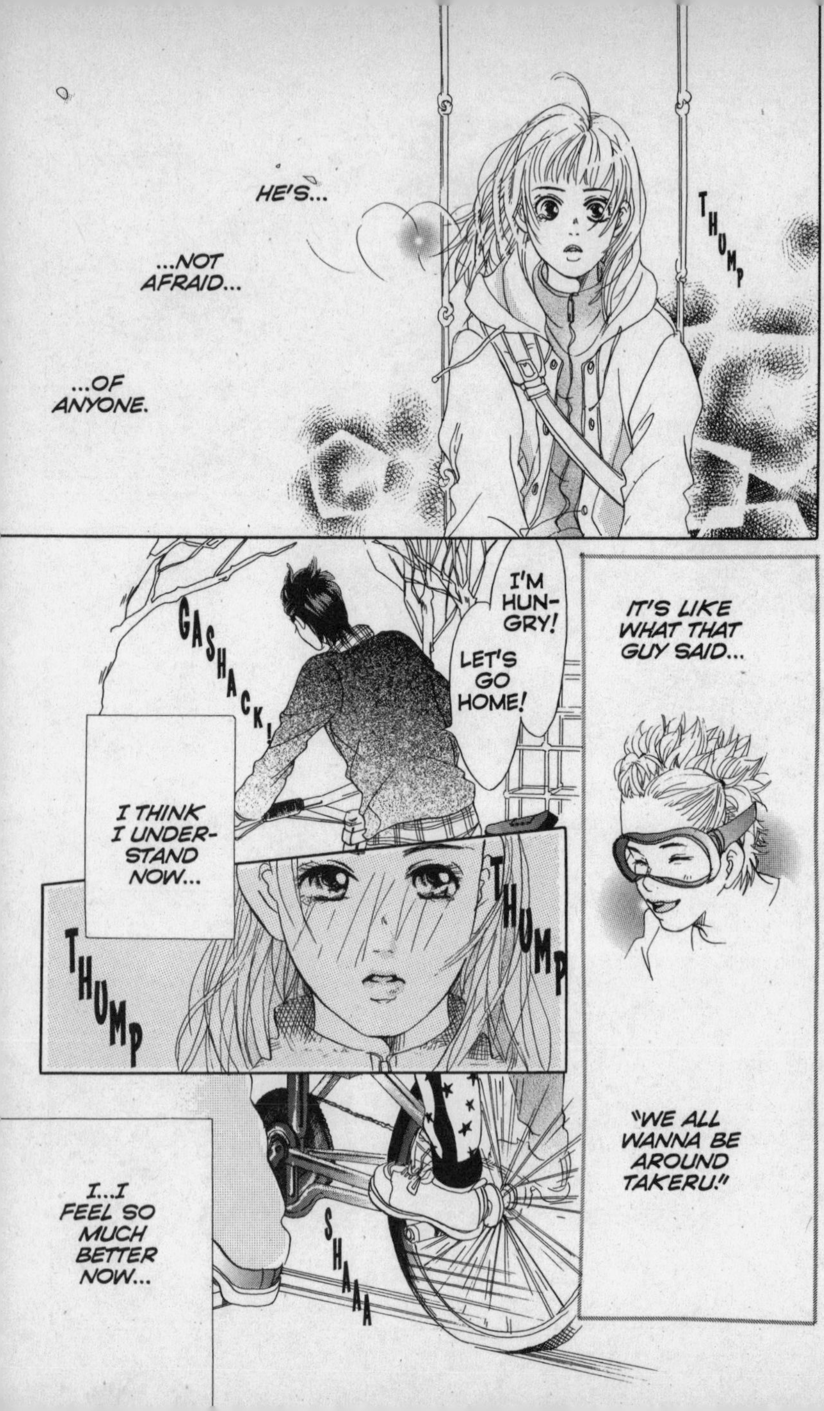
THUMP
HE'S...
...NOT AFRAID...
...OF ANYONE.
IT'S LIKE WHAT THAT GUY SAID...
"WE ALL WANNA BE AROUND TAKERU."
I'M HUN-GRY!
LET'S GO HOME!
GASHACK!
I THINK I UNDER-STAND NOW...
THUMP
THUMP
SHAAA
I...I FEEL SO MUCH BETTER NOW...

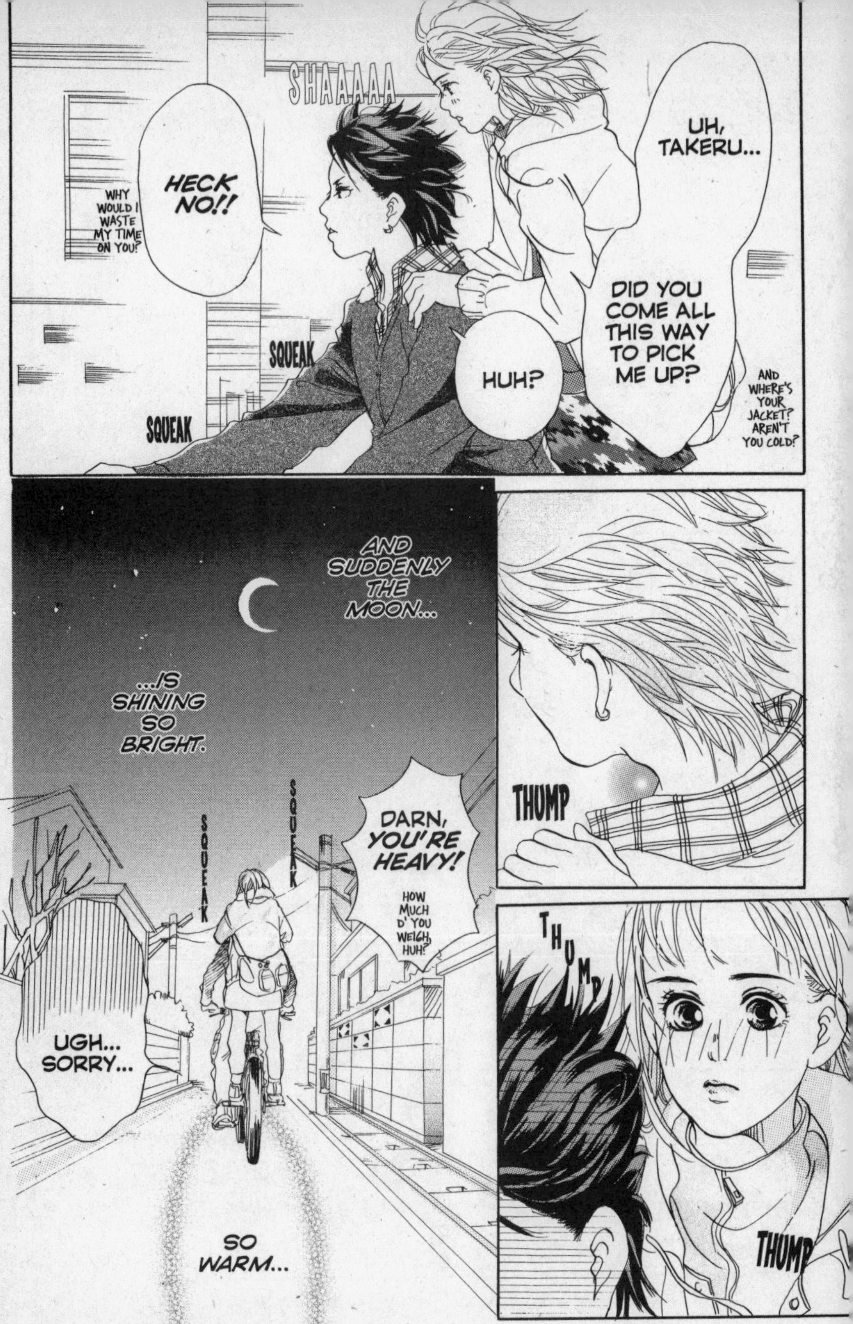
UH, TAKERU...
DID YOU COME ALL THIS WAY TO PICK ME UP?
AND WHERE'S YOUR JACKET? AREN'T YOU COLD?
SHAAAAA
HUH?
HECK NO!!
WHY WOULD I WASTE MY TIME ON YOU?
SQUEAK
SQUEAK
THUMP
THUMP
THUMP
AND SUDDENLY THE MOON...
...IS SHINING SO BRIGHT.
DARN, YOU'RE HEAVY!
HOW MUCH D' YOU WEIGH, HUH?
SQUEAK
SQUEAK
UGH... SORRY...
SO WARM...

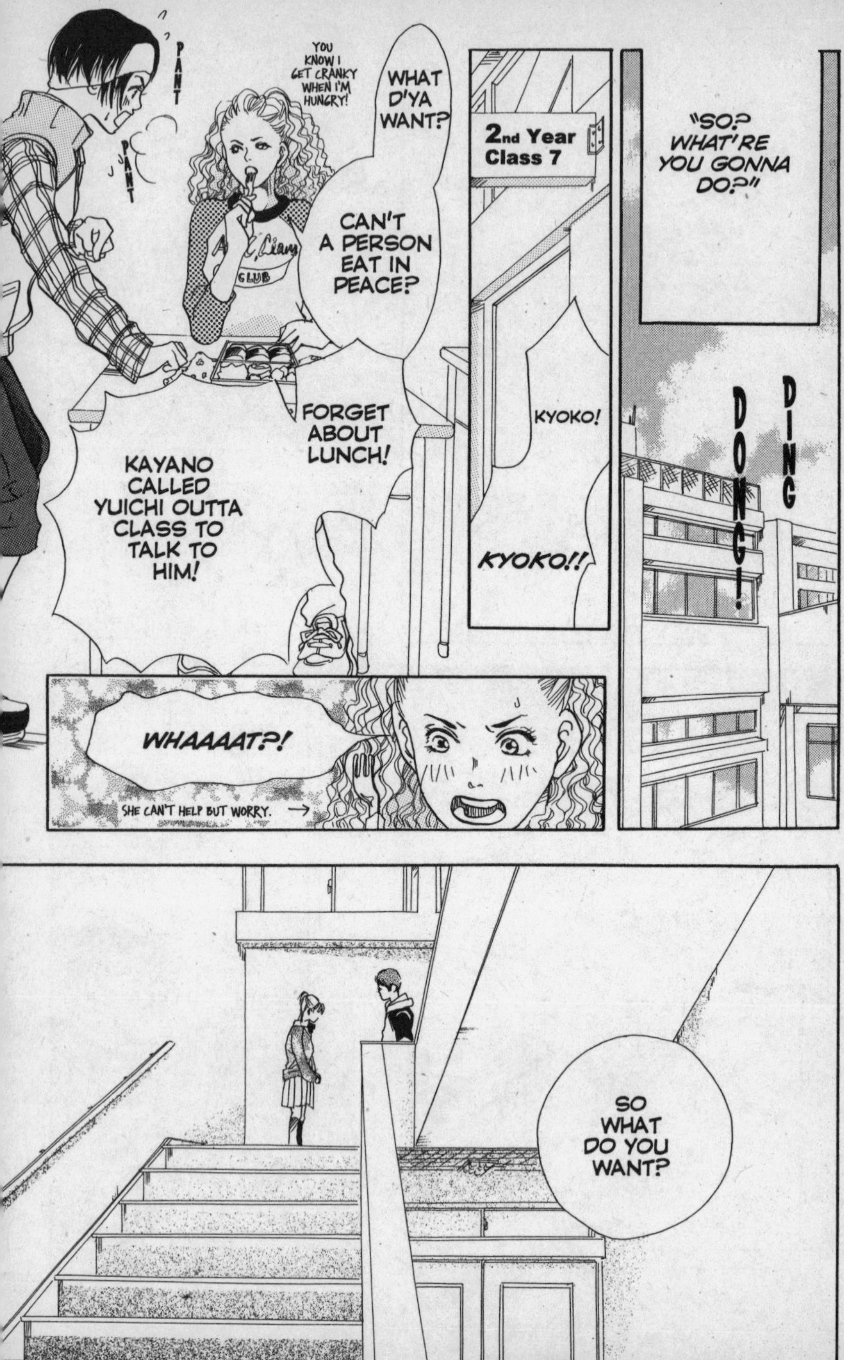
"SO? WHAT'RE YOU GONNA DO?"
DING
DONG!
2nd Year Class 7
KYOKO!
KYOKO!!
WHAT D'YA WANT?
YOU KNOW I GET CRANKY WHEN I'M HUNGRY!
CAN'T A PERSON EAT IN PEACE?
PANT
PANT
FORGET ABOUT LUNCH!
KAYANO CALLED YUICHI OUTTA CLASS TO TALK TO HIM!
WHAAAAT?!
SHE CAN'T HELP BUT WORRY. →
SO WHAT DO YOU WANT?

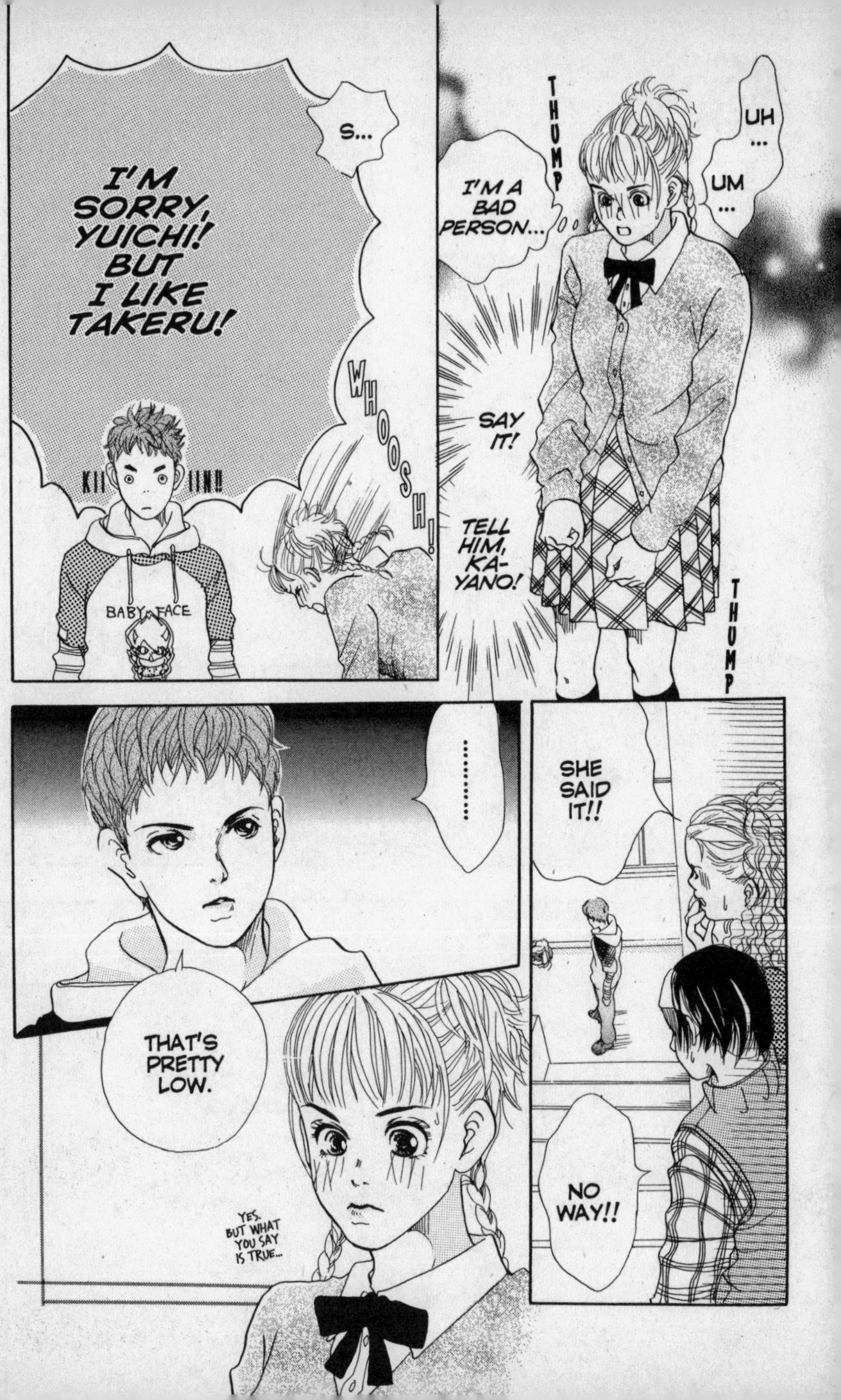

UH... UM...
THUMP
I'M A BAD PERSON...
SAY IT!
TELL HIM, KA-YANO!
THUMP
S...
I'M SORRY, YUICHI! BUT I LIKE TAKERU!
WHOOSH!
KII IIN!!
BABY FACE
SHE SAID IT!!
NO WAY!!
....
THAT'S PRETTY LOW.
YES. BUT WHAT YOU SAY IS TRUE...

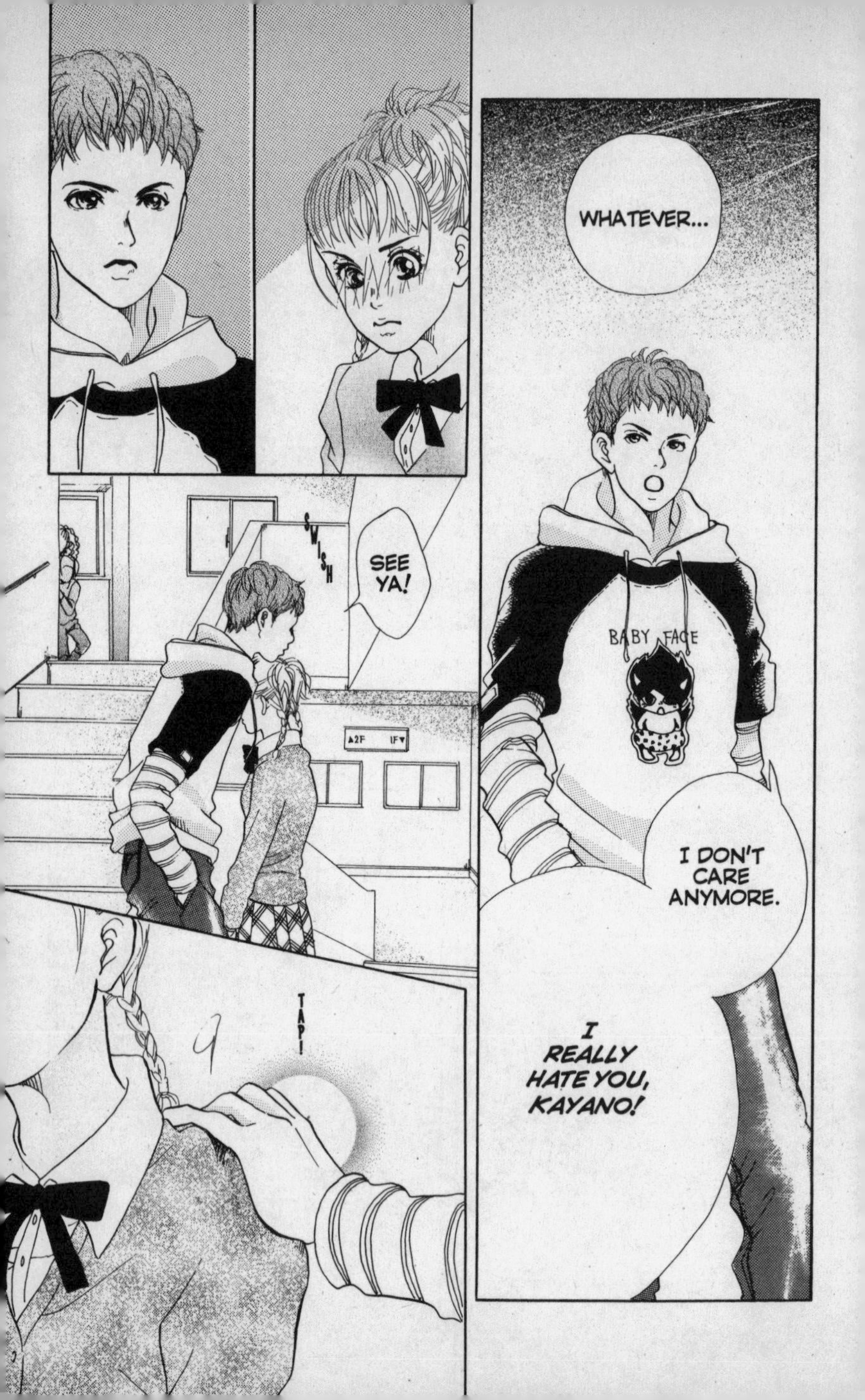
WHATEVER...
BABY FACE
I DON'T CARE ANYMORE.
I REALLY HATE YOU, KAYANO!
SWISH
SEE YA!
▲2F 1F▼
TAP!

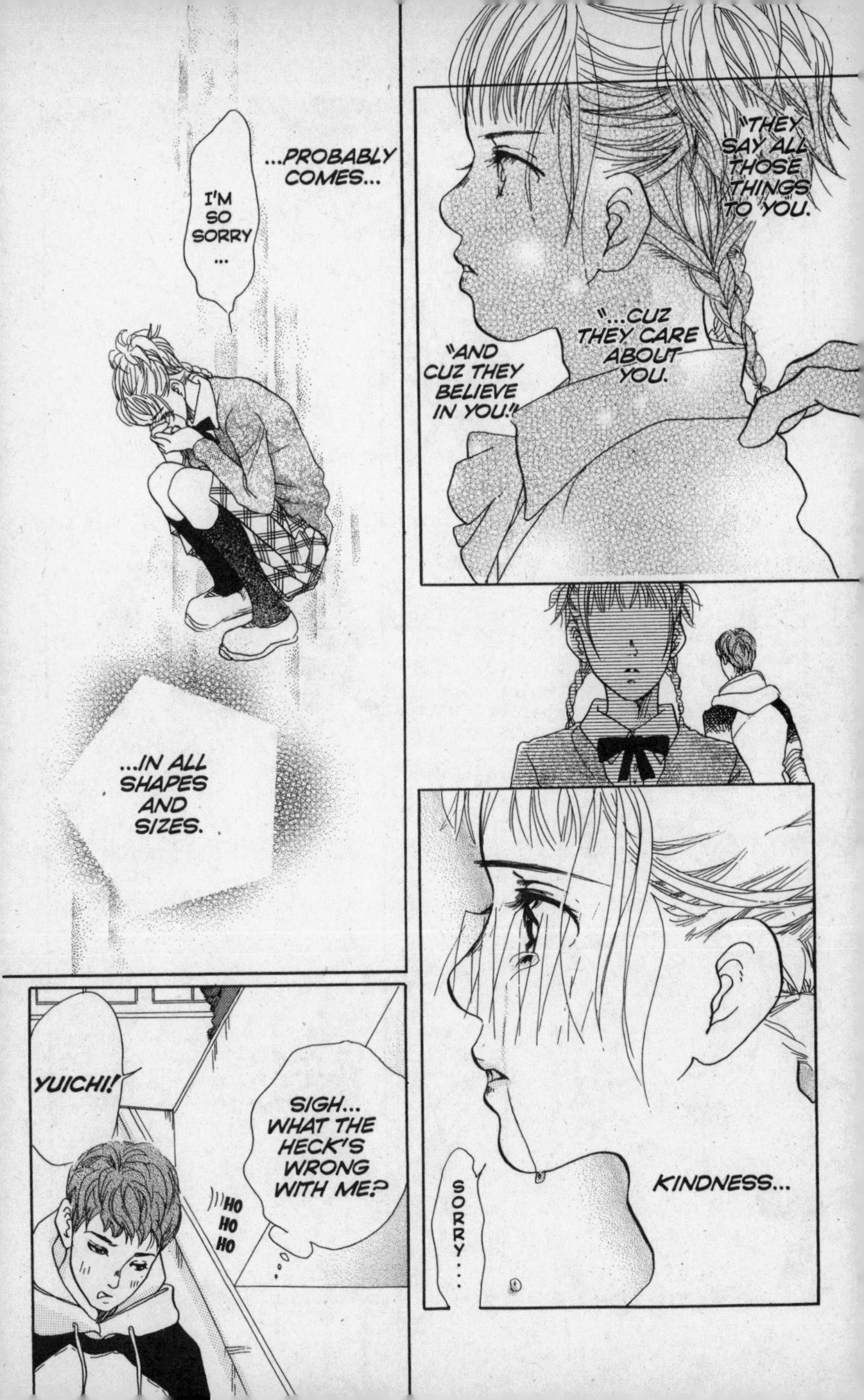
"THEY SAY ALL THOSE THINGS TO YOU.
"...CUZ THEY CARE ABOUT YOU.
"AND CUZ THEY BELIEVE IN YOU!"
KINDNESS...
SORRY...
...PROBABLY COMES...
I'M SO SORRY...
...IN ALL SHAPES AND SIZES.
SIGH... WHAT THE HECK'S WRONG WITH ME?
HO HO HO
YUICHI!

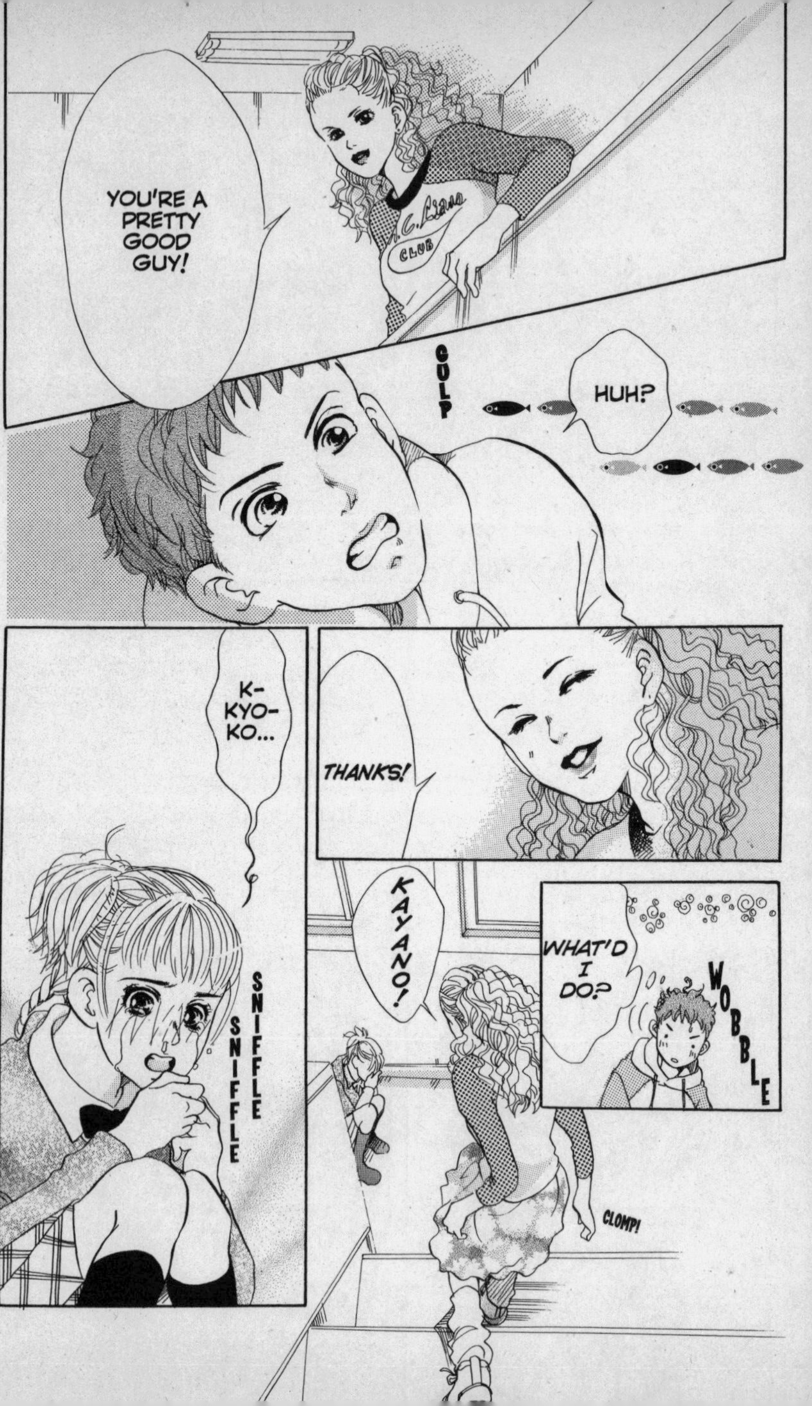
YOU'RE A PRETTY GOOD GUY!
HUH?
GULP
THANKS!
WHAT'D I DO?
WOBBLE
KAYANO!
CLOMP!
K-KYOKO...
SNIFFLE
SNIFFLE

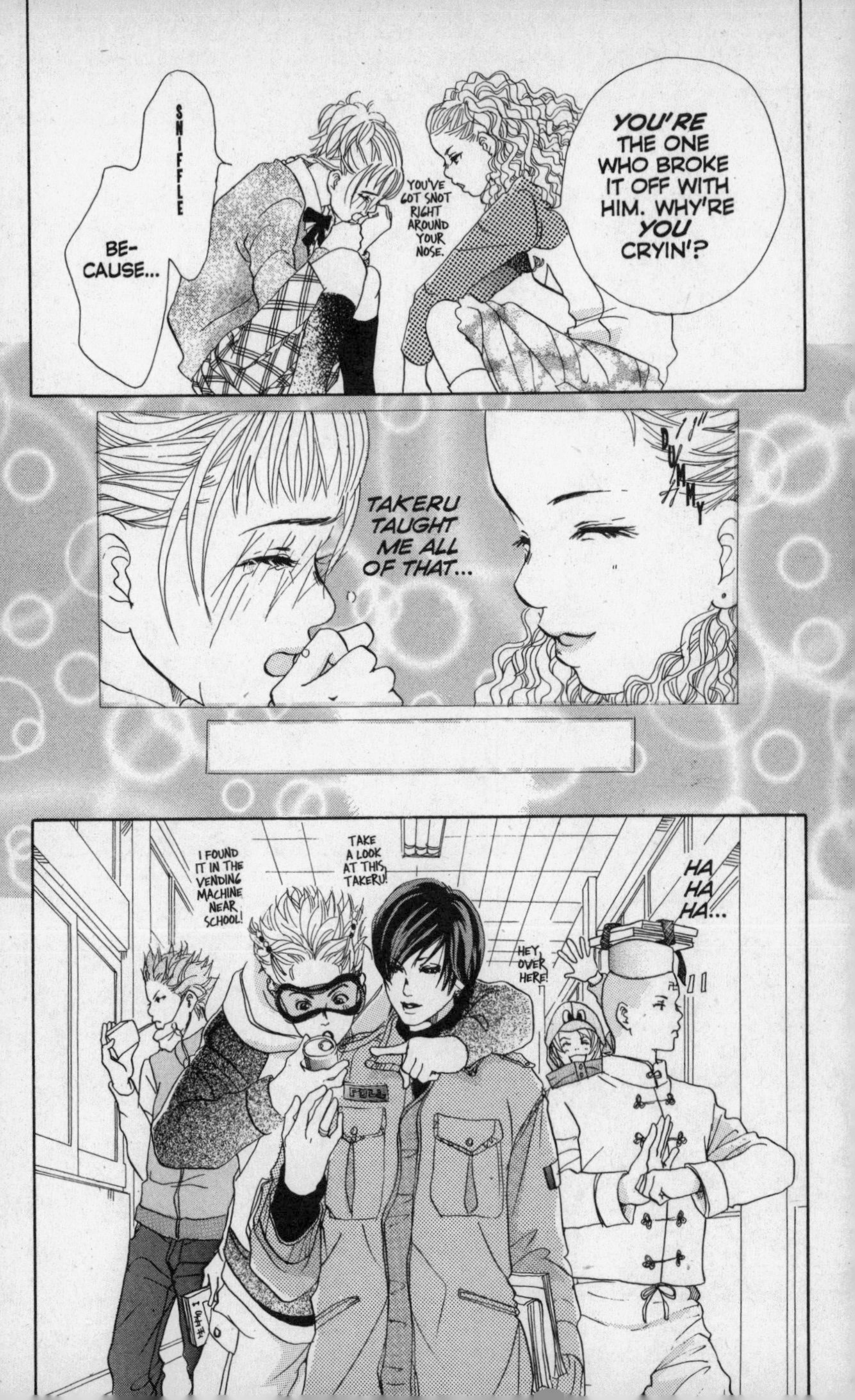
YOU'RE THE ONE WHO BROKE IT OFF WITH HIM. WHY'RE YOU CRYIN'?
YOU'VE GOT SNOT RIGHT AROUND YOUR NOSE.
SNIFFLE
BE-CAUSE...
DUMMY
TAKERU TAUGHT ME ALL OF THAT...
HA HA HA...
HEY, OVER HERE!
TAKE A LOOK AT THIS, TAKERU!
I FOUND IT IN THE VENDING MACHINE NEAR SCHOOL!

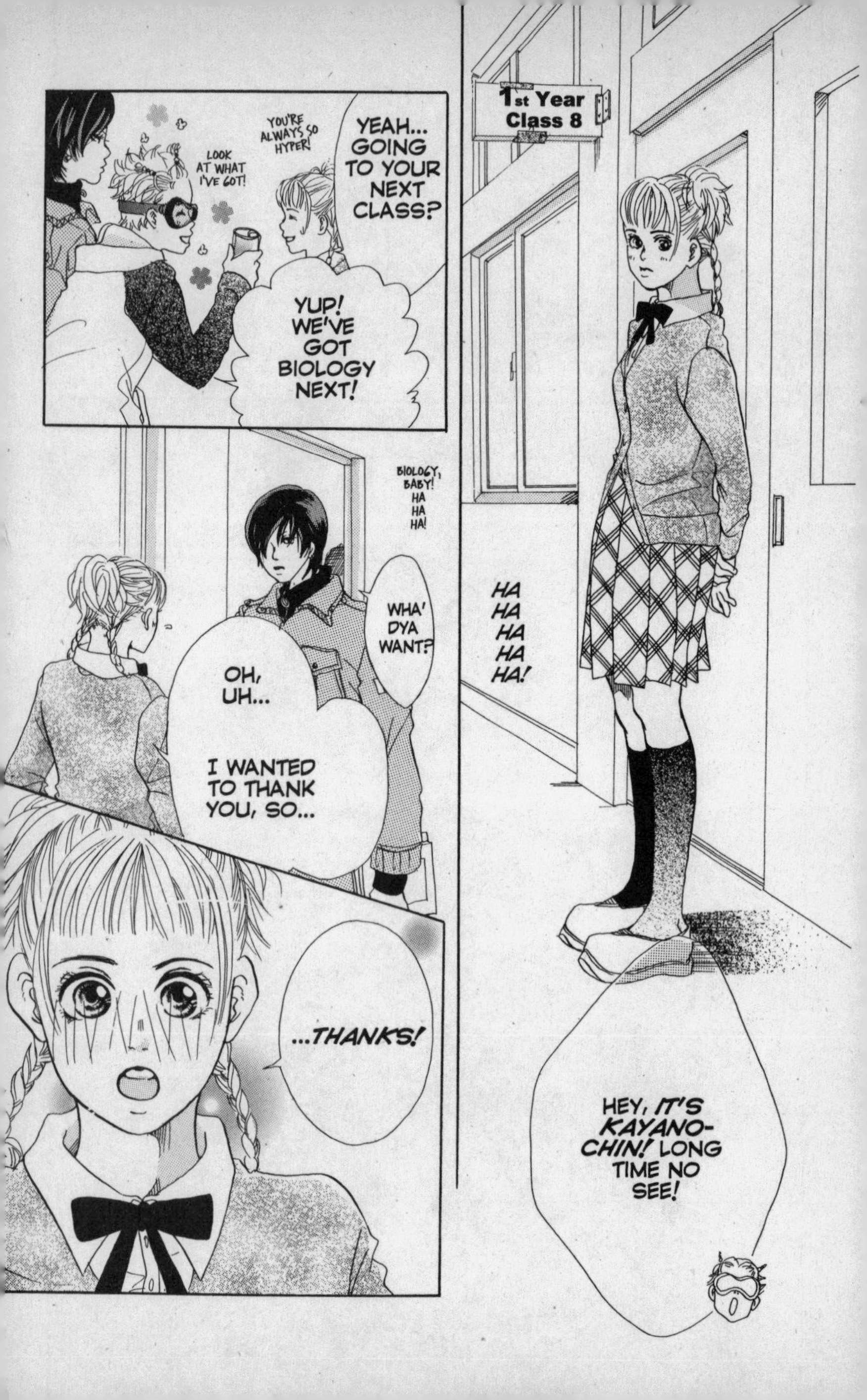
1st Year Class 8
HA HA HA HA HA!
HEY, IT'S KAYANO-CHIN! LONG TIME NO SEE!
YEAH... GOING TO YOUR NEXT CLASS?
YOU'RE ALWAYS SO HYPER!
LOOK AT WHAT I'VE GOT!
YUP! WE'VE GOT BIOLOGY NEXT!
BIOLOGY, BABY! HA HA HA!
WHA' DYA WANT?
OH, UH...
I WANTED TO THANK YOU, SO...
...THANKS!

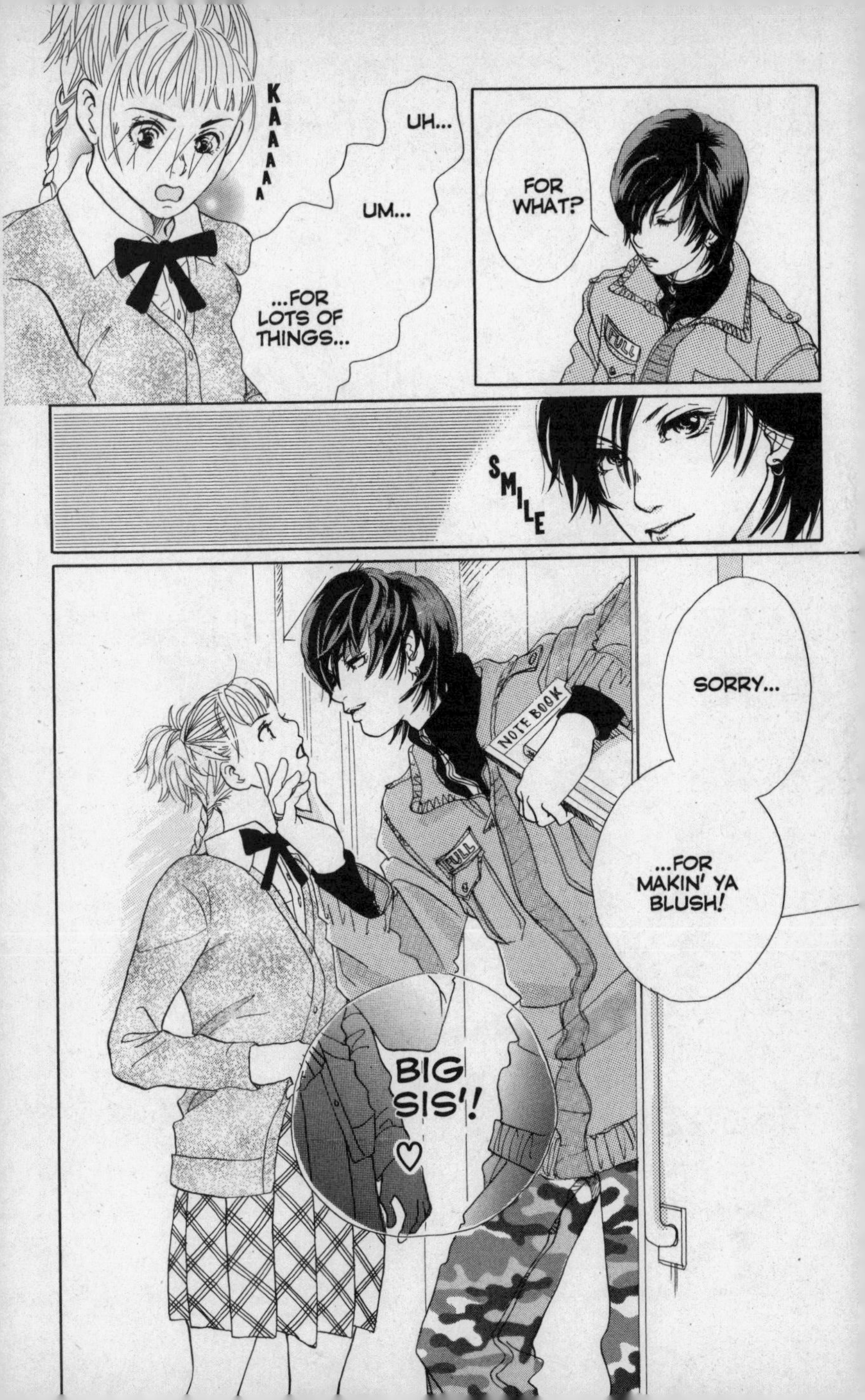
FOR WHAT?
UH...
UM...
...FOR LOTS OF THINGS...
KAAAAA
SMILE
SORRY...
...FOR MAKIN' YA BLUSH!
NOTE BOOK
BIG SIS'!
♥

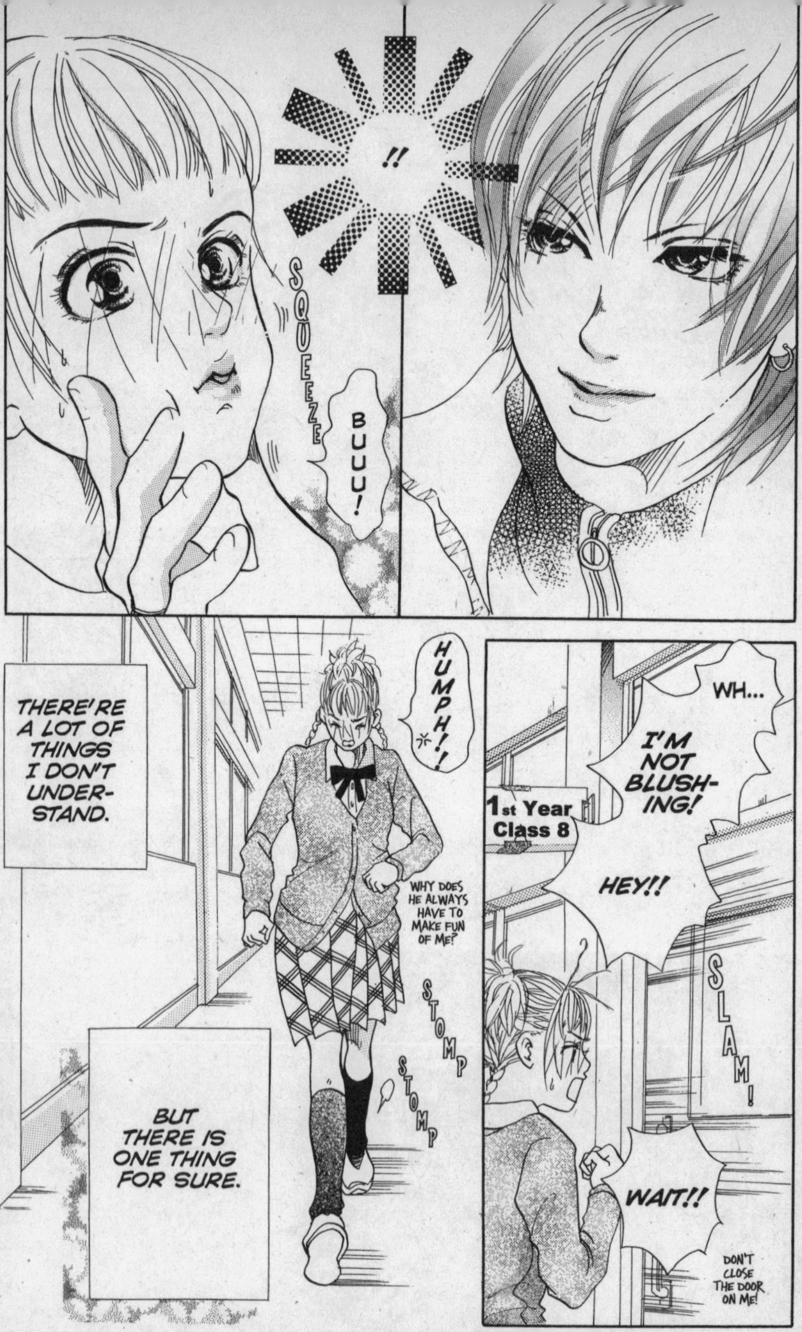
!!
SQUEEZE
BUUU!
WH... I'M NOT BLUSH-ING!
1st Year Class 8
HEY!!
SLAM!
WAIT!!
DON'T CLOSE THE DOOR ON ME!
HUMPH!!
THERE'RE A LOT OF THINGS I DON'T UNDER-STAND.
WHY DOES HE ALWAYS HAVE TO MAKE FUN OF ME?
STOMP
STOMP
BUT THERE IS ONE THING FOR SURE.

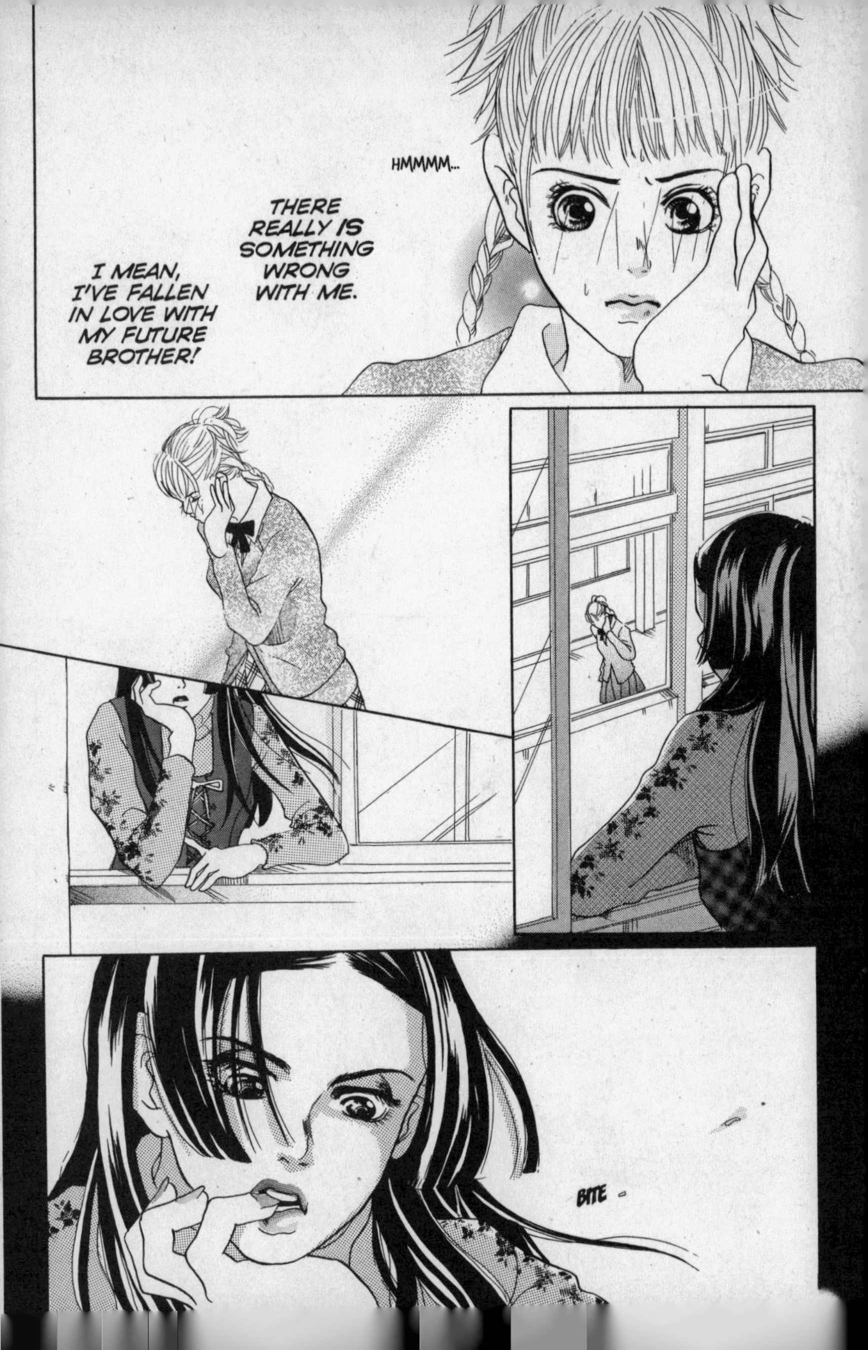
HMMMM...
THERE REALLY IS SOMETHING WRONG WITH ME.
I MEAN, I'VE FALLEN IN LOVE WITH MY FUTURE BROTHER!
BITE

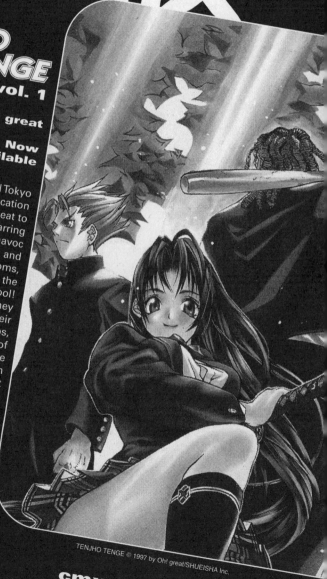

cmx

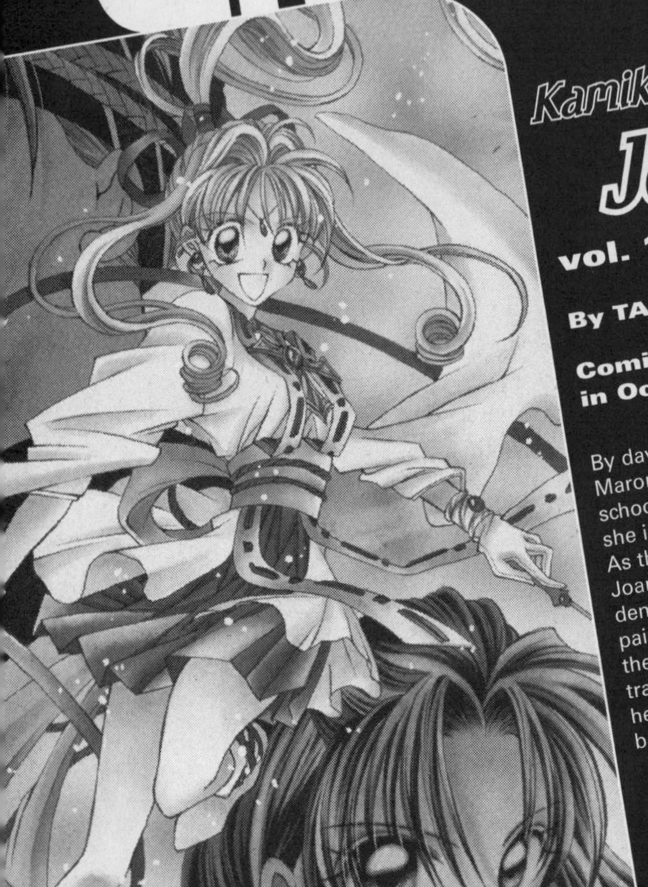

Kamikaze KAITO Jeanne

vol. 1

By TANEMURA Arina

**Coming
in October 2005**

By day, Kusakabe
Maron is an average
schoolgirl—but by night,
she is a Phantom Thief!
As the reincarnation of
Joan of Arc, she steals
demon-possessed
paintings and neutralizes
their evil. An angel-in-
training named Finn
helps Jeanne in the
battle against evil.

cmxmanga.com

CMX

Now available

Madara, vol.1

Created & Illustrated by Sho-u Tajima

Created & Written by Eiji Otsuka

When his village is attacked by demons, Madara, a blacksmith's apprentice, is awakened to his special powers and magical heritage. Now he must set out on a quest to free the land and defeat the evil king Miroku, who holds the secrets to Madara's past.

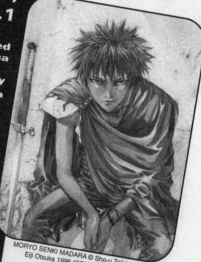

MORYO SENKI MADARA © Sho-u Tajima 1996 © Eiji Otsuka 1996 (OTSUKA EIJI OFFICE) KADOKAWA SHOTEN

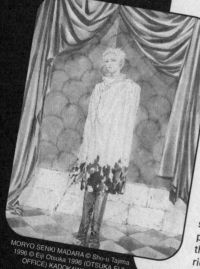

MORYO SENKI MADARA © Sho-u Tajima 1996 © Eiji Otsuka 1996 (OTSUKA EIJI OFFICE) KADOKAWA SHOTEN

Madara, vol. 2

Created & Illustrated by Sho-u Tajima

Created & Written by Eiji Otsuka

Madara and Kaos are similar creatures. Both are powerful fighters seeking to defeat the evil tyrant Emperor Miroku. Their only difference is one of destiny versus desire. Madara fits the prophecy, but Kaos covets the throne, and has far superior warrior training.

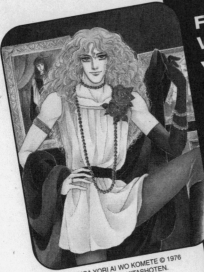
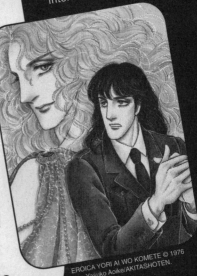

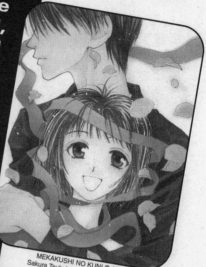

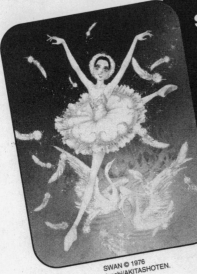
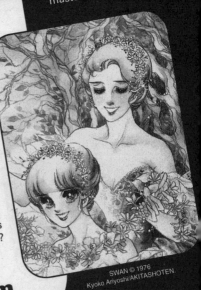

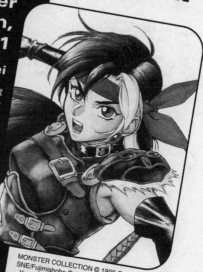
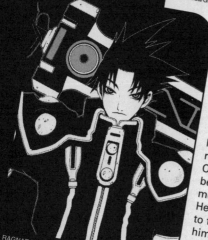

Coming in April

Madara, vol. 3

Created & Illustrated by Sho-u Tajima
Created & Written by Eiji Otsuka

While they wait for Madara's return, those who believe he is the true king have gathered to fight against Emperor Miroku and his Moki. Word spreads about a mighty warrior slaughtering Moki across the land, with a powerful sword able to slay demons with a single stroke. Who is this mysterious warrior?

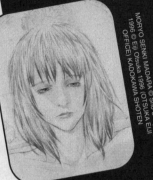

From Eroica with Love, vol. 3

by Aoike Yasuko

Eroica and Major Klaus steal into Iran. Tensions are high and *danger* is the byword, as this is Iran at the height of its Islamic Revolution. The Major is after military secrets and Eroica is after the Shah's treasures, both hidden within the Shah's palace.

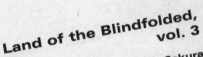

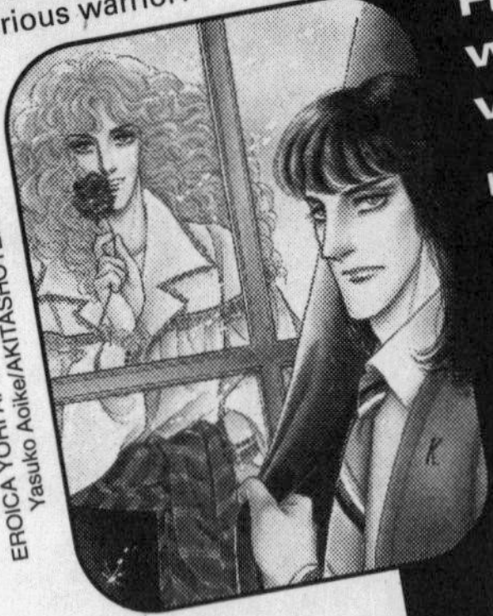

Land of the Blindfolded, vol. 3

by Tsukuba Sakura

After risking her life to help someone, Kanade confides in Arou and Namiki about how, as a young girl who was just discovering her supernatural talent, she "saw" her beloved grandfather die in a fire. Was Kanade able to change his fate? And how did that experience help make her what she is today?

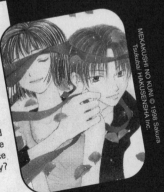

cmxmanga.com

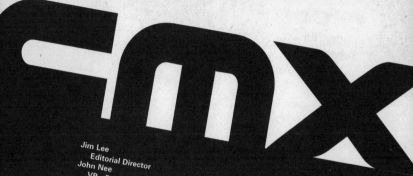

Jim Lee
    Editorial Director
John Nee
    VP—Business Development
Hank Kanalz
    VP—General Manager, WildStorm
Paul Levitz
    President & Publisher
Georg Brewer
    VP—Design & Retail Product Development
Richard Bruning
    Senior VP—Creative Director
Patrick Caldon
    Senior VP—Finance & Operations
Chris Caramalis
    VP—Finance
Terri Cunningham
    VP—Managing Editor
Stephanie Fierman
    Senior VP—Sales & Marketing
Alison Gill
    VP—Manufacturing
Rich Johnson
    VP—Book Trade Sales
Lillian Laserson
    Senior VP & General Counsel
Paula Lowitt
    Senior VP—Business & Legal Affairs
David McKillips
    VP—Advertising & Custom Publishing
Gregory Noveck
    Senior VP—Creative Affairs
Cheryl Rubin
    Senior VP—Brand Management
Bob Wayne
    VP—Sales

 DC Comics, a Warner Bros. Entertainment Company.

Translation and adaptation
by Michael Niyama

John Layman/Sno Cone — Lettering
John J. Hill — CMX Logo & Publication Design
Ed Roeder — Additional design

ISBN: 1-4012-0545-3

CMX
Rating System

Titles with this rating are appropriate for all age readers. They contain no offensive material. They may contain mild violence and/or some comic mischief.

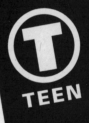

EVERYONE

Titles with this rating are appropriate for a teen audience and older. They may contain some violent content, language, and/or suggestive themes.

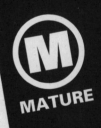

TEEN

Titles with this rating are appropriate for mature readers. They may contain graphic violence, nudity, sex and content suitable only for older readers.

MATURE

FLIP IT!!

All the pages in this book were created—and are printed here—in Japanese RIGHT-to-LEFT format. No artwork has been reversed or altered, so you can read the stories the way the creators meant for them to be read.

JAPANESE NAMES

Authentic Japanese name order is family name first, given name second. In CMX books we list the names of all characters as well as the manga creators in Japanese order, unless otherwise instructed by the author.

RIGHT TO LEFT?!

Traditional Japanese manga starts at the upper right-hand corner, and moves right-to-left as it goes down the page. Follow this guide for an easy understanding.

a
b
c
ed
f
g
h
i
j

Catch the latest at cmxmanga.com!

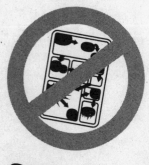

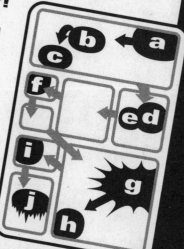